ZEN BAGGAGE

Also by Bill Porter/Red Pine

In Such Hard Times: The Poetry of Wei Ying-wu
The Platform Sutra
The Heart Sutra
Poems of the Masters
The Diamond Sutra
The Collected Songs of Cold Mountain
The Clouds Should Know Me by Now
The Zen Works of Stonehouse
Lao-tzu's Taoteching
Guide to Capturing a Plum Blossom
Road to Heaven: Encounters with Chinese Hermits
The Zen Teaching of Bodhidharma

ZEN BAGGAGE

A PILGRIMAGE TO CHINA

BILL PORTER

COUNTERP

BERKELEY

A Note on the Photographs: All photographs are those of the author, except the photograph of Empty Cloud and Yi-ch'ao at the end of Chapter Fifteen taken by an unknown photographer. All the author's photographs were taken with a variety of point-and-shoot cameras using Agfa black and white slide film and Ilford black and white print film and were scanned into digital format by Margaret Telfer and Ed McConaghay of PhotoBook Press and Patrick Barber of McGuire Barber Design.

Cover photo: A Monk entering the guest hall of Yunmen Temple. The author's bags are on the right. Photo by Bill Porter.
Dedication page photo: Pilgrims on the trail: Fall of 1991 at Stonehouse's hut. Copyright © 2009 by Bill Porter.

Library of Congress Cataloging-in-Publication Data
Porter, Bill, 1943–
  Zen baggage : a pilgrimage to China / Bill Porter.
  p. cm.
  ISBN-10: 1-59376-132-5
  ISBN-13: 978-1-59376-132-5
  1. Buddhist pilgrims and pilgrimages—China. 2. Zen Buddhism—
China. I. Title.

BQ6450.C6P67 2008
294.3'4350951—dc22

2008012043

COUNTERPOINT
2117 Fourth Street
Suite D
Berkeley, CA 94710
www.counterpointpress.com
Distributed by Publishers Group West
Printed in the United States of America
Text design by McGuire Barber Design

10 9 8 7 6 5 4 3 2 1

For my fellow pilgrims Finn Wilcox and Steve Johnson

So the 20th Century — so
whizzed the Limited — roared by and left
three men, still hungry on the tracks, ploddingly
watching the tail lights wizen and converge slip–
ping gimleted and neatly out of sight.

—from "The River" by Hart Crane (1899–1932)

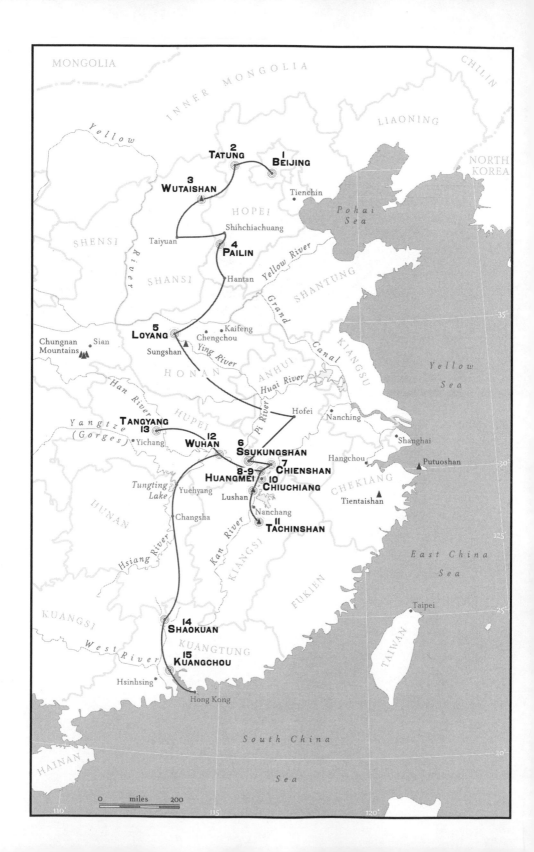

CONTENTS

ONE   **NO WORD**   1

TWO   **NO BUDDHA**   33

THREE   **NO MOUNTAIN**   53

FOUR   **NO HOME**   79

FIVE   **NO BEGINNING**   111

SIX   **NO FORM**   145

SEVEN   **NO MIND**   161

EIGHT   **NO WORK, NO FOOD**   177

NINE   **NO DUST OR MIRROR**   201

TEN   **NO DAY OFF**   215

ELEVEN   **NO PEACH BLOSSOMS**   229

TWELVE   **NO EAST OR WEST**   247

THIRTEEN   **NO NORTH OR SOUTH**   261

FOURTEEN   **NO FLOATING BELLY-UP**   277

FIFTEEN   **NO END IN SIGHT**   311

SIXTEEN   **NO GOING BACK**   331

CHINESE LEXICON   335

⏐ NO WORD

I finally returned home, just as the long twilight of a Northwest summer was beginning. A few hours earlier, I had been sitting in a plane flying so low over the town
where I live I could see the stand of doug fir next to my house. I wondered how high
the grass had grown. I had been away ten weeks. The plane banked, and the town
disappeared. Thirty minutes later, we landed in Seattle. A taxi to the Coleman Docks,
a ferry across Puget Sound, and two buses later, my friend Finn Wilcox picked me up
next to the Port Townsend Safeway and drove me to my side of that five-acre stand
of trees someone donated to the town as a bird sanctuary.

It was the Buddha's birthday, the eighth day of the fourth lunar month, which
fell on May 5 that year. Buddhists mark the day by pouring water over small statues of a standing, infant Shakyamuni. I celebrated in the clawfoot tub upstairs and
thought about the journey that just ended. Afterwards, I tried to sleep. But I was still
in China. So I got up and began writing this book, which begins in Beijing.

I arrived the night of February 26. It was spring. In China spring begins on New
Year's Day, which was January 29 in 2006. So it had been spring for nearly a month.
But the ancient Chinese who decided when spring began—on the first day of the new
moon closest to the midpoint between the winter solstice and the spring equinox—

lived along the Yellow River, three hundred miles to the south. In Beijing, it was still winter. While I was standing in the airport taxi line, I opened my pack and got out my parka. It was just a shell, and what I really needed were my long johns, but putting them on in public was not an option.

Normally I would have headed for a hotel. But my friend Ted Burger had offered a roommate's bedroom. His apartment was a sixth-floor walk-up at the top of a dark stairwell in a dark building in a dark compound in the eastern part of the city. The taxi driver found the right street and the right compound, but there were a dozen buildings in the compound and no outside lights. I couldn't see the numbers, and it took me three tries before I found the right building and the right stairwell.

Ted wasn't there. He was at a film festival in America showing his documentary on Chinese hermits, *Amongst White Clouds*, but his American roommate was home and let me in. The apartment was small and furnished as the young furnish their apartments everywhere, as if no one was planning to stay very long and money would be better spent on something more useful, like a bottle of wine. But the place was heated, and there was a radiator in every room. It was so warm I had to leave the window open in my bedroom that night. The bedroom belonged to Ted's Chinese roommate, who had offered to stay with her parents while I was there. There wasn't much in the room besides the bed, a bedside table, and a chest of drawers. But I was glad to begin my trip in something other than a hotel, and the accommodations seemed just right.

I was making a pilgrimage to places associated with the beginning of Zen in China, specifically its first six patriarchs: Bodhidharma, Hui-k'o, Seng-ts'an, Tao-hsin, Hung-jen, and Hui-neng. These were the men who put Zen on the map, and I wanted to pay my respects. None of the six ever made it to Beijing, but there were some under-lying issues I wanted to consider before I met the old masters. The first of those issues was language. And Beijing seemed like a good place to begin.

Zen was known for its cavalier, if not dismissive, attitude toward words. "To talk about it is to go right by it," those old Zenmen were fond of saying. And yet no school of Buddhism has generated as much literature. Thousands of books have been writ-ten, in the East as well as in the West, about what cannot be expressed by language. I didn't expect to find an answer to this conundrum, but I wanted to circle around from behind and maybe catch it unawares. So when I woke up the next morning, I called my friend Ming-yao. Ming-yao was the editor of the Buddhist magazine *Chan*, which was how the Mainland Chinese romanized the word "Zen."

Whenever I say *Zen*, people are always correcting me: "It's *Ch'an/Chan* (the Wade-Giles and Pin-yin romanizations of the word)." They say, "Zen is the Japanese form of Ch'an. Chinese Ch'an is different from Japanese Zen." That's one way of looking at Zen, as a cultural phenomenon. But Chinese Ch'an, Japanese Zen, and Korean Son all point to the same moon of the mind. And there aren't two kinds of mind.

The reason I like to point with *Zen*, as opposed to *Ch'an*, is that I love a good Z. Also, *zen* was how people pronounced this word back when Zen began (the reconstruction preferred by linguists is *dzian*). And the people who live in the Kan River watershed of Kiangsi Province, where zen became Zen, still pronounce it that way. The pronunciation used at court changed when the Manchus invaded China in the seventeenth century and established the Ch'ing dynasty and their own pronunciation as the arbiter of proper usage. But down in Zenland, it's still Zen. Besides, Zen isn't Chinese or Japanese anymore. It belongs to anyone willing to see their nature and become a buddha, anyone who lives the life of no-mind and laughs in these outrageous times.

So I called up Ming-yao, and he asked me to meet him for lunch. He said his wife Ming-chieh would be there too. Ming-chieh translated my book on Chinese hermits, *Road to Heaven*—except, of course, for the parts about politics, the military, and the police, which never made the Chinese edition. Everyone liked her title: *K'ung-ku-yu-lan*: "Hidden Orchids of Deserted Valleys." Strange as it sounds, no one had ever written a book about hermits in China, and the publication of *Kungkuyulan* had a noticeable impact. In the Sian area, it even resulted in the formation of a hermit association, which sounds ludicrous. But the association has since compiled a record of hut and cave locations in the Chungnan Mountains south of Sian where I conducted my interviews. And it now sends someone around periodically with medicine and food—and even mail.

Of course, that is not necessarily a good thing. The Cultural Revolution was nothing new. Times are good for monks and nuns right now in China, but everything changes. And when bad times come, someone will have to take the blame. Throughout Chinese history, that someone has often included its Buddhist and Taoist clerics: those unproductive slackers living off the sweat of others. Still, most of the hermits I talked to were not greatly affected even during the worst years of those decades everyone in China still wants to forget. The Buddhists and Taoists who felt the heat were the ones living in monasteries and nunneries, not the ones in huts—yet another advantage of seclusion and a low profile.

I met Ming-chieh and Ming-yao in the northeast part of Beijing, just off Liufang Nanli Street. They were waiting for me outside a vegetarian restaurant called Hotang Yuehszu (Lotus in the Moonlight). The calligraphy of Master Ching-hui hung over the doorway: EVERY DAY IS A GOOD DAY. Ching-hui was vice director of the Buddhist Association of China and our mutual connection. Ming-yao and Ming-chieh were his disciples, as was the woman who owned the place. She was there to greet us and led us into a private room. Ming-yao later told me she supplied a good deal of the money that paid for *Chan*. The magazine was the reason I called Ming-yao. I wanted to know more about what was involved in publishing a magazine about Zen in China, which he told me over a lunch of vegetarian dishes and an infusion made from freshly picked plum blossoms.

The magazine was started by Ching-hui. Ching-hui had turned *Fayin*, or *Voice of the Dharma*, into the leading Buddhist magazine in China. It featured articles focusing on Buddhist philosophy and sacred texts as well as news about the Buddhist community. But in the wake of the events of 1989, Ching-hui decided to launch another magazine. Ching-hui was also a Zen master, and he decided the times were right for a magazine about practice, especially a practice that wasn't separate from daily life, which was what Zen was all about. He kept it simple and called the magazine *Chan*, and Ming-yao offered to help.

In the beginning, he said, the magazine was a quarterly with a print run of three thousand copies. But it had since become a bimonthly, and its print run was up to twenty-five thousand. For a run of that size, he said, it cost around 60,000RMB ($7,500) to edit, print, and distribute, or about 2.5RMB ($0.30) per copy. Because the magazine was free, it was completely dependent on donations from people like the owner of Lotus in the Moonlight and the Hong Kong family that owned JeansWest. But ordinary readers also contributed.

Nearly all the money went to cover the costs of printing and mailing. The magazine had an office at Pailin Temple south of Beijing, but Ming-yao edited each issue wherever he and his wife happened to be living at the time. People either picked up a copy at their local temple, or they sent Ming-yao their name and address, and people at Pailin sent them a copy.

When I asked if the government ever interfered or censored the magazine, he said he had never had any problems. He didn't have to clear issues in advance, but he was required to send copies to the religious affairs authorities after it was printed. He said they actually encouraged the magazine's publication and considered *Chan* a model of what they hoped other religious organizations would do.

As for its content, Ming-yao said the magazine published articles sent in by Buddhist writers from around the country. But most of the material was from Ching-hui's disciples, both lay and monastic, who shared his emphasis on what he called *Sheng Huo Ch'an*, or "Daily Life Zen." The focus was on promoting a practice that could be cultivated in an apartment building as well as in a monastic setting.

Ming-yao said there was a revival of interest in Buddhism in China, but it was still superficial, and often misdirected. "Most people," he said, "are attracted by the magical powers of Vajrayana Buddhism or the devotional path of Pure Land Buddhism as a means of temporary escape, not complete liberation. But every practice is based on Zen, including Pure Land and Vajrayana. Zen is a buddha's mind. Sooner or later, anyone who practices Buddhism practices Zen. But Zen just about died out in China. It's making a comeback, but it's still uncertain how successful it will be.

"More and more people are becoming interested in Zen, especially young people and people with a college education. But it's going to take a while to reach a wider audience. Also, more and more Zen temples are being built, or rebuilt. But more important than restoring temples is restoring the spirit of Zen. That is what our magazine tries to do. There is no going back to the T'ang dynasty when Zen first began to flourish. It's going to take time to teach people how to manifest Zen in their daily lives in the modern world. That is really what Zen is about. Every place is a place to practice. Every time is a time to practice. Zen is concerned with the thought we have this moment rather than with rituals or rules of behavior developed in the past."

Ming-yao said that even though interest in Zen was growing, one of the problems was the lack of competent teachers. People didn't know where to begin or how to begin. The magazine helped. It provided knowledge and encouragement. But it couldn't take the place of a teacher. Ming-yao admitted that those truly able to teach were still far too few. Many people who claimed to teach Zen, he said, didn't. They just mouthed the words.

Finally I got around to the reason why I wanted to talk to him. I asked him how he dealt with the problem of language, since Zen masters traditionally showed such disdain for words. He said, "There is no way to teach people about Zen without using words. Our magazine uses language that makes sense to our readers. We try to put everything in terms they will understand. But the true Way transcends dialectical distinctions, and language is based on distinctions. From this standpoint, language is an obstacle to practice and needs to be overcome. But before we realize the truth, we need language to tell us how to realize the truth. Understanding the Way oneself and teaching the Way to others can't be separated from language. When Zen masters pointed directly at the mind and told their disciples not to get sidetracked by language, what they meant was that the Way doesn't exist in words. They didn't mean that we shouldn't read books or study scriptures. Words point to the truth, just as a finger points to the moon. This is what language is for. This is what our magazine is for. It points to the Way. People still have to see the moon for themselves if they want to know what it looks like."

It was a long lunch, and Ming-yao talked about other things as well. Afterwards, it was my turn. He asked me to come with him to meet some nuns. There were about a dozen of them, and they were staying in Beijing while their new nunnery was being built six hundred miles to the south, near Fourth Patriarch Temple outside Huangmei. The nuns were also disciples of Ching-hui. Ching-hui was a monk I had met in 1989 just before Tienanmen. It was Ching-hui who told me where to find the hermits who made *Road to Heaven* possible. So I, too, had a karmic connection with him. We were all dharma brothers and sisters.

Just inside the front door of the apartment that was their temporary abode, we took off our shoes and put on slippers, and the abbess, Master Hung-yung, invited us into the reception room. While several of her fellow nuns served us bowls of Uighur-style tea made from dried longan fruits and red dates, the abbess said they were all planning to attend the first recitation ever held of the six-hundred-chapter text of the *Mahaprajnaparamita Sutra*. Hsuan-tsang (602–664) brought this text back from India and translated it into Chinese in the middle of the seventh century. It was the longest single text in the Buddhist Canon and the granddaddy of all the scriptures that taught Prajnaparamita, the Perfection of Wisdom. The recitation was being organized by Ching-hui and was scheduled to take place in two days at Pailin Temple, three hours south of Beijing.

The abbess said she was hoping I would talk to her and her fellow nuns about *prajna*. I didn't know what to say. It was certainly unusual for a monk or nun to ask a layperson about Buddhism. Some monasteries and nunneries even had rules against laypeople giving Dharma talks. I thought she just wanted me to say a few words, a polite gesture to a visiting guest from afar. So I agreed. But I was mistaken about it being a polite gesture. The abbess got up from her chair and led us all into the living room, which had been turned into a meditation hall, and the other nuns followed us in. After we all sat down on meditation cushions, the abbess repeated her request. I took refuge in the *Heart Sutra*, the shortest of all presentations of the teaching of Prajnaparamita, and she and her fellow nuns were too kind in not demanding more than I was capable of explaining.

Prajna is the word around which Mahayana Buddhism formed in the Kushan Empire of Northwest India, Pakistan, and Afghanistan just before the beginning of the Christian Era. It means "what comes before knowledge" and refers to our original mind undefiled by discrimination or what passes for knowledge: Adam and Eve before the apple, religion before religion, the mind before mind. In a word, *prajna* means "wisdom." And adding the word *paramita* distinguishes it as "ultimate

Master Ching–hui

wisdom" or "the perfection of wisdom." It's the cultivation of such wisdom that enables a person to see things as they are, empty of self-existence and inseparable from the mind that conjures them into existence.

It was the arrival of Prajnaparamita scriptures in China in the second and third centuries that laid the philosophical basis for what later became Zen. But along with these scriptures emphasizing wisdom came others that taught *dhyana*, or meditation. When these Buddhist scriptures were first translated into Chinese, the Sanskrit word *dhyana* was transcribed *zen-na* and then shortened to *zen*. But it was the combination of dhyana (zen) with prajna that resulted in the tradition we know today as Zen. However, this didn't happen for several more centuries, not until Bodhidharma, Zen's First Patriarch, came to China at the end of the fifth century. Up until then, people cultivated meditation, or they cultivated wisdom, but they didn't practice Zen. They still made distinctions between the two—not to mention everything else. But the practice of Zen involves the manifestation of both simultaneously and without distinction, whether walking, standing, sitting, or lying down. Prajna without dhyana is Pie in the Sky Zen, while dhyana without prajna is Dead Tree Zen. Zen is the practice that eliminates the distinction between prajna and dhyana, between wisdom and meditation. But it is also the practice that is based on both. Thus, we take refuge in no mind, our buddha mind.

After I gave this simplistic explanation of prajna and followed it through the thirty or so lines of the *Heart Sutra*, Hung-yung and her fellow nuns bowed in thanks, and I got up to leave. But on the way out, the abbess told me that Ching-hui had invited me to join them for the recitation of the *Mahaprajnaparamita Sutra*. I had other plans, but it was an invitation I could not refuse, and we arranged to meet the following afternoon and go to Pailin Temple together.

Afterwards, I returned to Ted's apartment and waited for my friend Dave Murphy to get off work. Dave was first secretary at the U.S. Embassy and a fellow member of the Taiwan Expat Mafia. He picked me up at a hotel two blocks from Ted's apartment, and we drove out toward the airport to the Beijing International School, where his son and a hundred other students were performing a concert that evening for stringed instruments, meaning Western stringed instruments. There wasn't a Chinese lute or zither in sight. But even stringed instruments needed some accompaniment, and Dave's son played the drums. They were all quite good. I tried the violin once in the fifth grade, but my real passion was marbles—outside in the dirt or inside on the carpet. I tried to recall when I put my agate shooters away for the last time. I wondered what happened to them. They probably sank into the earth out of sadness. They were such good friends. They had magical properties. I wondered what I gave them up for. I think it was TV. It wasn't the violin.

On the way out after the concert, we met Dave's wife, Mao-hwa. She had been sitting near the back of the auditorium and hadn't seen us in front. We didn't dwell on the performance. It was late and we were all hungry, so we went to a Malaysian restaurant nearby. Mao-hwa had worked for Hewlett-Packard ever since I knew her, and she was now business manager of their China services division. She was always doing two things at once, not just walking and chewing gum, but carrying on two conversations at once, and in this case, three: with me, with Dave, and with their son, all different conversations. I feel as if I'm only half present when I try to talk to more than one person. I've never learned to juggle. I don't remember what we talked about or what we ate, except for the satay, of course, and the coconut brûlée.

By the time we finished, it was too late to go back to my overheated bedroom at Ted's, so Dave and Mao-hwa invited me to spend the night at their place. They lived close by in a gated compound of more than a hundred two-story villa-style houses— houses with yards, in Beijing. The place was called River Garden, and it was built by a Taiwanese woman whose own villa occupied a whole block. Her bedroom light was on when we drove by, and Mao-hwa whispered that she was divorced and still quite attractive. I don't know why she told me that, or why she whispered. They didn't stop to let me out—I could just imagine myself knocking on her door and asking for a snifter of port.

I woke up the next morning in the spare room and returned to the city with Dave when he went to work. It was snowing, and we drove back into a strangely muffled city. After Dave dropped me off at Ted's, I waited around for a couple hours, then took a taxi to meet Ming-yao and Ming-chieh and the nuns. We left in a convoy of three black Audis whose drivers took turns weaving through the expressway traffic at over seventy miles an hour. Even at that speed, it still took us more than three hours to reach Pailin Temple in the town of Chaohsien.

. . . . .

Chaohsien was where the Zen monk Chao-chou finally put down roots in 858 after wandering all over China for more than twenty years. All the regular roads leading to his old temple were being torn up for a new sewer line, and we had to come in through the south end of town by the Chaochou Bridge, the oldest stone-arch bridge in the world, built in AD 600. When someone once asked Chao-chou what kind of bridge it was, he answered, "The kind of bridge that donkeys cross and horses cross." That's what I mean about language and Zen. It's just a breath away from no language at all. And yet hundreds of thousands of Zen students have sat on their cushions and thought about that one, or Chao-chou's answer "No" to the question, "Does a dog have a buddha nature?" They all seemed to ignore the fact that on another occasion he answered "Yes." We turned into a dirt lane just past the bridge and wove through a part of town that recent development had left behind. We finally reappeared in front of the temple and parked behind the guest hall.

As we got out of our cars, one of the monks came out and ushered us along a series of corridors to the abbot's quarters near the back. The abbot, Ming-hai, graduated from Beijing University with a degree in philosophy in 1989 and managed to escape the wave of arrests that followed Tienanmen that year. He became a monk

Chaochou Bridge

soon afterwards. Ching-hui recognized his ability and turned over abbotship of the temple to him in 2003, when he was only thirty-five. Ming-hai saw us approaching and came out of the reception room to greet us, then led us inside.

Ching-hui was at the far end of the room talking to some wealthy patrons. As soon as he saw me, he got up, rushed over, and grabbed my arm, pulling me over to sit beside him. Ching-hui was always grabbing my arm, like my grandmother, and leading me around. Before I could say anything, he chided me for wearing a "Muslim cap." It was actually a Buddhist cap, the knitted kind worn by monks and nuns all over China during winter. But together with my beard, it often got me mistaken for a Uighur. The Uighurs weren't all that happy with the Chinese occupation and control of their section of the Silk Road, an occupation that began in 1949, and they were known to set off the occasional bomb in protest. I'm sure Chinese authorities wished they were more passive, like the country's other ethnic minorities. No doubt their activities caused problems for people like Ching-hui, who had to deal with the reaction of the central authorities to movements that had a religious component. The Uighurs were followers of Mohammed, not the Buddha. But the government tended to lump all practitioners together. It was an old trick. Lump everyone together and let them inform on each other. My cap must have reminded Ching-hui of the difficult position he found himself in whenever he had to attend meetings in Beijing.

He asked me what I had been working on, and I told him I had just finished a translation of the *Platform Sutra*, a text that records the teaching of Zen's Sixth Patriarch, Hui-neng. I volunteered that I had based my translation on the Tunhuang Museum copy recently edited by Yang Tseng-wen. Ching-hui cringed and shook his head. Suddenly I remembered he had written a book about the sutra and had given me a copy the previous year.

The sutra turned around a poem. One day Hung-jen, the Fifth Patriarch of Zen, told his disciples that whichever of them could write a poem that revealed their buddha nature would become the Sixth Patriarch. Hung-jen's chief disciple wrote:

The body is our Bodhi Tree
the mind is like a standing mirror
always try to keep it clean
don't let it gather dust.

An illiterate rice-pounder named Hui-neng responded with:

Bodhi doesn't have any trees
this mirror doesn't have a stand
our buddha nature is forever pure
how can it gather dust?

That was what Hung-jen was looking for, and Hui-neng became the sixth and most famous patriarch. His old home was the next-to-last stop on my pilgrimage itinerary. Suddenly the image of all the dust on the trail ahead of me came to mind, the mind that still gathered dust.

Ching-hui brought me back to the poem. He said the Tunhuang copies were wrong and that the third line should read *pen-lai-wu-yi-wu*: "actually there isn't a thing" (present in later copies). It was the very foundation of Zen. What bothered him was that both Tunhuang copies of the sutra, written less than a hundred years after Hui-neng died, had instead *fo-hsing-ch'ang-ch'ing-ching*: "our buddha nature is forever pure." Basically, it was Buddhism's School of Emptiness versus its Mind Only School, but Ching-hui shook his head and scolded me for translating the "wrong" version. I didn't know what to say. And it didn't matter. He grabbed my arm again and laughed, as if to say "gotcha."

Suddenly, and thankfully, I heard the sound of the dinner board being struck. We all got up and walked outside and made our way to the dining hall, the one reserved for guests of the abbot. The food was served buffet-style, and it was so good I went back for seconds. I used to lose weight when I traveled in China but not anymore. After dinner, one of the monks led Ming-yao and me and two other laymen to a set of bedrooms normally reserved for visiting monks. It wasn't that late, but we all went to bed, if only because it was too cold to do anything else. It was so cold I completely disappeared beneath a blanket filled with twelve pounds of cotton wadding. Fireworks celebrating the coming recitation were going off, but I went right to sleep. Tomorrow was going to be a big day. Morning services were scheduled to begin at three o'clock, and thousands of people were expected. I resolved to take refuge in a visitor's right to sleep in. I figured I could join the Prajna Chorus after the sun had warmed things up.

I figured wrong. Ming-yao woke me at 2:45. It was time, he said, to begin the opening ceremony. I didn't want to go, but when you're a guest "No" is not an option. In case I was wavering, he said the "Old Monk," meaning Ching–hui, was expecting me to attend. So I opened my cocoon and sat up. I was already wearing my socks, so all I had to do was put on my pants and shoes and grab my shirt and parka on the way out. I was still half-asleep, until I felt the air. It was freezing. Even the stars looked like they were shivering.

As we made our way across a courtyard the size of a football field, I finished buttoning my shirt and zipping up my parka. Finally we stepped into the huge, frigid hall. Over a thousand monks and laypeople were already inside and more were coming in behind us. Against the back wall there were five huge gilded buddha statues, and the surrounding walls were lined with ten thousand more, each about a foot high. It was the biggest buddha hall I had ever seen and cost the equivalent of five million U.S. dollars to build.

I soon found out that Ching–hui was serious about me being there. In the middle of the hall there were 108 small tables set up for the occasion. Each table was covered with yellow brocade and a set of three exquisite porcelains bowls: the one in the middle was for burning incense, the one on the left held sandalwood powder,

Hall of Ten Thousand Buddhas at Pailin Temple

and the one on the right was full of sandalwood sticks. Each of the tables also had a wooden book frame that held a copy of the text to be chanted. There was also a piece of paper taped to each altar cloth with the name of the person who was supposed to serve as officiant at that table. Someone led me to a table with a paper that read "Pi-er," or "Bill." There was no escape.

I hated ceremonies. When I was a kid, it was church. Later, it was military school, and later still, the Army. On my last day before shipping home in March of 1967, the sergeant major called me into his office and told me I was the worst soldier he had ever known. It was no secret. I didn't like ceremonies. As far as I was concerned, they were the denatured version of shamanistic rituals. Maybe if there was more dancing. But there I was, along with ten thousand buddhas and more would-be bodhisattvas than I could count. I heard later that three thousand people managed to crowd inside and a thousand more stood outside, as we called upon the deities of the ten directions to bless our communal efforts. I guess that was all any ceremony was meant to do anyway, instill a sense of community among participants. I think it must be my karmic heritage—as soon as I become part of a group, I'm looking for a way out.

It wasn't bad for the first hour or so. We were all still waking up. I kept busy building incense fires, sticking the pieces of sandalwood into the coals of the incense burner,

Bill's table

then sprinkling sandalwood powder over the fire and bowing and chanting in between. At one point, I decided I could build a better fire by crossing the pieces of sandalwood on top of each other, camp-style, instead of sticking them into the coals butt-end first, which was how everyone else was doing it. But a monk saw me doing this and came over and straightened out my little pyre. No playing around during ceremonies.

The smoke from our 108 sandalwood fires and the vapor from our collective breaths filled the cavernous hall. I thought so many bodies would begin to warm the place up, but my fingers and toes lost all feeling during the second hour. The only relief I felt was when I bowed down and touched my head to the kneeling cushion and stared at its embroidered lotuses and let my mud-borne, flower-scented thoughts rise and vanish into the smoky haze. Occasionally I found the place in the hymnal and chanted along. But mostly I just stood there teetering, like a lotus at the end of summer, waiting for the end, which finally came: after three hours, we took an hour break for breakfast. But it was only a break.

As soon as it was over, everyone began filing back into the buddha hall to begin chanting the six hundred chapters of the *Mahaprajnaparamita Sutra*. I made a quick dash to my room and put on my long johns and returned just in time for the bell that marked the start of the recitation ceremony. I felt better knowing that at least I wasn't going to freeze this time.

The printout of the sutra in the frame on my little altar included Chapters 510–513, as did that of several other officiants. The reason for the duplication was in case one of us missed a line or two, the others would make up the omission. It was a good thing, too, because I lingered over a number of passages, like this one in Chapter 510 at the bottom of page 604 in the standard edition of the Tripitaka:

On that occasion, each of the devas in the realms of Desire, Form, and Formlessness in the billion worlds of the universe scattered celestial flowers and incense around the Bhagavan as an offering from afar. Then they came before him and bowed at his feet and stood to one side and asked in unison, "When the Tathagata teaches the profound Prajnaparamita, what form does it take?"

The Buddha told the devas, "You should know that the profound Prajnaparamita takes emptiness, formlessness, and wishlessness as its form. The profound Prajnaparamita is not created. It is free of birth and destruction, defilement and purity, essence and attribute, impermanence and permanence, oneness and multiplicity, appearance and disappearance. It takes emptiness as its form. Thus does the profound Prajnaparamita have infinite forms. You devas should know that all such forms are taught by the buddhas according to the ways of the world and not according to their inexpressible meaning."

I read that passage over several times, especially the last line: "You devas should know that all such forms"—namely, the not-this, not-that, no-form type of forms—"are taught by buddhas according to the ways of the world and not according to their inexpressible meaning." When buddhas use language, they do so to make us let go of language. If buddhas taught according to the inexpressible meaning of the Prajnaparamita, there would be no language. There would be no tongues, no ears, no audience of thousands of would-be bodhisattvas. The whole hall and all of us in it would be a reflection in someone's teacup. Probably Chao-chou's. It was he who first built Pailin Temple and who made tea an essential part of Zen.

Thus did the sacred and mundane merge in our communal chorus as we expressed the inexpressible. This time we were supposed to chant silently, either standing or kneeling—whichever felt more comfortable, and at our own pace. But after a while people started mumbling, and the mumbling became louder, and pretty soon the buddha hall sounded like a pet store. The whole thing went a lot faster than I expected, and it was over in less than two hours. But then came another hour of chanting the names of the people who had contributed money or materials for the occasion: "May so-and-so be protected by the merit accrued here," followed by three bows. Hundreds of people were thus honored for their generosity.

Finally it ended. The monks filed out, and I was right behind them. As soon as I was outside, Chang Shun-p'ing and his boss waved and invited me to drive back to Beijing with them. His boss was a publisher. In fact, he was my publisher. He was planning to bring out a new Chinese edition of *Road to Heaven* later that fall, and Chang Shun-p'ing was the editor in charge of the project. Theirs was one of the black Audis in the convoy in which I had arrived the day before. Also joining us were two girls who were working on graduate degrees in art at Chinghai and Beijing universities. They sat with Shun-p'ing in the backseat, while I rode shotgun.

We hit the expressway just outside Chaohsien and headed north. While we sped toward Beijing, the two art students and Shun-p'ing discovered a mutual inter-est and started singing gathas from the *Platform Sutra*. I hadn't realized someone had set Hui-neng's poems to music. My car mates knew them by heart. It wasn't exactly "Froggy Went A-Courtin," but it was far sweeter than what we had been chanting and mumbling for six hours. They sang us all the way back to Beijing and through rush-hour traffic. I was still humming one of the gathas when I got back to Ted's apartment.

Ted was just back from the States. He said there was lots of interest in his hermit documentary, but no money. His American roommate was having a dinner party: spaghetti and red wine. China was actually producing some drinkable stuff, espe-cially cabernets. But I wasn't in the mood for wine and was too exhausted to carry on a conversation. I felt a cold coming on and went to bed. I think it was from standing in that freezing shrine hall for six hours.

The next morning I woke up again before dawn—no morning ceremony, just jet lag. I wasn't alone. There were already people down in the courtyard doing their morning exercises and talking loudly enough to hear on the sixth floor. I finally got tired of listening and got up to find the stuff in the kitchen to make a cup of cof-fee: filter, filter holder, ground coffee, cup. Instant coffee was usually what I drank in China—it was all that was available on the road. Making coffee with a filter felt strange. But it worked. Afterwards, I stretched out on the living room sofa and thumbed through an English magazine about the Beijing foreigner scene and waited for Ted to get up.

Foreigners got married in Beijing and had babies and announced promotions and had going-away parties and wrote about their travels. People can't keep from form-ing communities. And people who leave home and go abroad have an even greater need for the company of fellow countrymen. That was especially true in Asia, where relationships were everything.

About the time I was going through the classified ads for English teachers and masseuses (noting how much the former made, and how much the latter charged), Ted came down from his attic bedroom. I told him I had a big day planned and had some places in mind where language, I thought, would surely reveal its true nature. I invited him to join me. He was game, and after another cup of coffee, we sallied forth.

I decided to begin at the Ancient Bell Museum in northwest Beijing. It was across the city from Ted's apartment, and I wouldn't have attempted such an excursion in the past. But now there was a subway, and it worked great. Less than an hour later, we resurfaced at the stop for Big Bell Temple. In a previous incarnation, the museum was a Buddhist monastery. In 1733, only a few months after it was built, Emperor Yung-chung of the Ch'ing dynasty (1644–1911) ordered the Yungle Bell moved there. The single greatest treasure of the previous dynasty, the bell has been there ever since.

The story behind the big bell began when the man who founded the Ming dynasty (1368–1643) died suddenly in 1398, and his young grandson was chosen to succeed him. The grandson began trying to curtail the power of his uncles, the imperial princes. One of those uncles was Chu Ti. Chu Ti felt that he was the rightful heir to his father's throne, and he succeeded in overthrowing the grandson in 1402. Because Chu Ti's fief was centered in Beijing, he decided to move the capital there and ordered construction of the Forbidden City, the Temple of Heaven, and the Yungle Bell, which was rung for the first time in 1421, upon completion of the transfer of the capital.

The Chinese have been making bells a long time, apparently longer than anybody else. Where the Yellow River comes down from Inner Mongolia and cuts through the Loess Plateau then turns east for the sea, archaeologists have found bells dating back to 4000 BC. The people who lived there cultivated millet, raised pigs and dogs, and lived in mud houses. And they made bells out of clay and suspended a clay ball inside to produce the sort of sound made by a rattle. Because the bells were found in burial sites, archaeologists think they were used during shamanistic rituals for driving away malevolent spirits. When metal technology reached the area two thousand years later, their descendents made bronze versions of the same handheld bells and also buried them with their loved ones for use in the afterlife. As villages became towns and towns became cities, the bells kept getting bigger.

Inside the museum's first hall there was a set of bells cast around 500 BC, when Confucius was still a young man. They were unearthed during the excavation of a tomb, and there must have been fifty of them. They were suspended from wooden frames in graduated sizes ranging in height from six inches to three feet, and had been set up as if they were waiting upon the pleasure of their owner. The surface of each bell was ringed with bronze nipples designed to produce different tones. For a fee of 10RMB, or just over a dollar, the woman caretaker stopped knitting long enough to play a few ancient tunes with a long-handled wooden mallet. The bells were clearly meant for an ensemble, but the simple solos were entrancing.

Big Bell Temple didn't get many visitors. Except for the caretakers, the only other people we saw was a young couple who had probably come to be alone. As we entered what was once the temple's main shrine hall, we craned our necks upward. In the middle of the hall, where there normally would have been a statue of a buddha, there was now a bell: the Yungle Bell commissioned by Emperor Chu Ti. It was huge: over twenty feet high and more than ten feet wide at the lower rim. That ratio, according to the caretaker, gave it a deeper, more melodious tone than bells cast in the West, where the height and diameter were usually about the same. The reason I wanted to see this particular bell wasn't its tone or its size, but its use of language. Bells in China always had some sort of inscription on them: the name of the person who made the bell, or who commissioned it, or who owned it, or the name of the

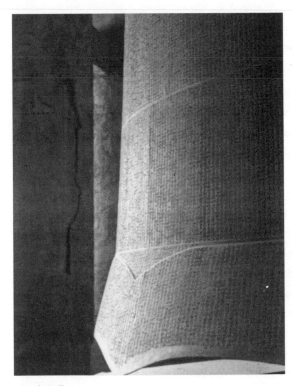

Yungle Bell

place where it was meant to hang, or perhaps a couplet to commemorate its creation and use. But the surface of this bell was covered with the text of nearly every major Buddhist sutra of its day.

The casting itself was an incredible achievement and has never been duplicated in China or anywhere else. First, the text of 108 Buddhist sutras containing over 230,000 characters, each nearly an inch in height, was written on rice paper. The paper was then applied to pieces of dried clay, the characters were carved into the clay, and the pieces of clay combined to form a mold. Then a bronze alloy of copper, tin, lead, zinc, aluminum, iron, magnesium, gold, and silver was poured into the mold at four points near the top. The resulting bell was welded to an armature through which a metal beam was placed, and the metal beam was then supported by a series of wooden beams that were themselves supported by eight large wooden pillars. The finished bell weighed forty-six tons, and there were no cracks, which made it fairly unique among bells of that size cast elsewhere in the world, either now or in the past.

Like most Chinese bells, it didn't have a tongue. It was struck from the outside with a log that hung horizontally from two chains. The caretaker said that for 100RMB, or twelve and a half dollars, visitors could pull back the log and heave it against the bell. But those who did, she said, seldom generated the kind of force bell ringers did in the past, when the bell could be heard thirty miles away. In the past it was struck every night, and it put Beijing to bed. During droughts, emperors came there together with their court and struck it for days on end while they burned incense and prayed for rain.

From the very beginning, bells have been used to communicate with the realm of spirits, regardless of how that realm and its inhabitants might be envisioned. Only lately have they been used for their musical qualities. Prior to modern times, they were used to reach distant and invisible realms where sound was the medium of communication, but sound far purer and more resonant than any earthly language.

Despite their use among shamans and court officials—or maybe because of it—it took a while before bells caught on with China's Buddhists. The earliest known bell made specifically for use in a Buddhist temple wasn't cast until 575, more than a century after Christian churches began using them in the West. But once Buddhists started using them, they insisted on them. You can't find a Buddhist temple in China from the T'ang dynasty onward (618–906) without one. When I lived in a monastery in Taiwan, listening to the song of the bell when I was waking up or going to sleep was my favorite time.

The bell was struck 108 times. The usual sequence was seven quick strokes, eight slow strokes, and twenty light strokes, repeated three times until a final three heavy strokes brought the number to 108. The most common explanation for the significance of the number is that it represents the number of our afflictions, broken down in this fashion: a bell for each of the Three Poisons of Greed, Anger, and Delusion during each of the Three Periods of the Past, Present, and Future throughout each of the Three Realms of Desire, Form, and Formlessness, and in each of the Four Directions: three times three times three times four, or one hundred and eight afflictions. Thus, this sea of suffering in which we all swim is also filled with the sound of liberation: one hundred and eight reminders every morning and every night. That was also why the Yungle Bell was covered with 108 sutras and why there were 108 tables set up for officiants at Pailin Temple.

A protective railing kept us at a distance, but I could make out parts of the *Lotus Sutra* and one of the *Perfection of Wisdom* texts—I couldn't tell which. Once sutras started talking about emptiness, they all sounded the same. But this bell represented an altogether different conception of how language can be transmitted and understood; in this case, as vibration. It occurred to me that this was an early form of radio. By covering the surface of the bell with these sutras, whoever designed it provided a means for the Dharma—the teaching of the Buddha—to enter the minds of all who heard it, but at a very elemental level: thirty miles for humans and even farther for those beings with more sensitive hearing.

According to Pure Land Buddhism, everything in the world where Amitabha Buddha teaches vibrates with the Dharma—the water, the wind, the trees, the birds, the sunlight and moonlight—everything vibrates with the teaching of suffering, impermanence, emptiness, and no self. This was language in its purest form: vibration. Nowadays we humans separate language and music into different realms. But whether we know it or not, we are still part of one realm that pervades the lives of all beings, the subatomic harmonics to which we still dance, though unknowingly. Now we say, "This is language and that's music." We have become so impoverished. Suffering, impermanence, emptiness, no self.

There were more halls with hundreds of bells from all over China. But I had seen enough, and it was nearly noon. When we went back outside the front gate, the black

Audi that brought me back from Pailin Temple the previous day was waiting for us. My publisher had sent his car and driver to take us to places beyond the range of the Beijing subway.

. . . . .

Fortunately, we didn't have to work our way through downtown traffic. Big Bell Temple was near one of the expressways that ringed the city, and we were soon headed out of Beijing. After less than an hour, we exited the expressway and continued southwest on Highway 107. A few miles later, we turned off and followed the signs to Choukoutian, the town at the base of the hill where the remains of Peking Man were found in 1929. It was thirty miles from Beijing, and maybe on a good night people there heard the dharma radio of the Yungle Bell when it was still being rung.

We stopped for noodles in what must have been the only restaurant in town, then drove up the hillside to the entrance of the Peking Man Museum and paid the admission fee of 30RMB. A young woman came out of the ticket office and introduced herself as Anita. She said she would be our guide, a free service for all visitors, funded by UNESCO. She led us up the hill to the main building. I had read that the museum was in bad shape, but that was an old report, or at least it was incorrect. The museum was in good repair, and the exhibits were well laid-out. They began with the series of skullcaps and teeth that made the place world-famous.

In 1899, a German physician named Haberer returned home from China with a collection of fossils he purchased from pharmacies around Beijing. He turned over his trunkloads of bones to a professor of paleontology in Munich named Strosser. And among the remains of over ninety mammalian species, Strosser found a human-like tooth he thought must be very old, perhaps as old as two million years. After Strosser published an account of his findings, a Swedish geologist on assignment in China named Gunnar Andersson read his report and began visiting the pharmacies of Beijing looking for similar fossils. He even sent letters to other foreigners in China to be on the lookout for what the Chinese called "dragon bones." Eventually he went to the sites where such bones had been found, and enlisted an Austrian paleontologist, Otto Zdansky, to help him excavate several promising locations.

In 1921, the two men tried their luck on Chicken Bone Hill, one mile southwest of the Choukoutian train station. Two years later, some locals told them about another location, and they moved their excavations to Dragon Bone Hill, 150 yards west of the train station. They unearthed hundreds of fossils at this second site, which Andersson sent back to Sweden to be examined by another paleontologist, Professor Carl Wiman. It took Wiman several years to go through the collection, but in 1926 he announced that it included two teeth similar to the one found by Haberer and reported by Strosser. He sent the teeth back to Andersson, who turned them over to Davidson Black at the Baptist-run Peking Union Medical College, hoping he would confirm Wiman's judgment. Black not only confirmed Wiman's finding, he joined in the search for more early human remains.

Several decades earlier, Eugene Dubois had astounded the world when he found a hominid skullcap in Java in 1891. These teeth were the second such find, thus seeming to confirm the authenticity of the first. At Black's behest, the Rockefeller Foundation agreed to fund further excavation at Choukoutian, and over the next decade a series of researchers, including Pei Wen-chung, Yang Chung-chien, and later Chia Lan-p'o found more than teeth. In December of 1929, Pei Wen-chung found a human skullcap, and in 1935 and 1936, Chia Lan-p'o found three skullcaps in another cave. Seventy years later, they were lined up in front of me, or at least their replicas were.

The explanation in the glass case didn't say when the replicas were made, but it was probably in 1937, the year the Japanese invaded China and occupied Beijing, and when work at Choukoutian stopped. At first the fossil remains of Peking Man were placed in the safe of the Cenozoic Laboratory at Peking Union Medical College. But as conditions in China deteriorated, it was decided to ship the fossils to the U.S. for safekeeping until the end of the war. In mid-November of 1941, they were packed into two crates and taken to the American Embassy. Then, on December 5, a contingent of U.S. Marines took them by train to Chinhuangtao Harbor, about eighty miles east of Beijing, where they planned to load the fossils onto the USS *President Harrison*, due to arrive from Shanghai on December 8, the Buddha's Day of Enlightenment. Unfortunately, it was also the same day Japan bombed Pearl Harbor (it was still December 7 in America). The Japanese sank the *President Harrison*, arrested the Marines in Chinhuangtao, and took possession of the two crates. Or did they? No one knows for sure what happened to the fossils.

Here is a typical tale: when the fossil remains of Peking Man first disappeared, the Japanese authorities went to a lot of trouble to locate them. Emperor Hirohito even issued an order in 1942 demanding they be found. Then that summer word came that they had been located in Tienchin, the next harbor south of Chinhuangtao. When a German woman who had worked as a secretary in the Cenozoic Laboratory went to Tienchin to identify them, she was turned back with the excuse that what had been found in Tienchin had nothing to do with Peking Man. That also marked the end of Japanese inquiry into the whereabouts of the fossils.

The obvious conclusion would seem to be that they were found and taken to Japan, where they have remained ever since, in some private collection or in that of the imperial family. After all, the emperor was very keen on locating the remains of what were also his own ancestors. In fact, at the end of the Second World War, there was a curious exchange of memoranda claiming that the fossils were found in Tokyo at the Imperial University, had been turned over to Allied Forces, and were on their way back to China. But they never arrived. There were dozens of such dead-end reports.

Fortunately, detailed casts were made of all the important fossils, including the

Entrance to cave where remains of Peking Man were first found (roof has fallen in)

skullcaps, and they were all on display in the museum. The original skullcaps dated from 500,000 to 200,000 years ago and showed the steady increase in the size of the frontal part of the brain associated with the development of language. Peking Man's average brain size was about 1,100 cubic centimeters, while that of modern humans is 1,400 cc, and that of the largest ape is 600 cc. I could imagine vowels and consonants echoing around those Peking Man craniums.

After we looked at the exhibits, Anita showed us the sites that had been excavated. The cave that yielded the first skullcap had a narrow opening that led down into a spacious rock floor. Prior to excavation, it had been steadily filled in with the debris of off-and-on human habitation for half a million years. After it was excavated, the roof collapsed, and now the cave looked like a small box canyon. It must have been a good place to hide and share the spoils of the hunt, which included an incredible variety of animals, including some very large and dangerous ones, such as the wooly rhinoceros, the straight-tusked elephant, and the saber-toothed tiger, any one of which would have required a great deal of coordination to kill. In addition to the skullcaps and other skeletal remains found in these caves, there were lots of flaked rocks that our early ancestors used to cut flesh from the bones and hides from the carcasses. There was also evidence of the use of fire dating back as far as five hundred thousand years ago.

It was an interesting site, but what had led me there was missing. I thought by standing on Dragon Bone Hill I could somehow imagine the sound of the people who left their skulls there. Anthropologists have spelled out in anatomical detail how changes in the way we walk and the way we eat also made it possible for us to talk. But the question few people ask, much less try to answer, is why we would have talked in the first place.

The most reasonable answer is still the one given by Charles Darwin in 1871 back when this question was first raised: "It appears probable that the progenitors of man, either the males or females or both sexes, before acquiring the power of expressing mutual love in articulate language, endeavored to charm each other with musical notes and rhythm." (*The Descent of Man*, p. 880) When we think of language, we usually think of it in terms of the information it conveys. But back before language came to dominate the human race, the sounds people made with their mouths conveyed emotion as much as information.

Nowadays we separate the two into music and language. And no society, however primitive, has ever been found in which either was lacking. But during Peking Man's day, music and language had not yet separated into the different realms they now occupy. Certainly the early humans who inhabited Choukoutian spoke, and they also sang and made music. But there would have been no reason to distinguish one from the other. Early humans lived in a sea of sound. It took a long time before language and music pulled us out of that ocean and we had to start using religion to find our way back to its shores. I like the way Lao-tzu put it, "When the Great Way disappears, we meet kindness and justice." (*Taoteching*: 18) And I would add: "When communication fails, we meet language and music." But at Choukoutian there were no casts of early human hearts.

We thanked Anita for showing us around and headed back toward Highway 107, but by a different road. About a mile from Choukoutian, we stopped in Shihlou Township and asked directions to the shrine of a man known for his concern with words. Just past Erchan Village, where the road crossed the railroad tracks, we came to a new wall encircling a set of new buildings and a sign that read: SHRINE OF LORD CHIA. That was what I was looking for. It was Chia Tao's shrine, a shrine to one of the great poets of China's golden age of poetry. It had been rebuilt in 2005 with funds supplied by a nearby factory, but word had not yet gotten around, and we were the only visitors. In addition to a caretaker, there was a guide, Ms. Chang. As she led us around, she sketched the events of Chia Tao's life and recited his poems.

Chia Tao (779–843) was born and grew up in this district. But all that was known of his early years was that his family was poor and he became a monk when he was still in his teens. The temple where he lived was still there in the hills just west of the Peking Man site. Among the advantages of monastic life was getting something to eat. It also meant having a chance to learn to read and write, and Chia Tao fell in love with words. The original meaning of the Chinese word for poetry (shih: 詩) was "words from the heart." And that was what Chia Tao excelled in. Among the poems Ms. Chang recited was one of my favorites: "Seeing Off Spring on the Last Day of April":

When April reaches its thirtieth day
your wind and light forsake a poor poet
I don't want to sleep with you tonight
until the dawn bell you're still spring.

When Chia Tao was thirty-two, he accompanied his master to the T'ang dynasty capitals of Ch'ang-an and Loyang. For Chia Tao, it must have been like dying and going to heaven. He met the country's most famous poets, men like Chang Chi, Meng Chiao, and Han Yu. The experience was overwhelming, and Chia Tao soon decided that monastic life was obstructing his craft. He returned to lay life so that he could devote himself to what he felt was his true calling: poetry.

But poetry rarely comes with a job. Chia Tao spent the rest of his life as an impoverished scholar, and it wasn't until he was in his fifties that he finally received his first appointment as a government official. But like all poets in China, he couldn't disconnect his mouth from his heart. He said or wrote the wrong thing at the wrong time and offended the wrong person and was banished, first to the middle reaches of the Yangtze, then to a tributary of its upper reaches. He died at his post in the town of Anyueh in 843 and was buried nearby. The life he chose gained him neither wealth nor power, but it did gain him the admiration of many. Following his death, the people in his hometown built a shrine for him. Although his body remained in far-off Szechuan Province, his possessions were sent home, and his hat and robe were buried at the shrine. After paying our respects at the memorial mound in which they were placed, Ted and I walked back to the car. On the way out, our guide recited one last poem: "Waiting at Night for a Flute Player Who Doesn't Come":

A recluse planned to spend the night in my shack
I unbarred the gate and faced the night sky
beneath the fall moon he played somewhere else
all night below the pines I listened to the wind.

Of all the stories told about Chia Tao, the one everyone hears, if they hear any at all, is the one about the day he was walking through a market in the capital while trying to decide which word to use in a poem, and he literally ran into Han Yu, the most famous literary figure of his day. When Chia Tao explained why he had been too distracted to know where he was walking, Han Yu suggested a solution, and the two became good friends. Ever since then, Chia Tao has been the hero of all those concerned with words, with the power of the right word, a word from the heart.

After saying goodbye to Ms. Chang, we returned to Highway 107 and resumed our southward journey. Twelve miles later, we turned west at a sign for Yunchu Temple. I still haven't gotten used to seeing signs to places I want to visit in China. In the past I always had to stop and ask directions from people along the roadside and work my way there in stages. But Chinese authorities were finally realizing the tourist potential of their own history. People had money and days off, and they wanted to go somewhere and see something. The Great Wall and the Forbidden City were no longer enough.

Ten minutes later, just before the entrance to Yunchu Temple, we turned north onto a side road. It was newly asphalted, but a platoon of soldiers was standing in the middle barring our way. We had to wait until the rest of their unit came running down the hill-side and fell into formation. After they marched off to their garrison, which was next to the temple, we drove to the place they had come down from and parked next to the small building that guarded the stone steps marking the trail to Thunder Cave.

We had to roust the man inside. Despite the sign on the highway, the temple didn't get many visitors, except on weekends, and the trail to the cave got even fewer. After paying the modest entry fee of 25RMB, or three bucks, we walked up the new steps, crossed the train tracks, and began hiking up a dirt trail. As we worked our way up the mountain, a passenger train passed below us. It was headed for Taiyuan, the capital of Shansi Province to the west.

Both the temple and the Army garrison guarded an old cart trail that led through the Taihang Mountains. Nowadays only trains made the passage. Halfway to Taiyuan the old cart trail, a new paved road from Beijing, and the railroad all passed just north of the sacred mountain Wutaishan, which was the residence of Manjushri, the patron bodhisattva of all those who cultivate wisdom. Wutaishan was—and still is—the big-gest pilgrimage center in North China. Fourteen hundred years ago, if you were look-ing for a location to build a temple, the entrance to the old trail through the Taihang Mountains would have been a good place to collect a few coppers from pilgrims.

The first temple built there was constructed in 605 by a Buddhist monk named Ching-wan (d. 639). According to his disciples, Ching-wan was a disciple of Hui-ssu (515–577), one of the founders of the Tientai School of Chinese Buddhism. One of the teachings Hui-ssu stressed to his disciples was that they were living in the Dharma Ending Age. In a number of sutras, the Buddha says the Dharma, or Truth, isn't subject to change, but humankind's ability to understand it decreases over time. He listed three ages of diminishing comprehension: the Age of the True Dharma, the Age of the Imitation Dharma, and the Dharma Ending Age. As far as Hui-ssu was concerned, the Dharma Ending Age had already begun, and he told his disciples to teach accordingly, which meant emphasizing devotional practices instead of the radical, direct approach of Zen—more prostrations, less tea.

Hui-ssu's teaching that humankind had entered the Dharma Ending Age probably had something to do with the anathema expressed by the rulers of the Northern Chou dynasty toward Buddhism. They were annoyed with the growing power of the Buddhist clergy and the loss of tax revenue from lands donated for monastic support. Finally in 574, Emperor Wu issued a decree ordering all Buddhist and Taoist clerics to return to lay life and their property confiscated or destroyed. His decree resulted in a major exodus of monks and nuns from the North to the South, among them Hui-k'o, the Second Patriarch of Zen. It also resulted in an end to the Northern Chou dynasty at the hands of its leading general, Yang Chien, who was raised by a Buddhist nun.

In 581, Yang Chien removed the last member of the Northern Chou imperial family from the throne and established the Sui dynasty in its place, with himself as its first emperor. He also reunited all of China for the first time in nearly three hundred years. With the country's reunification and the return of religious freedom, Buddhist monks in the North came out of hiding and many who had fled to the South returned. But many feared that this was only a break between persecutions—there had been an earlier one in 446—and they took this opportunity to prepare for the disappearance of the Dharma by copying sutras. Ching-wan was among them, and he decided that the rock of the Taihang Mountains was perfect for carving texts in a less perishable form.

He managed to fit fourteen of the most popular texts of his day, including most of the *Huayen Sutra*, into the cave he carved out of the mountain. Other monks began doing the same thing on other mountains in North China. But what distinguished Ching-wan's work was that it was carried on by others for another five hundred years.

The main reason for the continuity and extent of sutra carving at Yunchu Temple and Thunder Cave was its association with Fa-tsang, the Fourth Patriarch of the Huayen School of Chinese Buddhism. Fa-tsang came to Yunchu Temple in 697 at the behest of Empress Wu Tse-t'ien to conduct ceremonies aimed at defeating the nomadic Khitans. When the Khitans were defeated shortly afterwards, the imperial family considered Fa-tsang's efforts instrumental. Following his death in 712, the family sent a copy of the new Kaiyuan Edition of the Buddhist Canon in Fa-tsang's memory to Yunchu Temple, where he had conducted the ceremonies that had ensured the continuity of their dynasty. The volumes eventually arrived in 740 and became the basis for the carving that continued until around 1100, when the caves were finally sealed.

The caves were unsealed in 1956, and the importance of their contents is hard to overstate—at least for scholars and translators. Prior to their discovery, the earliest extant copy of the Chinese Buddhist Canon was a set of woodblocks carved in Korea around AD 1250. The Canon represented in the caves of Yunchu Temple was compiled five hundred years earlier. Altogether, more than fourteen thousand stone tablets containing more than a thousand sutras of the Kaiyuan Canon have been found, either in the nine caves on the mountain I was climbing or in a crypt adjacent to the temple.

Since my first visit to Stone Sutra Mountain two years earlier, motion sensors had been installed along the trail and also overlooking the caves. Even the secular authorities had come to recognize the importance of the place. The nine caves were spread across two levels just below the top of the mountain, less than a mile from the temple itself. The cave that Ching-wan carved out and filled with his favorite sutras was cave Number Five on the upper level. Everyone called it Thunder Cave because of the power of the Dharma to shatter delusions. The bricks that had once sealed it had been replaced by a steel door, which was locked. We looked around and finally

Interior of Thunder Cave

saw the caretaker near the top of the mountain with some other visitors. We yelled, and he started down.

A few minutes later, he arrived, unlocked the door, and led us inside. The cave was about thirty feet deep and twenty-five feet wide, and the ceiling was less than eight feet high. The walls were all lined with the sutras carved by Ching-wan, beginning with the *Lotus* on the right and ending with the *Vimalakirti* on the left. There were also four stone pillars in the middle of the cave to help support the roof. Instead of sutras, the pillars were lined with small buddhas, over a thousand of them, with their names carved on the pillars as well. Between the pillars there was a small altar with a statue of Maitreya Buddha, the Buddha of the Future. In 1981, a small crypt inside the altar was found to contain the relics of Shakyamuni, the Buddha of the Present Age. The relics consisted of two red granules to which small pearls had been attached. They had been brought from India and given to Yang Chien, the founder of the Sui dynasty, who in turn gave them to Ching-wan, who placed them inside his newly constructed cave at the beginning of the Dharma Ending Age.

The cave was a time capsule, and it was meant for us: beings from the future. But I couldn't help wondering how many of the sutras preserved there in stone meant anything to anyone other than the odd scholar or translator. I suppose that was why Ching-wan restricted his anthology to his fourteen favorite texts. His successors were not so careful. They made copies of every sutra in the Canon, whether they understood them or not. Clearly, the Dharma Ending Age had already begun. But since it had, how, I wondered, were we beings from the future expected to understand these words of the Buddha more than a thousand years later? There comes a time when language, even sacred language, becomes mumbo-jumbo.

When Bodhidharma started teaching Zen in China, he told his disciples the only text they needed to study was the *Lankavatara Sutra*. No doubt he earmarked the section in Chapter 76, in which the Buddha explained language and meaning to Mahamati Bodhisattva:

> Mahamati, fools say things like this, "Meaning accords with words. Words and meaning are not separate, because meaning has no existence of its own. There is no meaning outside of words." Mahamati, these benighted people do not know the nature of words. They do not know that words come and go, while meaning does not come and go. Mahamati, words are subject to birth and death. Meaning is not,

because it transcends existence and non-existence and is not subject to birth and death and is not an entity. Mahamati, the buddhas do not teach dharmas that are subject to birth or death. Because the existence or non-existence of language is indeterminate, they do not depend upon language but transcend it.

Mahamati, if someone says a buddha's teaching is dependent on language, they are mistaken. Such a teaching transcends language. Therefore, Mahamati, neither I nor any other buddha or bodhisattva utters a single word. And why not? Because everything we teach transcends language. We never fail to teach what accords with meaning, but we do so in accordance with the discriminations of beings. Mahamati, if we did not speak, our teaching would come to an end. And if our teaching came to an end, there would be no buddhas, bodhisattvas, pratyeka-buddhas, or shravakas. And if there were none, who would teach and who would listen?

Therefore, Mahamati, fearless bodhisattvas are not attached to language but teach according to what is appropriate. Because the aspirations and afflictions of beings are not the same, buddhas provide different teachings so that beings can get free of the mind, the will, and consciousness, so that they can attain the noble wisdom of self-realization, so that they can realize everything is a manifestation of the mind and does not exist outside of the mind, and so that they will abandon dualistic thinking. Mahamati, fearless bodhisattvas depend on meaning and not on words . . . Mahamati, a noble son or daughter should not become attached to words, because what is true is beyond words.

Mahamati, if someone points to something with their finger, and a fooish person looks at their finger, they won't see what it is pointing at. In the same manner, foolish people become so attached to the finger of words, they refuse to abandon it to grasp the truth, even at the point of death. The same is true, Mahamati, regarding what is not subject to birth or death. Those who don't cultivate skillful means cannot understand this. Thus, you should cultivate skillful means and not cling to words, as if you were looking at someone's finger.

But the *Lankavatara* was not among Ching-wan's favorites. After walking back down and returning to our car, we pulled onto the highway. I looked back at Stone Sutra Mountain. Why, I wondered, would anyone need a finger to point out the celestial lantern hanging just above the ridge?

2 NO BUDDHA

Having paid my respects to the words we hear when we think we hear a buddha, I turned to the image we see when we think we see a buddha. I suppose I could have done that in Beijing, but I wanted to visit China's most colossal attempt at rendering the image about which the Buddha once asked, "What do you think, Subhuti, can the Buddha be seen by means of the attributes he has acquired?" (*Diamond Sutra*: 5)

The Buddha urged his disciples to look within. But it was far easier for them to look at their teacher and imagine themselves with his golden-hued skin, his gossamer attire, his serene gaze, his radiance of awareness. Attachment to appearances not only plagues ordinary mortals, it also plagues those who would otherwise rise above the red dust of the world of sensation. Twelve hundred years after the Buddha's Nirvana, Lin-chi, the patriarch of the Linchi/Rinzai School of Zen, told his disciples, "When you meet the Buddha, kill the Buddha." That would be one solution. But I bore the Buddha no grudge, and I didn't think meeting him would be a problem. The place I had in mind was the old garrison town of Tatung, 225 miles west of Beijing, just inside that section of the Great Wall that separated Shansi Province from Inner Mongolia.

I considered the train, but taking the train in China was always such a hassle —

not the actual taking of the train, but the buying of the ticket, especially a ticket that promised a seat. Long-distance buses cost more, but they were faster, more comfortable, and far more frequent. Beijing had half a dozen long-distance bus stations, so I called Information and tracked down the right one. Buses for Tatung, it turned out, left from the Liuli Bridge Station, which was on the opposite side of town from Ted's apartment. But unlike Big Bell Temple, it was not near any subway stop. Before I headed off, Ted walked me down to the second-hand electronics mall on Ladies Street, where I bought a cell phone for ten bucks and enough minutes to get me started for another ten. I wished Ted luck on his next project—a shadow puppet documentary—then indulged in a 60RMB, or eight-dollar, taxi ride via one of the city's ring roads. I was at the Liuli Station in thirty minutes.

The station had just been renovated. The façade was made entirely of tinted glass, and the inside was even slicker. The ticket booths were computerized, and in less than a minute I had my ticket for the modest sum of 81RMB, or ten bucks. Buses for Tatung left every hour or so, and mine left in ten minutes, which gave me just enough time to visit the WC, buy a bottle of jasmine tea and a bag of peanuts, and climb on board.

Even though it was a Friday, there were only a dozen other passengers on the bus, which was as new as the station. I sat down near the back surrounded by empty seats. I felt privileged. An empty bus was rare in China, and an empty new one even rarer. Then I cringed. There was a TV and a DVD player set up behind the driver and speakers over every seat. But the gods smiled. The volume was set sufficiently low that the soap opera that began with our departure soon merged with the noise of the road.

We circled the northwest part of Beijing and at some point connected with the expressway to Changchiakou—the big city backdrop for Zhang Yimou's movie Not One Less. As we began snaking our way through the mountains, the section of the Great Wall at Pataling came into view. According to tourist authorities, between four and five million people visit Pataling every year. It occurred to me that if each visitor added but a single brick, they could rebuild the whole wall, from the sea to the Taklamakan Desert, in a matter of years. Put those tourists to work. Such was my bus ride reverie. I was tired from the previous few days and still suffering the effects of a cold. After we passed the Pataling exit, I tried to read a book about the history of buddha images in China but gave up. I got out my Air China pillow, propped it against the window, and fell asleep.

No one knows when the Buddha's followers began making images of their teacher. According to an account attributed to the early Buddhist sect known as the Mahasanghikas, when Shakyamuni left this earthly realm for a few months to teach his mother in the heavens atop Mount Sumeru, two kings from neighboring regions had their artisans fashion statues of the Buddha so that his followers wouldn't be distressed by his sudden disappearance. One of the statues was carved from sandalwood, and the other was made of burnished gold, and both were said to be life-size. (Cf. *Ekottara-agama-sutra*: 28)

This account was compiled within two or three hundred years of the Buddha's Nirvana, which occurred in 383 BC, and it may or may not be true, but it suggests how important the Buddha's image was to his followers. According to the archaeological evidence currently available, the earliest representations of the Buddha were not statues but shadow images suggesting his presence: the fig tree beneath which he sat at Bodhgaya, the lion seat from which he delivered his sermons, the eight-spoked wheel that represented his teaching of the Noble Eightfold Path, a stupa that held his remains, or his footprints, which showed he had left the dust of delusion and its karmic wake behind. It wasn't until the first century BC and the first century AD that artisans in Gandhara (Pakistan) and Bactria (Afghanistan)—and slightly later in Mathura (Uttar Pradesh)—worked their way up from footprints to a human figure.

In these earliest representations, the soft protuberance in the middle of the Buddha's head became a topknot of wavy hair, his earlobes came to resemble a young elephant's, his long arms looked like an orangutan's, his eyes were like lotus petals, he wore a robe that covered not one, but both, shoulders, and he usually stood, rather than sat, with his right hand held up and his palm facing outward in a gesture of fearlessness, a big hello to all beings. Although scholars continue to debate the cultural origin of such anthropomorphic representations (were they Indian or Greek?), iconic sculpture in the subcontinent was previously limited to local deities. The early Mahasanghika text known as the *Ekottara-agama* notwithstanding, in the beginning the teaching was considered more important than the teacher. We encounter this refrain in such early Buddhist texts as the *Samyutta Nikaya*, where the Buddha tells Anathapindika, "Who sees the Dharma, sees me. And who sees me, sees the Dharma." (Cf. v. 3, p. 120, Pali Text Society edition)

But the Buddha also told his disciples that five hundred years after his Nirvana, his followers would turn from the teaching to its representation in images. He was right, but they didn't wait that long. As early as the first century BC, we find likenesses of Shakyamuni carved in relief on the burial caskets and coins of the Greco-Indian and Kushan rulers of Gandhara and Bactria, and we see more sophisticated rock sculptures in Mathura during the following two centuries.

This development was no accident. It was in this area bounded by Bactria, Gandhara, and Mathura that Mahayana Buddhism arose, with its emphasis on devotional practices aimed at gaining access to the sacred through the accrual of merit rather than meditation. As the merchants and rulers in that part of the world began to fund this new, lay-oriented movement, the Buddha took on an Apollonian guise. And by the fourth and fifth centuries, he appeared not simply as another god but as a superman of monumental proportions. Now that the buddhas of Bamyan have been reduced to rubble, nowhere is this vision of the Buddha's likeness presented on such a colossal scale as it is in Tatung, toward which I sped until the conductress woke me.

Two hours after leaving Beijing, we pulled into a Sinopec station for a toilet break. Although the petroleum industry in China had been privatized, Sinopec had pretty much locked up the North China market. At least their stations had toilets now. In the old days, all they had was a wall with a trench behind it. While my fellow passengers availed themselves of the opportunity, I tried to go back to sleep, but without success. Usually these long-distance buses stopped long enough for passengers to smoke a cigarette as well, but this time, as soon as people came out of the WC, the conductress yelled for them to get back on board, and we rolled on.

Just before the exit to Hsuanhua, we turned off the Changchiakou Expressway onto the Tatung Expressway and headed southwest. The Chinese call them "expressways" and not "freeways," because all roads of any significance in China are toll roads, which was why the country had been able to build up its system of paved roads so quickly. Whatever they cost to use, they were always worth it. Of course, they were getting beat to hell by never-ending columns of overloaded trucks, but so were the old roads, which were one pothole after another. I used to consider myself lucky if the bus I was on averaged more than twenty-five miles an hour. On the expressways now, buses averaged over fifty and private cars sixty. They may have made traveling in China less adventurous, but they made traveling long distances practical.

As we continued southwest, the road cut through the vast desiccated landscape of the Nihowan Basin. In recent years, it had become more famous than Choukoutian among those who studied early human remains. Just off the highway, about seventy-five miles from Beijing, Chinese archaeologists had pushed back the date of hominid habitation and tool making in that part of the world to 1.7 million years, more than a million years earlier than Choukoutian and just about as early as anywhere else. I considered the distance we'd traveled, from stone tools to language, to buddhas, to rock-and-roll. Suddenly and inexplicably, I imagined Little Richard as a second-century Gandharan buddha: pencil-thin mustache, wavy hair all knotted up on top, transmitting the teaching of "wop bop a loo bop a lop bam boom." Such was my tutti-frutti reverie as we crossed a landscape now devoid of human habitation, but not of daydreams.

The road was as desolate as the landscape. There weren't even any trucks. It was eerie. At some point we crossed a series of rivers. I hadn't expected rivers in such an arid region. And all of them were frozen. Black and white magpies hopped awkwardly across the ice, looking for an opening. In the middle of one river, an old man sat on a folding stool fishing through a hole in the ice. The nomads who once roamed that part of China made a big deal about catching the first fish of spring. After a winter of mutton, fish had been a treat, and apparently still was.

The only other breaks in the landscape of brown on brown were fields of last year's cornstalks and windblown plastic bags. It wasn't until we were approaching Tatung that we finally passed something green. It was a pine forest, and it stretched several miles. It looked completely out of place. Then we were back to brown on brown.

Ever since the Indian Plate slipped under the Eurasian Plate and lifted up what is now Central Asia, the monsoons stopped making their annual visit to this part of the world. It was dry and getting drier. But it wasn't a desert, at least not yet. This was the southern edge of what was once an endless grassland, where nomads grazed their herds and lived off the wealth of the slow-moving people who lived in towns the color of mud. China's early history is the history of the relationship between these two groups: the grain-growing Chinese who settled the watershed of the Yellow River and the pastoral tribes who followed their animals across the grasslands to the north.

Nomadic peoples didn't develop from Neolithic hunter-gatherers. They arose from civilization, or at least from the transitional phase preceding it that involved the domestication of animals that needed room to graze, such as sheep and cattle and horses. It was never an easy relationship, but both groups depended on the other. The nomads depended on the civilized world for grain and manufactured goods, such as textiles and metals. The civilized world depended on the nomads for horses and hides but even more for their military skills, which the nomads themselves used to extort goods and wealth from the Chinese, but which the Chinese just as often employed to defend themselves against their enemies, who were sometimes other nomads and sometimes other Chinese.

When China first became a unified political entity under the Ch'in dynasty in the third century BC, their nomad neighbors also produced their first great tribal confederation, the Hsiung-nu. And as Chinese dynasties rose and fell, so did nomad confederations: the Hsiung-nu gave way to the Hsien-pi, and the Hsien-pi gave way to the Toba. For the most part, the Chinese were the dominant member in this relationship. At least they were until the Toba inaugurated a new phase. The Toba not only raided the Chinese, they conquered them and established the first non-Chinese dynasty, the Northern Wei, in AD 386. The Toba have long since disappeared, but they left their traces around their old capital, where we finally arrived four and a half hours after leaving Beijing.

Before I left the Tatung bus station, I checked on buses to my next destination, the sacred mountain of Wutaishan. It was an old habit: always making sure I knew how to get out of town. The lady at the ticket window said there was only one bus a day. It left at 7:30 in the morning but from a different station. I made a note and walked outside, threw my pack into a waiting taxi, and asked the driver to take me to a good hotel—I was just beginning my journey and still feeling flush. The city had changed since my first visit in 1989, when local transportation presented visitors with a choice between pony carts and public buses held together by slogans like ADVANCE BEHIND THE LEADERSHIP OF THE COMMUNIST PARTY.

The taxi driver overestimated what I meant by a "good hotel" and took me to the Huayuan, a four-star establishment where rooms cost 420RMB, or more than fifty bucks. The two young receptionists seemed surprised that a foreigner couldn't afford the price, but they tried to help and called the Yunkang, which at 360RMB was still beyond my reach. Finally, and somewhat reluctantly, they suggested the Taihochun. It was a three-star, they confided, as if they were embarrassed to send me there. But rooms were only 200RMB, which was the price I was hoping for. It was at the east edge of town, but the town wasn't that big, and I was there in a few minutes. After I checked in I came back outside to get my pack and asked the driver if he would take me to see the sights the following day. We agreed on a fee equivalent to twenty bucks, which was a third of what taxi drivers charged in Beijing, and I went up to my room.

The room was a good deal for twenty-five bucks. Even the carpet was clean—not a single cigarette burn. After congratulating myself on my good fortune, I boiled some water in the hot pot that had lately replaced the thermos in most Chinese hotels. While I was waiting, I took out my tea gear: a clay pot the size of a small mandarin orange and two small porcelain cups—the second one for a guest or just another one for me, a bag of oolong from Taiwan, and a round, handmade wooden tray I bought in a thrift store on Bainbridge Island across from Seattle. It had a carving of a mountain, a pavilion overlooking a waterfall, and a poem in Japanese I've never been able to make out. It looked like someone had tried to dream their way to another world, which was what I did myself. This was my first night in a hotel, and I enjoyed the luxury.

The next morning I switched to coffee, if only for its laxative effects, and got ready to meet the Toba. The Toba were a Turkish tribe, and like other nomadic groups, their religious beliefs were shamanistic. But like other nomadic groups that conquered sedentary civilizations, those who stayed to rule adopted the beliefs of those they conquered. The Toba found Buddhism especially useful. They not only supported the Buddhist clergy, they took for themselves the role of living buddhas and thereby ensured their control of a devoted populace.

But this arrangement also had a downside. Monks and monasteries were exempt from taxation, which more and more people began using as a subterfuge, increasing the burden on those unable to find similar shelter. The Toba emperor T'ai-wu finally became so annoyed at this state of affairs that he launched China's first persecution of Buddhists in 446. Temples were destroyed and monks and nuns who didn't flee were forced to return to lay life. But when T'ai-wu died in 452, his grandson and successor, Wen-ch'eng, reversed the policy and tried to make up for it by rebuilding the temples his grandfather had destroyed. He also initiated the largest art project ever undertaken in China, in the sandstone cliffs just west of the Toba capital. The place was sacred among the local people and was called Yunkang: "Cloud Bluff." It was a place where people went for visions, and Emperor Wen-ch'eng carved his there in stone.

The original plan, conceived by the Buddhist monk T'an-yao and approved by the emperor, was to carve out five caves, each with a different buddha inside. They represented the five kinds of knowledge acquired by every buddha: the knowledge of reality, the knowledge of perfect reflection, the knowledge of equanimity, the knowledge of subtle discrimination, and the knowledge of what works. And since the imperial family was funding the project, the buddhas were made to resemble four of the five Toba emperors up to that point and Emperor Wen-ch'eng's deceased son, who became Maitreya, the Buddha of the Future. Since the Toba rulers had adopted the role of living buddhas, the statues were simply a confirmation in stone. According to dynastic annals, over forty thousand workers took part, and artisans were brought from sites along the Silk Road and as far away as India. Work began in 460, and by the time it ended in 524, the final tally was over fifty thousand statues in more than fifty caves. The Chinese added a few more buddhas during the T'ang dynasty, but except for a single huge statue of Amitabha, the resident Buddha of the Western Paradise, they didn't compare with those left by the Toba.

Mr. Chang was waiting outside the hotel to take me to the caves, and he wasn't alone. Sitting with him in the front seat was his daughter, Lili. She was twenty-three and was studying at the local teachers' college just outside of town. Normally she lived in the college dorm, but it was a Saturday, and her father thought this would be a good chance for her to practice her English. I agreed, but had to remind myself not to stare. It was like having the moon in the car.

When Mr. Chang asked if I had eaten, and I told him I had had a cup of coffee, he insisted we stop at his favorite restaurant. It was a noodle joint, but it wasn't the usual noodle joint: it was indoors behind big glass windows, had a tiled floor, and was spotless. As we sat down, Mr. Chang waved to the proprietor, and bowls of noodles appeared a minute later. They were the wide, flat variety, and were topped with coriander, shredded turnip, and a meat sauce of ground pork. Mr. Chang insisted on paying, which wasn't much, but it was his way of demonstrating the hospitality I have received so often in China. In America, I'm just another guy in line, but in China I'm so well cared for, if not watched over, I have to wonder what wonderful deeds I must have performed in a previous life.

After we finished our noodles, it took maybe twenty minutes to drive the ten miles to the Yunkang Caves west of town. The entry fee was 60RMB, or nearly eight dollars. It was a major tourist site, but it wasn't the tourist season. There was only one tour bus parked outside the gate in a parking lot with room for a hundred. March was obviously a good time to visit—even if it was on the chilly side. I bought Lili a ticket and offered to buy her father one as well, but he declined, saying he needed to keep an eye on his taxi.

Yunkang was such a special place I decided to splurge on a guide as well, which cost another 80RMB. I walked inside the travel service office next to the ticket window. There were about forty guides waiting for tours that were at least a month away. I had my pick and chose Ms. Chiang. She spoke English, and I thought an English-language tour would be a good experience for Lili. It turned out Ms. Chiang had graduated from the same college Lili was attending, so they chatted about school while we went to see the buddhas.

We began with the caves at the eastern end of the bluff. Each cave had a number, and these were caves 16–20. I'm not sure what the numerical sequence was based on, because these were the first ones carved there in 460. As we walked inside the earliest one, I was surprised how cold the air was. I had to zip up my parka. Our guide said the caves stayed cool year-round, even in the middle of hundred-degree summer days.

Except for one cave, where part of the front wall had collapsed during an earthquake, none of the buddhas in these first five caves could be seen from the outside—only after passing through a portico. Inside, the caves opened up into huge chambers that had been hollowed out of the rock. The buddhas that remained after the carving was done were among the largest figures ever carved out of stone. Some were seated, and some were standing, and they all ranged from forty-five to fifty feet in height—about the same size as the heads of the U.S. presidents carved at Mount Rushmore. But due to the lack of space in front of them, they could only be viewed by craning our necks upward, which turned us all into supplicants.

Halfway up the front walls, large openings let in sunlight that lit up the carved faces and made them appear detached from their bodies. I noticed that wherever the backs of the statues were connected to the rock walls, they showed signs of water damage. The rock was quite porous, and when it rained around Tatung, it poured. The summer storms in that part of China—the deforested, denuded part—supplied the Yellow River with most of the silt that made it five times muddier than any other river in the world.

As with monumental portrayals of the human form elsewhere, the proportions didn't seem quite right. Maybe it was just the viewer's perspective, looking up rather than at the same level. Or perhaps it was because the artisans were still feeling their way through the rock. No one had ever attempted to render the human form on such a massive scale before. The buddhas at Bamyan weren't carved until the following century. Some of the buddha statues at Yunkang were so big the carvers had to use attendant bodhisattvas as pillars to hold up the buddhas' outstretched hands.

Back in the Northern Wei dynasty 1,500 years ago, worshippers who entered these caves would have been awestruck and would doubtlessly have redoubled their devotion to their living buddha emperors. That was what came to mind, as I walked through those first five caves. This was not art for art's sake, nor was it about the Buddhist goal of liberation from suffering. This was about inspiring awe and submission to authority. Coming before these supermen in stone, worshippers

Yungang Cave entrance and interior detail

would have felt a profound and insurmountable sense of spiritual separation between themselves and the Buddha. Who among them would have asked, "How do I become a buddha?"

We moved on to the buddhas in caves 9–13 carved in the decades that followed. These were commissioned by the Toba nobility, and the emphasis was not so much on impressing worshippers with the size of the statues—though they were still huge—as with their design and artistry. Ms. Chiang pointed out Iranian and Byzantine motifs in the clothing and wall carvings, as well as the modeling of figures that was clearly Greco-Roman. Each of these caves was a jewel with a thousand facets, and walking into them was like giving a kaleidoscope another turn. Almost every inch of wall space was covered with a buddha or a heavenly deity or a scene from Shakyamuni's life, or just a rosette. And Buddhism wasn't the only subject represented. Persia and Central Asia were the source of many of the musical instruments used in Chinese music, and the walls of one cave were covered with deities playing celestial tunes—some on instruments I had never seen before.

Another unique feature of this second group of caves was that they were colored. About a thousand years after they were carved, someone had covered the statues with a layer of straw and clay and then painted the clay. The result was to turn the austerity of monochromatic sandstone into a rococo tableau of pastels. It was gorgeous. In some places, the clay had fallen off and exposed the holes into which wooden pegs were inserted to hold the straw and clay in place. This second set of caves also differed in general layout. The caves in the first set were round or ovate and resembled huge huts—or perhaps yurts—and the buddhas inside looked as if they had turned into stone during meditation. The caves in the second set were square or rectangular and closer in design to a throne room in a palace, and the buddhas inside looked as if they were teaching the Dharma to those who came before them. Clearly, the greater refinement of the second set of caves reflected a change in emphasis: art over awe.

As we continued westward into caves 5–8, we began to encounter pairs of buddhas. The carving in these caves had been funded by the Toba nobility and the local Chinese elite, and the pairs were meant to represent the couples who funded construction. These too had been colored. Cave 6 was especially beautiful and included over three thousand statues of all sizes. Another feature of these later caves was that the rock around the central figures had been removed all the way down to the floor so that worshippers could circumambulate the object of their devotion. This wouldn't have been important for emperors and court officials but would have been an essential part of any ceremony involving the Buddhist faithful. As with some of the earlier caves, another nice touch was the large windows carved out of the rock to expose the faces of the buddhas from a distance, but only the faces, not the bodies. This is what we think of when we think of a person. Arms and legs and torsos aren't important. The face reveals who we are. Thus Zen masters ask their disciples to show them their original face, their face before they were born, not their original hand or their original foot.

At this point, Ms. Chiang left us to continue on by ourselves to the caves at the western end. These final caves were carved out during the T'ang dynasty (618–906), long after the Toba had left, when buddhas became Chinese and were not as muscular or austere as those commissioned by the Toba. Finally, the caves petered out in a series of undistinguished buddhas carved by local nobles when Tatung's glory years were long gone.

Before leaving, I took a picture of the big T'ang-dynasty statue of Amitabha, the Buddha of the Western Paradise, looking out from the bluff. I couldn't help feeling the weight of this monumental testament to our quest to portray the sacred. It was

T'ang dynasty Amitabha Buddha at the Yunkang Caves

great art on a great scale, and I felt honored to have seen it. But I couldn't help wondering if such representations helped people on the road to liberation from the world of red dust or if they only furthered their enslavement to the objects of sensation. I could hear Subhuti answering the Buddha, telling him that the Buddha could not be seen by means of the attributes he had acquired. And I could hear the Buddha adding, "Since the acquisition of attributes is an illusion, Subhuti, the non-acquisition of attributes is not an illusion. Hence, by means of attributes that are not attributes the Buddha can, indeed, be seen." (*Diamond Sutra*: 5) All I saw were buddhas with attributes. The attributes that were not attributes would have to wait for another day.

. . . . .

I walked with Lili back out the front gate, and we woke up her father who was dozing in his taxi. We climbed in and headed back to town, but we didn't go far. I saw an archway on the side of the road announcing the Chinhuakung Coal Mine and asked Mr. Chang to stop. It was one of the biggest mines in the Tatung area, and I had read that they had tours of their underground operations. We drove inside and finally found the officials in charge of public relations. Unfortunately, they were not receptive to the idea of a one-person tour, especially when I let slip that I was gathering material for a book. What was I thinking?

We returned to the main road. But less than a mile later, Mr. Chang pulled off at the entrance to another mine: the Chingtzuyao Mine. Mr. Chang said that was where his father had worked, and he used to come there every day when he was a boy. He knew the people. He said sometimes he went down into the shafts with his father, and sometimes he just waited at the top and played in the dirt with the sons of the other miners. But it was noon when we arrived, and everyone in the office was on their two-hour lunchbreak. Since no one was around to object, Mr. Chang led me into the building that housed the main elevator shaft.

It was dark, but I could see half a dozen miners getting ready to take some drilling equipment down. When my eyes finally adjusted to the light, or lack of it, I walked over and asked them how far down they were going. They said the shaft they were working in was five hundred feet below, and it took the elevator two minutes to get there. Except for their faces, there wasn't much else I could make out. They were completely covered with coal dust.

Their safety equipment bordered on the absurd. Their hard hats were made of the flimsiest plastic and outfitted with tiny headlamps that were wired to battery packs on their belts, to which canteens were also attached. That was it. I'm not sure what else they should have had, but they looked so hopeless. Still, they joked around like soldiers do when they know they could die at any moment. They said they made 50RMB, or about six bucks, for a ten-hour shift. No one knows how many people die in China's mines every year. Different sources put the figure between five and ten thousand. The government liked to claim it was a regulated industry, but it wasn't—at least not the smaller mines, and it was in those smaller mines that most of the deaths occurred. Suddenly, the foreman appeared and yelled at the men to get a move on. They smiled and waved as they disappeared down the shaft to the 140-million-year-old Jurassic swamp below to spend another day mining the rock that burns.

Back outside, I saw train cars arriving on a track that ran through the mining area. They were piled high with pine logs. Mr. Chang said the logs were used to support the roofs of the mineshafts. So now I knew what that pine forest was for that I had seen on the way into town. As we drove back down to the main road, we passed several donkey carts coming up. Mr. Chang said donkeys still hauled most of the coal

Tatung coal miners taking drilling equipment below

and most of the mining equipment in the smaller mines, not only aboveground, but also belowground. I could feel the air from the flick of the whip above my ears. I'm not sure who had it worse, the donkeys or the men. The hillsides around the mine were covered with thousands of mud–brick hovels where the miners lived with their families between shifts in the earth below. It looked like a refugee camp. This was not a union town. If it wasn't one enslavement, it was another: the rock that burns, the rock that looks like a buddha.

After we returned to Tatung, Mr. Chang said he wanted to invite me to his home for lunch. We parked in an alleyway somewhere on the south side of town and walked up to his third–floor apartment. His wife met us at the door. As I took off my shoes, she handed me a pair of plastic slippers. They were hopelessly small, but I put them on anyway and entered. The floor was cement, and there wasn't much in the way of décor. The only gesture at art was a wall calendar with a picture of the Swiss Alps. The Changs also had a teenage son, but he was away at high school. His school was two hours from Tatung, and they couldn't afford to pay his bus fare, so he stayed in the school dorm, even on weekends.

Mrs. Chang made dumplings. They were filling, but that was all I would say about them. Dessert, though, was special. She took several persimmons out from the freezer. They were leftover treats from New Year. She sliced their tops open, and we sucked out the pulp: fruit sorbet in its purest form. It was delicious. Afterwards, we retired to the Changs' bedroom, which doubled as the living room. While Mrs. Chang did the dishes and otherwise stayed busy, Mr. Chang stretched out on the bed, and Lili and I sat in the two chairs that filled the room's remaining floor space.

I haven't mentioned that the whole time we were together, Mr. Chang kept criticiz–ing Lili for her timidness. "Speak English," he kept saying. She tried, but having never spoken to a foreigner before, she was understandably shy and usually responded to my English with Chinese. But her father reserved his strongest criticism for her deci–sion to waste her education preparing for a career as a teacher. His daughter glowed with the intent hopefulness of which youth is so capable. I told her to ignore her father. He meant well, but life was too precious to let someone else live it.

When I suggested she could use the same education to do other things, like the tour guides we met earlier at the caves, Mr. Chang said they were probably bored, and it wasn't a good job anyway. Lili finally showed some mettle and interjected that every job was a good job. It all depended on your attitude. I seconded her. Realizing he was outnumbered and verging on becoming unhostlike, Mr. Chang changed the subject. He said the reason Tatung was so poor was that all the big shots had taken the money from the mines and moved to Beijing or Tienchin, Beijing's port city. Finally, he sighed: today had been a good day, but what about tomorrow?

Indeed, it had been a good day, but it wasn't over. After our siesta, I told Mr. Chang there was one more place I wanted to visit, a temple built by the nomad successors to the Tobas. The hegemony of the Tobas ended when the Chinese reestablished control over the North as well as the South with the Sui (581–618) and then the T'ang dynasty (618–906). But when the T'ang collapsed, another series of nomad confederations took control of the North, and they maintained their control for the next five hundred years.

This five hundred-year period began with the Khitans. The Khitans were a confederation of tribes from the upper reaches of the Liao River in Manchuria that traced its origin to a man on a white horse and a woman in a cart pulled by a black ox. The man on the horse obviously represented a herder, and the woman in the cart a villager, which was a fair summary of the relationship between these two societies as well as of the origin of nomads in general. The man and the woman had eight sons, and they founded the eight tribes that made up the Khitan confederation.

The Khitans established the Liao dynasty (907–1125), with Beijing as their main capital and Tatung as their auxiliary capital. And about the same time William the Conqueror was invading England, the Khitans built a set of shrine halls in Tatung on a sufficiently grand scale to accommodate imperial ceremonies. And the halls were still there, as were the buddhas inside. That was where we went after our afternoon siesta.

The halls were near the middle of the old part of town in a compound that was so large it had since been divided into two separate temples: Upper Huayen and Lower Huayen. *Hua-yen* was a translation of the Sanskrit *avatamsaka*: "garland," the name of a Buddhist sutra and the school of Chinese Buddhism based on it that developed on the sacred mountain of Wutaishan south of Tatung. The sutra was a phantasmagoria of Mahayana teaching taught by the Buddha to an audience of deities just after his Enlightenment, when he wasn't sure his fellow humans were ready to hear what he had to say. In it he recounted a journey to dozens of other realms—if only to show how limited the human understanding of reality was. The shrine halls of Upper and Lower Huayen that portrayed this teaching in art were still among the biggest and oldest such structures in China.

Mr. Chang dropped me and Lili off at the entrance of Upper Huayen and parked out in the street. The entrance was on the east side instead of the south side, toward which the Chinese preferred to orient things. This was because the Khitans worshipped the rising sun (it got cold up there in the grasslands) instead of the midday sun. Once inside the gate, we walked across a vast deserted courtyard toward the two huge halls that dominated the grounds. The lighting inside was no better than that of the mining shaft. But in this case, the treasures were above ground, and the lack of light was meant to preserve their pigments.

The main shrine hall of Upper Huayen was first built in the eleventh century, but its murals and statues had been damaged during the series of wars that saw one nomad dynasty replace another until the Chinese finally reestablished control in the fifteenth century, which was when the interior was redone. I could hardly make out anything, but what I could see was impressive. Seated at the back were five huge, gilded, wooden buddhas seated on lotus thrones—the lotus being the flower that rises above the mud before it opens. Like the five buddhas of the Yunkang Caves, these represented the five kinds of knowledge. But the carving in this case was more lifelike and the faces more serene. Flanking them on either side were twenty standing deities, twice life-size and all leaning forward, as if in anticipation of instruction in the Dharma. Surrounding them on the walls were murals of the most important events in the Buddha's life and an attendant audience of five thousand disciples.

The artistry was breathtaking. But the day was late, and there was more to see in the halls next door. As we walked back out the front gate, evening services at Upper Huayen were just beginning. They were being held in a new hall built so the monks and laypeople wouldn't risk damaging the temple's architectural and artistic treasures. At least Upper Huayen was still under the control of monks. When we entered the front gate of Lower Huayen, there were no monks in sight. The temple was under the control of the cultural preservation officials.

As we approached the main shrine hall of Lower Huayen, I saw a man copying an inscription from a Liao-dynasty stele. When I went over to talk to him, he sighed at the futile attempt of the monks to regain control over Lower Huayen. It was a common problem I encountered at sites that had historic or artistic value. I was only surprised that the government had allowed the monks to keep control of Upper Huayen. I guess they had to give them some place to live.

The caretakers said they were about to close, and I had just enough time to take a quick look inside the main shrine hall, which was also built in the eleventh century, but hadn't been damaged in the intervening years and still contained its original eleventh-century statuary. I was stunned by what I saw: thirty-one of the most beautifully carved standing Buddhist deities, all larger than life and all surrounding three huge seated wooden buddhas: the Buddhas of the Past, the Present, and the Future. I've visited hundreds of Buddhist temples in China, but none of their statues or murals compared in conception or execution to those in the shrine halls of Huayen Temple. Michelangelo would have sighed. One bodhisattva statue in the main shrine hall of Lower Huayen so impressed China's great scholar Kuo Mo-juo (1892–1978) that he called it the Venus of the East.

I only regretted I hadn't come at dawn, when sunlight would have been streaming through the hall's huge doors. It was late afternoon, the sun was going down behind the halls, and the caretakers were anxious to go home. It was like leaving the Louvre after ten minutes. But I had seen what I had come to see. Having tasted an unforgettable wine, I felt no need to drink the whole bottle. I went back outside with Lili, got into her father's taxi, and we drove toward the hotel. It had been a long day; a long day but a good day. I had seen enough buddhas to last a few lifetimes. And though they were all impressive, a poem by the twelfth-century Zen master Tao-ch'uan kept coming to mind:

> Make it out of clay or wood or silk
> paint it blue or green and gild it with gold
> but if you think a buddha looks like this
> the Goddess of Mercy will die from laughter.

On the way to the hotel, we drove past Tatung's Nine Dragon Wall. Even though it was after five o'clock, the front gate was still open, so I asked Mr. Chang to stop. The caretaker's watch must have been at least fifteen minutes slow. He was still there. So I paid the admission fee of 10RMB apiece for Lili and me, and we entered a huge, vacant lot. The only thing there was one very large wall that took up most of the south end of the lot. It was 135 feet long, 25 feet high, and 6 feet thick. But it wasn't just a wall. Its surface was tiled with dragons, nine purple, blue, green, yellow, and orange dragons in ceramic relief playing between the curling waves and roiling clouds that surrounded Mount Sumeru, the center of the Buddhist universe. It was a magnificent piece of work.

It was built by Chu Kuei (1374–1446), one of the sons of the founder of the Ming dynasty, which replaced the Yuan dynasty of the Mongols, which replaced the Chin dynasty of the Jurchens, which replaced the Liao dynasty of the Khitans. The Ming was the first Chinese dynasty to regain control of North China in five hundred years, and its founder was intent on making sure the Chinese stayed in control. In 1392 he sent Chu Kuei to Tatung to help guard the northern frontier from nomad incursions, and Chu Kuei built this wall the same year. The heir-apparent had died the previous year, and the wall of nine dragons represented Chu Kuei's aspiration to succeed him.

Chinese have been worshipping dragons since Neolithic times and consider themselves the descendents of dragons. Their primordial Adam and Eve were Fu Hsi and Nu Wa, who were half-human and half-dragon. It was Nu Wa (Noah) who saved humankind from the Great Flood. And it was her husband and brother, Fu Hsi, who developed the system of trigrams of yin and yang lines that formed the basis of the *Yiching*, or *Book of Changes*.

Nine Dragon Wall

The Chinese see the dragon as the ultimate yang creature and the number nine as the ultimate yang number, and both as symbols of power. I was surprised by Chu Kuei's temerity to build such a blatant representation of his ambition. He was only eighteen at the time. Some years later, two similar dragon walls were built in Beijing, but neither was as big as Chu Kuei's. Like its counterparts in Beijing, he built his wall facing north, toward the entrance of his own south-facing version of the Forbidden City, of which nothing remained but swirling dust.

When the caretaker yelled that it was time to close, we returned to our taxi, and a minute later, we were at the hotel. I asked Lili and her father to join me for dinner, but they feigned having other plans and politely declined. After we said goodbye, I went inside and had my usual problem ordering a meal for one. I forget what else I ordered, but the dish I remember because I hadn't seen it before and haven't seen it since was a two-tone, white and orange pyramid of mashed potatoes and some kind of squash. It looked like Mount Sumeru, and I ate my way through the realms of hungry ghosts, humans, and gods. I swallowed the whole universe, and nobody noticed.

Wall detail of dragon above Mount Sumeru

3 NO MOUNTAIN

I checked out of the hotel in Tatung so early I had to wake the night clerk. By the time I walked outside, it was six o'clock. Since it was only the fifth of March, there was just a hint of light in the east. My bus wasn't scheduled to leave until 7:30. But the night before, I came across a Tatung tourist brochure in my room that mentioned the Luyehyuan (Deer Park) Caves. It called them "Zen caves" and said they were three miles north of town.

When someone says "Zen" in China, they usually mean meditation rather than what Bodhidharma had in mind, which is not unusual, since meditation is what the word meant originally. But I couldn't help wonder if in this case it might have been a memento left behind by China's First Zen Patriarch. Bodhidharma was the Indian monk who brought Zen to China, and there was a good chance he spent some time in Tatung. According to an account written around 650 by the monk Tao-hsuan (596–667), Bodhidharma arrived in Kuangchou by sea from South India around 475, give or take a few years. When he didn't find the reception he was looking for in the Liu Sung dynasty that controlled South China, he traveled north. If, in fact, he arrived in China around that time, he would have come to Tatung, which was the capital of North China in those days. The Toba later moved their capital to Loyang in 494, and Bodhidharma would have moved with them, but I felt obliged to pay the Zen caves a visit, just in case.

The street outside the hotel was deserted, and it was 6:20 before a taxi finally appeared. I waved, and it pulled around, and I told the driver where I wanted to go. He said he had heard of the caves but had never been there. The only thing either of us knew was that it was north of town. So we headed out of Tatung on the only road that led in that direction. The road was a work in progress. It was dirt and badly rutted, and "three miles" was either a mistake or calculated from the city's administrative limits.

After about six miles, the road forked at the village of Hsiaoshihtzu ("Little Rock"). We took the road on the left, if only because it was paved. According to a sign, it led to the village of Hsinjung, wherever that was. The driver had never heard of it either. The road to Hsinjung led up a ravine. As we started to climb, I began to wonder if I was going to get back in time to catch my bus, much less find Bodhidharma's rock cushion. A mile later, there was a small sign on the side of the road. We stopped to read it. It said: DEER PARK ZEN CAVES. On a bluff overlooking the bend in the road there was a small temple.

The driver said the reason he had heard of the place was that he knew people who came there to make offerings. Like most Chinese who grew up during the Cultural Revolution, his religious practice was limited to burning incense and paper money for his ancestors a couple of times a year. He didn't know why people had to go to a Buddhist temple to do what they could do at home. It was a point well taken, but I didn't pursue it. I was more interested in the temple, or at least in its caves.

The driver said the people who came there told him the caves were along the sides of a canyon behind the temple and there were buddhas in some of them. While I was wondering which were the Zen caves, the caves with or without buddhas, I reached into my shoulder bag and pulled out my alarm clock, which also served as my watch when I traveled in China. It had taken us thirty minutes to get there, and it was already 6:50. I was out of time. Bodhidharma would have to wait for another day. I took a waypoint with my GPS device and resolved to return in the future. We flew over the ruts back to Tatung and arrived at the bus station at 7:15. The daily bus for Wutaishan was still there. I tipped the taxi driver for getting me back in time and walked over to the outdoor ticket window. A ticket to Wutaishan cost 62RMB, or eight bucks. Since I still had a few minutes, I bought a fried-egg flatbread, still hot from the griddle, and joined the other passengers on board.

While the driver was warming up the engine, I asked him why there was only one bus a day to Wutaishan. He said there were four a day between April and October, the tourist season. But I was there in March. There were maybe ten other passengers on board, and none of them was going to Wutaishan to see the sights. I grabbed a couple of rows near the back—one for me and one for my bag. The last two rows of seats and the aisle between them were buried beneath cardboard boxes containing vegetarian shrimp, vegetarian scallops, vegetarian crab, vegetarian abalone, vegetarian liver, vegetarian sweet-and-sour spare ribs, you name it—all made from soybeans and wheat gluten by a company near Hong Kong. It was for the pilgrims, in case they came early.

Wutaishan was a sacred mountain, the most famous sacred mountain north of the Yellow River. It was on every Buddhist's pilgrimage itinerary, but not in March. Most pilgrims arrived in summer, and most of them arrived in stages via Shihchiachuang, Taiyuan, or Tatung, all of which were 120 miles away—Beijing was 250. In the case of Tatung, our bus was scheduled to get us there in four hours, or just before noon, but that was under ideal conditions.

As we pulled out of the station parking lot, I could see the road through the floorboards. Before we were out of town, my feet were numb. I had to get my wool socks out of my pack and put them on over my regular socks. Apparently someone else complained, and a few minutes later I smelled something burning. It smelled like rubber. After a few more minutes, the smell began to fade, and I felt heat coming from the conduit that ran along the floor next to the wall. But the warmth that brought feeling back to my toes didn't last long. Less than thirty minutes out of Tatung, the bus broke down. And it kept breaking down. We stopped six or seven times. And each time, the driver took off the engine cowling next to his seat and tinkered with the transmission or the linkage. I'm not sure what was wrong. My understanding of vehicle mechanics never recovered after I went AWOL from the Army.

The week before we were due to graduate from jeep-vehicle mechanic school at Fort Benning, Georgia, we got orders sending our whole class to Vietnam. I couldn't believe how gung-ho a bunch of teenagers were to kill people who posed less danger to them than their neighbors. Everyone cheered when we got the news. It was the summer of 1964, and they weren't showing body bags on TV yet. Having flunked out of my third college in three years, I had received my draft notice that spring. But instead of going into the Army for two years, which was what the draft required, I volunteered for a third year so that I could go to Germany. That was the deal in those days: your choice of training or duty station for an extra year. Suddenly faced with the prospect of going to Vietnam and still serving an extra year, I decided our deal was off, and I left Fort Benning the next day, which just happened to be payday.

A private's pay in those days was $78. That and the money left over from the previous two months was enough to get me out of Georgia and halfway across the country. Not quite a month later, after surviving a car wreck, detention by the police, and a nymphomaniac, I got caught in a freak snowstorm as I was hitchhiking through Montana in late August. Cold and broke, with no ride or sanctuary in sight, I walked into the nearest town and turned myself in at the local sheriff's office. Their jail had one cell with two bunks, one of which was taken. As I sat down in the empty bunk and turned to talk to my cellmate, I nearly jumped back up. He didn't look human. There wasn't a place on his face or body that wasn't cut, bruised, or swollen. He turned out to be a hobo. The train bull had thrown him off a freight while it was going full speed, and someone had found him on the side of the tracks and brought him to the jail to recover. He should have been in a hospital. But that wasn't going to happen.

Later that day, one of the cops drove me to Miles City, the biggest town in the vast prairie land of eastern Montana. I didn't know what was going to happen next and prepared for the worst. The worst turned out to be the Miles City jail, which had no bedding of any kind, only metal racks and just enough magazines to make a small pillow. They didn't like to encourage drifters. It took the Army a week to send someone around to collect me. That was a long week, a week of long, cold nights—every one of which was interrupted by the cops shooting in the firing range across from the cells—and long days, which I spent reading and rereading the magazines that made up my pillow. They were about hunting and fishing and sailing the seas looking for sunken treasure, which I resolved to do if I ever got out of the Army.

Finally, someone based at a nearby Air Force missile silo came around and put me on a train. Since I had turned myself in, the Army didn't bother sending an escort. Four or five days later, I reported back to my unit at Fort Benning. When the sergeant major asked me why I had gone AWOL, I told him. For reasons I'll never understand, especially in light of my subsequent experience with the military, he made good on the Army's promise. Instead of a court-martial, he assigned me to KP for a month. Then he sent me to clerk school and following that to Germany, where I ended up working in the headquarters of a medical battalion. And my knowledge of vehicle mechanics never progressed beyond its pre-AWOL level: transmission or linkage, linkage or transmission.

Such were my thoughts while the driver worked on our bus. Other than having to wait, I never worry when buses break down in China. Chinese drivers can fix anything. Ours started off using a screwdriver for interim tinkering, then finally got serious and went underneath with pliers and a wrench and some wire. Thirty minutes later, he reemerged, and off we went, up and over the big brown-shouldered mountains that rose in the distance southeast of Tatung.

While we were working our way up a second set of mountains, we entered a gorge and drove past Hsuankung Temple. As its name suggested in Chinese, it hung (*hsuan*), as if in space (*k'ung*), from the side of a cliff. It was a stop on every tourist itinerary in that part of China, and I had been there twice myself. Despite its templelike appearance, it was built for the military so they could have a convenient place to light incense to the various deities that helped them keep the nomads out of

Hsuankung (Hanging) Temple

China. Since ours was not a tour bus, we didn't stop. The temple did look ethereal, though, in the morning light.

While I was still gazing at its suspended façade, we entered a long tunnel and eventually came out on the edge of a reservoir that was frozen over. It was so white it looked like one of the salt lakes I had once driven across on my way to find the source of the Yellow River. But there were no tire tracks. Nor was anyone skating or even fishing. The reservoir looked as bleak as the mountains that surrounded it. Not long afterwards, the bleakness was interrupted by farmers with their mattocks breaking up the cornstalks from last fall's harvest. Their oxen stood looking on, wondering, no doubt, when they would be called upon to plow the detritus under and begin another year on the domesticated animal treadmill. At some point we passed a huge herd of black and white goats. There must have been five hundred of them. Mutton was the meat of choice in that part of China.

At the 70 km marker we passed an annex of the Chintzuyao Coal Mine, where farmers worked in the off-season and some poor souls worked year-round. After zigzagging our way down our second mountain, we turned west and began driving down a valley so wide and flat it must have been leveled by the mother of all glaciers. Suddenly the driver pulled over again. He went outside and gave one of the tires a few kicks. It was losing air. Again, that was no problem. Along roadsides in China, there were always places that fixed tires, even in the middle of nowhere. Sure enough, a couple of hundred yards down the road, there was a mud-brick hovel with a *pu-t'ai*: "tire repair" sign.

While the driver jacked up the bus, took off the tire, and rolled it down the road, everyone else went outside to smoke or pee or just stretch their legs. I struck up a conversation with the man who had been sitting in front of me. He was a Mongol and in his eighties. He only had two teeth, at least that I could see, and I figured he must have lived on millet gruel and steamed buns. He thought I was a Uighur, and I thought he was a Tibetan. After straightening out our identities, he said he had an arrangement with a lama at one of the monasteries on Wutaishan. For the past seven years, he came up every spring to sit in the meditation hall, then went back down to Tatung in the fall. I asked him about places to stay, and he suggested a couple of pilgrim hostels.

While we were talking, another Mongol passed him a bottle of white lightning, which he passed on to me. I laughed and passed it back. I couldn't imagine why anyone would want to drink so early in the day, especially on a bus. Besides, Chinese white lightning was my least favorite alcohol. I shudder just thinking about it. After I handed the bottle back, I walked over and talked to a monk who was standing by himself fingering his beads. He said he lived on Wutaishan at Paohua Temple. He was on his way back after visiting some fellow monks at Upper Huayen in Tatung. He said Paohua was at the foot of North Peak, up a side valley from Pishan Temple. I told him I knew where Pishan was, but I'd never heard of Paohua. He said there were only a dozen monks there, and they didn't get many visitors. But it was a good place to practice, he said. He invited me to come and stay awhile, I told him I had other plans. Maybe next time.

After the driver returned and replaced the tire, we continued west and before long passed through the ramshackle town of Shahe. The driver slowed down just enough to avoid pedestrians. Shahe was where the two daily trains that ran between Beijing and Taiyuan dropped off pilgrims and tourists bound for Wutaishan. It didn't look like the place had changed much since the first time I passed through in 1989. Shahe was a town without any discernible order, other than what the road that ran through it provided. We didn't stop, even when a few potential passengers tried to wave us down. Normally buses in China picked up anyone and everyone, even if there wasn't room to stand, much less sit. When I wondered out loud why we weren't stopping, the Mongol sitting in front of me turned and said passengers in Shahe had to take Shahe buses. That was the arrangement.

Our driver did his part to maintain the arrangement and continued on. Just outside of town, we turned south again and began following a river into the mountains. As we started climbing higher, we passed snowdrifts on the side of the road, and the river turned to ice. We zigged and zagged our way up the north slope of Wutaishan and started driving across the river, frozen or not. The snow on the side of the road became snow in the middle of the road. I noticed there were piles of sand every fifty feet or so. I thought maybe I should have taken a swig of that white lightning when I had the chance. As we were working our way up one icy patch, a mini SUV coming down the mountain lost control as it approached us. It skidded 270° and ended up just short of a three-hundred-foot cliff. In order to avoid the car, our driver had to swerve as well, and we ended up stuck in a snowdrift on the mountain side of the road.

Everyone on the bus got out to survey the situation—as did the people in the SUV, which included one old monk and three young monks. They were all wearing their yellow, going-to-town robes. They said they were from Chulin Temple, and they were on their way to the Shahe train station to drop off the old monk and one of the young monks. As they surveyed the situation, all they could think of to say was the name of the buddha who welcomes devotees to the Western Paradise: *Omitofo*, which was the current Mandarin pronunciation of Amitabha. It was the standard response among Chinese Buddhists to any situation, good or bad. No sense in getting upset when something bad happens: Omitofo. And no sense in getting excited when something good happens: Omitofo. All things are made of mind: Omitofo. Including this mountain: Omitofo. The young monk who was driving finally got back inside and put the SUV in reverse, and half a dozen of us very carefully helped push it back into the middle of the road. The other monks then bowed in thanks and got back inside, and they all continued on their way down the mountain made of mind.

Meanwhile, we turned to address our own dilemma. At first we tried to push the bus forward out of the snow. Then we dug around the wheels and put down sand, but the tires couldn't get any traction. Finally, we tried rocking the bus and managed to gain just enough momentum to rock it backwards and out into the middle of the road. We all climbed back on board, and the driver started forward. But as the bus began going uphill, it started to fishtail on the ice. Given the proximity and height of the cliff on the other side of the road, it was too dangerous to stay inside. We all got out and walked behind the bus, sometimes pushing, sometimes just following along, until it finally found dry pavement.

Once we were past that one bad stretch, things improved. Not long afterwards, we crossed the summit and headed down the mountain's mostly snow-free southern slope. Halfway down, we had to stop at a checkpoint, and I had to get out and pay 75RMB for the Wutaishan entry fee. The official who took my money said the fee was due to double in May during the tourist season. Monks, nuns, and people over seventy were free, as were all those who lived or worked on the mountain, which apparently included all of my fellow passengers. Twenty minutes later, we finally arrived at the pilgrimage center of Taihuai in the valley below. It was, as *huai* indicated in Chinese, "embraced" by the surrounding *t'ai* (terraces) of Wutaishan. Instead of just before noon, we arrived just after three o'clock, or nearly eight hours after leaving Tatung. But we arrived.

The air outside was cold, and the wind made it feel a lot colder. The village was nearly deserted. Other than a handful of monks and nuns, the only people walking around were the locals who ran the few businesses still open. If any other pilgrims or tourists were there, they were done for the day and either gone or holed up in their hotels. I thanked the bus driver for getting us there safely and walked down a lane off the main street to check out a couple of hostels. Unfortunately, none of them had bathtubs, and I really wanted a hot bath. I finally gave up on the village and walked across the bridge spanning the river that ran along the east side of Taihuai.

Against the foot of the mountain on the other side of the bridge was the three-story Chinchieh Shanchuang (Golden Realm Resort). It was a two-star hotel, and rooms, of which it had well over a hundred, were 400RMB. Since I was the only guest that day, they didn't argue with my offer of 160RMB, or twenty bucks. I dropped my bag in my room, walked back across the bridge into the village, and bought a couple of books about the mountain at the local bookstore. I also mailed a letter—even on Sunday the post office was open. Then I walked down an alley on the other side of the street and checked my e-mail at the local Internet cafe and brothel, which was full of young monks and kids playing video games and middle-aged men getting blow jobs.

Once I was done, I walked back out to the only street in town and began looking for an open restaurant. While I was walking along, I met two nuns, and we started talking. The older nun said they lived at Wutaishan's Pushou Temple, which was the most famous training nunnery in China. When I told them I was looking for some-where to eat, they led me to their favorite place, the Shansi Restaurant. They said they had already eaten but sat down to keep me company. I ordered a plate of spinach with garlic and another of fried potatoes with tree ears and onion stalks. While I waited for my food, I asked the two nuns why they lived on Wutaishan. It was so cold in the winter and so overwhelmed with tourists in the summer.

They said they didn't mind the cold. They just put on more clothes in win-ter. And tourists didn't visit their nunnery. It was a good place to practice. But the reason it was a good place to practice, they said, was that the mountain was under the protection of Manjushri. I asked them if they had ever seen Buddhism's Bodhisattva of Wisdom. They said they had seen him twice, both times at Hsientung Monastery, which was the oldest monastery on the mountain. They said they had also seen the balls of fire that Wutaishan was known for and that appeared from time to time above the peaks. When I asked how they differed from the Northern

Lights, they said the balls of fire were much brighter, and they appeared over all five peaks, even South Peak.

When I mentioned that I wanted to visit one of the peaks the next day, the woman who ran the restaurant overheard me and said she had a friend who had an SUV, and she would pick me up at my hotel the next morning. She didn't know how much it would cost but said we could discuss that then. The nuns said they had made a pilgrimage to all five peaks the previous year along with their abbess and sixty-five laypeople from Inner Mongolia. They did it all on foot, which took them three days. But that was in the summer.

The bill for dinner was 27RMB, or three and a half bucks, which wasn't bad for a place set up for tourism. I said goodbye to the nuns, and they crossed the street and disappeared down an alley. Their nunnery was a mile up the road, but they had to catch an early morning bus and were spending the night at a smaller temple in the village. I walked back across the village bridge to my own accommodations under a purple vault of fading light and shining stars.

. . . . .

I tried to take a bath, but the water wasn't even close to hot, and I was too tired to complain. I settled for a very quick, very lukewarm shower. Since I was the only guest in the hotel, they didn't turn on the heat in the rooms that night either. It was so cold I kept trying to get my head further under the covers but regrettably needed to breathe. It was a long night, and I was glad to see the light outside the window the next morning. I finally got out of bed at seven o'clock just long enough to get dressed, make some coffee, and get back into bed. About an hour later, the woman from the restaurant knocked on my door. She was there with a driver and a local cop. The cop was there to ensure my safety. I wasn't going to be doing anything dangerous, but officials in China hate filling out reports when a foreigner gets injured or killed. The cop wasn't taking any chances, and no doubt he was also expecting a piece of the action.

The pilgrimage village of Taihuai was surrounded by five (which was where the *wu* in Wutaishan came from) not very impressive peaks, which was why the Chinese called them *t'ai*: "terraces," rather than *feng*: "peaks." And all five were now accessible by road. When I asked the driver about road conditions, he said the only peaks he thought he could reach were East Terrace and South Terrace. There was too much snow on the roads to the other peaks. But the only peak I was interested in visiting was North Terrace. North Terrace was the highest of the five, and it was where Han-shan Te-ch'ing (1546–1623) lived for eight years when he was a young monk. His were among the first Buddhist texts I ever read in Chinese, and he had become a prominent figure in my pantheon of Buddhist heroes. The driver said he could get me to within an hour's hike of the peak, but he wanted 1,000RMB. He must have thought I was from Mars. We negotiated, and the price dropped. But he wouldn't go below 300RMB, which was still outrageous, but what was I going to do?

We drove out of Taihuai on the same road on which I had arrived the day before. As we began to climb toward the pass, whenever we approached an icy stretch, the driver turned on a battery-operated device that chanted *Namo Omitofo*: "Homage to Amitabha." And as soon as we hit dry pavement again, he turned it off. No sense wasting the Buddha's protection. When we finally reached the pass, we turned off on a side road that followed the ridgeline west to North Terrace. Some wealthy lay benefactor from Taiwan had paid to have the road, all seven miles of it, set with paving stones that were expected to do a better job of withstanding the freezing and thawing of winter and spring than cement or asphalt.

But we didn't get a chance to see the new surface, or if it worked. After less than a hundred yards, the road became impassable. The snow was too deep. When I got out to see for myself, I sank down to my waist and had to thrash around for a while before I found snow that was only knee-deep. It looked hopeless. Still, I wanted to make an effort, however feeble, at paying my respects to those who had chosen this snow-swept ridge for their huts. I told the driver I would be back in an hour—two at the most. Confident that I wouldn't get far enough to get lost or into trouble, the cop stayed in the SUV, and I trudged off alone through the drifts.

Whenever I could, I took advantage of rocky outcrops and finally came across an animal trail that was only ankle-deep. The larger tracks looked like those of a mountain sheep, and the smaller ones appeared to be made by a rabbit. Wutaishan was now a national park, and its wildlife was enjoying the benefits of such protection. I followed their trail for half a mile or so to a rocky promontory from which I could see the mountain's North Terrace in the distance. I was beginning to feel dizzy from hiking in deep snow at that elevation—it was over 8,500 feet, and I decided I was close enough. I bowed to Han-shan Te-ch'ing and the lineage of practitioners he represented and congratulated them on their choice of residence.

Looking out on the white landscape, I recalled a poem Te-ch'ing wrote at the other end of his life on another mountain:

Snow covers earth and sky and everything is new
my body is concealed inside a silver world
suddenly I enter a treasury of light
a place forever free of any trace of dust.

During his eight years on Wutaishan, North Terrace became so much a part of him, Te-ch'ing added its local name, Hanshan, to his own, and he has been known as Han-shan Te-ch'ing ever since. Hanshan was the name the Mongols gave it. It reminded them of a sacred peak of the same name in what was now Mongolia on whose summit their tribal confederations were once formed and sanctified back in the days of Genghis and Kublai Khan.

After paying my respects to all past, present, and future practitioners on the mountain, human or otherwise, I trudged back to the SUV, and we headed back down to Taihuai. The driver offered to take me to South Terrace at no additional charge to make up for not being able to get me any closer to North Terrace. But I told him I wasn't disappointed, I did what I wanted to do, and one terrace was enough. I asked him to drop me off in the village near the entrance to Hsientung Temple, which was at the foot of a solitary hill that overlooked all of Taihuai.

Wutaishan was the first place Buddhist pilgrims came in China, and Hsientung was the first temple they built on the mountain. One of the books I bought at the village bookstore told the story of how that came about. One night in AD 64, Emperor Ming of the Han dynasty dreamt he saw a golden man fly off toward the setting sun. After consulting with his advisors, the emperor sent a delegation to the Western Regions to investigate. Three years later, his envoys returned with two Buddhist monks, Matanga and Dharmaraksha. The two arrived in the capital of Loyang leading white horses laden with scriptures and images of the golden-hued Enlightened One the emperor had seen in his dream. The emperor installed the monks in the residence normally reserved for foreign dignitaries just outside the capital's West Gate. This residence later became the first Buddhist temple in China, known as White Horse Temple.

But Matanga and Dharmaraksha were not done with their travels. According to an account not written down until a thousand years later, as soon as winter snows melted from the passes, the two monks left Loyang the following spring and made the long journey north to Wutaishan to pay their respects to Manjushri, whose residence they knew to be on the mountain. Taoists, however, considered Wutaishan a Taoist sanctuary. They called it Tzukungshan (Purple Palace Mountain). When the two monks arrived, the Taoists told them to leave. Being foreigners, they had no choice.

Upon returning to Loyang, they reported this to the emperor. In AD 71, the emperor convened a contest between the Taoists and Buddhists, during the course of which the scriptures of both religions were set on fire. Why this was done wasn't explained, only that it took place. At White Horse Temple, there's a mound that still marks the spot. In any case, when the smoke cleared, the only texts to survive the flames were those brought to China by the two monks. Since the gods had obviously spoken, Matanga and Dharmaraksha were given permission to erect a temple on Wutaishan, which they did the following year.

The temple they built on Wutaishan was called Gridakuta (Vulture Peak), after the mountain in India where the Buddha delivered many of his sermons. They also

View of Taihuai pilgrimage center from Bodhisattva Summit

placed relics of Shakyamuni inside a stupa next to the temple. Stupas started out in India as burial mounds for spiritual teachers. But by the time they were built in China, they were brick towers. The stupa on Wutaishan was the first of the thousands that were built in China during the next thousand years. Over the centuries, the name of the temple was changed to Hsientung (Manifest Power), and the stupa was expanded to the point where it became the huge 180-foot-high dagoba (Vajrayana-style stupa) that dominated the valley. Ever since then, Wutaishan has been the destination of pilgrims seeking to pay their respects to Manjushri, the Bodhisattva of Wisdom and patron saint of Zen.

When that first temple was constructed on the mountain, there were no written records concerning Manjushri, only the oral tradition brought to China by Matanga and Dharmaraksha. The Chinese didn't read about him until he made his appearance in early Mahayana sutras translated into Chinese in the second and third centuries. In such texts as *The Perfection of Wisdom in 25,000 Lines* (translated into English by Conze: *The Large Sutra on Perfect Wisdom*), Manjushri was the chief advocate for a new teaching called Prajnaparamita, or the Perfection of Wisdom.

In the fourth and early fifth centuries, several other sutras explained his connection with this teaching. According to the *Sutra on the Purity and Wonder of the Buddhaland of Manjushri* and the *Vaipulya Sutra on the Pure Precepts*, Manjushri came to this world from another buddhaland far to the east to pay his respects to Shakyamuni. After hearing Shakyamuni teach, he decided to stay and help spread the Dharma. But because the teaching taught by the buddha with whom he had previously studied focused on ultimate truth rather than provisional truth, the Dharma taught by Manjushri in this world was Prajnaparamita. After the Buddha's Nirvana in 383 BC, Manjushri continued to teach this teaching, but he eventually returned east and settled on Wutaishan. He has been there ever since and still appears from time to time, but always in a different guise, and always in such a way that people don't realize they've met him until afterwards. I've seen him twice myself, or so I've concluded: once he was hitchhiking near the pass; another time he was helping rebuild a monastery.

By the end of the fourth century, Wutaishan was the biggest pilgrimage center in North China, and it was around that time that the Northern Wei emperors in Tatung began contributing vast sums for temple construction on the mountain. During the next two hundred years, the number of temples on Wutaishan increased to more than three hundred. Of course, many of them were little more than modest shrines with a few caretaker monks or nuns. But many of them were huge complexes that housed several thousand monks or nuns. As recently as a hundred years ago, the monastic population on Wutaishan was still over ten thousand. The last hundred years, though, have not been kind. Only a handful of temples managed to survive the Second World War and the Cultural Revolution. And it is only in the last few decades that a dozen or so major temples have been rebuilt and the mountain has seen a resurgence in pilgrimage.

However, it is a form of pilgrimage coupled with the bullhorns of tour guides explaining Buddhist iconography to busloads of the curious. The society that once made a pilgrimage center like Wutaishan possible has changed. There are still plenty of Buddhists in China, and there are more every day. But most Chinese have internalized the old Communist Party attitude toward religion. When asked, they say they have no religious beliefs, at least that they are willing to acknowledge. Hence, they visit religious sites as tourists rather than as pilgrims. The monks and nuns living in temples welcome them anyway, up to a point, figuring it is going to take another generation to reintroduce Buddhist practice to a traumatized, and now materialistic, public.

I was glad I was there in March, before the tourist season began. Still, I was not alone. As I worked my way through the shrine halls of Hsientung Temple and the temples on the slope above it, lighting incense to the thought of Enlightenment and to those who manifested it, I had to wait outside each hall for a dozen Chinese tourists from Taiyuan to finish listening to their guide's comments concerning the date of the buildings and the identity of the various deities honored inside. As they moved on, I followed in their wake until I finally reached the shrine to Manjushri at Bodhisattva Summit. After paying my respects before his statue, I walked back outside and placed three sticks of sandalwood in the incense burner in the courtyard: one for Shou-yeh, my first Buddhist teacher, one for Han-shan Te-ch'ing, and one for Hsu-yun (1840–1959), another Zen hero of mine.

Hsu-yun, or Empty Cloud, was the most famous Chinese Zen monk of modern times. He was also an admirer of Han-shan Te-ch'ing. At one point he even called himself Te-ch'ing. And some say he was his reincarnation. In 1882, following a pilgrimage to Putuoshan, the island home of Kuan-yin, the Bodhisattva of Compassion, Hsu-yun resolved to travel to Wutaishan to pay homage to the Bodhisattva of Wisdom in hopes that any merit he might accrue would benefit his parents in their next lives.

From the port of Ningpo, on the other side of Hangchou Bay south of Shanghai, he made a full prostration for every three steps he took. It took him two years to make the twelve-hundred-mile journey. During the last winter, he nearly died of hunger, cold, and illness but was repeatedly rescued by an incarnation of Manjushri, who even carried his pack for him part of the way. Years later, looking back on that pilgrimage, Hsu-yun said it was not until then that he was finally able to free himself of delusions and understand the teaching of Manjushri.

There are dozens of texts in which Manjushri explained this teaching, but the one studied and quoted by early Zen masters more than any other was *The Prajnaparamita Sutra Spoken by Manjushri* (translated into English by Garma Chang in *A Treasury of Mahayana Sutras*) in which he tells the Buddha,

> Those who cultivate Prajnaparamita do not reject the dharmas (truths) of fools,
> nor do they grasp the dharmas of sages, because in the light of Prajnaparamita,
> there are no dharmas to be grasped or rejected. Moreover, those who cul-
> tivate Prajnaparamita do not delight in nirvana, nor do they detest sansara
> (life and death), because they do not perceive sansara, much less detest it,
> nor do they perceive nirvana, much less delight in it. Those who thus culti-
> vate Prajnaparamita do not perceive any defilement to eliminate or any merit
> to acquire. Their minds neither expand nor contract in regard to any dharma,
> because they do not perceive expansion or contraction in the dharma realm.
> Those who can do this cultivate Prajnaparamita.

The teaching of Manjushri was what Shou-yeh, Han-shan Te-ch'ing, and Hsu-yun all cultivated. That was where Zen came from. It was my path too.

While I was sitting in the sun outside Manjushri's shrine hall watching my sticks of incense burn down and the smoke curl through the frigid air, I heard another group of Chinese tourists coming up the steps and decided to leave. At least I wasn't there during the summer, and at least I had half an incense stick's worth of time with my Zen friends. I walked back down to the village and stopped in a restaurant for a bowl of noodles. While I was eating, the abbot from one of the monasteries dragged an old nun inside and sat her down and ordered a bowl of noodles for her. She tried to refuse on the grounds that the oil used to cook the noodles was sure to have lard in it. But the owner insisted he used a separate wok for his vegetarian customers. Finally, she relented. As soon as she did, the abbot had the owner add a couple of steamed buns to her meal. She was there on pilgrimage, and the abbot said she hadn't eaten in two days.

The noodles were good, with or without lard. Afterwards, I walked back across the village bridge, checked out of the Golden Realm, and took a taxi for 10RMB to Pishan Temple. Pishan was over a mile up the same road that led back to Tatung and where most visiting monks stayed when they came to Wutaishan. It was first built at the end of the fourth century and had seen many renovations. I walked through its ancient gate and went straight to the guest hall. I had stayed at Pishan the previous year, and I knew the abbot, but he was off somewhere on the mountain taking care of temple business. Since lunch was over, and it was siesta time, the guest manager took me to the building near the front gate that had accommodations for guests. He showed me to a room with six beds, all with boards for mattresses. I chose one next to the window that was warmed by the sunlight, and fell into a two-hour nap. It must have been my morning hike in the snow.

. . . . .

After I woke up, I checked at the guest hall again, but the abbot still wasn't back. I didn't feel like waiting around, so I walked back out the front gate and up the road a hundred yards, then followed the faintest of dirt trails across a frozen stream and up a steep slope through a forest of leafless trees. The abbot led me there the previous year when I just happened to visit on Shou-yeh's birthday. The trail ended at a set of five stupas that had been erected for Pishan's recent abbots. The last one on the right held Shou-yeh's remains. Shou-yeh was the monk I met when I was a graduate student at Columbia University who introduced me to the Dharma. The only English word he knew was "watermelon." And my Chinese was only slightly better. But that didn't stop him from inspiring me to take refuge in the Three Treasures of the Buddha, the Dharma, and the Sangha (the community of practitioners).

I had no idea who Shou-yeh was at the time. It was only much later, when I mentioned his name in Taiwan and China, that I learned something about him. He was born in 1908 at the end of the Ch'ing dynasty near the Grand Canal city of Wuhsi. His parents were shopkeepers, and he was the youngest of five children. His father died when he was still a child, and by the time Shou-yeh was twelve he was working as an apprentice at an iron works in Shanghai. While he was there, he developed an interest in martial arts and practiced every day with a fifty-pound iron staff he made for the purpose.

When he was twenty, his mother told him she had arranged a bride for him. But Shou-yeh had no interest in the pleasures of the red dust. A month before he was due to get married, he quit his job and disappeared. When he didn't show up for the wedding, his sister had to dress up as a man and go through with the ceremony. Afterwards, his mother found a suitable replacement, but Shou-yeh did not return. He decided, instead, to become a monk, and he found a master in Shanghai who agreed to take him in. The master's name was Te-sung. He took Shou-yeh to Hangchou to have his head shaved and to Paohua Temple near Nanching for ordination and then to Wutaishan, where Shou-yeh paid his respects to Manjushri in a snowstorm that lasted the whole time he and his master were there.

Several years later, Shou-yeh returned to Wutaishan alone and built a hut near the mountain's South Terrace. In the realm of spiritual cultivation, mountains are tantamount to what we call graduate school in the West. Mountains are where people go to make a teaching their own, a teaching they first study with a teacher in a monastery or a nunnery or, in the past, in a Confucian academy. Of course, this period of independent study could just as easily be carried out on other marginal land beyond the noise of civilization, such as a swamp or a desert. But mountains seem to be everyone's first choice. The key is solitude. Solitude isn't for everyone, but it's essential for anyone who hopes to go beyond written accounts of the spiritual path or an intellectual understanding of it. The purpose, as practiced in China, isn't to turn one's back on others but to develop the ability to help others by first helping oneself. And Wutaishan has seen more monks and nuns practicing in icy solitude over the past two thousand years than any other mountain in China. It isn't an especially scenic mountain, just a powerful one.

After spending a year on South Terrace, Shou-yeh returned briefly to Shanghai to accept abbotship of his master's temple but then came back to Wutaishan and resumed his study of martial arts at Kuangchi Hermitage. The abbot of Kuangchi was Hai-ch'an, who had been one of China's most famous martial arts practitioners before becoming a monk in 1888. But after a few months of training in Shaolin and Tibetan forms with Hai-ch'an, Shou-yeh decided he still needed more time alone. He built another hut nearby, and he began a period of isolation during which he focused on the study of the *Huayen Sutra*. Wutaishan has always had a close association with this text. This was the sutra in which the mountain was first mentioned as the residence of Manjushri, and Wutaishan was the place where the Huayen School of Buddhism developed in the seventh and eighth centuries.

The Buddha considered his presentation of the interpenetration of all levels of truth, the mundane and the sacred, as too difficult for humans to understand, and he never taught this teaching again. Shou-yeh felt drawn to this sutra, and he thought the best way to study such a profound and all-encompassing, all-penetrating teaching would be to write it out—not in ink, but in his own blood.

In the fall of 1936, he began writing out the six hundred thousand Chinese characters that made up the text. Every day he cut his fingertips or his tongue and used the blood mixed with an herbal tincture that kept it from coagulating. He tried to write between five hundred and a thousand characters a day. These weren't the small variety but were as big as silver dollars. Over the next few years, he became so weak he nearly died. But he persisted, and finally, in the summer of 1940, he reached the end. Then he wrote it out three more times in ink.

Shou-yeh's devotion to his practice and his utter disregard for the illusory line separating life and death so impressed others that he was asked to take over as abbot of both Pishan Temple and Kuangchi Hermitage—at the age of thirty-two. Other temples on Wutaishan were lineage temples, which required a connection with the abbot in order to stay. Pishan and Kuangchi were the only temples open to anyone with an ordination certificate, and that was where most monks stayed, whether they came for a few days or a few years. It was a turbulent time, during the Second World War. But besides overcoming the difficulties involved in simply staying alive, Shou-yeh managed to have the surplus income from his master's old temple in Shanghai sent to Wutaishan, and he was able to support hundreds of monks who sought refuge on the mountain during those years.

But when the Communists drove the Nationalists out of the country in 1949 and established the People's Republic, Shou-yeh decided it was time to leave, and he was among the tens of thousands of Buddhist monks and nuns who fled. Instead of going to Taiwan, as many prominent monks did, he divided his time between Hong Kong and Saigon. He thought the Communist repression of religion would ease once things settled down and he could go back. But the situation only got worse. In 1970 he finally accepted an invitation to go to New York. That was where I met him in the fall of 1971, at a weekend retreat he conducted at a Buddhist temple in the countryside north of the city.

According to the records at Pishan Temple, the copy of the *Huayen Sutra* Shou-yeh wrote in blood was destroyed during the Cultural Revolution, as were those he wrote in ink. But during that first retreat, Shou-yeh took the sutra he had written in blood out of a cabinet behind the altar and showed it to me. I didn't know what to think. He was the first Buddhist monk I had ever met, and I was impressed by his demeanor. I took refuge with him the next day.

Since he never learned English, he never developed a large following among Americans. Most of his disciples were overseas Chinese living in the New York area. I later heard that he took a liking to feeding pigeons and taking drives through the countryside. After the Cultural Revolution ended, and the Chinese government reaffirmed its support of religious freedom—up to a point—he came back to China several times, and I have seen his calligraphy on many of the country's sacred mountains. But for some reason, Shou-yeh always returned to New York, and that was where he died in 2001 at the age of ninety-four. The night he died, which was the full moon of the third lunar month, there was a heavy snowstorm on Wutaishan. The mountain missed him. So did I.

I sat in the sunlight before the stupa that contained Shou-yeh's remains until the afternoon shadows covered the hillside and reminded me it was time to return to his old temple. I lit some incense and bowed to my old teacher. It wasn't the season for watermelon, so I left a cookie at the base of his stupa. I've always regretted not being able to thank him for connecting me with the living Dharma, not just the Dharma in books. As I turned to leave, I saw some magpies eyeing the cookie from a nearby tree. I also noticed mountain sheep tracks in front of his stupa. Apparently, I wasn't the only one who came there. Sometimes we give, and sometimes we receive, but we're all connected.

The abbot was waiting for me back at the guest hall. His name was Miao-chiang, and we were dharma brothers. We had no sooner greeted each other and grabbed each other's hands at our good fortune in meeting again than six laypeople from Tatung also arrived. They spoke the same dialect as the abbot, of which I couldn't understand more than a few words. So I just sat down off to the side and waited for them to finish.

Miao-chiang was born in 1952 in Yangkao County, about thirty miles northeast of Tatung. His parents were farmers, and they were also devout Buddhists. Not long after he was born, his father became a monk, and his mother became a nun, and they gave Miao-chiang to a local temple to raise. He was three at the time. When he was ten, his mother took him to Tatung to live with the monks who took care of the Yunkang Caves. And in 1969, Ts'ang-t'ung, the monk in charge of the Caves, shaved Miao-chiang's head, and he became a novice.

Not long afterwards, the Cultural Revolution kicked into high gear, and he was forced back to his village for reeducation. He said he maintained his practice by reciting the *Diamond Sutra* from memory every day. He said it only took him nine minutes to recite all seven thousand characters. I should have asked him if he could still do it that fast. Most people need at least half an hour, and I would probably need

Master Shou-yeh's Stupa

an hour or more. When the Cultural Revolution finally ended in 1976, Miao-chiang returned to Yunkang. And in 1981, Ts'ang-t'ung sent him to Wutaishan to receive full ordination from his dharma brother, Ts'ang-ming, the abbot of Puhua Temple.

The next year, the Wutaishan Buddhist Association sent Miao-chiang to Chihsia Temple near Nanching for training. When he returned in 1984, he was given control over a series of temples and was asked to restore monastic order as well as the buildings. Several years later, he was sent south again, this time to Kanlu Temple on Chiuhuashan, to attend a special six-month course in monastery management. Upon his return to Wutaishan, he was made abbot of Pishan Temple. It was a big deal. Shou-yeh even returned from America to take part in the ceremony. Since then Miao-chiang had not only rebuilt and revitalized Pishan, he had also rebuilt Chulin Temple from scratch and had established Wutaishan's only Buddhist academy for monks.

I listened to Miao-chiang regale the group of laypeople with his take on Chinese Buddhism. He had just returned from Burma and was very impressed with the level of practice of the Theravadin monks there. The Chinese usually refer to the Theravada Buddhism of Southeast Asia as the Small Vehicle and their own Mahayana Buddhism as the Great Vehicle. But Miao-chiang said that from what he had seen in Burma and China, the Buddhism of the Small Vehicle was not necessarily that small, and the Buddhism of the Great Vehicle was not necessarily that great. His accent, though, was so heavy, I had a hard time understanding, and I wondered how he communicated when he traveled outside Shansi Province.

Finally, at 4:40 he jumped up and said, "Let's eat," and led us to the mess hall. We were too late for the regular dinner, which was served at 3:30 in the winter and spring. But we sat down anyway on the mess hall's long benches, and a few minutes later bowls of mixed vegetables and steamed bread appeared. It was spartan fare but filling. When we were done, Miao-chiang led us outside. He told me to get into the temple's SUV and his other lay visitors to follow us in their SUV. Then we drove back through the village of Taihuai and southwest three or four miles to Chulin Temple, which was located on a hillside off by itself.

According to Miao-chiang, Chulin was first built during the Northern Wei dynasty about the same time as Pishan Temple. But it became a city unto itself at the end of the eighth century when a monk named Fa-chao expanded the place in accordance with visions he experienced. By the time he was done, the temple housed over 7,000 monks in 120 buildings that completely covered the hills. When Miao-chiang was appointed abbot in 1992, all that was left was a Ming-dynasty stupa. The rest was rubble. Since then, he had built several shrine halls and a four-story building that housed a Buddhist academy and had enough rooms for fifty monks. That, he said, was only the first stage of a much larger complex that would house several hundred monks.

After we arrived, one of the novices led me to a room on the fourth floor facing the snow-covered hillside to the south. Below, just outside the monastery wall, I watched a coal truck arrive and unload its cargo in a side courtyard. All the rooms had radiators, and there were shower stalls down the hall. It was nothing like the old temples, where monks bathed once a month in one mammoth bathtub, in order of seniority.

About an hour after we arrived at Chulin, a monk came to my room and said Miao-ching had time to see me. I followed him downstairs into the monastery's reception room. The laypeople from Tatung were also there, as were half a dozen senior monks from Chulin. As soon as I entered the room, one of the laymen came up to me and gave me a bracelet of beads. He said he used them to chant the name of Amitabha. At first I didn't know what to say and simply thanked him. But when I looked at them more closely, they turned out to be the most unusual beads I had ever seen. They were some kind of fruit pit whose seeds were visible through five small holes at the end of each pit. I didn't have time to ask what kind of fruit they were from. While I was admiring them, Miao-chiang came over and grabbed my hand. Then he led me to a chair next to his and asked me if I had any questions. During the Ch'ing dynasty, Wutaishan became a center for Vajrayana Buddhism, the variety of Buddhism practiced in Tibet and Mongolia and by the Manchus, the founders of the Ch'ing dynasty, so I asked him if anyone still practiced Zen.

He said there were only three monasteries that had meditation halls: Hsientung, Puhua, and Pishan. But there were dozens of smaller temples where monks and nuns meditated and cultivated Zen, where they did research, he said. He loved to use the word "research." Zen practice, he said, was research, research into the here and now, into the Five Skandhas, the Eighteen Dhatus, the Twelve Ayatanas, into the mind. "Every thought is practice," he said. "We don't have to read books to find out about Buddhism. Every thought is Buddhism. Consider existence. Consider nonexistence. Anyone who does research practices Zen. We practice Zen when we drink a cup of tea or when we eat a bowl of rice. Zen is the basis for all forms of practice." That's about all I understood. And I only understood that because he scribbled it down on a piece of paper.

He talked for more than an hour. And maybe I understood 5 percent of what he said, if that much. He had one of the most difficult accents I had ever encountered. I wasn't alone. I've talked to other monks who have met Miao-chiang, and they all agree. It takes time to get used to him. But I didn't have time, and it was late. We were all tired. I went back to my room, lay down in my bed next to the window, and looked out at the twinkling sky. The elevation of my room on the fourth floor was over 5,500 feet, and the stars looked close enough to touch.

There is a story that has been told in China and other parts of Asia for the past two thousand years or so, about how the world was created through the efforts of a creature named P'an-ku. After eighteen thousand years of chiseling away and creating the vault between heaven and earth, P'an-ku finally died, and his body became the world's mountains. As I lay there, I wondered why some mountains were more sacred than others. Looking out the window, the thought occurred to me that maybe some mountains were more sacred because there were more stars above their peaks. But then maybe there were more stars because the mountains were sacred. In a number of sutras, the Buddha says the tongues of buddhas cover every world throughout the ten directions and constantly speak the Dharma: "suffering, impermanence, emptiness, no self." Maybe their voices were just clearer on some mountains. I finally closed my eyes and went to sleep listening to the temple's drum and bell enumerate the passions that bind us to the Wheel of Existence, including the passion for knowledge.

I woke up the next morning an hour before dawn. I had told Miao-chiang the night before that I wanted to catch the seven o'clock bus to Shihchiachuang. Miao-chiang was waiting for me downstairs and led me outside. While we were waiting for his driver to bring his SUV around, he tried once more to talk to me about Zen. Everything was Zen, he said. But his dialect was impenetrable, and standing outside in the freezing cold before dawn didn't make it any clearer. I figured that not understanding was also Zen. His driver finally arrived, and Miao-chiang and I said good-bye. Even though I hardly understood a word he said, I felt a strong connection with him, and I knew we would see each other again.

A few minutes later, I was back in the village of Taihuai, where I soon discovered that the daily bus to Shihchiachuang only operated from May to October, and it was March. I would have to take a bus to the provincial capital of Taiyuan and then transfer to another bus to Shihchiachuang, which meant an additional three hours or so. What the hell. At least Miao-chiang's driver kept me from jumping into one of the empty buses that cruised the village's only street looking for passengers. He steered me to a small van that was already half full and that eventually left at 7:30.

That was what China got when it lifted its restrictions on public transportation. Anyone who could get the money together for a van and the necessary permit was in business. These private vans and mini-buses didn't operate out of bus stations but cruised certain routes. Usually they waited near transportation hubs, such as train stations or bus stations or markets or crossroads. They didn't leave until they were full, or close to it. And once they were underway, they continued to troll for more passengers, which slowed things down, but which made it possible for people to

Master Miao-chiang

stand on the side of a road just about anywhere in China and flag down some form of transportation heading their way. This was one of those runs, with people getting on and off almost the whole way to Taiyuan. Finally, at 11:10, we pulled up outside the city's North Station.

When I asked the van driver if I could get a bus from there to Shihchiachuang, he told me I would have to go to the city's South Station. I should have gotten a second opinion. The ticket sellers at the South Station sent me back to the North Station. And the ticket sellers at the North Station sent me to the Main Station, the one down the street from the train station. That turned out to be the right station, and there was a bus leaving for Shihchiachuang fifteen minutes after I got there. It left at noon and cost 50RMB, or six bucks, and was only half full. Even though it was a public bus, it drove slowly out of town, trolling for more passengers. But once it hit the expressway, it cruised all the way to Shihchiachuang. As we headed into the Taihang Mountains, I read over an inscription I had recorded in my journal from a fifteenth-century stele in the courtyard of Pishan Temple: "A place doesn't become sacred by itself. It's people that make it sacred." It occurred to me that the corollary would be that the reason a place isn't sacred is also people. It was a hopeless thought, and I let it pass.

4 NO HOME

The conductress woke me as we came out of the Taihang Mountains onto the end-less expanse of the Yellow River floodplain (which makes up about two-thirds of the North China Plain):from Beijing in the north to Loyang in the south, from the Taihang Mountains in the west to the Pohai Sea in the east, nothing but mud. Ever since the Yellow River formed over a million years ago, it has been bringing down soil from the Loess Plateau one summer storm at a time, and filling in 150,000 square miles of ocean. Imagine an uncontrolled fire hose shooting out a billion tons of mud per year. This was where Chinese civilization began around 3000 BC, on the fringes of the Yellow River's steadily expanding empire of mud.

I was sitting near the back of the bus asleep on my Air China pillow when we pulled into a Sinopec station. The conductress leaned over in her tailored blue uni-form and matching hat and said it was time to pee. I got up and followed her down the aisle and outside and wondered if I was still dreaming. There was so much dust in the air, the gas station looked like a Martian movie set. As we walked across the pavement to the WC, I had to look down to keep the dust out of my eyes, and I only reached the station's white-tiled oasis by focusing on the conductress's knee-high black boots.

An hour later and eight hours after leaving Wutaishan, I arrived in Shihchia-chuang, the capital of Hopei. I had passed through its urban sprawl of ten million people a dozen times without stopping except to change buses. But it was too late in the day to continue on to Pailin Monastery, which was my next destination. And I wanted a hot bath. Outside the bus station, I flagged down a taxi and told the driver to take me to a hotel near the provincial museum. I thought about visiting the museum every time I passed through Shihchiachuang but never did. This, I decided, would be the time. The driver took me to the International, right across the street from the monolithic building that housed the treasures of Hopei that I hoped to see.

The International was a four-star hotel, and I hesitated as I entered its vast marble-lined lobby. But the price turned out to be a reasonable 290RMB, or thirty-five bucks. There was even a computer terminal in my room. The Internet browser didn't work, but it made me appreciate the four-star difference. There was also a porcelain tea set and an electric water kettle. And while I was making myself a pot of oolong, the concierge knocked and brought in a plate of fruit. That sort of thing didn't happen in the lesser-starred or unstarred hotels where I usually stayed.

As I sipped my tea and looked out the window, I was glad to be indoors and out of the dust. But I hadn't eaten all day, and something had happened to my lower back during the bus ride. I had to clench my teeth just to walk hunched over, and standing upright was impossible. So I ventured forth in quest of relief. Downstairs, I asked the doorman where I could find a blind masseuse—if there was one occupation blind people excelled at in China it was the art of massage. Every city in China had a lane where they congregated. But in this case it was too far from my hotel, and the doorman pointed me instead toward a regular massage parlor.

I followed his finger across the street and north a couple of blocks to a sign for a "health spa." Just inside the door, five women dressed in short white frocks were sitting on an orange vinyl sofa. The place looked like a brothel, and I felt somewhat embarrassed asking if they gave massages. They said, "Sure." What did I expect? Like they were really going to say, "No." Realizing the silliness of my question, I said I didn't want a girl and turned to leave. One of them laughed and said they weren't girls. It was so funny, the way she said it, I turned around and asked her how much. She said 15RMB—less than two bucks—for forty-five minutes. At that price and for that amount of time, it had to be a massage. The woman who quoted the price lifted a white curtain, and I followed her into a room with four massage tables, all of them covered with white sheets. I hung up my jacket, took off my shoes, emptied the contents of my pockets onto an adjacent stool, and lay down on my stomach. I told her my lower back was in spasm, and she went to work.

When she asked me where it hurt, her accent sounded different—not as stilted as Beijing Mandarin. So I asked her where she was from. She said she was from a town near the Korean border. When I asked what brought her to Shihchiachuang, she wouldn't say. She was so good with her hands, she couldn't have just picked up that kind of skill to make ends meet. When I asked how long she had been working as a masseuse, she said seven years. She was in her late thirties, and I wondered what happened that led to the career change. At first I thought a failed marriage: she came there with her husband, got divorced, and didn't want to go back home. But that was too easy. Then it hit me. She had been in prison. Seven years earlier would have been 1999. In the wake of the democracy movement, ten-year sentences were handed out like traffic tickets in 1989. And prisons in the Shihchiachuang area specialized in political dissidents. The Falunkung/Falungong had complained for years about imprisoned members having their organs harvested in Shihchiachuang. That was too dismal a prospect. I switched back to the minor trauma of a failed marriage. She had too much spirit to have been in prison.

Finally, she rescued me from my imagination and asked me where I was from. I thought it was obvious, but sometimes it wasn't. When I told her I was from America, she called over the other "girls" and asked them where they thought I was from. They all said "Hsinchiang," the province formerly known as Chinese Turkestan. It was my beard. I was mistaken for a Uighur once again. She laughed and said they were wrong. I was from America. They still didn't believe me until I showed them my passport when I paid. The massage parlor was so close to the International, I thought surely some foreigner had wandered in before. But they said I was the first. And when they saw the date of birth on my passport, they said I looked at least fifteen years younger. That coupled with the massage made me feel so much better. I entered hunched over and left standing up and feeling like I was maybe forty-five.

On the way out, I asked my masseuse to recommend a restaurant. She led me outside and pointed at the place next door. It looked clean and had a tiled floor—always a good sign. It was typical of the new kind of restaurant that would have been a noodle joint in the past but was now à la carte. A young couple was sitting at one of its five orange-topped tables, and a young girl was doing her homework at another.

The proprietress, who turned out to be the girl's mother, was standing behind a counter at the back. I walked inside and sat down, and she brought me the menu.

I never know what to order in restaurants in China anymore. Even the simplest hole-in-the-wall place has a menu that runs several pages with descriptions so fanciful only a regular customer knows what they refer to. I was too tired to ask for explanations and told the owner to recommend something. She suggested a plate of deep-fried mushrooms and another of tofu skin with green peppers. That sounded great.

While I was waiting, the owner's daughter came over and introduced herself. She was ten years old, and she was already studying English. She didn't know enough to ask questions, but she was not at all shy about asking me in Chinese where I was from and what I was doing in China. And she was actually interested in my answers. She asked about everything but politics. The Chinese learn at an early age to stay away from the tiger's mouth. I was almost disappointed when the food arrived and she returned to her homework.

Her mother's recommendations were superb, especially the mushrooms. When I commented on them, she said she used *mo-ku* (*Agaricus bisporus*) instead of *hsiang-ku* (regular shitakes). They held up better when deep-fried. That and the tofu skin with green peppers and a bowl of rice cost another 15RMB, the same as the massage. After such a thrifty evening, surely an indulgence was in order. Next to the hotel, I stopped at a Häagen-Dazs and blew the day's savings on a scoop of green tea ice cream, which cost 28RMB. While I licked my treat, I congratulated myself on making it all the way from Wutaishan. And I was walking upright. And the hot bath that ended my day was as hot as I would ever want a bath to be. And I was finally able to wash my clothes. I was a happy traveler.

I was still happy the next morning when I woke up and could still stand up straight. I felt fortunate to live in a time and a place where there were massages and hot baths and ice cream on the pilgrim trail. After the *de rigueur* morning coffee and a journal-worthy dump—can anything be more important to a traveler at the start of a day?—I walked across the street and the adjacent square to the Hopei Provincial Museum.

In the middle of the square, there was a group of a dozen people with red sashes around their waists waving red scarves and dancing in unison to a beat set by another member on a big skin drum. It was a Yangke folk dance club and a great improvement on the ballroom dance clubs that took over from Taichi in the morning exercise scene in China when the Falunkung was outlawed. The reason for the shift to other forms of exercise was that *ch'i-kung* routines similar to those used in Taichi were part of the daily Falunkung regimen. And no one wanted to be suspected as a member. Taichi, however, was making a comeback, but in less traditional forms, so as not to arouse suspicion. Joining the folk dance club on the square were two such groups. One of them was racing through its routine, while the other was doing its forms so slowly, I couldn't bear to watch.

The museum looming behind them was typical of the 1950s Soviet-style architecture in provincial capitals throughout China: big, imposing, meant to make people outside think there was something important inside, something too important for the likes of them. And it worked. There was no one inside except me and the guards. In my travels around the province, I was always being told that the stele or statue or sarcophagus I was looking for had been moved to the provincial museum for safekeeping. So I was expecting to see some of these cultural treasures that had thus far eluded me. But it was not to be.

The ground floor was taken up by "Hopei Today": everything from motorbikes to tractors, from synthetics to electronics. I passed it all up for "Ancient Hopei" on the second floor. I guess I could say the pieces were carefully chosen and well displayed, with good explanations in Chinese. But it was the poorest example of a provincial museum I had seen anywhere in China. And this was Hopei, one of the five most important provinces of ancient China—the others being Shantung, Honan, Shansi, and Shensi, the provinces that bordered the mud hose of the Yellow River. According to the guard at the front door, everything I had hoped to see was in storage, awaiting the construction of a new museum. I was a few years early.

When I walked back outside, the dance club and Taichi groups were gone. In their place were a dozen tables. And sitting in chairs behind each table were white-jacketed men and women. They looked like health care workers, and I thought maybe they were handing out information about the latest viral infection. But I was wrong. A huge banner hanging from poles directly behind them said, FIND OUT HOW YOUR GOVERNMENT WORKS. What a concept. I couldn't help noticing that the Property Bureau table was surrounded by people asking questions, while the Tax Bureau table looked awfully lonesome. Signs of the times.

Since I really didn't want to know how the government worked, I passed up its emissaries. I went back to the hotel, said goodbye to its four-star comfort, and walked outside again beneath the Martian sky. I briefly considered another massage but instead decided to head for the monastery where a week earlier I chanted the *Mahaprajnaparamita Sutra*. The air was no longer freezing, which was a relief, but the sky had disappeared behind a veil of dust. I hadn't traveled in North China in March before and thought it was just a passing condition. But what the Chinese call *huang-t'u*: "yellow-dust" would be all I would see of the sky until I reached Loyang and left the Yellow River floodplain.

From the hotel, I took a taxi to the city's South Station and five minutes later boarded a bus for Chaohsien, which was twenty-five miles southeast and where Pailin Monastery was located. I love the public transportation system in China. It goes everywhere. Of course, it takes a country of a billion people to make it work. But it's why I enjoy traveling in China. I couldn't understand why everyone was buying a car. And what happened to all the bicycles? At least there were buses, and more of them than there used to be, and paved roads. Less than an hour after leaving my hotel, I walked through the front gate of Pailin and down its east wing to the guest hall, where would-be lodgers were expected to report for accommodations.

. . . . .

Pailin Temple was first built in 857 by Chao-chou, a disciple of a disciple (Nan-chuan) of Ma-tsu. Ma-tsu was responsible for introducing nonlinguistic means of instruction into Zen: the shout, the nose twist, the slap were all among his favorite devices. Chao-chou wasn't any easier on disciples hoping for an answer in words, but he was more grandmotherly. His favorite reply to a question about Zen was *ch'ih-ch'a-ch'u*: "Have a cup of tea."

As I entered, I saw Ming-hai standing in the middle of the guest hall talking to another monk. Ming-hai was the abbot. We both waved, and I went over to say hello. I'm not sure why I always waved when I saw him instead of bowing, or why he always waved back. Waving just seemed more appropriate. We hadn't had time to talk when we met the previous week at the big chanting ceremony. Unfortunately, Ming-hai didn't have time to talk this time either. He was leaving for a meeting in Beijing and introduced me to a tall young monk named Ch'ung-tu, who, he said, would take care of me in his absence.

After we said goodbye, I told Ch'ung-tu what I was hoping to do and asked him if he could arrange for me to talk with some of the senior monks, beginning with the *tien-tso,* or food manager. We exchanged cell phone numbers, and he led me outside and across the courtyard to the temple's west wing and turned me over to Laywoman Liu, who had been in charge of lay guest quarters at Pailin for the past twelve years. The temple was pretty much destroyed during the Second World War. Not long after rebuilding began, so did the Cultural Revolution, and the monastery became a teacher's college. Since being returned to the monks in 1988, it had been rebuilt on a grand, but not ostentatious, scale by Ching-hui, the previous abbot. It was one of the biggest monasteries in China and normally housed anywhere from one hundred to two hundred monks, sometimes more.

Pailin Temple courtyard with Chao-chou's pagoda in background

The monastic way of life was just about eliminated during the Cultural Revolution, but you would never know it to travel in China today. Temples are everywhere, and it would be hard to find a town or a mountain in China without one, if not several. The Chinese word for them is *ssu*. Originally, that was the word for a midlevel government agency, of which there were dozens in ancient China, such as the Agency for Imperial Dependents or the Agency for Imperial Sacrifices. When the first monks arrived in China in AD 67, they were lodged at one of these. In their case, it was the Agency for Tributary Envoys, or Hung-lu-ssu.

In ancient times foreigners were not allowed to spend the night in a Chinese city, hence this agency was located outside one of the city gates. As the number of monks lodged there increased, the Agency for Tributary Envoys was moved, and the original compound of the Hung-lu-ssu was turned over to the monks and renamed Pai-ma-ssu, or White Horse Agency/Temple, in honor of the steeds that accompanied the first monks. Despite having nothing to do with Buddhism, the word *ssu* has been used for Buddhist temples in China ever since.

Once these first Buddhist *ssu* were established in the capital of Loyang, similar *ssu* started to appear wherever foreign merchants traveled and wherever the Chinese with whom they did business were attracted to the Dharma. As in India, these early monasteries were places where the Buddhist *sangha*, or community of practitioners, could live apart from the world of red dust, where they could devote themselves to meditation, the study of texts, and the performance of rituals, and where they could also instruct others.

But unlike in India, the residents of these monasteries did not support themselves by begging. The Chinese did not respect people who begged, and monks had to rely instead on donations from lay supporters. Since the monks' lay supporters included both the merchants in whose company they came to China and their Chinese trading partners, getting enough to eat was not a problem. Nor was it a problem when Buddhism became the preferred religion of the rulers of a series of dynasties that controlled North China between the third and sixth centuries and South China in the fifth and sixth centuries.

Within a relatively short time, Buddhist monasteries appeared everywhere in China. But these were not Zen monasteries. Zen had not yet arrived in China. This monastic way of life was dependent on others, rather than being self-sustaining. It was not until the early part of the seventh century that Tao-hsin, the Fourth

Zen Patriarch, established the first Zen monastery. And it was not until the end of the eighth century that Pai-chang finally established the monastic system that has remained the way of life in Zen monasteries ever since.

Pai-chang called his system *Ch'ing Kuei*: "Rules of Purity." Unlike the Buddhist monastic system in other parts of the world, he insisted monks be self-supporting and that they live and work together. He even insisted they pay taxes on their crops, the same as regular farmers. His rules have sometimes been summarized as "No work, no food." Although Pailin, like most monasteries nowadays in China, had lost its land and was no longer self-supporting, in all other respects it followed the rules of communal living and communal practice established by Pai-chang. Since I knew the abbot, I figured this would be as good a place as any to find out more about how such a community worked.

Laywoman Liu led me through an archway whose calligraphic inscription declared that the red dust of delusion stopped there. That did not, however, apply to the yellow dust of Mongolia, which turned midday to dusk. She led me down a long corridor on the west wing to a room with three beds and told me to take my pick. Ch'ung-tu had told her I would be doing some writing, so she reappeared a few minutes later with a desk lamp and two thermoses of hot water.

That reminded me that I was out of coffee. Fortunately, a source was close by. I walked back outside the monastery's front gate and waited at the curb for the street traffic to clear. As I stood there, Ming-hai drove past on his way to Beijing in a convoy of three black sedans. We waved again, and I wondered how monks managed to put up with all the meetings they had to attend. I tried to imagine Shakyamuni riding in an oxcart on his way to meet with officials in charge of begging permits.

Once across the street, I walked past the shops that lined a weed-covered square toward the department store at the other end. Along the way, I stopped to look at three huge, wooden buddha statues sitting outside one of the shops. They were twelve feet high, and each of them was made of a dozen large chunks of camphor and fir that had been mortised together. The surface of the wood was finely carved but still bare, and I assumed it would remain that way until the future owners decided on a color scheme, or until the statues reached their new home. I walked inside and asked the salesgirl how much they cost. She said 15,000RMB, or less than two thousand dollars. The store could ship them anywhere in the world. My living room ceiling was too low, but I took the shop's name card, just in case I ran into someone with a fifteen-foot-high ceiling who wanted a really big buddha.

At the far end of the square, I entered the department store doorway and pushed aside the heavy plastic strips meant to keep out dust and flies. I was surprised how dark it was inside. Then I realized the lights weren't on. The woman at the counter where I checked my shoulder bag said electricity was off everywhere in town. Today was their turn. Since the register scanners didn't work, clerks had to call out for prices. Otherwise, it was business as usual, and no one seemed concerned. I replenished my supply of instant coffee (small packets that included sugar and the white powder they call "creamer"). I also added a bag of cookies (chocolate with almonds). Back in my room, I enjoyed a midday indulgence and took a long nap. Either I was still tired from Wutaishan, or I was coming down with something.

When I finally woke up, I tracked down Ch'ung-tu. He said he had arranged for me to talk with the *tien-tso* and to meet him in the guest hall. I had stayed at Pailin many times, but this time I actually had a purpose. I wanted to get a better sense of how the monastery worked, how it functioned as a community in support of the spiritual life. I had never asked about that before but just enjoyed the smooth operation of the sangha. How that came about was a mystery to me. Now I wanted to know more; not everything, just more.

I wasn't the only one. As I walked across the monastery grounds to the guest hall, I passed several large groups of visitors. They were being led around by lay guides who were showing them how to act in a monastery. For Buddhists this all began when Shakyamuni tasted the fruit of Enlightenment in 432 BC. Over the years that followed, he gathered a community of practitioners around him. That was the beginning of the Buddhist *sangha*, which is the Sanskrit word for an assembly of individuals who come together for a common purpose. For early Buddhists, that purpose was Nirvana. For later Buddhists, it was Enlightenment. Either way, it meant liberation from the suffering inherent in the endless round of birth and death.

As the Buddha wandered from town to town, the size of his following grew, and he was often approached by lay devotees with the question, "Now where could the Bhagavan dwell that would be neither too far nor too near our village, where disciples could come and go freely, that would be accessible to all by day and quiet by night and sufficiently secluded for meditation?" Once such a place was decided upon, it was given to the sangha and retained for its use as a *vihara*, or resting place. Over time, certain viharas became places where monks rested year-round. By the time of the Buddha's Nirvana in the spring of 383 BC, some of these viharas had become permanent monasteries capable of housing hundreds of monks. Thus, Buddhist life became communal. Monks still wandered from place to place, but the places they wandered to and from were monastic enclosures.

It was a transition characteristic of many religious movements, whereby an individual quest was eventually provided with a social setting designed to support others who took up the same quest. During his ministry, the Buddha taught his disciples that the path to liberation rested on the cultivation of wisdom and wisdom rested on meditation and meditation rested on morality, on leading the sort of life that was conducive to liberation.

Just before the Buddha passed into Nirvana, when his disciples asked what final instructions he had for them, he did not mention wisdom or meditation. He told them their guide should be the *pratimoksha*, the code of conduct he had devised during his forty-nine years as a teacher. The rest was up to them, and still is. Unless people live in harmony with others, how can they expect to cultivate the necessary peace of mind to see through the delusions they have accumulated over countless lifetimes?

Commenting on the communal way of life of the typical Buddhist monastery in China, Holmes Welch wrote, "It was intended to create a model society that the whole world could copy. Thus it has the fascination of all utopias. The ideal is alluring, its realization is astonishing, and its failure is consoling." (*The Practice of Chinese Buddhism 1900–1950*, p. 3)

But even members of a utopia need to eat. Maybe it's just me, but I've always thought the most important place in any community was its kitchen. Hence, the first interview I arranged was with the monastery's *tien-tso*, or food manager. His name was Ming-ch'ing, and he was waiting for me in the guest hall. He was about forty, maybe younger, and he was on the thin side. I joked that I was expecting someone fatter. He laughed and said he was too busy to take advantage of his position. I asked him to tell me about his daily routine.

He said the kitchen crew got up at four-thirty, the same as everyone else. But instead of going to the shrine hall at five o'clock to take part in the morning ceremony, they came to the kitchen and began making breakfast. They were usually done cleaning up by seven and took a two-hour break. Then they returned at nine to get lunch ready. After lunch, they took another two-hour break and returned at three.

Dinner began at four-thirty, and by the time they cleaned up, it was six. Some of the crew then returned to their rooms to study or take care of personal matters, and others joined the evening meditation.

Normally, the number of monks and laypeople at Pailin averaged around two hundred. As long as the numbers didn't go much beyond that, the kitchen crew consisted of five or six monks and an equal number of laymen from the local community. During Buddhist festivals, which occurred half a dozen times during the year, they had to feed upwards of two thousand people, and on those occasions the size of the kitchen crew doubled. In either case, the laymen were paid a salary. It was their job. The monks were assigned by one of the guest managers for several months or more, depending on need. Of course, anyone who wanted could stay on, and some did, like Ming-ch'ing, who had been food manager for three years. It taught him humility and self-control, he said, because things were always going haywire. It wasn't just his place of work. It was his place of practice. In talking with him about his responsibilities, Ming-ch'ing kept stressing this, the conjunction of spiritual practice and community service.

After we shared a cup of tea, Ming-ch'ing led me into the kitchen, and I watched two monks making steamed buns (*mantou*) and two layworkers making an herbal soup in woks bigger than my entire stove. We arrived near the end of the two-hour break between meals, so there wasn't much going on just yet. The actual cooking, he said, didn't begin until fifteen or twenty minutes before meals. But it took more than an hour to get everything ready.

In addition to kitchen operations, the food manager was in charge of the menu. In a more traditional setting, he would have also been in charge of the monastery's fields and orchards, and even its flower gardens. But Pailin was on the edge of what was becoming a small city. It had lost its fields, and all food supplies had to be ordered from local wholesalers or from laypeople who had made it known that they would like to donate something like rice or flour or cooking oil or dried mushrooms or fruit, or something to round out a meal.

I asked Ming-ch'ing how he decided what to cook, if he used a recipe book. He said he made it up as he went along. Most of the dishes were standard fare, but he liked to experiment with new combinations. It was trial and error, he said. But since all dishes were vegetarian, even errors weren't bad. Ever since Chinese Buddhists gave up the Indian custom of begging for their food and became directly responsible for what they ate, they have avoided eating meat and eggs and also such aphrodisiacs as onions, garlic, and tomatoes. There was a difference of opinion, however, concerning the last item, and I always smile when a shred of red appears in my bowl: the work of a rebel food manager.

In a niche on the wall overlooking the kitchen's institutional-sized woks and preparation tables, there was a small statue of a blue-skinned, red-haired Chienchai (Meal Watching) Bodhisattva. Inscribed on white paper pasted beside the niche were reminders that no one was allowed to eat food prepared there unless they had done something to deserve it and no one was allowed to take food prepared there to eat outside the mess hall, for example, in their own room. Private

Cooks in action at Pailin Temple

provisions and personal snacks, of course, were exempt. But when I happened to walk through later, I watched several older monks in their sixties and seventies come into the kitchen, fill up their mess kits, and return to their rooms to eat in private. I decided not to ask about this. I'm sure the explanation would have been that it wasn't food but "medicine."

From the kitchen, Ming-ch'ing led me to an open-ended room. It was open-ended because its doors were never closed. This was where water was boiled for drinking. At the far end of the room, there were two huge boilers, each of which held about five hundred gallons. In the past the boilers would have been wood- or coal-fired, but these were electric. Each had a pipe leading to a dozen spigots lined up above a long cement trough designed to catch the overflow. This was where people came every day to fill their thermoses. On the side of each boiler was a temperature gauge so people knew which one to use.

Ming-ch'ing then led me into the mess hall. Like all mess halls, it was huge. It was about thirty feet wide and a hundred and fifty feet long, and a single central aisle divided it into left and right sections. At the end of the aisle was an altar with a statue of Kuan-yin, the Bodhisattva of Compassion, and below the altar were a raised thronelike chair and tabletop where the abbot ate. On either side of the aisle were rows of benches and tables where everyone else sat and ate.

The seating arrangement, and this was true throughout China, placed monks on the front benches of both sides of the central aisle, laymen on the back benches on the right, and nuns and laywomen on the back benches on the left. Left was *yin*, and right was *yang*. There was room, according to Ming-ch'ing, for about four hundred people in the main mess hall. There were also two smaller dining halls in an adjacent building with room for another hundred, but these were usually reserved for important visitors. Ming-ch'ing said that during major assemblies, when the number of participants reached two or three thousand, people ate in shifts, with fifteen to twenty minutes between shifts.

According to the way of life followed by Buddhists in ancient India, monks and nuns restricted themselves to one meal a day, and that before midday. But because China's colder climate required more food, Chinese monastics ate breakfast in addition to lunch, and some ate an evening meal as well. Still, to remind themselves of the ancient proscription against eating after midday, they called the food they ate at dinner "medicine," which was often simply leftovers from lunch with one additional dish to liven things up. Most of the younger monks, I noticed, skipped that meal.

Since mealtime was approaching, I thanked Ming-ch'ing for explaining how things worked and walked back outside the monastery and down the street to check my e-mail at an Internet hole-in-the-wall. I returned just in time for dinner and took my place at the back of the mess hall on the right side with the lay workers and other lay visitors. There were about twenty benches on each side of the central aisle and about ten people to a bench. In front of each row of benches was an equally long row of tables on which the servers set chopsticks and two bowls before each of the places where people were expected to sit. As soon as the meal chant was over, eight servers began circulating among the tables spooning rice into one of the bowls and tofu and mixed vegetables into the other. Another server gave everyone a steamed bun. Toward the end of dinner, another server came by and handed out apples. Talking was not allowed during the meal. Even though everyone knew this, several lay workers couldn't resist whispering to each other. As soon as they did, the monk in charge of patrolling the mess hall came around and shushed the offenders.

During breakfast and lunch, no one could leave until the monks left, which they did in unison and in single file. But since dinner wasn't really a "meal," people were allowed to leave as soon as they were done. As I got up, the layman sitting beside me also got up and followed me outside and started talking to me without any prompting. After introducing himself, he told me he had been imprisoned for ten years for his involvement at Tienanmen. After he was arrested, he said, he wore leg shackles and was beaten and shocked with an electric cattle prod every day for years. It ruined his legs, his back, and his heart, he said. Since his release, he hadn't been able to work, and he was waiting to talk to Ming-hai, whom he had known when they were both students at Beijing University. He said he had tried life as a monk, but only for a short period. He couldn't bear the manual work. He was hoping for something easier, and he thought Ming-hai might be able to help him. I presumed he was hoping for an introduction to one of the monastery's patrons and a sinecure of some kind.

As we took an after-dinner stroll around the temple grounds, another monk came up and introduced himself. His name was Ming-yen. He said he was the dean of the Buddhist academy that occupied the northwest part of the monastery, and invited us to follow him to the academy's reception room for a chat and some tea. I took this to be a polite way of silencing my new companion, but neither of us was in a position to object. We followed Ming-yen inside, and he got out some high-mountain Taiwan oolong and made tea in what has become the way preferred by most tea connoisseurs in China: he took a small unglazed clay teapot and filled it about a third full of tea leaves. After pouring in boiling water and immediately pouring it out—to wash the leaves—he poured in water that was just below boiling, and after about twenty seconds, poured the tea into as many small cups as it took to drain the pot, in this case four: one for me, one for my dinner companion, one for Ming-yen, and one for a student who joined us.

Ming-yen said there were more than sixty monks studying in the academy, and they were enrolled in programs that ranged from three to six years. Dozens of such academies had opened in China in recent years, and monks and nuns nowadays were encouraged to attend one of them at some point in their careers. It wasn't absolutely essential, and some monks and nuns didn't feel qualified or weren't interested, but attendance was encouraged. Studying texts was another door to Enlightenment. And every Zen master, even the ones who didn't think much of textual study, quoted from texts when they taught. But I didn't stay to find out which texts they studied or what courses they offered. I was definitely coming down with something. After a courtesy cup of tea, I bid the dean and my tea companions goodnight.

· · · · ·

When I woke up the next morning, I felt like I had hit a wall. Something was wrong with my sinuses. I had never encountered anything like it. They didn't stop draining, and I was up most of the night. Finally around dawn, I slipped into a sleep that lasted until around eight o'clock, when Ch'ung-tu called me on my cell phone. I was glad I had the foresight to buy one before leaving Beijing. In this case, it allowed me to talk without getting out of bed. My reprieve, however, was short-lived. Ch'ung-tu asked me if I had time to meet with the monastery's master-at-arms. It wasn't really a question. That was why I was there. I got dressed and dragged myself outside and across the courtyard to the guest hall, where Ming-yi was waiting.

There were two principal positions associated with the guest hall in a monastery: the master-at-arms (*seng-chih*) and the guest manager (*chih-k'o*). Ming-yi had been serving as one of the guest managers, but due to the sudden departure of the previous master-at-arms, he was asked to take over. Normally appointments were made on the fifteenth, or full moon, of the first lunar month or, failing that, on the full moon of the seventh month. But provisional appointments, like Ming-yi's, were made whenever the need arose.

After exchanging introductions, we sat down, and Ming-yi poured me a cup of tea. He had a full-moon face and looked like he was in his mid-thirties. He said he moved to Pailin the previous year from Fourth Patriarch Monastery outside Huangmei. The abbot there was Ching-hui, the same monk responsible for rebuilding Pailin. Once Ching-hui was finished at Pailin, he turned the monastery over to Ming-hai. Hence, these temples and their residents were connected by a master-disciple relationship, and monks often moved between them. The "Ming" that began so many names at Pailin indicated the generation of Ching-hui's disciples to which they belonged. Connections were just as important in the Chinese Buddhist world as they were in the world outside. Who your spiritual teachers were made a difference. It was always a subject of inquiry during the interviews that every visiting monk or nun had to go through, whether they wanted to spend the night or a few years.

Ming-yi began by saying that the guest hall wasn't only concerned with guests but with all areas of monastic activity. Its master-at-arms, he said, was the monastery's policeman. He was in charge of ensuring order and adherence to the monastic code. Before every ceremony, he inspected the premises. He watched over the participants during every ceremony, and at all communal events, including meals, as well.

If someone violated a rule of order, he told the offender to correct his behavior. If the offender was guilty of repeated infractions and showed no signs of rectifying his behavior, the master-at-arms could expel the person from the monastery without consulting the abbot. Ming-yi said he had to be everywhere to ensure adherence to the rules. When I asked him who made the rules, he said Pai-chang compiled the first code for Zen monasteries in the ninth century, but it had been revised many times, and every monastery was free to add or change any part as conditions warranted.

He said the best current compilation he had seen was that of Chenju Temple on Yunchushan. Chenju was the monastery where Hsu-yun, or Empty Cloud, spent the last decade of his life. It was Empty Cloud who was responsible more than anyone else for revitalizing the practice of Zen in China, and the revised code he developed at Chenju was universally admired. Unfortunately, it had never been published. Ming-yi said he had tried to copy it once when he was taking part in a winter retreat there, but he didn't have enough time. He said the principle underlying the code at Chenju or any other Zen monastery was that it ensure a good environment for spiritual cultivation. It wasn't just a set of rules.

I asked Ming-yi if enforcing the rules interfered with his own practice, if he wished he could spend more time meditating. He said he was still learning about Buddhism and wasn't ready for prolonged periods of meditation, but he hoped to spend more time in the meditation hall in the future. Right now, he said, he was still learning how to be a proper monk. In that respect, he shared a characteristic I noticed in a lot of young monks. They weren't in a hurry in terms of their meditation practice. They were happy to have been able to enter the sangha as disciples of a monk they respected, and they were content with the practice of service in the new community in which they had chosen to spend their lives. Every place is your place of practice, Ming-yi said. Later at lunch, he circled the mess hall, not so much looking for offenders as letting everyone know he was there, practicing.

After lunch I checked in at the guest hall again. This time, I met Ming-chi, the supply manager. He was pushing seventy, short, wiry, and extraordinarily friendly. He was from Paoting, just north of Shihchiachuang, and Pailin was the only monastery where he had ever lived. Unlike the other monks who occupied positions of authority in the monastery, Ming-chi had never been to college. In fact, he had never finished grade school. But he was perfect for the job—a jack-of-all-trades and with enough energy to do them all justice. He began by showing me his room. It was on the second floor above the mess hall and included a cot with a pole at each corner for a mosquito net, a very large desk with nothing on it but a vase with a spray of plastic orchids, and a small wardrobe for his clothes and personal possessions, which were sufficiently few to fit inside with room to spare. Just outside his door there was a litter box for the supply section cat.

The rest of the second floor consisted of room after room of the things the monastery needed to keep on hand. No one was allowed to take anything without the permission of the abbot or his representative—except in one room, where there was a large supply of used clothing that people could choose from anytime they needed something. Despite the amount of stuff stored in all the rooms, Ming-chi only had one assistant. But whenever a truckload arrived or something needed moving, he said he could call on other monks, especially the novices.

While he was showing me around, he kept asking me about Buddhism in

America. Were there monasteries in America? What were they like? What kind of people practiced Buddhism? Was the practice different? I told him that, yes, there were a few Buddhist monasteries in America, but that most of them were for training monks or nuns who then lived in lay settings, that most of the people attracted to Buddhism had been to college, that they also practiced meditation and conducted rituals, but that they practiced as lay communities rather than monastic communities, and that as a result, sexual relationships and earning a living were the big issues, as they were for everyone else in America. He nodded, not as if he understood, but as if he was glad to have asked and to have received an answer, however superficial.

Just inside the doorway of the first room, there was a statue of a two-armed Daheitien (Mahakala) Bodhisattva brandishing a mallet in one hand and a bag in the other, standing on two ingots of gold and silver denoting his protection of the wealth and material goods bestowed upon the monastery. The supply section cat darted in and out while Ming-chi led me through aisles crammed with tables and chairs and ritual paraphernalia, cabinets full of monastic clothing, blankets, and bolts of fabric for making more of the same. There was also a large supply of electric fans for use during summer, and there were lots of mosquito nets, also for summer, and lanterns, and thermoses.

When I asked Ming-chi if there was something he was short of, he said he could use a better sewing machine. The new ones weren't as good as the old ones, and the old one he had was too old. He asked me if I could help him get a new serger. He said he needed it to sew the seams of robes. I wondered why he couldn't just request one. He was supply manager. When I was in the Army, whoever was in charge of supplies was second only to the sergeant major in terms of actual power in any battalion-sized unit. But Ming-chi was shy. And I imagined he felt intimidated by the college-educated monks who occupied the other positions of authority. I told him my daughter was studying fashion design and should know what kind to buy. I told him I'd look into it for him. He suggested a Number 26, whatever that meant.

Later that night at dinner, he tugged my sleeve and told me to forget it—he couldn't afford it. I still didn't understand why he needed to pay for it himself or why he couldn't just buy one and get reimbursed. But he was embarrassed he had asked me to help. I agreed to forget it, but I decided I would ask the abbot on Ming-chi's behalf. Also at dinner, I was relieved to see the former political prisoner. He had disappeared all day after talking with me the night before. This time he made no attempt to approach me. I assumed he had been instructed not to talk about his "reeducation," especially to a foreigner.

After dinner, I wandered into the guest hall once more. I was hoping to meet the guest manager, and I was in luck. He was talking to another monk, and he asked me to sit down and have a cup of tea with him. I waved off the tea. I was still eating the apple I got at dinner. The guest hall was the first place anyone came if they wanted to stay at a monastery. It served as the monastery's connection with the outside world, and the person who oversaw that connection was the guest manager (*chih-k'o*). At Pailin, the chief guest manager was Li-sheng. He was from the coastal city of Fuchou and was about forty years old. He had been a monk for twenty years and the guest manager of Pailin for the past five.

Li-sheng knew what I was there for and didn't wait for me to ask questions. He started by telling me what he did. As the chief guest manager, he was in charge of overseeing monastery activities in general. But due to the size and complexity of operations at Pailin, there were three other guest managers under him: one who received important guests, such as government officials and prominent patrons, one who assigned duties within the monastery, and one who oversaw the maintenance of the monastery's physical plant, such as its plumbing and wiring and so on. Each of the four guest managers also had monks assigned to assist them whenever large numbers of people came to take part in a ceremony or celebration.

In addition to overseeing the work of the other guest managers, Li-sheng said he was in charge of interviewing visiting monks. He said it usually went something like this: When a monk arrived who wanted to stay at the monastery, he first came to the guest hall to inquire about accommodations. In the past, he would have left his bag just outside the threshold of the hall. To take his bag inside would have been presumptuous. But nowadays, given the mix of people coming and going in many monasteries, Li-sheng said this rule was usually dispensed with so that a monk could keep his possessions in view. In any case, after stepping inside and making three prostrations before the guest hall altar, the monk then sat down on a long bench and waited to be called for an audience with the chief guest manager—who was usually off taking care of other business.

Once the chief guest manager showed up and called the visitor over, he asked to see the monk's identification card, which was issued by the government, and his ordination certificate, which was issued by the Buddhist Association. He also asked a few questions to verify that the visitor was who he claimed to be. If the guest manager suspected something wasn't right, he asked the person to leave. There was no appeal. But if everything was in order, he arranged for appropriate accommodations, depending, of course, on availability.

Li-sheng said at other temples a visiting monk might share a room with a dozen or more monks. But at Pailin, there were only two or three monks to a room. If a monk wanted to stay longer than three nights, he had to have another, longer interview. Agreeing to provide another person with food and lodging on a permanent basis was not done lightly. Also, during the second interview, the guest manager found out more about the person's background and character and judged how he might fit into the daily life of the monastery. If the interview did not go well, the person applying had to leave that day. In a large monastery such as Pailin, nuns could also stay, but only for three nights, unless they were there to take part in a ceremony that lasted longer than that.

The guest hall, he said, also functioned as a reception center for laypeople who came to make a donation or to pay for some religious service, such as a funeral. For many monasteries, funerals and memorial services provided their main means of support. While Li-sheng was telling me all this, his cell phone rang, and he said there was something that needed his attention. But before getting up to leave, he asked me if there was anyone else I wanted to talk to. I told him I was hoping to talk with the *wei-nuo*, or religious affairs manager. While I was blowing my nose for the hundredth time that day, he made another call and said the *wei-nuo* would be waiting for me outside the meditation hall.

The meditation hall was off-limits to visitors, but I knew where it was. I walked past it whenever I visited Ming-hai. It was next to the abbot's compound. As I walked into the walled-in courtyard, I looked up. Over the doorway of the meditation hall was a sign with the characters WU-MEN-KUAN: GATE WITH NO DOOR. The *wei-nuo* was waiting for me underneath and introduced himself. His name was Shang-hui, but that was all he told me about himself. He was on the shy side. Like most of the other administrators at Pailin, he was also in his forties. There was a conscious effort at Buddhist monasteries and nunneries throughout China to appoint more of the younger generation to positions of authority than in the past. Of course, part of the reason was that the previous generation of spiritual practitioners—those in their fifties or sixties who would have become monks or nuns between 1960 and 1980—was missing. That generation never happened.

The first thing Shang-hui told me was that the religious affairs manager was in charge not only of the meditation hall but of all the monastery's shrine halls as well. In addition to maintaining order in the halls, he was in charge of instructing novices how to behave in each of them. The rules were complex, he said, and it took several months to learn just the basics. The choreography had developed over many centuries. For the most part, he said, the meditation halls at Pailin followed the rules developed by Pen-huan at Kuanghsiao Temple in Kuangchou and by Hsu-yun and later Yi-ch'eng at Chenju Temple on Yunchushan.

The only conversations I ever had with Pen-huan were brief. Every time I met him in Kuangchou, he was surrounded by disciples. But he was always up for calligraphy. Calligraphy and Zen, he once told me, were the same. And I enjoyed watching him wield his brush. After he was released from prison and the dust of the Cultural Revolution settled, he was instrumental in rebuilding a number of major Zen monasteries in China. I once saw a book he published with photographs and illustrations showing in great detail how to conduct a meditation retreat. It was, indeed, a fine example of choreography. Unfortunately, the book was a mammoth tome, and I was traveling light, and I've never seen it again. It must have been a very limited edition intended for Zen monasteries.

Yi-ch'eng was a different kind of artist. He was the current director of the Buddhist Association of China. But the first time I heard about Yi-ch'eng, he was referred to by another name: Ch'i-fo, "the Eccentric Buddha." When I finally met him a few years later at Chenju Temple, true to his nickname, he asked me and my friend Steve Johnson to go inside the meditation hall and photograph the monks while they were meditating, just to see how they reacted. All rules aside, Yi-ch'eng knew what a meditation hall was for, and monks in China considered participating in one of his retreats a highlight of their careers.

Shang-hui said the meditation hall was the heart of every Zen monastery. Many monasteries didn't have a meditation hall. That was because they weren't Zen monasteries. The other major school of Buddhism in China was Pure Land. At Pure Land temples, the meditation hall was replaced by a hall where monks and nuns chanted the name of Amitabha (Omitofo), the Buddha of the Western Paradise, or the name of Kuan-yin, the Bodhisattva of Compassion, who welcomes new arrivals to Amitabha's Pure Land. If people wanted to meditate at such monasteries or nunneries, they did so in their rooms.

At Pailin there wasn't just one meditation hall but several, to accommodate visiting monks and nuns as well as laypeople. When I asked Shang-hui about the routine, he said meditation periods during a retreat began with a ninety-minute sit. My knees ached at the thought. That was twice as long as I was used to. He said the ninety-minute period was followed by periods that were successively shorter but never less than thirty minutes. Altogether, there were eleven such periods a day during a retreat,

Meditation hall of Pailin Temple

the longest of which was the five-week winter retreat. During the rest of the year, there were usually only three sixty-minute periods a day: one in the morning, one in the afternoon, and one in the evening. But sometimes there were more. All residents whose monastic duties didn't require them to be elsewhere were supposed to take part. That was why anyone who lived there lived there. It was a Zen monastery.

Shang-hui pushed aside the hanging mat that blocked the doorway and led me inside the main hall. As we walked around, I counted seventy-eight seats. Since there were anywhere from one hundred to two hundred monks in residence at any one time, I asked where the rest of them sat. Shang-hui said that many of the monks had other duties, but if they had time, they could sit in one of the other halls. There was, however, one curious twist to all this. Because this was a Zen monastery, any monk who wanted to sit in the meditation hall could not only do so but could decline to do anything else. And, in fact, there were several monks at Pailin who basically lived in the meditation hall. Shang-hui pointed out their well-worn cushions.

All the seats in the hall were assigned, and on the wall over each seat was the name of the person who sat there. The instructors and their assistants occupied the seats immediately to the left of the doorway. Directly across the hall from the doorway was an enclosed seat for the abbot and a seat on either side for his two attendants. Immediately to the right of the doorway, there were two seats divided from each other by a wooden table. These seats were reserved for the *wei-nuo*, or religious affairs manager, and his counterpart, the *shou-tso*, the monastery's chief instructor, who was gone the week I was there. The table was for the incense that was burned to gauge the length of meditation periods and for the small hand bell used to bring a meditation period to a close. Above the table hung the sounding board. There were five different Zen lineages in China, and each had its own board. Pailin belonged to the Linchi (Rinzai) lineage, hence its board was rectangular with the top two corners lopped off. The sound was basically the same, but every school had its own design.

Shang-hui said that when monks entered the hall, they had to be fully robed, and they couldn't bring anything else into the hall, not even beads. Monks whose prac-tice involved using a mala while reciting the name of a buddha or bodhisattva could always sit in the hall used by laypeople. Even if they recited silently, it was still con-sidered distracting if it involved any movement, even something as slight as the fin-gering of beads. Hence, everyone put away their beads before they entered.

Likewise, the hall was bare of any decoration. The only thing in the hall besides the sitting platform that ran along all four walls was a small altar. It was in the middle of the hall and had just enough room for a small alabaster statue of a seated Shakyamuni. On either side of the statue there were two flat wooden sticks that were used by the monks who patrolled the hall to strike the shoulders of dozing monks.

The altar also had a practical function. It provided the hall with a center. Between meditation periods, the monks slipped their shoes back on and stood up, faced left, and walked around in a clockwise direction to get some circulation back in their legs. Unlike Zen halls in Japan or in the West, where people walked around single-file, in China everyone walked at their own speed and in any orbit that suited them. In the halls where I've been allowed to take part, they looked like a bunch of electrons circling a buddha nucleus. Of course, anyone who wanted to continue sitting could do so. Some people were born to sit. But most welcomed the relief.

Shang-hui said that normally everyone sat with their legs folded in the lotus position, but if someone couldn't bear the pain, they could assume a more relaxed posture. If their legs still hurt, they could stand up and walk over to the buddha statue and do standing meditation or kneeling meditation—but they had to be very quiet so that they didn't distract the other monks. Everyone, he said, used whatever meditation technique they liked, counting breaths, focusing on a koan, or reciting the name of Amitabha, but to themselves.

While we were talking, another monk entered the hall and struck the wooden sounding board. As soon as he did, someone outside the hall struck a gong. The evening sit was about to begin. I thanked Shang-hui and went back to my room. I was exhausted and went straight to bed. But my sinuses never stopped draining, and I only slept intermittently.

. . . . .

The next morning I considered whether or not I had the energy to interview a few more monks. I had only met with a handful of the monks involved in the monastery administration. I hadn't talked with any of the instructors (*pan-shou*), the monks responsible for teaching younger monks how to meditate and how to manifest what they learned in the meditation hall in their daily lives. But I also knew that if I was going to visit all the places on the pilgrimage I had planned, I had to move on. Kuangchou, my final stop, was over twelve hundred miles away.

After breakfast, I went to say goodbye to the abbot. Ming-hai had returned from Beijing the previous night and was sitting in his reception room talking to half a dozen reporters from the provincial capital. After introducing us, he motioned for me to sit down in the empty seat next to him and asked me if I had talked to everyone I wanted to. I decided not to ask about the meditation instructors. But while his attendant poured me a cup of tea, I said I had hoped to talk with the *chien-yuan*, or temple manager. Next to the abbot, the *chien-yuan* was the most important person in the monastery administration, especially in terms of whether things ran smoothly. The temple manager knew how to get things done. If the abbot was the president of the monastic corporation, the temple manager was the chief executive officer.

Ming-hai said unfortunately the temple manager was away for the week. But he offered to answer any questions I had. I didn't really have any. But since Ming-hai was one of the most knowledgeable and forthcoming abbots I knew, I asked him if he could tell me about the legal status of Buddhist monasteries in China. As soon as I asked, Ming-hai slipped off his shoes and gathered his legs under him in the full lotus position and told the reporters to turn off their video cameras and voice recorders. Since he knew I was gathering material for a book, and it wouldn't be appearing in the local media, he told me to leave my recorder on.

After pausing for a few moments to gather his thoughts, he said, "At the end of the Cultural Revolution, the government issued a directive declaring all temples that had been occupied by schools, factories, or government agencies be returned to clerics. For example, during the Cultural Revolution, Pailin had become a teachers' college. Once this policy of restoring temples to the sangha was announced, the college had to move. But because the school had built a number of buildings on monastery land, the monks that took back the place had to come up with 'key money.'

"However, this return of temples to the sangha didn't happen everywhere. There were simply too many temples and not enough monks and nuns left to take care of them. Hence, temples that had historic or aesthetic value or that were located in scenic places were taken over by the Cultural Affairs Ministry or the Tourism Ministry or even the Department of Forestry. There were many such temples that weren't returned to the sangha.

"Also, Buddhists had never been interested in going through the bureaucratic process of updating their rights according to modern standards. So most Buddhist temples had no legal standing. That was not the case with churches. They were established by foreigners, and foreigners were familiar with such bureaucratic procedures. Hence, they were able to reestablish their legal claims after the Cultural Revolution, whereas Buddhists and Taoists have not been so fortunate."

I asked, "Then who does this monastery belong to?"

Ming-hai said, "That's a good question. In the case of Muslims and Christians, their mosques and churches belong to their religious organizations, and not to the individuals who live in them. But this is not the case for Buddhists, or for Taoists either. Even though we have a Buddhist Association and also a Taoist Association, they have no legal claim to any of their members' monasteries or nunneries. Every monastery and nunnery is on its own. But strange as it may sound, no individual or group living in a monastery or nunnery has any legal claim either.

"For example, during the Cultural Revolution, the monks who were living at Pailin were forced back into lay life. So after the Cultural Revolution, the monks who came here were not the same monks as before. There was no continuity. And the monastery was never registered as such, not legally. So if someone came here today and took over our monastery, we would have no legal recourse in terms of being able to take them to court."

Although monasteries and nunneries were in legal limbo in China, the Chinese were not only adept at surviving ambiguity, they cultivated and even relished it. Much of their culture was based on ambiguity and still depended on it. Ambiguity had allowed them to remain a nation where relationships were still more important than laws. Despite the absence of any legal standing, monasteries and nunneries were able to operate as if they were just another corporate entity—depending, of course, on the relationships they maintained. And like any other corporate entity, there was someone in charge, someone who made the final decisions. That person was the abbot. So I asked Ming-hai how abbots were chosen.

He said, "Nowadays the outgoing abbot usually chooses his successor. But even that requires the approval of the monastery's senior monks as well as the monastery's lay supporters. The old abbot usually discusses his choice with these people first. Also, once he makes his selection, it still has to be approved by the Buddhist Association and finally by the Ministry of Religious Affairs and the Ministry of Propaganda—but they usually go along with the Buddhist Association."

I asked Ming-hai how he would describe the abbot's role in the monastic hierarchy, and if it had changed. He said, "The abbot is still the administrative and the spiritual head of the monastery. That hasn't changed. Below him on the administrative side, he has a series of managers chosen for their ability to over-see the activities necessary for the functioning and welfare of the community: the temple manager, the guest manager, the master-at-arms, the religious affairs manager, the food manager, the supply manager, and so on. And below him on the spiritual side, he has a series of instructors chosen according to their seniority, their knowledge of Buddhism, and their spiritual attainments. All of these people represent the abbot both inside and outside the monastery. Hence, they're chosen very carefully.

"Appointments to all administrative posts end every year on the eighth day of the first lunar month and are reassigned, or reconfirmed, on the fifteenth, or full moon. This gives the abbot a week to hold meetings and consultations to consider what changes, if any, should be made. In cases where waiting until the first month would be inconvenient, appointments can also be made on the full moon of the sev-enth month. But spiritual positions in the monastery hierarchy only change over a long period of time and are dependent on general recognition of a person's spiritual practice as much as on the abbot's approval.

"The abbot's position, too, is subject to review. In the old days, his term was three years, but nowadays it's five. Many abbots prefer not to serve beyond that, and I would include myself in that group. However, others feel comfortable being an abbot. And every time their term is up, they're reconfirmed by the monastery's sangha and lay supporters. But once the abbot does step down, he often moves to another monastery to give the new abbot more room to act without feeling the need to consult him. I myself hope to step down after my current term is complete, but it's possible I'll be asked to continue for another five years. After a second term, though, I would not agree to stay on. There are other things I hope to do."

I didn't ask Ming-hai about what other things, but he once told me that he would like to spend several years in seclusion. He even had a mountain in mind in the nearby Taihang Range. I asked, instead, what attracted so many monks to Pailin and why they chose to stay there. He said, "The reason they come here and the rea-son they stay is that this is a good place to live and also a good place to practice. Everything they need is provided here: good food, clean rooms, even hot water for bathing. We also give everyone a monthly stipend of 100RMB ($12.50) to buy personal items they might need. And if they want, they can earn an additional 200RMB or so per month by reciting sutras or mantras at the occasional memorial service. But the reason they stay here is to practice.

"This is a Zen monastery. And the heart of every Zen monastery is its meditation hall. All activities revolve around it. And the heart of the meditation hall is the sounding board, which is struck to regulate the periods of meditation. When this board is struck, its sound carries outside the hall, where someone is waiting who then beats an iron gong to let everyone know that a meditation period is about to begin. There are different sounds from the different boards and drums and gongs, each of which sends a different message throughout the monastery. You could say that the activities of a Zen monastery don't depend on words, only sounds. As the meditation hall resonates, so does the rest of the monastery. This is why anyone lives here.

"In ancient times, Zen monasteries, unlike other Buddhist monasteries, were agricultural communes. They were self-supporting. They grew their own food on land someone donated. But when Buddhism first came to China, most monasteries were located near cities, and the lives of their residents revolved around studying texts and performing ceremonies. It wasn't until much later that Zen developed its own style of communal living that combined manual work with spiritual cultivation. Zen is about direct understanding, not about studying texts or performing ceremonies. Words and rituals are useful. But they can also become obstructions. Zen monasteries focus on daily living, on cultivating an understanding not dependent on words or concepts.

"Of course things are different nowadays. When the government began giving monasteries back to the monks after the Cultural Revolution, one of the conditions set by the authorities was that the monks take care of cadres too old to transfer to other jobs. The cadres stayed on in the monasteries as 'laymen.' So the monks had to come up with a way of generating extra income to support the lay cadres as well as themselves, and they started selling entrance tickets to visitors. At monasteries whose buildings possessed some historic or aesthetic value or that were located in scenic places, the government had already begun doing that, and it was hard to stop the practice in cases where those monasteries were given back to the sangha. Another source of income that is becoming more important is the monastery store, which sells books and incense and statues and religious paraphernalia. But for many monasteries, the most important source of income is still the performance of ceremonies for laypeople, especially funerals and memorial services.

"But the problem for a Zen monastery that supports itself by selling entrance tickets or by performing funerals and memorial services is that this distracts the residents from their practice. The purpose of living in a Zen monastery is spiritual development, not economic development. Naturally, the two have to be balanced. If we don't have any means of support, we can't practice. But if we're too distracted by the way we earn money, what is the purpose of living in a monastery?

"Of course, not all monasteries need to be places for practice. Some monasteries, like Shaolin, for example, are so overwhelmed with visitors the monks are too busy taking care of people to practice. Still, they manage to spread the culture of Buddhism to others, and this is also a form of practice. But that can become a problem. Sometimes people invest in temple construction for the purpose of making money—not the monks but businesspeople who offer their support for

Master Ming–hai instructing monks on Arbor Day

reconstruction, at a price. The Buddhist Association now forbids private investment in temple construction. But it still happens."

I asked if there was any movement toward becoming smaller. Most of the monasteries I had seen were being rebuilt on a large scale. Ming-hai said, "Living in a small monastery only works for practitioners who already have a good foundation in Zen. First people need to live in a larger community to develop the discipline and necessary focus. Without a good foundation, if you live in a small monastery, you are likely to become slack and lazy about your practice. So right now, we are putting more emphasis on reestablishing the communal way of life in larger monasteries and nunneries."

Just then a young monk came in and said, "The trees are here." Ming-hai got up and asked us all to follow him outside and across the courtyard to the open land behind the main buddha hall. A huge crowd was assembled: monks, laypeople, and students, about five hundred people. They were all looking on as cedar saplings were being unloaded from several trucks. Suddenly I realized it was Arbor Day, which was celebrated in China on March 12 to commemorate the death of Sun Yat-sen, the founder of the Republic. Trees symbolized new life. By the time the workers were done unloading, there was a pile of six hundred saplings averaging six feet in height. Coincidentally, that was one for every chapter in the *Mahaprajnaparamita Sutra* we had chanted together at Pailin nearly two weeks earlier. There was also a big pile of shovels.

Ming-hai gathered everyone around and explained how to plant the trees: "Don't put in the debris left over from the construction of the buddha hall because it contains lime. And put in loose dirt in the bottom of each hole before you plant the tree." While he was explaining this, another contingent of more than two hundred people arrived. They were high school students from Shihchiachuang and were led by several students holding a huge banner announcing the celebration of Arbor Day. As soon as they joined the crowd, people started planting. The name of the monastery, *Pai-lin*, meant "Cedar Grove." It was finally getting back its trees.

After I helped plant one of the saplings, I told Ming-hai I needed to be going. I had a long way to go and needed to catch a series of buses to my next destination, which was Hantan. Ming-hai told me that wouldn't be necessary. He had already arranged for my transportation. I didn't know what to say. I'm always being embarrassed by the generosity of the sangha in China.

As I went back to my room to collect my gear, I heard someone strike the gong outside the meditation hall, announcing the beginning of a meditation period for all those not engaged in planting trees or other monastery work. The whole monastery was ordered around such sounds: time to get up, time to meditate, time to chant, time to eat, time to work, time to sleep. A person could live out their life and never say a word. It was a land beyond language. And it was time for me to leave.

5 NO BEGINNING

My next stop was Hantan, ninety miles south of Pailin, not the city itself but the countryside nearby where the first Chinese Zen master taught and where he died. By the time I collected my gear, Ming-hai was waiting for me behind the guest hall where several vehicles belonging to the monastery were parked. He helped me load my pack into the trunk of a black sedan, introduced me to my companions for the day, wished me a safe journey, and off I went—into the dust.

The sky had been obscured for days, but the four directions had now disappeared as well. Mongolia was migrating south. If not for the operation of gravity, I would have had to guess which way was up. Visibility was no more than a hundred yards, if that. But I was the only one in the car who seemed concerned. It certainly didn't bother the driver, who managed to find the expressway, and who drove as if he could see forever. My sinuses were in full spate, and I was wedged in the backseat between a yellow-robed monk and a Buddhist Association official. I would have preferred the bus, but this was a ride I couldn't refuse.

The monk's name was Hai-ju. He was about forty and portly for a monk. He said he lived in a small temple a couple of hours north of Beijing and was visiting Pailin to confer with Ming-hai about the first World Buddhist Forum. It was scheduled to take place in Hangchou the following month, and several hundred foreign Buddhists were expected to attend. Hai-ju said he wanted to talk to them about spreading the Dharma. Reestablishing Buddhism in China, he said, wasn't enough. The Wheel of the Dharma had to keep rolling, across the sea and around the world. He had some ideas he planned to present in Hangchou. He said the best way to transmit the Dharma to the West was to build temples, and he hoped to begin a fundraising drive at the Forum.

When he asked me what I thought, I was feeling so miserable, I didn't have the energy to be polite. I told him building temples in the West would be a waste of money. Temples would attract spiritual dilettantes and the curious. I suggested bringing Westerners to China for retreats, not conferences. And instead of building temples, why not send monks who could speak English and set them up in houses or apartments where they could teach informally and where they could learn how to adapt Chinese Buddhism to Western needs? Chinese Buddhism, I said, had almost no impact in the West because those engaged in its transmission insisted on its Chinese forms, the external rigamarole. My suggestions went right by him. He had already made up his mind.

Sitting on the other side of me was Kao Shih-t'ao, the deputy director of the Buddhist Association of Hopei. Since he seemed to be listening to my conversation with Hai-ju, I turned to him and explained that if Chinese Buddhists built temples in America, it would provide nice places for Chinese Americans and Chinese in America to light incense and to take part in ceremonies and maybe even to meditate, just as if they were back home. But the cultural moats and linguistic drawbridges would be too forbidding for Westerners trying to put an end to suffering. He agreed, which surprised me. It turned out we were both of the opinion that it was necessary to free the Dharma of as much cultural baggage as possible in transmitting it to other countries. The West didn't need Chinese temples, but it certainly needed the Dharma. I turned back to Hai-ju and said if he was determined to build temples to build them without walls. That silenced everyone, for which I was only too glad. I was feeling so miserable I didn't want to talk anymore.

After weaving through truck convoys for ninety minutes, we finally exited the expressway at Hantan and followed a local road east for twelve miles. As we approached the town of Chengan, we turned south at a Christian church painted pastel blue. Two hundred yards later, we pulled into the front gate of Kuangchiao

Temple. That was where Hui-k'o, Zen's Second Patriarch, taught. Chao P'u-ch'u, the late director of the Buddhist Association of China, once said, "Without Hui-k'o, there would be no Zen in China." That was because there was no Zen in China until Bodhidharma showed up in the late fifth century, and Hui-k'o was his dharma heir.

Hui-k'o didn't leave behind much information about himself. According to the earliest accounts of his life, he was born in 487 near the town of Jungyang, sixty miles east of Loyang, in the stretch of hills that separates the Yellow River from the sacred mountain of Sungshan to the south. Hui-k'o's parents were Taoists, but he studied the Confucian classics in his youth with a view to becoming a government official. And he seemed destined to become one until his parents died and he lost heart in a worldly career and turned to Buddhism.

In 519, at the age of thirty-two, he became a monk and studied with Master Pao-ching at Hsiangshan Temple near Loyang. The kind of Buddhism practiced in North China at that time was not Zen but a mixture of Hinayana and early Mahayana prac-tices aimed at eliminating the passions. What Hui-k'o first studied was what Zen masters would later call Dead Tree Zen, as opposed to Living Zen. It was Buddhism for a warrior elite, not for a civilian militia. And like Shakyamuni before him, it left Hui-k'o unsatisfied.

After eight years with Pao-ching, Hui-k'o decided to look elsewhere for instruc-tion. He didn't have to look far. The sacred mountain of Sungshan was a two-day walk southeast of Loyang, and at Sungshan's Shaolin Temple Hui-k'o heard about an Indian monk named Bodhidharma. The most popular version of what happened next—first recorded in an inscription written by Fa-lin in 634—has Hui-k'o hik-ing up the trail behind the temple to a cave where Bodhidharma was meditating and asking the First Patriarch for instruction. When Bodhidharma paid no attention to his visitor, Hui-k'o continued to stand outside the cave and wait. He stood there for several days. Even when it started snowing, he continued to stand there.

Finally, in an act of utter desperation, Hui-k'o cut off his left forearm and put it before Bodhidharma as an offering. This got Bodhidharma's attention, and he asked the Chinese monk what he wanted. Hui-k'o said he couldn't still his mind, and he asked for Bodhidharma's help. When Bodhidharma asked him to show him this mind he couldn't still, Hui-k'o said he had tried everything, but he couldn't get hold of it. Bodhidharma said if that was true, then he had already stilled his mind. Hui-k'o suddenly realized the true nature of mind and became Bodhidharma's disciple.

Hui-k'o stayed with Bodhidharma for six years. Finally, in 534, the Indian Zen master gave Hui-k'o his robe and bowl as symbols of authority to teach in his place, and the two monks parted company. His advice to Hui-k'o was to spread the teaching of Zen wherever he found a receptive audience, and he gave him a copy of Gunabhadra's translation of the *Lankavatara Sutra* to use should he feel the need for a text.

A civil war had been going on in the Loyang area for a number of years, as various claimants vied for the throne. Finally, the same year Bodhidharma and Hui-k'o parted company, the two major political factions put an end to the Northern Wei dynasty and divided North China into a Toba-dominated Western Wei, which established its capital in Ch'ang-an, and a Chinese-dominated Eastern Wei, which moved its capital from Loyang to the safer location of Yeh, two hundred miles to the north and not far from Hantan.

Bodhidharma remained in the Loyang area, where he died two years later. What happened to Hui-k'o is unclear. Some sources claim he served as abbot of Shaolin Temple for several years. But at some point he traveled to Yeh, and he taught in and

Bodhidharma's cave

around the new capital for over thirty years. There is no mention in any record as to which years. The only thing certain is that while Hui-k'o was in the Yeh area, he aroused the anger of other monks who found the Zen teaching of Bodhidharma anathema, if not absurd. How could we all be buddhas? And how could Enlightenment be less than a thought away, since everyone knew it took lifetimes to achieve? They were also annoyed to see their students flocking to hear another teacher whose teaching they themselves didn't understand and couldn't compete with.

If the stories of Hui-k'o's reception in Yeh were even partly true, he was lucky to live as long as he did. In fact, Tao-hsuan's biographical record of early Buddhist monks in China, written only a few years after Fa-lin's account, says it was during Hui-k'o's stay north of the Yellow River that his forearm was cut off by bandits. If that was true, it's quite possible the "bandits" were simply the henchmen of jealous monks. It was not a good time for Zen. The Buddhists of North China were into works: ascetic practices, meditation aimed at suppressing the passions, shamanistic incantations, and magic. The emphasis was on doing something and getting something in return. They could not comprehend the usefulness of doing nothing and getting nothing. Zen was crazy, if not dangerous, for it called into question the understanding of those who considered themselves the purveyors of the means to liberation. It was said that when Bodhidharma died in 536, it was the result of the sixth attempt on his life—all by poison. Assassinations were common, even in religious circles.

Meanwhile in North China, the Western Wei was succeeded by the Northern Chou, and the Eastern Wei was succeeded by the Northern Ch'i. Then in 574, the ruler of the Northern Chou launched a religious persecution against Buddhists and Taoists, and in 577 he extended it to all of North China, when he conquered the Northern Ch'i. At some point, Hui-k'o decided it was too dangerous to remain in Yeh, and he fled south to the region along the Yangtze controlled by the more hospitable Ch'en dynasty (557–588).

It wasn't until 580 that a Northern Chou general, who fittingly had been raised by a Buddhist nun, put an end to the persecution and the dynasty responsible for it and established the Sui dynasty (581–618) with himself as Emperor Wen and his capital in Ch'ang-an. With the country reunited for the first time in more than three hundred years and an end to the religious persecution, conditions improved, and Hui-k'o returned to the North. But again, we don't know when. All we know is that he crossed the Yellow River and returned to where he had taught for over three decades

(c. 534–577). But Yeh was gone, destroyed during the war that brought an end to the Northern Ch'i. Hui-k'o's followers, though, were still there, and he decided to stay in the area and teach.

Twenty-five miles northwest of the old capital's ruins, he found a warm reception at Kuangchiao Temple, whose abbot even built a platform from which Hui-k'o could address large audiences. Unfortunately, his success as a teacher aroused the enmity of a monk named Pien-ho, who convinced the government official in charge of the region that Hui-k'o was blaspheming the Dharma and stirring up trouble. Despite the reunification of the country by the Sui, conditions in the countryside were still chaotic, and justice was often at the mercy of local leaders. It was said that Hui-k'o remained unmoved both when these false charges were leveled against him and also when he was executed, which occurred in 593 when he was 107. Like Bodhidharma, he seemed to acquiesce to what he perceived was a sentence imposed by his own karma. Fortunately, his dharma heir, Seng-ts'an, stayed in the South and was able to continue the transmission of Zen. But that's another story.

As we parked in the courtyard of Kuangchiao Temple, a dozen nuns came out to greet us. The monastery had become a nunnery. Ming-hai had called ahead, and they were expecting us. One of them even spoke English. Her name was Hui-k'ung, and she was from Singapore. She was a graduate of the Buddhist academy at Pushou Nunnery on Wutaishan and couldn't have been more than thirty-five. She had taken over as abbess of Kuangchiao from Wu-ming, who had died the previous year at the age of seventy-seven. Hui-k'ung led us into the reception room and showed us a wall covered with color photographs of her master's cremation relics, or *sarira* as they're called in Sanskrit.

I wanted to talk to Hui-k'ung about her teacher and also about her own practice. But just then a delegation of local authorities showed up in two black sedans. They were led by Wang Yu-fu, who was in charge of religious affairs for Chengan County. His office had made a video of the sites in the area associated with Hui-k'o, and he wanted us to see it. He led us back into the reception hall and put his disc into the temple's DVD player, and we all sat down and watched. It was set to music and included footage of the area, but it was also a promo for investing in the county. At least it was short. Afterwards, we thanked the nuns for their hospitality and proceeded to Hui-k'o's gravesite, which was six miles northwest of Chengan down some very, very bad roads.

Their ruts ended just north of Second Patriarch Village at a brick wall built to protect five acres of weeds. We pulled up to the only building in the compound and got out. I looked for Kuo-le, the monk who was there the last time I visited, but I didn't see him. I didn't see the rosebushes he had planted in front of the building either.

While I was looking for traces of the roses, two monks came out to greet us. The older of the two introduced himself as Kuo-ming. He was about seventy-five, and he smiled the whole time we were there. He said Kuo-le had left to take care of another temple of which he was also abbot and would be back, but not anytime soon. The other monk was about forty-five and was as energetic as the older monk was happy. As he guided us around, he said he and Kuo-ming were there to oversee construction of a new temple at the gravesite—although it wasn't too clear if and when anything would ever be built. Previously, someone had begun work on a shrine hall at the far end of the property but had given up when they ran out of funds.

There wasn't much else, other than the dilapidated two-story building where Kuo-le and the two caretaker-monks lived. They slept on the second floor and used the first floor for everything from daily ceremonies to meals and, of course, storage. Before showing us the excavation site, the younger monk unlocked a small room where they stored food, tools, and all sorts of junk, or what looked like junk. He lifted a tarp and presto, there was the small stone sarcophagus that had been found at the bottom of Hui-k'o's stupa. Inside the sarcophagus was a small silver casket, and inside the casket were Hui-k'o's relics.

The stupa where the relics were found wasn't built until 732, and it had been restored several times but was now gone. Damaged over the centuries by warfare and earthquakes, it was finally taken down in 1969 when local authorities decided to excavate the site. During the excavation, the relics were discovered in an underground burial chamber. They had since been moved to the vaults of the Hopei Cultural Affairs Institute in Shichiachuang and were due to be returned if and when the stupa was rebuilt. In the video we saw earlier, the relics looked like hundreds of tiny mud balls and reminded me of a line in a poem by Cold Mountain: "Drop a ball of mud in water and behold the thoughtless mind." (*The Collected Songs of Cold Mountain*, p. 95)

After showing us the sarcophagus and the lid that listed the donors who financed its Sung-dynasty reinterment, our guide led us to the huge pit where it had been found. The pit was about a hundred feet on a side and maybe twelve feet deep. There was also another smaller pit to the north that contained a T'ang–dynasty stele. It had been buried by floods, and its base was nearly ten feet below the present ground level, which was a good indication of how much sediment the Yellow River had deposited over the past twelve hundred years.

We slid down the slope into the pit and examined the inscription. On the front side, it said it was erected in 817 as a replacement for an earlier stele erected around the same year the pagoda was built, and it repeated the epitaph to Bodhidharma written by Emperor Wu of the Liang dynasty in 538. The inscription on the backside rambled on about Zen, but it gave the order of transmission in China from Bodhidharma through Hui–neng, which made it the earliest tangible record of the traditional Zen lineage I had seen anywhere.

Besides a lack of biographical information, Hui–k'o didn't leave much behind in the way of written material either. About the only thing we have is a brief collection of statements found a hundred years ago in the Tunhuang Caves in a text called the *Leng–ch'ieh–shih–tzu–chi* (Record of the Masters of the Lankavatara). In this account of China's early Zen masters, he says,

Site where Second Patriarch's relics were found

Though buddhas fill the ten directions, no one has ever become a buddha without practicing Zen. Practitioners who rely on written or spoken words for the Way are like lanterns in the wind. They flicker and go out and are unable to dispel the darkness. If they would meditate instead of running around, they would be like lanterns inside a closed room. They would dispel the darkness and illuminate everything clearly.

Once you understand that the mind is originally pure, all your wishes will be fulfilled, all your undertakings will succeed, you will have done what needed to be done, and you will not suffer another existence. Unless you're honest with yourself, even if you meet countless buddhas, they will be of no help. Beings liberate themselves by knowing their own mind. Buddhas don't liberate anyone. If buddhas could liberate beings, since you've already met countless buddhas, why haven't you become a buddha? It's because you haven't been honest with yourself. With your mouth you say you understand, but in your mind you don't understand. You'll never escape the Wheel of Rebirth. Your buddha nature is like the sun and moon in the sky, like fire in a piece of wood. Everyone has a buddha nature. What comes from practicing Zen is something you yourself realize. Talking about food will never satisfy your hunger. If you don't quit hanging out with those who study words, you'll be no different from someone who boils water to get ice or who creates steam to make snow. Sometimes the buddhas teach by speaking and sometimes by not speaking. But the true form of all dharmas isn't found in what they say, nor is it found in what they don't say.

Since we had seen what there was to see, and since my companions were anxious to get back to Pailin, we thanked the two monks and returned to the paved road. But before we hit the expressway, I asked the driver to drop me off in Hantan. Whenever I heard the name, I thought of the song Cold Mountain once sang,

> This maid is from Hantan
> her singing has the lilt
> make use of her refuge
> her songs go on forever
> you're drunk don't talk of goin
> stay till the morning comes

where you sleep tonight
her quilt fills a silver bed.
    (*The Collected Songs of Cold Mountain,* p. 55)

I didn't plan to spend the night, just catch a bus to Loyang. Mr. Kao used his cell phone to call ahead and told me there was one leaving for Loyang in less than an hour. Once again, I was grateful to travel in a country where public transportation was so good, or at least so available. After my companions dropped me off and we said goodbye, I went inside and bought my ticket. Since I still had twenty minutes, I walked down the street to a pharmacy and got some allergy medicine. I decided my problem wasn't a cold but a reaction to the dust. I should have realized that earlier. I began to envision relief on the horizon.

Back at the bus station, I had no trouble spotting my conveyance in the parking lot. It was the oldest bus in the fleet—relegated to the minor route that Loyang represented. Once the capital of a dozen dynasties, Loyang was now only the fifth biggest city in Honan, and it was expected to drop to eighth place by the end of the decade. I was just happy there was a bus that went there. I got on board and took my usual seat toward the back. A woman came down the aisle behind me selling peanuts. She said she planted them herself: planted them in the third lunar month, harvested them in the eighth, stir-fried them in a wok, and added salt and seasonings that were a family secret. Peanuts were my favorite long-distance bus food—they filled the belly and clogged the colon, and I bought three bags. I was expecting a long ride—Loyang was over two hundred miles away. At least the bus left on time. Counting me, there were eight passengers. We picked up another six on the way out of town, but once we hit the expressway, that was it—fourteen people in a bus with seats for more than sixty.

After we had been on the road for an hour, two kids who couldn't have been more than twenty came back and sat down in the seat in front of me and asked me where I was from. They thought I was from India. That was new. When I told them I was from America and was visiting places associated with the early history of Zen, one of them asked me what was the essential teaching of Zen. I was surprised by the question. It was so direct. I told them that the only way out of this bitter sea—and where wasn't it on the salty side—was to see things as they are, made of your own mind. As far as I knew, that was the most essential teaching of Zen. They looked puzzled.

What do you mean, things as they are? How else would things be than the way they are? I told them the way they saw things was not the way things were but only the way they appeared through the lens of delusions constructed over lifetimes. This was always hard for people who were simply curious. There was nothing at stake. Why shouldn't they keep seeing things the way they saw them? I didn't have an answer. They finally got up and moved back to their original seats. Not long afterwards, the medicine kicked in. I was right. It was a dust allergy. I slept the rest of the way, rising only briefly to note the Yellow River, which we crossed at dusk. The mud dragon that gave birth to Chinese civilization looked harmless. It was close to a mile from the dikes on either side—still hibernating, and dreaming, no doubt, of summer storms on the Loess Plateau.

We arrived in Loyang around seven o'clock, five hours after leaving Hantan. Not bad for an old bus. And only the first part of that was on an expressway. After checking on buses to my next destination, I took a taxi to the New Chuho, on Liberation Road—close to the bus station, but not too close. The girls at the front desk were the happiest crew I saw the whole trip. They actually delighted in lowering the price of a room from 400RMB to 235RMB, or thirty bucks, and they even seemed to take pleasure in finding me a room with a bathtub. Dinner in the hotel restaurant sucked, but I was too tired to care. All I wanted was a hot bath. Afterwards, I washed my clothes and went to bed happy, knowing that the medicine had worked and that I had made it far enough south to escape the dust that had made me feel so miserable and so helpless.

. . . . .

I may have eluded the dust, but not the cold. A front followed me south during the night. When I went outside the next morning, the wind hurt. I had to go back to my room and get my parka. Once I was properly attired, I grabbed a taxi from the hotel taxi pool and began the Loyang portion of my pilgrimage with a visit to White Horse Temple, where Buddhism first arrived in China. It was at the eastern edge of the city and took about thirty minutes to drive there. In ancient times, it had been at the western edge. The city kept moving around. Every time it was destroyed, the Chinese built it back up. The city had such a great location, in the very middle of the Middle Kingdom, less than six hundred miles from anywhere in the empire, except the extreme south and the farthest outposts on the Silk Road. Loyang's geomantic position was also auspicious. The ancient Chinese claimed there was no better place to be buried. Of course, times had changed, but despite falling behind other cities in the province in terms of economic development, Loyang's current incarnation still had a population of six million, and not everyone was there to work in the East Is Red tractor factory. Mining equipment, construction equipment, and glass manufacturing were all big draws, as was tourism.

We parked just outside the temple gate, and I walked past the stone replicas of the two horses that brought the first monks, the first sutras, and the first images of the Buddha to China. Two thousand years ago, Loyang was the eastern terminus of the Silk Road, and Buddhism arrived along with the merchandise. Although the first members of the sangha were not officially noted until the first century AD, once they made their formal appearance, it didn't take long for them to make an impression. In Chang Heng's "Rhapsody on the Western Capital," which he wrote in AD 130 about Ch'ang-an, his description of the women in the palace included these memorable lines:

One look and a city might fall at their feet
Liu Hsia-hui or a passionless monk
could not but fall in love.

That pretty much summed up Buddhist practice in those days: out with the passion, in with the Nirvana.

Those first monks happened to arrive during the Han dynasty (206 BC–AD 220), when the Chinese established the sense of cultural identity they have managed to maintain ever since. The Chinese still call themselves "Han" Chinese, to distinguish themselves from other ethnic groups in the Middle Kingdom, and they look back on the Han as their first Golden Age—the T'ang being the second. The Han was when the first monks arrived whose names we know: Matanga and Dharmaraksha, the same monks who later traveled to Wutaishan and built the first temple there.

Just inside the front gate of the former Agency for Tributary Envoys, I stopped to pay my respects at their graves, which I did every time I came there, and this was my seventh or eighth visit. Matanga's grave was against the east wall, and

Dharmaraksha's against the west wall. Thousands of tourists, foreign and domestic, visited White Horse Temple every day, but I don't recall ever seeing anyone at either grave. Visitors were only interested in the main corridor of shrine halls and the statues inside them. There were no statues of the two monks, but someone had carved their likenesses on steles in front of their graves. They were done in the fanciful, almost comical, manner more commonly associated with the T'ang-dynasty poets of Tientaishan: Cold Mountain and Pickup. Looking at their images, it was easy to imagine one of them composing poems like Pickup's poem about merchants and their handheld scales:

> Silver stars dot the beam
> green silk marks the weight
> buyers move it forward
> sellers move it back
> never mind the other's anger
> just as long as you prevail

Grave of Matanga at White Horse Temple

when you die and meet Old Yama
up your butt he'll stick a broom.
> (*The Collected Songs of Cold Mountain*, p. 285)

Good old Pickup.

The reason I always stopped to pay my respects was that Matanga and Dharmaraksha not only brought the first sutras to China, they also produced the first translations into Chinese. And I was a translator. One of the translations attributed to them was a Buddhist primer. They titled their text *The Forty-two Passage Sutra*. The reason for the number was that there were forty-two letters in the Sanskrit alphabet, each of which had magical properties if written or pronounced properly. So in a sense, the sutra represented the entire corpus of Buddhist teachings.

The passages they translated were short summaries and most of them reflected the Hinayana teachings of early Buddhism. But Passage Two was clearly moving in the direction of the Mahayana:

> The Buddha said, "Those who leave home and become monks put an end to
> desire and passion, discover the wellspring of their own mind, penetrate the
> profound truths of all buddhas, and awaken to the Unconditioned Dharma.
> Free of internal attainments and external quests, they are tied to neither dhar-
> mas nor to karma. The Path they follow is without thought, without action,
> without cultivation, without realization, without stages and is alone worthy of
> veneration."

This must have made a few people stop and think, but not for long, and only a few.

Matanga was buried there in AD 73, and Dharmaraksha not long afterwards—the year wasn't given. It was said that Emperor T'ai-tsung of the Sung dynasty ordered their graves opened in 993 to ask their spirits for assistance in alleviating a drought. Their bodies were said to look as if they had just been buried. A thousand years later, the forsythia growing from their graves was just beginning to bloom.

After paying my respects to my esteemed predecessors, I skirted the throng of visitors in the shrine halls and walked over to the guest hall along the eastern corridor. I was hoping to meet the abbot of White Horse Temple, whom I had always managed to miss on my previous visits. The guest manager said he was there but he was busy. He told me to come back in half an hour. He would ask. I went back outside and walked among the gardens.

I watched a monk tilling the soil around the peonies. The peony was to China what the rose was to America, tantamount to a national flower. Loyang was the country's center of peony cultivation and had been for over a thousand years. People came from all over the country during the last two weeks of April for the city's annual peony festival. The plants in the monastery garden were just beginning to put forth their big, fat buds. The middle of April was still a month away.

I was going to question the monk who was gardening and maybe learn a trick or two to try on my own peonies. But just then the guest manager tracked me down and said the abbot would see me. I followed him to the building just past the guest hall and into a spacious room at the end of a long corridor. The abbot was standing in the middle of the room waiting. After we greeted each other, he motioned for me to follow him over to a huge burl-top tea table, and we sat down on seats made from stumps. He opened a new bag of Iron Goddess and started brewing us some tea.

His name was Yin-le, and he was born in 1965, he said, at the foot of Tungpaishan. Tungpaishan was the name of a range of mountains northeast of Nanyang and about 120 miles south of Loyang. It was the location of dozens of monasteries in the past and the site of Buddhist rock carvings dating back to the Northern Wei dynasty. It was also a place known for its seclusion, and many famous Buddhist masters had lived there as hermits at some point during their careers. Yin-le said there were still lots of hermits on the mountain, and if I wanted, he would take me there and find a hut for me. Living in a hut, he said, was a good way to learn to put aside material concerns and concentrate on the spiritual life.

He said when he was a boy, monks often stopped to eat and even sleep in his parents' home on their way up the mountain. When he wasn't in school, he spent his days in the monasteries where his parents worked as volunteers. He felt very much at home in monasteries, and when he was seventeen, he became a monk. That was in 1982. He spent the next seven years studying in Buddhist academies, first in Nanching, then in Beijing. After that he lived for thirteen years at a temple in Chengchou, the same temple that also housed the headquarters of the Buddhist Association of Honan Province. In 2002, he was invited to spend a year at a Chinese Buddhist temple in Denver. And in 2003, he was asked to come back to China and take over as abbot of White Horse Temple.

As he recounted all this, it occurred to me that Miao-chiang, the abbot of Pishan Monastery on Wutaishan, had also studied in Nanching, so I asked Yin-le if he knew him. His eyes lit up, and he jerked his head back. He said he and Miao-chiang were old friends, dharma brothers. They were in the same class in Nanching. He asked me how I knew him, and I recounted my connection via Master Shou-yeh. So it turned out we were also dharma brothers. We both laughed about that. I asked Yin-le if he understood Miao-chiang. He laughed again and said as long as he didn't speak too fast or too much. As he began pouring us some tea, Yin-le said one of the great teachings of the Buddha was that of karma. We both must have done something special, he said, to meet this lifetime at the same temple where Buddhism arrived in China.

I was interested in his American experience and asked him what impressed him most. He said, "The environment." He said he was surprised how much attention Americans paid to protecting their environment. He said the Chinese government was also concerned about that now, and it was one of his own concerns. He said China had developed so fast over the past few decades, the environment had been neglected, but not anymore. This was not said idly—at least not on his part. Yin-le, I learned later, had recently been appointed to the central government's highest policy advisory board. He was a very busy man, and we barely had time for a second pot of tea before one of his assistants appeared with a bag of gifts. That was always a sign that it was time to leave.

The bag included a fancy book about the temple with color photos, a boxed edition of *The Forty-two Passage Sutra* printed in gold leaf, and a set of sandalwood beads with the name of the temple burned onto the middle bead. I thanked Yin-le for his kindness, and he invited me to return. I told him I would be back to take him up on his offer of a hut, but I still had a few things to take care of first. He laughed again and saw me to the door.

After we said goodbye, I walked past the shrine halls and the throngs of tourists and out the front gate. My driver was still there, so I got in and asked him to go back out to the main road and continue east. Half a mile later, I told him to pull over. I got out and crossed the railroad tracks next to the road and slid down the embankment to the former site of Yungning Temple. There was now a wall surrounding the site, and it was too high to scale. But through the padlocked gate, I could see the former temple's raised foundation.

By the time the Han dynasty collapsed at the beginning of the third century, people were sufficiently alienated from Confucian orthodoxy to consider alternative views of the world and their place in it. People flocked to Taoist movements and also to Buddhism, which was viewed by many as a foreign variety of Taoism. A century later, when the nomadic Toba conquered North China, a foreign religion suited the new rulers just fine, especially a religion whose practitioners were adept at calling forth spells to their advantage.

When the Toba later moved their capital from Tatung to Loyang in 494, the city became a mecca for Buddhist monks, and hundreds of temples were built, of which Yungning was the biggest. When Buddhist temples first appeared in China, they were built, as in India, around a stupa or pagoda, and Yungning featured the most incredible pagoda ever constructed. It was built by Empress Hu in 516 and was over three hundred feet high. It could be seen from thirty miles away, and the sound of the golden wind chimes that hung from its eaves could be heard across the entire city. The pagoda was built of wood, mountains of wood, and when it caught fire in 534, it burned for three months.

According to a record of the city's temples completed in 547 by Yang Hsuan-chih, an Indian monk named Bodhidharma called the pagoda the most incredible piece of architecture he had ever seen. What I found remarkable was that its foundation had been preserved for nearly fifteen hundred years and that nothing else had been built on the site. And it looked like nothing was going to be. As I returned to my taxi, the image of Bodhidharma staring up at that soaring tower of wood wouldn't go away. I decided to call Yen-tzu, the temple manager of Kunghsiang Monastery, where Bodhidharma was buried. It was a good thing I did. Yen-tzu said he had time to see me that morning—it was just after nine o'clock—but he would be too busy the rest of the week. I told the driver where I wanted to go, and we agreed on a roundtrip price of 350RMB, or less than fifty bucks. It was over sixty miles each way, and I would have had to pay twice that in Beijing. Considering how reasonable his rates were, I asked the driver for his name card. He didn't have one, but he took out someone else's, crossed out their last name and wrote down his, which was Yang, and he did the same with the phone number.

From White Horse Temple, we headed back toward Loyang, then turned onto the expressway and continued west in the direction of the ancient capital of Ch'ang-an and modern city of Sian. As soon as we were beyond the city's industrial-zone suburbs, we began a gradual ascent out of the Yellow River floodplain into the pla-teau country that had formed over the past million years from the windblown loess, or "yellow dust," that couldn't get past the Chungnan Mountains. In the past, the only road west was a rutted snake of a highway that followed every contour of the desiccated plateau. The expressway was not only paved, it was straight and cut through every hill it encountered. It took just over an hour to reach the Kuanyintang exit. From there we drove south on another paved road. The wind was howling, and at one point, Mr. Yang had to stop and take the taxi sign down from his roof to keep it from blowing off. After about two miles, the monastery appeared below the bar-ren peak of Bear Ear Mountain. We parked just outside the front gate, and I got out. There was no one in sight. It was too cold to be outside.

Kunghsiang was one of the first Buddhist monasteries built in China. It began as a way station for monks on the old road from Ch'ang-an to Loyang, and it gradually developed into a major monastery where as many as eight hundred monks lived and where countless pilgrims came to light incense. Bodhidharma was said to have spent a number of years there after the Toba moved their capital from Tatung to Loyang. It was still forested then, and the Zen patriarch must have liked the spot. It was probably at his request that his remains were interred there following his death in Loyang in 536. In 538 the temple's abbot, Master Chi-an, built a stupa over the Zen patriarch's coffin—his body wasn't cremated. That same year the abbot also erected a stele with Bodhidharma's likeness and another one with Emperor Wu's epitaph to the First Patriarch, the same epitaph as the one found at the Second Patriarch's grave.

The temple was originally called Tinglin: "Meditation Grove." It was, and still is, a fine place to cultivate a meditative life—although it could use a few trees. There was nothing but farmland in all directions, and the nearest village was four miles away. The change in the temple's name came about when a Chinese official reported meeting Bodhidharma on the Silk Road several years after his death. When the emperor heard this, he ordered the Zen patriarch's crypt opened. The only thing they found was a single sandal. And as a result, the name of the temple was changed to Kunghsiang, or Empty Form. Or so the story goes.

The first time I heard about Bodhidharma's grave, I was giving a talk about the *Diamond Sutra* at the Berkeley Zen Center in 2000, and one of the members gave me a newspaper clipping from Japan about a group of Japanese Buddhist scholars who had been there. When I finally managed to locate the place two years later, the only improvement since the Japanese had visited was a wall around the site. Now there was a simple residential compound, and a large shrine hall and a mausoleum further up the slope.

During that first visit, I met the man in charge of the office of cultural affairs in the nearby county seat of Sanhsiamen, and he showed me the steles that had been unearthed there, including the Sung-dynasty copies of Emperor Wu's epitaph and Chi-an's portrait of Bodhidharma; the original steles of 538 had been destroyed long ago. The surviving steles were kept under lock and key, but the official let me photograph them. Apparently, someone had used the portrait for rock practice, and it was chipped in places. Otherwise, it showed the Indian patriarch with heavy stubble and thick eyebrows but without the usual bushy beard and bulging eyes.

Bodhidharma's stupa at Kunghsiang Temple

Although the Sung-dynasty steles were gone from the gravesite, several later ones not important enough to haul off for safekeeping had been left to memorialize the place. I paused briefly to pay my respects at Bodhidharma's old stupa. But I had seen everything before, and it was too cold to linger. I ran for the shelter of the one-story compound where the monks lived. As I walked along an interior corridor, I heard voices coming from one of the rooms. I knocked on the door, and a young novice opened it. I asked him if he could direct me to the temple manager's room. He pointed to the adjacent compound, where I knocked at random and got lucky. Yentzu opened the door. He was one of the guest managers at Shaolin Temple and had been assigned to Kunghsiang as temple manager to train novices in everything from deportment to meditation and, of course, martial arts. The abbot of Kunghsiang Temple was Yung-hsing, who was also abbot of Shaolin. Since Yung-hsing rarely visited, Yen-tzu was tantamount to acting abbot.

I was glad to get out of the cold, and Yen-tzu's room felt warm when I first stepped inside. I was surprised to see that on top of his winter-weight robes, he was also wearing a full-length padded robe. But within minutes of sitting down on the vinyl sofa across from him, I was rezipping my parka and reaching out my hands to warm them above the small coal brazier on the floor between us. It was the only source of heat in the room, and I was glad I was there in spring and not winter.

While he poured me a cup of tea, I reached into my shoulder bag and pulled out a copy of the Bodhidharma translations I had published twenty years earlier. On my previous visit he had given me a book about Kunghsiang Temple, and I wanted to give him something in return. As I handed him the book, which was bilingual, he smiled and turned to his bookshelf and pulled out a photocopy of the same book. He said someone had given it to him in Shanghai the year before.

The book contained four relatively short pieces attributed to the First Patriarch. How much of it was actually by Bodhidharma was unknown, but even scholars agree the one called *Four Practices* was most likely his. It was the shortest of the four and began:

Many roads lead to the Path, but basically there are two: reason and practice. To enter by reason means to realize the principle through instruction and to believe that all living beings share the same true nature, which isn't apparent because it's shrouded by sensation and delusion. Those who turn from delusion back to reality, who meditate on walls, the absence of self and other, the oneness of mortal and sage, and who remain unmoved, even by scriptures, are in unspoken agreement with reason. Free of discrimination and effort, they enter, we say, by reason.

To enter by practice refers to four all-inclusive practices: suffering injustice, adapting to conditions, seeking nothing, and practicing according to the Dharma.

After a few lines about the first three, it concluded: "But while practicing the Six Paramitas (generosity, morality, forbearance, devotion, meditation, and wisdom) to eliminate delusion, practitioners practice nothing at all. This is what is meant by 'practicing according to the Dharma.'"

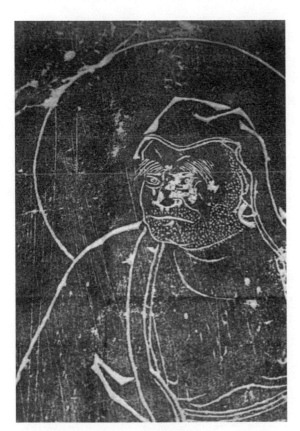

Rubbing of earliest likeness of Bodhidharma

These two entrances to realization, through intuitive understanding and through experience, were not meant to exclude each other. They were Bodhidharma's two feet, even if only one of them got to wear the sandal he put on when he headed home.

I figured Yen-tzu could always use another copy and gave him the published version to go with his photocopy. He had been a monk since 1989. A lot of young men and women became monks and nuns that year in the wake of the events at Tienanmen. He had been at Shaolin ever since. Back then Shaolin did not have a good reputation. I had met monks who disguised the fact that they had ever been there to avoid being associated with what was viewed as a life too soft and too distracting to justify leaving home. Shaolin was one of the biggest tourist attractions in China. Around two million tourists walked through the temple's front gate every year—that was six thousand a day. It didn't leave much time or reason for the monastic way of life.

But Yen-tzu said things had changed at Shaolin. There was a new set of buildings being built to which tourists would not have access. There was also a meditation hall now and a winter retreat. Yen-tzu said that before they started using the new hall, the abbot sent him and several other monks to Shanghai to study the operation of a meditation hall with Nan Huai-chin. Master Nan was the most famous lay Buddhist in China, and it was one of his disciples who gave Yen-tzu a copy of my book. Yen-tzu said he came away from that week with a completely different understanding of how a meditation hall worked. It wasn't so much the rules, he said, as it was the practice of Zen that he learned.

Another thing that had changed at Shaolin, he said, was the development of subsidiary temples for training and practice. He said Shaolin received 10 percent of the 100RMB entrance fee the government charged tourists. I calculated to myself: 10 percent of 100RMB times 6,000 people a day. That was 60,000RMB, or US$8,000 per day, which was three million dollars a year. And that didn't include donations, funerals, and the sale of merchandise. The temple was a cash cow. According to Yen-tzu, one of the things Shaolin was using the money for was the development of places like Kunghsiang Temple. He said Shaolin was doing the same thing at half a dozen other places where its monks were now able to spend more time practicing meditation and martial arts away from the crowds.

Kunghsiang, he said, was being used as a training center for novices. It was remote, and there were no distractions. Novices came there for six months, then returned to Shaolin. There were more than twenty of them at the time of my visit, and Yen-tzu was in charge of all aspects of their training. On my way through the compound, I noticed shoes with soles at least six inches thick outside every door and in the middle of each courtyard padded structures for practicing kicks.

I asked him if the training had changed. He said, "External circumstances have changed, but external circumstances aren't important. Zen is about cultivating the mind. The mind hasn't changed, and the way we cultivate hasn't changed. When Bodhidharma arrived in China, Buddhism had already been in China for more than four hundred years. But people who practiced Buddhism then were concerned with the translation and study of sutras and the attainment of spiritual powers. And most monks lived in cities, not in the mountains. So when Zen was first taught in China, it didn't make much of an impression. It took two hundred years before it really began to flourish. But since then, Zen has become central to all Buddhist practice in China. Zen is about the cultivation of the mind and is basic to all schools of Buddhism, not just Zen. It's basic to Pure Land and Tantric Buddhism as well. But Zen isn't something you can see. It's how you see. You can't find it in a book. Zen is your mind, your buddha mind. That hasn't changed."

We talked a while longer, but the whole time I was there, which wasn't more than thirty minutes, I sensed Yen-tzu had something else he wanted to be doing, and I was keeping him from it. After a third cup of tea, I thanked him for taking the time to see me and got up to leave. It was so cold outside we said goodbye at his door. But after I drove off, I had to tell Mr. Yang to go back. I knocked on Yen-tzu's door again and told him I had forgotten my staff, which I had leaned against the wall. It had accompanied me in China ever since 1991, when I found it on a hillside near Hangchou's West Lake lying beside a T'ang-dynasty stone buddha. Someone had ripped it from a tree and just tossed it on the ground. It had the most unusual properties. It was incredibly light and also incredibly strong. It had saved my butt on many trails. People were always surprised when I told them what it was. It was the aerial root of a banyan. Best staff in the world. It flew into my hand. I thanked Yen-tzu again and headed back toward Loyang.

We returned to the expressway, but twelve miles later, Mr. Yang switched to the old highway. Mr. Yang said he used to drive trucks on that route, and he wanted to introduce me to his favorite lunch stop in the county seat of Hsinan. Twenty minutes later we were there. The specialty of the place was Chengchou noodles. It wasn't the noodles that were so special but the sauce. It was made with twenty-nine medicinal herbs. I could taste the angelica. And there was mutton in it as well. The broth was a perfect accompaniment to the weather. For the first time that day, I felt warm, and from the inside out.

By the time we returned to Loyang, it was too late in the day to do more than engage in my usual end-of-the-day ritual: eat dinner, wash clothes, take a bath. But I did make two phone calls. The first one was to Mr. Cheng, the chief custodian of Pai Chu-yi's grave. Pai Chu-yi (772–846) was one of China's greatest poets and one of my favorites. And whenever I was in Loyang I tried to visit his grave. As soon as I called, Mr. Cheng said he would come to my hotel. I didn't know why, but I couldn't say no. He came straight from work and was still covered with the dust that always distinguished him. It clung to him like dew to a lotus leaf. His hands were black from calligraphy ink, and his glasses were still broken and taped together, and I think he was missing another tooth since I had seen him last. I still had to stand back a bit when he talked, until I got used to his smell.

Mr. Cheng had worked at Pai Chu-yi's grave for thirty years. When he wasn't sweeping or cleaning up, he sat by the tomb, even in the rain, and sold his calligraphic renderings of Pai Chu-yi's poems to whoever showed up. Sometimes he just gave them away. That was how I first met him in 1989, and we had met a half dozen more times since then. The reason he came all the way to the hotel, he said, was to extend a formal invitation to the annual celebration at Pai Chu-yi's grave. The next day was Pai Chu-yi's birthday, and hundreds of his descendents would be there. That was exciting news. He said the ceremony would begin at ten o'clock. I promised to be there and escorted him back downstairs. Mr. Yang was still outside, and I paid him to take Mr. Cheng home. Otherwise, it would have taken him an hour to get there by bus.

The second phone call was to Yen-ying, whose number I had gotten from Yen-tzu at Kunghsiang Temple. I had hoped to talk to one of the senior monks at Shaolin Temple, and Yen-ying was Shaolin's *seng-chih*, or master-at-arms. When I called, he didn't sound very receptive. In fact, he said he had no time. He said a former abbot had died the day before, and there were going to be ceremonies all week. I suddenly realized why Yen-tzu had seemed preoccupied. He was one of the guest managers at Shaolin, and there would be thousands of mourners over the course of the week.

Everyone was going to be busy, but especially Yen-ying, who was in charge of the funeral. However, before he hung up, he said with all the goings-on that night he would be sleeping late the next morning, until six or so, and if I could get there before seven, he would see me. I told him I would be there. I went outside the hotel and corralled Mr. Yang again. He had just returned from taking Mr. Cheng home. He said there was road construction on the way to Shaolin, but he could get me there in ninety minutes. We agreed on a price, and he said he would pick me up the next morning at five o'clock.

. . . . .

By the time I got downstairs the next morning, it was already 5:15. Mr. Yang was waiting with his motor running—to keep from freezing. As soon as we took off, I lay down in the back. My room was above the hotel's entertainment center, which didn't wrap things up until one o'clock, and the couple in the next room got into a fight that lasted until two. Through the car window I watched the full moon follow us out of town. About the time we began working our way into the mountains, I fell asleep again.

Mr. Yang woke me just as we reached the entrance of what was now called Sung-shan National Park. We drove past the parking lot and through the main gate. No one was there to stop us. It was too early for tourists. I was glad to save the 100RMB admission fee but even gladder that I didn't have to walk. Normally, visitors had to park in the lot and walk half a mile to Shaolin or take the shuttle, if it was running. We drove all the way to the temple's front gate and parked next to the stupa cemetery. It was 6:30. I walked over to the temporary shrine that had been set up next to the temple's east wall for the funeral. There were two young monks putting things in order, and I asked one of them if he could direct me to Yen-ying's quarters. He dropped what he was doing and led me up a cobblestone alley that ran between the temple's shrine halls and the monks' quarters. Most of the halls had been torn down and were being rebuilt. Tourist dollars at work. My guide said Shaolin had been closed all year and wouldn't reopen until later that fall.

At the very back of the complex, we entered a small compound where the senior monks lived. The young monk banged on Yen-ying's door. I was surprised at his temerity. When he didn't hear anything, he banged again. Finally, Yen-ying answered.

He had been asleep and needed a minute to get dressed. I laughed to myself, happy in the thought that I had actually woken up Shaolin's master-at-arms. Gary Snyder's poem "Why Log Truck Drivers Rise Earlier Than Students of Zen" came to mind:

In the high seat, before-dawn dark,
Polished hubs gleam
And the shiny diesel stack
Warms and flutters
Up the Tyler Road grade
To the logging on Poorman Creek.
Thirty miles of dust.

There is no other life.

The polished hub gleamed in the starless sky, and I, too, would not have wanted any other life. After a minute, Yen-ying opened the door and invited me in.

The room was larger than I had expected, about twelve feet on a side. There was a full-sized bed at the far corner of the room and a smaller one, presumably for an attendant, near the door. I sat down on the standard vinyl sofa, and Yen-ying reached underneath his bed and pulled out a kilo bag of Kuanyinwang, the goddess of Iron Goddesses, and he didn't skimp when he filled his clay teapot. There was barely room for water. He said it was a present from a layman and cost over 1,000RMB, or $125, a kilo. When Chinese buy or sell things by the kilo, they don't actually mean a thousand grams. They mean six hundred. It's called a "market kilo," and it's equivalent to about twenty ounces. When I told Yen-ying not to waste it on me—not that I really meant it—he lifted the blanket hanging over the edge of his bed and showed me his tea supply underneath. There were several dozen more bags, presumably of equally fine tea—presents from patrons and well-wishers. I was envious. He smiled then sat down beside me. Once the tea was ready, he poured me the tiniest of cups and a mug-sized cup for himself. We both sat there for a minute enjoying the fragrance and then the taste.

Yen-ying didn't wait for me to ask questions. He jumped right in. He said, "When new monks at Shaolin ask me about the Dharma, I tell them to have a cup of tea. If they still don't understand, I tell them to taste the tea. The Way is in everything we do. Drinking a cup of tea, eating, shitting, it doesn't matter, it's all the Way. You can read all the books you want, but unless you find the Way in your daily life, you're wasting your time. It's the same with martial arts. Every kick, every blow is the Way. You can't separate yourself from what you do. If you do, it's not the Way. At Shaolin, we don't separate the inside from the outside. We must have a karmic connection for you to show up here in my room and be drinking tea with me. Have another cup."

Yen-ying was from Szechuan and looked to be about forty. He said when he first arrived at Shaolin as a young novice in 1991, he didn't have any previous training in martial arts. But he wanted to learn. That was why he came there. He learned fast. Seven years later he was appointed Shaolin's master-at-arms, and he had been reappointed to the post every year for the past eight years, which was a long time to hold any position in a monastery. He was good at what he did. When Shaolin monks

Interior of Master Yen-ying's room at Shaolin Temple

were invited to perform, whether at state functions or abroad, Yen-ying was their leader and their featured performer. The government's new admission ticket for Sungshan National Park showed him striking a pose reminiscent of Sun Wu-k'ung, the Monkey King, one of the heroes in *Journey to the West*—a novel and later an opera that recounted the monk Hsuan-tsang's adventures on his journey to India to collect Buddhist scriptures.

As Yen-ying became more comfortable with me sitting next to him, he started punctuating what he said by flashing his fists in front of my face. He was so fast, I never actually saw his fists, but I felt the wind. And each time he did this, he leaned back to observe my reaction, and then laughed.

When Shaolin was first built by Emperor Hsiao-wen in 496, it wasn't for Bodhidharma but for another Indian monk whose name was Buddha. Neither Buddha nor his disciples were Zen monks. They were representatives of that amalgamation of Hinayana and early Mahayana Buddhism that emphasized meditation and knowledge but not wisdom, and ascetic practices and supernatural powers but not everyday affairs.

The temple first became associated with martial arts a little more than a hundred years after it was built. In the battle to succeed the Sui dynasty, a group of Shaolin monks used their fighting skills to protect Li Shih-min, whose father eventually founded the T'ang dynasty in 618. When Li Shih-min succeeded his father, the temple became the recipient of imperial patronage. There was no further mention of martial arts at Shaolin until the sixteenth century, when historians finally took note of its unique style of Zen. But the Second World War and the Cultural Revolution were not kind, and the temple was down to a handful of monks until Bruce Lee put martial arts and Shaolin Temple on the world map. Since then, privately run martial arts academies in the area have flourished, while the temple itself has had to struggle to reestablish its own unique style that combined martial arts and Zen. Yen-ying said, "We don't teach external forms, we teach a way of life."

He said that at any one time there were between two and three hundred monks at Shaolin. But Shaolin, he said, wasn't a "public monastery." Monks couldn't just show up and stay for a couple of nights as they could at some monasteries. It was too much of a distraction to have monks coming and going. There were enough other distractions. Anyone who wanted to stay had to agree to stay at least a year. Those who did, he said, were trained in both meditation and martial arts as one and the same practice. He said, "Sitting and kicking are the same. The mind and the body are one, not two. The monks here practice whatever style they feel is right for them. But they don't have to practice martial arts if they don't want to. The main thing is for them to practice Zen in whatever they do."

When I asked him about the new meditation hall, he said it was just a temporary hall, and that a much larger hall was being built behind the monastery. Strange as it sounds, Shaolin actually hadn't had a meditation hall in modern times until now. Monks meditated in their rooms. So I asked Yen-ying if the monks who were using the new hall for the first time approached their practice any differently, and if they talked to their instructors more now about their states of mind.

He laughed, "You can't talk about a state of mind. States of mind are delusions. Zen is about being free of delusions. People read books and analyze their meaning and develop all sorts of ideas about a state of mind. But a state of mind is a delusion. Zen isn't analysis. If someone at Shaolin asks about their state of mind, they're more likely to get a beating than an answer. Zen isn't something you study. It's not something you analyze. We tell the monks here not to make Zen into another delusion, not to make the Buddha into another delusion, to wake up to their real mind, their original mind, their mind free of delusions, including the delusion of mind." Then he snapped his fist past my face again and in the same motion reached down and poured me another cup of tea. He continued, "Some people like to seek out monks who have read a lot of books and who know a lot about Buddhism and ask them how to practice. But they're wasting their time. Practice doesn't come out of a book. Practice comes out of the mind. Zen doesn't depend on words."

Just then another monk knocked and entered without waiting for Yen-ying to answer. Yen-ying turned to me and said, "This is our religious affairs manager. He's in charge of the meditation hall." On any other occasion, I wouldn't have left without talking with him. But I could see that their day—and the former abbot's funeral—was about to begin, which was why the religious affairs manager was there. I thanked Yen-ying for his kindness and for the tea. As the master-at-arms, he was responsible for ensuring compliance with the rules in the monastery, but he was clearly more interested in expedience than in rules. That was what I tasted in his tea.

After we said goodbye, I walked back down the cobblestone alley and came out again beside the funeral shrine. The sunlight hadn't quite reached the temple, but there were already a few tourists photographing each other in front of its closed gate. Mr. Yang was waiting in his taxi on the other side of the forested courtyard on the dirt road that separated the monastery from its cemetery of rocket-ship stupas. When I walked over to get in, I paused and looked up at the peak behind the temple. The morning light was shining on the cave just below the summit. That was where Bodhidharma faced a rock wall for nine years and where Hui-k'o stood in the snow and where the teaching of Zen began in China. It was about the size of the cave at Pragbodhi where Shakyamuni meditated until he had the good sense to come down the mountain and sit under a tree. I was glad Zen masters finally discovered tea.

It was a perfectly clear but freezing day, and I didn't linger. Mr. Cheng had asked me to meet him at Pai Chu-yi's grave at ten o'clock, and it was just after eight when I left Shaolin. Mr. Yang said not to worry, he would get me there on time. I lay down in the back again and tried to sleep. The old highway was under repair, and we had to detour through a few villages and negotiate several traffic jams. It took nearly two hours, but we arrived at the south end of the Yi River Bridge a few minutes before ten. I paid Mr. Yang and told him not to wait for me this time, that I would take a bus back to Loyang.

The Pai Gardens, as the grounds around Pai Chu-yi's tomb were now called, were located across the Yi River from the Lungmen Caves, which was where all the tourists went. Hardly anyone visited the Pai Gardens. Mr. Cheng was waiting at the entrance. He waved and led me inside, up a stone path to the back. Instead of garden scenery, which was lovely enough, he wanted to show me the calligraphy. Famous calligraphers from all over China had written out dozens of Pai Chu-yi's poems and essays, and their calligraphy had been carved onto stone and set up around the rear of the garden. Mr. Cheng was only the janitor, but he was also the chief custodian of Pai Chu-yi's spirit. It always took a minute to get used to the dust and stench that accompanied him, but it was always a pleasure to be with him, and I was always sad to say goodbye.

After pointing out a few of his favorites, he led me over to a pillar on which Pai Chu-yi's advice to his descendents was inscribed, and we read it out loud together: "Don't envy those above you or disdain those below you, don't be swayed by flattery or deterred by criticism. Cultivate friendships, and be true to the Way in all that you do." I don't remember the rest, except for the conclusion: "Those who don't follow my advice are no descendents of mine."

The pillar was erected at the spot where a stupa once stood that contained the remains of Pai Chu-yi's best friend, the monk Ju-man. Mr. Cheng didn't know what happened to the stupa or when it disappeared, but the pillar was a worthy substitute. While we were standing there admiring the calligraphy, we heard the ceremony beginning, and made our way to the tomb. The noise was deafening. Drums and horns usually reserved for funerals were blaring forth such a cacophonic din, the accompanying firecrackers failed to drown them out. If Pai Chu-yi was residing in the highest heaven, he was now surely aware of what was going on at his grave below.

Pai Chu-yi was born in 772 and grew up east of Loyang in Jungyang, the same town as Hui-k'o, the Second Zen Patriarch. His parents later sent him to live with relatives near Ch'ang-an to study for the imperial exams. It took him a while, but Pai Chu-yi finally passed and became a government official. However, he was too outspoken for his own good, and spent much of his career in exile far from the capital. His poetry, though, made up for his failure to effect social reform through the normal channels. He was one of the first poets to write in a language everyone could understand. People from all walks of life knew his poems by heart, even while he was alive. And his poems did make a difference.

Between exiles, he lived briefly in Loyang in 824. It was then that he added two ladies to his household that so brightened his life and his poetry: she with the ruby lips, and she with the willow waist. He returned to Loyang again in 829 to serve as governor of the province of which Loyang was the capital. And a few years later, he built a small house for himself near Hsiangshan Temple across from the Lungmen Caves. He raised the money by writing epitaphs for people of means. He was, after all, the most famous poet of his day. But he was also a man of great moral character and refused to use public funds for the project. And so he began his retirement in the company of monks. It was a fine place with a fine view. The huge stone buddhas in the Lungmen Caves on the other side of the river must have been quite a sight in the moonlight.

Over the years, Pai Chu-yi had kept copies of all the poems he wrote, which was what other poets did and still do, and he spent his last years putting them together. By the time he was done, he had compiled an edition of 3,800 poems, which was a lot of poems. He had the brilliant idea of sending copies to the chief monasteries of the day, which was why his poetic corpus was so well preserved. In his will, he asked to be buried near the stupa of his old friend, Ju-man, the stupa that had since been replaced by a pillar with his advice to his descendents. One of the poems that always came to mind when I thought of Pai Chu-yi was one that was later collected in *Three Hundred Poems of the T'ang*: "A Question for Liu Nineteen":

I have a new batch of emerald wine
and a small stove made of cinnabar clay
it feels like it's going to snow tonight
can you come by for a cup or two?

It was cold enough to snow, but there wasn't a cloud in the sky. Ever since Pai Chu-yi died there in 846, his descendents have gathered every year to honor their ancestor on his birthday, which they celebrate on the full moon of the second month, and which fell on March 14 that year. Scholars put his birth a month or so earlier, but his descendents have their own records. And they were out in force. Hundreds of people taking part in the ceremony crowded around his stone-encircled tomb. In front of the tombstone, there were a dozen or so people dressed in the white sheets

Pai Chu-yi's descendents at his grave in Loyang

and hempen hats that were standard attire for mourners. It was a birthday and also a deathday celebration.

With some difficulty, Mr. Cheng led me through the crowd, introducing me to some of the poet's descendents, of which there were an estimated forty thousand in Loyang alone. The oldest was in the forty-eighth generation and was over a hundred, and the youngest was in the fifty-seventh generation and only a few months old. When I asked how ten generations could be alive at the same time, one of his descendents explained that there were sixteen lines of descent, not just one. People in some of the lines had lived longer than others. He said there was a representative from each line in front of the tomb offering incense to their esteemed ancestor, which was what the people dressed in white were doing.

As I went around meeting Pai Chu-yi's descendents, at some point I became separated from Mr. Cheng and wandered away from the grave along the ridge of the hill that faced the Lungmen Caves across the Yi River. The path ended at Hsiangshan Temple. It had been moved from its original location, which was further south, and rebuilt for tourists. There were no monks. The only thing of interest was a set of statues of Pai Chu-yi's nine friends, including the monk Ju-man. I lit some incense, walked back to the bridgehead, and took the next bus back to Loyang.

Later that night, the oddest thing happened. The chairman of the Pai Chu-yi Research Association and another man came to my hotel room and conferred on me a certificate making me an honorary member, with all rights and privileges thereto. I was so surprised I couldn't think of anything to say except to thank them for the honor. As we said goodbye at the door, they encouraged me to translate Pai Chu-yi's poems and make them better known in the West. I told them I planned to do exactly that, but not until my old age. I was planning to build a hut, I told them, close enough to a monastery to hear the dinner board. But not yet.

6 NO FORM

It was time to leave Loyang and the happy crew of the New Chuho Hotel. I could have walked to the bus station, it was that close. But I wanted to thank Mr. Yang, the taxi driver who worked out of the hotel parking lot, so I asked him to take me there. Loyang was the capital of twelve dynasties, and I was always finding myself in one of them. And few connections are more important in China than a reliable driver. After he dropped me off, I went inside and bought a ticket. My bus wasn't due to leave for thirty minutes, so I went back out into the morning air. The weather was warmer— not warm, but at least not freezing. For the first time since arriving in Beijing, I stood outside and unzipped my parka. Then I took it off. While I was standing there wondering if I had gone too far, Mr. Yang drove up and honked. He lowered the passenger window and handed me a bag of snacks I had left in the backseat. My protective deities were on the job early.

A few minutes later, I boarded my bus. It was bound for Hofei, the capital of Anhui Province miles to the southeast. There was only one bus a day from Loyang, and it left at nine o'clock, which was fairly late for a bus that had to go so far. Still, I was glad I didn't have to get up at six or seven, which was when most one-bus-a-day runs departed. I kept waiting for it to fill up, but when we left, there were only six of us. I really didn't understand what was going on. I was traveling on empty buses . . . in China. Apparently, I had discovered a break in what I had previously experienced as a constant flood of human migration. I resolved to travel in the first half of March again.

Other than the intermittent gunfire from the Hong Kong gangster flicks, it was a fine ride, mostly on expressways. I had the entire back half of the bus to myself, and I stretched out on the last row and went to sleep. My dust allergy was gone, so the accumulated exhaustion of more than two weeks on the road must have finally caught up with me—I slept for more than four hours and didn't wake until we stopped for lunch at one of the new expressway travel centers. There were easily twenty buses parked outside the restaurant and more than five hundred people inside. I went in, took one look at the cafeteria-style food, and walked back out. I decided to stick with my snacks. I sat down on the steps to wait for my fellow passengers to finish eating—buses were locked during meal breaks.

While I was sitting there, an old man came by collecting beer bottles—left by passengers, I assumed. He asked me why I wasn't inside eating. I told him I didn't like the looks of the food. He grinned and said the food wasn't up to his standards either and he ate better at home. He was dressed in several layers of rags and only had a few teeth to work with. I had to laugh. He laughed too. We both kept chuckling at the thought of him eating better than all the folks in the fancy new travel center cafeteria.

Not long after my fellow gourmand wandered off looking for bottles to finance his next repast, we reboarded our ghost bus. A few minutes later, we turned off the expressway onto a regular highway. Both sides of the road were lined with farmers selling strawberries. I suddenly realized I wasn't in North China anymore. I had fallen asleep about the time we left the Yellow River watershed just south of Loyang. I was in the Huai River watershed now, and I was on the heels of the Second Patriarch.

When Hui-k'o and his disciples fled the religious persecution of 574–580, they would have traveled by boat. After stopping at Shaolin to say goodbye to those who stayed behind, they would have followed the Ying River southeast all the way from Sungshan to the lakes and marshes formed by the Huai River just west of Huainan. The Huai drained the watershed between the Yellow River and the Yangtze and was one of China's four great rivers—the fourth being the West River that drained most of southwest China.

Once across the Huai, Hui-k'o and his disciples would have continued south up the Pi River to its headwaters in the Tapieh Range, where they finally stopped when they reached a mountain called Ssukungshan. That was where they hid out until things settled down in the North, and that was where I was heading. The bus I was on followed the same route, but not all the way to the Tapieh Range. Hofei was the end of the line.

Until recently, Hofei was a provincial backwater, a regional distribution center for agricultural products. But Hofei was centrally located, which was why it was chosen as the new capital of Anhui after Liberation. And it was booming. The city had gone from fifty thousand people in 1949 to anywhere from four to six million, depending on which month you counted. There were regular migrations between the countryside and cities that fluctuated with the seasons, mainly the retail seasons that drove China's manufacturing industries. Like provincial capitals elsewhere in China, Hofei looked like a cicada coming out of the ground. I didn't know which was more depressing, the shell it was trying to leave behind or its new comic-book façade.

At least it was dark. It was seven o'clock when we finally arrived, and I was ready for a hotel. But first I asked where I could get a bus to Yuehhsi, which would put me close to my next destination, Ssukungshan. One of the ticket sellers said buses left from the city's West Gate Station, and so I proceeded there by taxi. Just up the street from the station and towering over everything was the twenty-two-story Fengle International. It looked like it was out of my price range but it was the only hotel in the area, and after ten hours on the road, I couldn't say no, especially when they only charged 200RMB, or twenty-five bucks, for a very swank room.

After dropping my bag, I went back downstairs and inquired about an Internet cafe. The hotel bellboy didn't just point, he walked me outside and down a long winding alley to his favorite place. I answered a few e-mails, but there was still no word from the Gug. The Guggenheim Foundation sent out award letters in March, and it was already the fifteenth. This was the seventh time I'd applied. It wasn't the annual rejection letter I minded—the fantasy would have otherwise been worth it. What I minded was having to ask people, some of whom I didn't even know, to write letters of recommendation every time I applied.

The Gug had already turned down my proposals for a book about China's hermits, a book version of the thousand radio programs I did for a Hong Kong radio station about my travels in China, a translation of the *Buddhacharita* (the earliest epic poem about the Buddha's life)—for which I applied twice, a translation of the *Lankavatara Sutra* (the text Bodhidharma gave Hui-k'o), a translation of the poems of the T'ang poet Wei Ying-wu; and now they were about to turn down a book about a pilgrimage to Zen sites in China. Except for the Gug, there really wasn't much grant money out there for whatever category it was I fit into. But I promised myself this was going to be the last time.

I also checked on the Mariners. They were at spring training in Phoenix, and they, too, were hoping for more from the gods than they were going to get. Afterwards, I stopped in a hole-in-the-wall restaurant for some fried noodles, then went back and took a bath. I finally made use of the body lotion that was always in hotel bathrooms. My skin had become so dry in the North, it hurt when I got into the bath. Afterwards, I put on the robe that came with the room and sat on the chaise longue—did I mention how swank the place was? Through the room's huge curved window, I watched the moon cross half the sky. By the time I said goodnight, the port I had brought from America was almost gone, as were the fun-size Snickers left over from Halloween. No one ever came by our house—it was on a hill. But we had to be ready, just in case.

The next morning I discovered there were no buses to Yuehhsi from Hofei's West Gate Station. I keep telling myself to get a second opinion, but I always forget. After some running around, I finally found the right place—the Hsinya Station, near the city's East train station. Buses to Yuehhsi left every hour, and mine left a few minutes after I arrived.

It took nearly an hour to get out of town, but once we were rolling through the countryside, everything I saw was green. It was such a relief. I had slept through most of it the day before. The North was so brown it was depressing. But there was more to the scenery south of Hofei than green. After another hour, we turned off the main highway at the town of Shucheng onto a much narrower road that led southwest through the mountains. The view was so unexpected, even my fellow passengers kept looking out the windows, admiring the forested slopes of pine and fir and hillsides of bamboo and rushing mountain streams.

I was also impressed with the driver and the conductor. They didn't allow smoking. Nor did they allow anyone to lie down across the seats, as I foolishly attempted. They said it was too dangerous—too many unexpected moments involving oncoming traffic on curves. There were, in fact, a number of such moments, and I was relieved when we finally came out of the mountains and turned south again onto a regular highway. The last hour was all hillsides of fruit trees in bloom, wave upon wave of tea bushes, and lone farmers turning the soil in their terraced fields. Spring had arrived in Anhui.

Four and a half hours after leaving Hofei, we pulled into Yuehhsi. It had grown since my last visit in 1999 from little more than an intersection of two highways to a town with a dozen paved roads. But Yuehhsi was not my final destination. I was headed for Ssukungshan, which was another forty-five miles to the southwest, near the village of Tienchien. There were no buses from the long-distance station, but there were from the local station right across the street. Half a dozen minivans were waiting in the station's dirt parking lot for passengers bound for villages in the area. I climbed aboard one with a sign for Tienchien. It was waiting for just one more passenger to justify the run, and I was that passenger.

The road was mostly paved, but it was far more tortuous than the earlier one between Shucheng and Yuehhsi. There were so many switchbacks, the woman sitting behind me got carsick. Fortunately, another woman had a piece of ginger and gave it to her to chew. That seemed to do the trick. The scenery was even more spectacular. At one point we passed a series of weathered magmatic domes that had extruded upward and then cooled to form huge folded clouds of rock on which a few determined pines embraced the wind. This was all part of the Tapieh Range that separated Anhui from Hupei Province. It would have been a great place to hide out, and still would.

It took two hours, but we finally arrived at the one-street village of Tienchien at the bottom of a long valley. For an extra 5RMB, the driver took me the remaining two or three miles to Wuhsiang Temple halfway up the slope of Ssukungshan. As I walked through the parking lot and into the temple courtyard, I saw an old nun sitting in the sun trying to thread a needle. I went over and asked her if the abbot was there. I had visited seven years earlier and was impressed with the group of young monks in charge of the place. When I showed her a photograph I took of them, she said they had all moved away. There was a new abbot. His name was Neng-wen. But he was gone too. He was conducting a ceremony at a temple near Yuehhsi, and he wouldn't be back for a while—maybe next week.

I was disappointed. Zen may have begun in North China, but it was lucky to get out of the North alive. And this mountain was where it ended up. I was hoping to talk with the abbot to resolve a few issues surrounding the Second Patriarch, such as the different dates suggested for his stay there. Local records only say he came there during the Northern Ch'i dynasty (550–577), which would mean before the Northern Chou put an end to the Northern Ch'i in 577. My own feeling was that he wouldn't have had reason to come south until after the Northern Chou began its persecution of Buddhists in 574. Later accounts, though, say he came to Ssukungshan in the 550s and returned to the North before the persecution began, which didn't make sense, at least not to me.

But the minivan that had brought me there and that could have taken me back to Yuehhsi had already left, so I was stuck. Since it was clear that I would be spending the night, the nun led me over to the two-story building I had stayed in before. It was in bad shape when I visited seven years earlier, and it had only gotten worse. She looked inside one of the guest rooms and quickly closed the door. She decided to put me in the abbot's room instead. It was the only room with a full complement

Old entrance of Wuhsiang Temple on Ssukungshan

of bedding: a sheet on another board mattress, a couple of blankets filled with cotton wadding, and a couple of pillows filled with chaff. None of the bedding had been washed in a very long time. But if it was good enough for the abbot, how could I object? Besides, it wasn't like I had a choice.

Since I was obviously taking the rest of the day off, I did what I do at home every afternoon. I took a nap. It was my first one in a week, and it felt like such a luxury. After I woke up, I decided there was no reason to get out of bed. So I propped myself up with one of the pillows and wrote in my journal. I hadn't gotten very far when the nun knocked on the door. I got up and opened it, and she handed me two thermoses of hot water. Tea seemed like a good idea, so I invited her to join me. She was only too glad for the company. She said the abbot didn't spend much time there, and she was usually alone. I cleared off the desk by the window and pulled out two stools from underneath. Then I got out my tea set and made us some tea.

The nun said her name was Jen-ming, and she was from Yuehhsi. She was sixty-three, but she didn't look a day under seventy-three. She had clearly had a hard life, but I'm not sure what wore her down. She said she had never married and never had children. When she said this, she pointed to her head, as if to say she was nuts and nobody would have wanted to marry her. I nodded, as if I understood. But being nuts didn't seem to keep other people from getting married. It must have been something else, but whatever it was, she didn't say.

I asked her what sort of Buddhism she had studied. She said that even though she had been a nun for ten years she had never actually studied Buddhism. The way she said *fo-chiao*: "Buddhism" reminded me of my aunt Pearline, who was raised on a cotton farm in Arkansas and was always making fun of my interest in "Buddhasm," as she called it. Jen-ming had such a wonderful open and simple manner, I'm sure studying Buddhism would only have done her harm. We chatted about everything but Buddhism, although I only understood half of what she said. The local dialect was beyond me. But it didn't matter. I couldn't help smiling every time she laughed, which was often. She was so unpretentious. She said she had never had such good tea, and it was, indeed, pretty good tea—a high-mountain oolong from Taiwan. Everything tastes better when you're having a good time.

After the fourth pot, she said she had some sewing she wanted to finish before the sun went down, and she went back to the spot where she was sitting when I arrived, and I returned to my journal. While we were both engaged in our respective use of the fading light, a laywoman arrived on her motorbike. Her Buddhist name was Ming-shen, and she came up from the village twice a day to cook breakfast and dinner and to help Jen-ming perform the two ceremonies that marked the temple day. It didn't take her long to cook what she brought. Less than an hour after arriving, she beat the wooden board that was every monastery's dinner bell, and the three of us sat down to a meal of cabbage, mustard greens, and a variety of wild mushroom that seemed to confirm my suspicion that mushrooms were the food of the gods, who had inadvertently left some spores behind when they moved on to a more peaceful planet.

After dinner, I followed Jen-ming and Ming-shen up the cement steps to the main shrine hall for the evening ceremony. The hall wasn't there when I visited before, but it was basically the same as buddha halls elsewhere in China—cement and tile in the imperial style. The Chinese can be incredibly conservative when it comes to outward appearances. I keep waiting for someone to design a buddha hall that doesn't require a pile of money—glazed tiles aren't cheap—and that reflects the teachings of the Buddha rather than the extravagance of its insecure builders. I'm sure I'll be waiting a long time, especially in China.

The old nun went up to the altar and lit some incense, which was standard procedure. But then she burned some paper money, which was her own addition to the proceedings. Perhaps it was for her parents or perhaps it was for some departed donor. The only place such currency could be redeemed, according to the design printed on the notes, was at the Bank of Hell. Of course, not everyone who died would be needing that money. It was a worst case scenario. Everything was free in Paradise. After the flames died down, she went over to one corner of the hall and started ringing the temple bell, which was held up by a wooden scaffold, and the laywoman from the village went over to the opposite corner and started beating a huge drum, which was also suspended from a wooden frame.

The last time I was there, the bell was sitting in the courtyard waiting for a place to be hung. It was cast with the temple's name prominently displayed: WUHSIANG SSU. *Ssu* meant "temple," and *wu-hsiang* meant "no form." That was the teaching of Zen and the teaching of Hui-k'o. Nothing up the sleeve. No sleeve. While Ming-shen beat the drum with all the strength she could muster, Jen-ming rang the bell of formlessness 108 times, once for every trouble and way out of trouble. The two always go together. Affliction and Enlightenment. As the two women shook the ten directions and roused practitioners down in the valley, they sang the evening song of offering. I sat there on the floor against the wall and just hummed along:

> *May the sound of the bell and drum dispel afflictions*
> *may it nourish the roots of wisdom*
> *and give rise to the fruit of awareness*
> *may it carry to the depths of Hell*
> *and echo through the Three Realms (i.e. Desire, Form, and Formlessness)*
> *and may all who hear it become buddhas*
> *and vow to liberate others.*

Afterwards, Ming–shen went back down the mountain on her motorbike, and Jen–ming and I adjourned to our respective lodgings for the night. I poured myself the last of the port, said goodnight to the moon, and went to sleep in the abbot's bed.

. . . . .

Wuhsiang Temple bell

Sometime during the night, the moon disappeared, and the weather changed. A cold front moved in. Once more I felt as if I was being pursued by the weather gods. When I woke up the next morning, out came the old parka again. But it wasn't just cold. It was also damp. I could tell that rain wasn't far behind and decided I'd better visit the places near the temple associated with Hui-k'o while I still could.

When Hui-k'o led his disciples to Ssukungshan to escape the religious persecution in North China, there were no temples on the mountain. But Ssukungshan had a reputation as a good place to hide out, which is why he chose it. In fact, that was how it got its name, which was an odd one. *Ssu-k'ung* meant "Minister of Works." It was the title of an official who hid there around the time of Confucius, and the mountain had been called Ssukungshan ever since. It was also one of Li Pai's favorite haunts. In 758, shortly before he reportedly tried to embrace the moon in the Yangtze and drowned, China's Poetry Immortal wrote a poem entitled "Thinking of My Hideout on Ssukungshan."

There were lots of places to hide, and Hui-k'o and his disciples disappeared into the mountain. It wasn't until Pen-ching (667–761) settled there that a monastery was built. Pen-ching was a dharma heir of Hui-neng, the Sixth Patriarch of Zen. When Emperor Hsuan-tsung heard about him, he invited the monk to lecture at court in 743 and was so impressed that he elevated Pen-ching to the status of National Master and bestowed on him enough funds to build the biggest monastic complex in China. That was the origin of Wuhsiang Temple, which nowadays wasn't even a shadow of a shadow of a shadow of its T'ang-dynasty incarnation, when records say seven thousand monks lived there.

No one knows how long Hui-k'o stayed on the mountain before he headed back north. He didn't leave any records. But just behind the present shrine hall, there was a stone platform where he lectured. And further up the trail, there was a large gourd-shaped boulder where he was said to have transmitted his robe and bowl to Seng-ts'an, making him Zen's Third Patriarch. The last time I was there I also visited a couple of caves and stone huts near the top of the mountain where Hui-k'o and his disciples lived. But that was it as far as earthly traces.

Hui-k'o took to heart Bodhidharma's teaching that an understanding of Zen did not rely on texts but on the mind. He preferred to teach face-to-face. Until the brief collection of statements attributed to him in *Record of the Masters of the Lankavatara* came to light, some scholars even doubted his existence. While he was on this mountain, though, he did leave a poem behind in which he recounted his journey there:

Past the lakes and swamps I journeyed
with the moon on my shoulders I reached Ssukung
where a cloud patch holds my robe together
and the snow fills me up when I'm hungry.

Hui-k'o was a tough old bird. After transmitting the Dharma to Seng-ts'an, he insisted on returning to North China—even though he was over a hundred. He said he had a karmic debt, which he presumably repaid when he was executed near Hantan in 593. His other disciples accompanied him north, but he told Seng-ts'an to stay in the South, which was why Zen not only survived but flourished.

This time, I only hiked up as far as the gourd-shaped rock where Seng-ts'an received the robe and bowl of the patriarchship. There was some mist in the air, and I decided I had pushed my luck with the weather. After paying my respects where one mind met another, I hiked back down to the temple. As I walked across the courtyard, Jen-ming came out of the building she lived in and told me she had telephoned down to the village. She said the next minivan going to Yuehhsi would swing up the mountain pick me up on the way, which it did less than an hour later. While I was waiting, I snuck into her room and left her the rest of my oolong and enough money to go nuts on her next trip to Yuehhsi.

When the minivan pulled into the parking lot, I climbed aboard and took the seat in front across from the driver. As soon as I sat down, the old nun hurried out of the gate and over to the window next to my seat and told me that Neng-wen was at Fayun Temple. It was only six miles from Yuehhsi, and she suggested I go there. Maybe the abbot had some information about Hui-k'o's years on Ssukungshan, she said. I agreed to try, and we waved goodbye. Off I went down the mountain and through the village of Tienchien and up and over the ridges of the Tapieh Range.

Halfway to Yuehhsi, the mist turned to rain, and the temperature started dropping. It was a long, cold two-hour ride. When it was over, I discovered there was no public transportation to Fayun Temple, and the two taxi drivers I was able to track down—the town was that small—weren't willing to risk it. The last part of the road, they said, was too rough or nonexistent. Since I was out of options, I walked over to the long-distance bus station to buy a ticket to my next destination. But while I was checking the schedule on the station wall, the minivan driver who had brought me there from Ssukungshan caught up with me. He said he knew someone who would take me to the temple.

A few minutes later, a sixteen-year-old kid appeared out in the street with a motorcycle-driven carryall, and off I went for 15RMB, or two bucks. At least the carryall part was covered, and amid all the bouncing I was able to reach into my pack and pull out my wool socks, and tried to resuscitate my half-frozen feet. The last mile or two of the road was, as advertised, rough or nonexistent, depending on one's definition of those terms. But the road gods relented just enough to grant us passage.

Fayun Temple was at the foot of a forested hill, and its entrance was dominated by a tall, unusually thin pagoda whose bricks were covered with buddhas in relief. A sign at the base called it THOUSAND BUDDHA PAGODA. I didn't have time to find out anything more than that. I was cold, and it was raining, and my parka was no longer waterproof. Also, the carryall driver insisted on walking beside me trying to hold an umbrella over both of us, which wasn't doing either of us any good. He was just a kid, but he was trying, and I didn't linger. I walked up the steps next to the pagoda and through a tunnel, coming out into a small courtyard below the main shrine hall.

There were about a dozen monks and an equal number of laypeople standing inside the hall chanting. Off to the right in what served as the guest hall and the office for keeping track of donations, there were half a dozen laywomen sitting on stools warming their hands and feet around a charcoal brazier. I walked over and asked if Neng-wen was there. They said he was conducting the ceremony. When I asked when it would be over, they said in two or three hours. I sighed. I didn't feel like waiting in the cold that long, and I turned to leave. As I headed out the doorway, they said to wait, that there would be a break in half an hour. I figured if Hui-k'o could stand in the snow for a few days, the least I could do was wait in the cold for thirty minutes. But I didn't even have to do that. The women invited me to join them around the small floor stove, and I was finally able to restore feeling to my fingers and toes.

They said that Neng-wen was the abbot of Fayun Temple as well as the abbot of Wuhsiang Temple but that he spent most of his time at Fayun, where the living conditions were better and where more laypeople came to take part in the merit-accruing ceremonies. Ssukungshan, they said, was too far away for most people. When I asked them about the history of Fayun Temple, they said it was built around 300, and the pagoda a couple of decades later. But they didn't know whose remains it contained.

They were right about the break. After thirty minutes, the chanting stopped. As soon as it did, one of the women told me to wait outside the guest hall while she walked up to the shrine hall. Shortly afterwards, Neng-wen came out and walked down to where I was standing and asked me what I wanted. He was a thin man of about sixty-five, and he was wearing his red ceremonial cassock. Someone came over and handed him a cup of tea, and while he quenched his thirst, I told him I was visiting the places where the early patriarchs of Zen lived and taught. Neng-wen motioned for me to sit down on a stone bench in the courtyard garden. As I did so, he also began to sit down. But the odd thing was that there was nothing for him to sit down on. For a moment he appeared to be falling. Then out of nowhere, a disciple slid a wooden bench under him just before he reached the point of no return. Eerie.

When I asked Neng-wen what he knew about Hui-k'o, he more or less repeated the standard account. But he grabbed my hands when I told him that Hui-k'o's relics had been found. After I assured him that this was true, he said their discovery would signal a renaissance of Zen in China. It was important, he said. When I asked him what he knew about Hui-k'o's teaching, he said Hui-k'o left no writings because his teaching was beyond form. He said there was no Zen school when Hui-k'o was alive. All he had to rely on was his mind, and that was what he did. He taught mind-to-mind. Other teachers relied on texts or ascetic practices. Their teachings were based on form. Hui-k'o taught a formless teaching. The form wasn't important. Only the mind was important.

It wasn't entirely true that Hui-k'o left no records of his teaching. There were the statements in *Record of the Masters of the Lankavatara* and the poem he left on Ssukungshan. And there was one more item. It was a response to a letter from someone named Layman Hsiang, who many believe was the man who eventually became the Third Patriarch. The date given for this exchange was 550–551, when both men were still in North China. Layman Hsiang wrote,

> Our body creates a shadow, and our voice produces an echo. And yet people
> exhaust their body to chase their shadow without realizing that their shadow

comes from their body. And people raise their voice to stop its echo unaware that the echo comes from their voice. Getting rid of affliction to attain nirvana is like trying to find one's shadow apart from one's body. And abandoning one's humanity to achieve buddhahood is like stilling one's voice and listening for its echo. Thus we know that delusion and awareness are the same and ignorance and wisdom aren't different. From what has no name, we make names. And once we have names, right and wrong appear. From what has no principle, we make principles. And once we have principles, arguments arise. Illusions aren't real. So who is right and who is wrong? Delusions aren't true. So are they empty or do they exist? I would know how to gain what cannot be gained and how to lose what cannot be lost. Unable to pay you a visit, I send these thoughts and dare hope for a reply.

Hui-k'o's response was in the form of a poem:

> I have read your words and they are true
> indistinct from the deepest truths
> at first we mistake this magic gem as rubble
> then suddenly we see it is a jewel
> ignorance and wisdom aren't different
> the ten thousand dharmas are simply so
> but for those who cling to dualistic views
> I take out my brush and write down these words
> don't see yourself as anything but a buddha
> why search for a place where nothing at all remains [i.e. nirvana]?
> (Hsukaosengchuan: 16)

The idea that we are all buddhas was introduced to the Chinese by the *Nirvana Sutra* and promoted by Tao-sheng as early as the fourth century, but as an idea, not as a realization that affected one's life. This was the difference that such Zen masters as Bodhidharma and Hui-k'o conveyed to their students: look within yourself for the truth and not in a book.

Just then someone banged the drum inside the shrine hall. The break was over. Neng-wen stood up and apologized for not offering me any tea. I told him I hadn't come for the tea and thanked him for taking the time to talk with me. He invited me to come again, when he had more time. The next day was Kuan-yin's birthday, he said, and he was busy. In China, her birthday was celebrated on the nineteenth day of the second lunar month. But the party for the Goddess of Mercy was already under way in some quarters. I said goodbye, and the young boy who drove me there led me back down to his rig, trying to keep me as dry as he could. At least we didn't have to go all the way back to Yuehhsi. I got out where the rough or nonexistent road met the highway a mile or so from the temple. The boy waited with me, holding his umbrella over us both, while we looked down the highway for a bus.

7 NO MIND

I was traveling south again, but so was the weather. At least I didn't have to wait long to wave down a highway bus, and at least it was only thirty miles to my next destination, and at least I had the sense to call ahead. I was planning to stay at Third Patriarch Temple and phoned K'uan-jung, the abbot. He said the place was full. Over a thousand people had come to help him celebrate Kuan-yin's two-day birthday, and more than a hundred of them were sleeping over. He suggested I stay instead at a hotel in nearby Chienshan and come late the next day, after the crowds had left. He gave me the name of a hotel and said he would call ahead and make a reservation.

The bus that picked me up wound its way up and over the easternmost spur of the Tapieh Range and came down along a river that was more sand than water. It was called the Chienshui, or Shallow Water. Now that it was out of the mountains, it was taking its time. The Yangtze wasn't far away. Not long after we started following the river, we drove past the overwhelmed parking lot of Third Patriarch Temple. I was glad to be passing it by.

The bus I was on was headed for the Yangtze port of Anching, but it stopped on its way through Chienshan to let me and several other passengers off. Chienshan hadn't completely made the transition into the motorized world. Local transportation still included bicycle-powered rickshaws. They were lined up waiting for us to disembark at what passed for a bus stop. I climbed aboard one and asked the driver to take me to the Chienyang International. I had to smile as I said the name. It sounded absurd for such a nondescript town.

My rickshaw driver looked like he was in his seventies, and even the slightly inclined roadway was a struggle for him. I thought about getting out and walking, but he clearly needed the fare, which was 3RMB. Besides, my back was giving me trouble again, a light mist was falling, and his rig had an awning that more or less covered us both. And so I eased my way into another afternoon off on the pilgrim trail.

At the front desk of the International, they said they were expecting me. The abbot had, indeed, called ahead and had asked them to give me the preferential room rate of 160RMB, which was half the normal rate. The hotel was only two years old and far better than I would have expected for a modest-sized county seat like Chienshan. I felt like I had landed in the god realm again. And the room they gave me was in the quiet wing, facing away from the horn-honking street. After dropping my bag in the room, I went in search of something sweet. At a small dry goods store a couple of blocks away, I discovered a new treat. They were called *nan-kua-ping*: "pumpkin cookies." But they were so much more than cookies. They were pumpkin-filled, poppy-seed-coated, and deep-fried—the perfect accompaniment to an afternoon cup of instant espresso—actually, two cups.

After the *de rigueur* nap, I walked down the street toward the middle of town and found a place to eat. There were lots of small family restaurants offering wild specialties from the nearby slopes of Tienchushan. Pictures of deer, boar, and pheasants looked out from their signs. I chose the smallest and cleanest of the bunch and ordered a dish of tree ears (*Auricularia aricula*) with scrambled eggs and another one of wild mushrooms. The mushrooms were the size of portabellos and sufficiently excellent that I felt impelled to convey my appreciation to the proprietor and also to the chef.

On the way back to the hotel, I stopped at a small grocery store and replaced my recently defunct port supply with a bottle of wild gooseberry wine. I often came across wild patches of Chinese gooseberries (what we call kiwifruit in the West) while visiting hermit friends in the mountains, and I tried to imagine someone trying to collect enough to make wine. As an alcoholic beverage, it was only 7 percent—not even half as strong as port, but it was delicious. It tasted like an amontillado sherry. I drank a glass while reclining in a long, hot bath and a second glass to make sure the first one was as good as I thought. After writing a few pages in my journal, I got into bed, turned out the light, and began a long, strange night.

The room was haunted. I'd never encountered spirits before, so it took some getting used to. Actually, I didn't get used to it. I could hear things dropping, heavy things, and paper rattling and loud scratching. I called the front desk, but they insisted I was the only person staying in the "quiet" wing. The noises came from different parts of the room, and I looked everywhere for the source, but in vain. And no, it wasn't mice. But it did keep moving around. Sometimes it was under the bed, sometimes below a chair, sometimes on top of the desk, sometimes behind the curtains, and sometimes in thin air, as if something was happening in another world, and the sound was crossing over into mine. I didn't fall asleep until three o'clock. Once I did, though, I slept until eleven.

I don't think I had ever slept so late in China before. But it was a good day for a slow start. I opened the drapes and looked out the window. The rain had stopped. When I went outside, I discovered the cold was gone too. I had finally outrun the weather that met me when I landed in Beijing. There was still a lot of moisture in the air, but I was confident the sun was just on the other side of the haze. I took off my parka one more time.

Since I didn't want to arrive at Third Patriarch Temple too early, I went to an Internet cafe to check my e-mail. My daughter informed me that the dreaded envelope from the Guggenheim had arrived. She said the answer was once more "thanks for applying." At least I hadn't spent the money this time. At least I had learned that much over the years. So I would have to continue juggling credit cards for another year. Big deal. Like, who doesn't? I halfheartedly resolved to start buying lottery tickets when I got home. I knew I wouldn't, but I also knew that the end of one fantasy required a quick replacement, however lame.

Meanwhile, back on the street, I walked down to the town's main intersection and climbed aboard one of the minivans that cruised the road I had come in on the day before. We retraced the sandy Chienshui for six miles, and I got out at the foot of Tienchushan, the home of all those deer and boar and pheasants and wild mushrooms. It was also the home of Third Patriarch Temple and had been for the past fifteen hundred years. The temple's parking lot was still half-full of sedans and tour buses, so I decided to take a walk along the gorge to the left of the front gate. It was the gorge for which the temple was first named.

It all began in 106 BC, when Emperor Wu (r. 141–87 BC) of the Han dynasty chose Tienchushan (it was called Huoshan in those days) as one of China's five sacred mountains. The emperor was a firm believer in the Taoist conception of Five Elements, which held that all things were part of a never-ending interplay of earth, metal, water, wood, and fire. Tienchushan, being the southernmost of the five mountains, represented fire. Emperor Wu built an altar half a mile up the gorge, and he conducted sacrifices there to Heaven and Earth and to all the manifestations of fire, such as the color red, the southern quadrant, and, of course, the mountain. Tienchushan was thereafter known as China's Nanyueh, or Southern

Third Patriarch Temple at the foot of Tienchushan

Peak, a title it held until 589, when that honor was transferred to Hengshan in Hunan Province.

Having been elevated to such a prestigious position, Tienchushan attracted hermits and recluses but no one of note until a monk named Pao-chih came there in 505. Pao-chih (417–514) was a wild and disruptive character. Emperor Wu (r. 483–494) of the short-lived Ch'i dynasty (based in Nanching) was so annoyed by him, he ordered him imprisoned for "crazy talk and sowing confusion." He wasn't released until twenty years later, when another Emperor Wu (r. 502–550) ascended the throne, this time of the Liang dynasty.

Pao-chih was eighty-five at the time, but he was still fit enough to travel, and he wandered around looking for a good place to meditate. When he came to Tienchushan, he decided that was the place. But a Taoist priest named Pai-ho, or White Crane, objected. He told Pao-chih to find another place. I'm not sure why the mountain wasn't big enough for both men. Perhaps the disagreement represented the more fundamental conflict between Buddhists and Taoists over access to patronage and to a pilgrimage site that must have generated a significant income for somebody.

Emperor Wu refused to take sides and resolved the conflict by telling the two men whichever of them could send an object from Nanching to Tienchushan first could lay claim to it. Pai-ho sent his white crane flying through the sky, and Pao-chih sent his magic staff. The staff won, and Pao-chih chose a cave at the foot of the mountain for his residence. A few years later, three brothers built a hermitage for Pao-chih just below his cave, and Emperor Wu gave it a name: Shankussu, or Mountain Gorge Temple.

Emperor Wu called himself the Bodhisattva Emperor and funded construction of 480 Buddhist temples and shrines during his long reign. He was the same Emperor Wu with whom Bodhidharma reportedly had an audience and who asked the Indian patriarch how much merit he was earning through all his temple construction. When Bodhidharma said, "None," the emperor expelled him from his kingdom, which was why Bodhidharma ended up in North China instead of in the otherwise more hospitable South.

As I walked along the gorge, I paused to read the graffiti carved onto its boulders and rock walls by visitors. To make the inscriptions easier to read, the temple's abbot had the characters painted red. The Sung-dynasty prime minister, Wang An-shih (1021–1086), left this poem:

The water has no mind and just winds along
the mountain has a shape that circles all around
the seclusion never ends and only grows deeper
sitting on a boulder I forget the way home.

Another Sung poet, Huang T'ing-chien (1045–1105), left this one:

Babbling and gurgling rock gorge water
drumming and rumbling mountain tree wind
460 incense-filled years
all of them thanks to Old Pao-chih.

Huang visited the gorge in 1080 on his way into one of several exiles and miscalculated the founding of the temple by a hundred years—it was closer to 560 years. He came there, as many did and many still do, to pay his respects to the author of the 146-line poem *On Trusting the Mind*, which was written by Seng-ts'an, the Third Patriarch.

As with his teacher and his teacher's teacher, Seng-ts'an left few traces. The little we know of him, and much of it is conjecture, is that he was born in North China in 519 near the city of Kaifeng 120 miles east of Loyang. And his surname was Hsiang. But that, too, is conjecture. It was Hsiang if we accept the letter written to Hui-k'o around 551, and translated in the previous chapter, as his. The only other record we have is an account of his meeting with Hui-k'o in 559 at the age of forty.

One day a layman, presumably Layman Hsiang, told Hui-k'o he suffered from madness, and he asked the Zen master to absolve him of the sin he surely must have committed in a previous life. Hui-k'o asked the layman to show him this sin, and he would gladly absolve him of it. When the layman said he had searched for it, but without success, Hui-k'o said, "Then I have absolved you of your sin, and you should now take refuge in the Three Treasures of the Buddha, the Dharma, and the Sangha."

The layman said, "Seeing you here before me, I know what 'Sangha' means. But what does 'Buddha' or 'Dharma' mean?"

Hui-k'o said, "This mind is the Buddha. And this mind is the Dharma. The Buddha and the Dharma are not two different things. It's the same with the Sangha."

As he heard the patriarch's words, the layman suddenly understood and answered, "Today I finally realize that the nature of sin is neither inside me, nor outside me, nor somewhere in between—that is just how the mind is—and the Buddha and the Dharma are not two different things."

Hui-k'o could see that this layman was a worthy disciple and welcomed him into his band of followers. He then shaved the layman's head and said, "Since you are sure to become a treasure of the sangha, I will call you Seng-ts'an [seng-ts'an: 'sangha-jewel']."

Seng-ts'an followed Hui-k'o in his wanderings across North China, until the religious persecution of 574–580 sent them fleeing south. During the brief period that it lasted, monasteries throughout North China were destroyed, and five million Buddhist and Taoist clerics were forced to return to lay life—but not in the South. Once Hui-k'o and his disciples reached the safety of Ssukungshan, they stayed there for more than a decade, until the religious persecution ended and the dynastic struggle that followed it subsided. With the reunification of China under the Sui dynasty in 581 and the subsequent pacification of the countryside, Hui-k'o eventually returned to the North, but not until he transmitted the patriarchship to Seng-ts'an.

Once Hui-k'o was gone, Seng-ts'an began his career as the Third Patriarch. In 590 he left the seclusion of Ssukungshan and traveled to the nearby pilgrimage center of Tienchushan. His decision to come to Tienchushan was clearly a sign that he was ready to expand his instruction beyond teaching the occasional herb collector he would have met on Ssukungshan. Despite losing its appellation as the Southern Peak the previous year, Tienchushan still saw a constant stream of travelers and pilgrims. And what better place to talk to them about the Dharma than Pao-chih's old hermitage at the foot of the trail?

But if records are any indication, Seng-ts'an did not attract many disciples. According to the commemorative inscriptions left at the temple by officials of the Sui and T'ang dynasties and repeated in subsequent accounts, he only had one disciple of note—and he was just a boy. Seng-t'san's future dharma heir came to the temple in 592 when he was only twelve. His name was Tao-hsin, or He Who Trusts the Way. Despite his youth, he impressed the Third Patriarch. He asked Seng-ts'an, "What is the mind of a buddha like?"

Seng-ts'an asked back, "What is your mind like?"

Tao-hsin replied, "Right now, there is nothing in my mind."

Seng-ts'an said, "If there is nothing in your mind, how could there be anything in a buddha's mind?"

Another account of that meeting has Tao-hsin and Seng-ts'an repeating an exchange similar to that of Hui-k'o and Bodhidharma at the cave above Shaolin. According to this second account, Tao-hsin asked Seng-ts'an to liberate him from bondage. And Seng-ts'an asked, "Who is holding you in bondage?"

Tao-hsin answered, "No one is holding me in bondage."

Seng-ts'an said, "Since no one is holding you in bondage, why do you want me to liberate you from bondage?" On hearing this, Tao-hsin was liberated and became Seng-ts'an's disciple and dharma heir.

On another occasion, Seng-ts'an told Tao-hsin, "The *Lotus Sutra* says, 'There is only this one mind. There is no second or third.' You should realize that the sacred Way is traveled in mystery and not fathomed by explanations. The dharma body is perfectly still and empty and not something the senses can apprehend. And it is a waste of effort to write or talk about it."

And, except for the Third Patriarch's 146-line poem, he didn't write about it.

Finally in 601, at the age of eighty-two, Seng-ts'an gave the robe and bowl he had received from Hui-k'o to Tao-hsin, who was only twenty-one. Near the back gate of the temple, there was a cave where Seng-ts'an often meditated and where the transmission of the patriarchship was said to have taken place.

Despite his age, or perhaps because of it, Seng-ts'an then left Chienshan and traveled all the way to Lofushan, near Kuangchou in South China. It was said that he went there to spread the Dharma. But Lofushan was over six hundred miles away, and there were plenty of places nearby where he could have done that. I've often wondered if his journey wasn't connected with Lofushan's fame as a place for compounding elixirs that could lengthen one's life. It was on Lofushan that the great alchemist Ke Hung (284–343) became one with the Tao.

In any case, just as inexplicably Seng-ts'an returned to Chienshan two years later and resumed teaching. Apparently, the elixirs weren't all they were cracked up to be. Not long afterwards, in 606, while standing beneath a tree at Shanku Temple and lecturing on the Dharma, he pressed his hands together and passed away. His body was kept at the temple in a mummified state until 745, when it was cremated and his relics placed inside the pagoda that still stands above what is now called Third Patriarch Temple.

The only teaching the Third Patriarch left behind was the long poem known as *Hsin-hsin-ming*: "On Trusting the Mind." Some scholars have contended it was written by someone else—and they have suggested half a dozen possibilities. Lately, however, the pendulum has swung back toward Seng-ts'an, at least among scholars in China. Certainly there was no doubt among the Chinese of the following century concerning its authorship. The Tientai master Chan-jan (711–787) was a great admirer of Seng-ts'an's poem and visited Third Patriarch Temple in 757 to pay his respects. He was only one of many to do so during the T'ang and Sung dynasties.

The first line pretty much summed up Seng-ts'an's teaching: "Attaining the Way isn't hard / just avoid choosing." Until the advent of Zen, the Chinese considered Buddhism a religion for the spiritual elite. Attaining nirvana was hard, really hard. And those magic powers that practitioners acquired along the way didn't just fall from the sky. Buddhism's inner sanctum was not for everyone; it was for the few, the proud, the ascetic. Even the first Zen patriarchs were presented in that light: tough as nails, able to look at a rock wall for nine years, or to stand in the snow for days and cut off their own arm. That was what Buddhist masters did; not your average monk, mind you, but the masters to whom disciples looked for inspiration.

Then Zen went south. No more rock walls, no more amputations. Beginning with Seng-ts'an, attaining the Way was presented as something within anyone's reach. All a person had to do was stop dividing their mind from the world. Of course, the teaching of not choosing, of nonduality, of nondiscrimination, the teaching that one's very mind was all a person needed to be a buddha, the teaching that the only difference between a deluded person and a buddha was the delusions of the deluded person, this had been taught by Bodhidharma and by Hui-k'o. And someone must have understood their message—both Bodhidharma and Hui-k'o had other disciples. But the teaching of Zen didn't make much of an impact until it traveled south, until Seng-ts'an passed it on to Tao-hsin. I have a theory why this was so. But that will have to wait until we meet Tao-hsin.

Meanwhile, I saw a side trail leading away from the babble-babble gurgle-gurgle and followed it to a forested ridge. After wandering through the trees for a while, I found a cliff that overlooked the temple and sat down on a rocky ledge and finished off the last of my pumpkin cookies. I was glad the people who built monasteries chose the spots they chose. I stretched out on the rocks and fell asleep in the sun.

It must have been an hour later that the honking in the parking lot woke me. In the distance, I could see the tour buses pulling out. It was time to visit the abbot. I worked my way back down to the gorge and to the temple's front gate and up the long series of steps that led through one archway, then another. Over the years, the temple had expanded up the hillside and spread out along several levels. I had been there before and knew the way. When I reached the middle level, I walked over to the dharma hall, where the abbot's quarters were located.

Through the doorway, I saw the abbot talking to another visitor, so I waited outside until the visitor left, then I went in. The abbot's name was K'uan-jung. Two years earlier, we spent several days traveling together visiting other temples in the area. As soon as he saw me, K'uan-jung came over, grabbed my hand, and led me over to a pair of armchairs. After we both sat down, he asked me how the hotel room was, and I told him about my night. I was surprised that he wasn't surprised, and we moved on to other subjects. The human world was mysterious enough without trying to figure out the spirit world.

K'uan-jung had one of the most placid manners I have ever encountered in anyone, not just in monks. He had an innocent aloofness and seemed to be floating a few inches off the ground, even when he was sitting down. He was born in 1970, sixty miles west of Sian, and he became a monk when he was eighteen. His parents were Buddhists, and their parents were Buddhists, and his siblings were Buddhists too. So his family didn't object, especially since the Cultural Revolution was over.

When I asked him what led him to set forth on the homeless path, he said there were many reasons, but the main reason was that the Buddha taught people how to transcend life and death. That was what concerned him most, even as a young man. He wanted to get free of the endless round of suffering and help others do the same. And he thought the acquisition of knowledge was the way to do that. He said, "The more I learn, the better prepared I'll be to help others."

He was only thirty-six, but in the eighteen years since becoming a monk, he had not only graduated from the Buddhist academy on the nearby Buddhist mountain of Chiuhuashan, he had received a BA in education and school administration from Szechuan University, an MA in business administration from South China University, another MA in literature from Nanching University, and a PhD in philosophy from Western Pacific University.

And now he was abbot of a monastery that was once again becoming a major pilgrimage destination. In 1980, the year after the government reaffirmed the freedom of religious practice, the number of pilgrims who came to offer incense at Third Patriarch Temple was a thousand. In 1990 it was ninety thousand. And in 1996 it was 240,000, which was the last year for which I could find records. It was probably double that by now.

Having to take care of so many visitors obviously was a distraction, as it was at Shaolin. But K'uan-jung said that right now it was necessary to reacquaint people with Buddhism, and he expected it would be another ten years before he could teach people Zen. The practice of Zen, he said, hadn't changed, but not everyone was up to it. Right now he was more concerned with reestablishing an understanding and appreciation of Buddhism among the general public and with reestablishing the monastic system in which practice could flourish in the future.

He planned to make Third Patriarch Temple into a Zen monastery once more, but he said it was still in a transitional stage and everyone there was on their own as far as their spiritual practice was concerned. There were only about fifty resident monks at the temple and usually a dozen or so visiting monks. In addition to giving me a book about the temple and another one with the Third Patriarch's poem, K'uan-jung showed me architectural drawings of a planned expansion he said would accommodate another two hundred monks in a separate complex. Those plans, though, were a few years from realization. He was still collecting funds.

While we were talking, a thirty-member group of Korean Buddhists touring Buddhist sites in China arrived. K'uan-jung had been expecting them. Our conversation ended, and K'uan-jung joined the Koreans around a huge table set up in the dharma hall for visiting delegations. Once greetings were translated back and forth into Chinese and Korean, the monk who was the leader of the delegation asked K'uan-jung what the monks at the temple used in their meditation practice. K'uan-jung said those who practiced Zen used the last line of On Trusting the Mind: "Trusting the mind means no duality." Everyone pressed their hands together and bowed. What more was there to say?

To show his appreciation, the monk who posed the question asked for paper and ink—and what temple didn't have such things on hand at all times? An attendant brought over a sheet of calligraphy paper, an inkstone, and a brush holder and put them on the table in front of the monk, who stood up and chose a brush, dipped it in the well of the inkstone, where someone had already prepared ink, and wrote the characters for "Dancer in a Dream." He signed the calligraphy "Korean Master Hui-yuan" and dated it "Birthday of Kuan-yin, Year of the Dog." Then he lifted it up and presented it to K'uan-jung.

That marked the beginning of an exchange of gifts between the delegation and the abbot, whose attendants entered with thirty bags, each of which included a lidded teacup in a protective box, a pilgrim's shoulder bag, and a canister of tea, all of which were emblazoned with the temple's name. If there was one skill universally practiced by abbots in China, it was the fine art of public relations. They knew how to treat people regardless of their background and how to establish and cultivate a relationship.

K'uan-jung then led the group outside on a tour of the temple grounds, and I took this opportunity to pay my respects to K'uan-jung's predecessors who had made this a welcome way station on the Dharma Highway. From behind the dharma hall, I continued up the steps to the temple's upper level. Along the way, I took a short side trail to Pao-chih's old cave, where he had spent his summers. He spent his winters in Nanching, which was where he died in 514 at the age of ninety-seven.

After bowing to the shadows inside his old cave, I returned to the main trail and continued to the pagoda at the top that contained Seng-ts'an's remains. I paid my respects and walked over to read the stele next to the pagoda. It was inscribed with the words of *On Trusting the Mind*. Two visiting monks were reading the words out loud, and I joined in. When we got to the end, we all laughed: pilgrims on the trail, trusting our minds. Just then K'uan-jung appeared with the Korean delegation. When they also stopped to read the poem, I went over to K'uan-jung and said goodbye.

After I took a parting photograph of K'uan-jung in front of the Third Patriarch's pagoda, he continued on with his visitors, and I walked back down to the road and took the next minivan back to Chienshan. Since my time there was almost over, I stopped in the store near my hotel and bought all the pumpkin cookies they had— all four of them. A good thing, too. I didn't see any more the entire trip. On my way back, I noticed a large sign on the other side of the street for *t'ui-na*, or acupressure massage. It was a sign I was ready for. The muscles in my lower back were in spasm again.

When I walked in, a woman behind the counter asked me what was wrong. She could see that I wasn't able to stand up straight, but she asked anyway. I told her it was my lower back. It happened every time I traveled in China, partly because of the long bus rides but also because of my pack. I accumulated more and more books as I went along. I tried to send them back periodically, but not often enough.

The woman yelled to someone down the hallway, and another woman appeared. She was dressed like a nurse and led me into a cubicle. She told me to take off my shirt and lie down on my stomach. She was thirty-five, and she had been doing this for eight years. Most people, she said, had to tell her to ease up. Her hands were incredibly strong. I told her to do her worst, and she did. Her hands weren't just strong, they were intuitive. They knew where to go and what to do. I winced a few times but nearly nodded off listening to the background music: a Spanish guitar, an Irish flute, and an instrumental version of "The Sound of Silence" were all I remembered.

Master K'uan-jung and Third Patriarch's Stupa

After nearly an hour, she stopped. But she wasn't done. She heated the air in four glass cups, then placed them lid-side down along my lower back. As they cooled, they created a vacuum that sucked my skin as it had never been sucked before. The idea was to draw the blood up from below the skin. It was painful, and it left four large blue moons on my back. What the hell, I thought. It was for a good cause. The treatment wasn't cheap: 88RMB, or eleven bucks. But it was worth every RMB. I was able to walk erect again.

Since the day was drawing to a close, I decided to eat at the first restaurant I saw. Just past the acupressure clinic, I looked down a deserted side street and saw red lanterns hanging from some eaves, which was usually a good sign suggesting it might be the sort of place where people came on festive occasions, perhaps for a wedding banquet. The restaurant probably did cater to the occasional banquet, but certainly not one that was high-end, or even somewhere in the middle. It turned out to be a working-class restaurant. But it was clean, and that was all I ever asked. I had experienced hepatitis before, and once was one time too many.

I thought I would keep it simple and ordered a plate of fried rice with a bunch of vegetables mixed in. At least that was how I explained it to the proprietor. While I was waiting, half a dozen neighborhood kids came in and gathered around to watch me write in my journal. English looked just as strange to them as Chinese once did to me.

Every once in a while, I think back to the day I was filling out an application for graduate school. After the Army, I studied anthropology at UC Santa Barbara. As graduation approached, I saw no reason to get a job, not if I could go to grad school, and I decided to apply to Columbia, whose anthropology faculty included Margaret Mead and Ruth Benedict, among others. I checked all the boxes for money, including one for a fellowship that required the applicant to choose a language. Having just read Alan Watts' *The Way of Zen* and feeling inspired, I wrote the word "Chinese." I had never really looked at Chinese characters before. People say to be careful what you wish for. They should also say to be careful of what boxes you check. Six months later, I was overwhelmed.

The class was Intensive Chinese, which was required by the fellowship. And the teacher was the Dragon Lady, or so she was called by those who survived her as well as by those who didn't. She started with twenty students, and within a month she was down to four. Then one day she asked me to stay after class and told me she only had time for three (two of whom she couldn't get rid of because they had been sent there by the CIA), and I was not one of the three. When I told her I couldn't drop the class, that my fellowship required it, she simply pretended I wasn't there. I became invisible. After a month, the chairman of the East Asian Studies Department finally had to intervene. But the Dragon Lady exacted her revenge. She gave me a D for the class, which would have cancelled my fellowship had I not been able to challenge the class and replace the D with a B. I survived. But to call Chinese "strange" would not be to do it justice.

While the kids were marveling at the ease with which I wrote the tiniest of English words recounting my day, seven or eight men came into the restaurant, one at a time. They were all drivers, and their rigs soon filled what was once a deserted street. This was apparently their hangout and also where they ate. But before any of them did anything else, they walked into the kitchen and disappeared. I could hear them continuing up a set of stairs to the second floor and a woman's voice. Then after a few minutes, they came back down smiling.

I've always thought blow jobs were overrated. I'll take a pain-free back any day, even one covered with blue moons. It was another good day, except for the news from the Gug. And I expected that. Back at the hotel, I even succeeded in getting my room changed. During the night, I woke up once when something touched my out-stretched hand. But this time my heart wasn't in it. I pulled my hand back under the covers, rolled over, and lay down in a field of tall, dry grass with someone I knew but didn't remember the next morning.

8 NO WORK, NO FOOD

I hate traveling without a maid. After washing my clothes and hanging them up the night before, I had neglected to turn on the ventilation system in the room and had also forgotten that I was now in the more humid Yangtze watershed. They were still wet in the morning. I like to save my second set of clothes for emergencies or for evening wear on days that end early, and I don't carry a third set. So I began putting on one item at a time, then getting back into bed, trying to distract myself during the drying process by writing in my journal.

A brief account of Third Patriarch Temple got me through the socks, and my meeting with the abbot got me through the T-shirt. Finally, for the pants, I opened the edition of *On Trusting the Mind* K'uan-jung had given me before the Korean delegation arrived. I couldn't believe my good fortune. It included three commentaries, all of them exceptional. I began to envision another translation project and another book advance and another paid-off credit card. Before I knew it, my pants looked dry enough that only I would know they weren't. Whoever cleaned the room was going to wonder about the wet sheets, but the sheets had to be washed anyway. And maybe they would blame the ghosts.

After checking out, I walked outside and waved down a motorized rickshaw, as opposed to the pedaled variety that also plied the streets of Chienshan. I wanted to get to the bus station as fast as possible. My next destination was Huangmei, sixty miles to the west, and the hotel desk clerk said there was only one bus a day. It was already ten o'clock, and I thought I might have missed it. But when I got to the station, they said it wasn't due to leave until one. I should have been relieved, but I wasn't. I could have slept longer and let my clothes dry a bit more and saved my journal entries for when they weren't quite so forced. But there was no turning back. Since I didn't want to wait three hours, I did what I normally do when one mode of transport fails in China. I walked back outside and looked for another.

My rickshaw driver was still there, so I asked him if there were any buses passing through Chienshan in the direction of Huangmei I could flag down. He said all the long-distance traffic was on the expressway now. But he said there was a break in the fence three miles south of town that locals used to gain access. That was good enough for me, and off we went. Ten minutes later, he dropped me off next to the expressway in the middle of nowhere. As promised, someone had used wire-cutters to make an opening in the fence. I threw my pack over the top and squeezed through and inched up the embankment. It was so steep I wouldn't have made it without my trusty staff. Who was it who said, "A gentleman doesn't travel without his port and his walking stick?" Surely someone said it. And I would leave the port before I would leave the walking stick.

But my paean to the walking stick ended at the guardrail. When I climbed onto the pavement, there was no traffic. It was eerie. I wondered if the expressway had only recently opened and word hadn't gotten around. After about ten minutes, a long-distance bus came along, and I waved in relief. The driver waved back and kept going, as did the next driver and the driver after that. Finally, a bus bound for Changsha stopped. Changsha was the capital of Hunan Province 350 miles to the southwest. When the door opened, and the conductor asked where I was going, and I said "Huangmei," the door closed, and the bus left without me. About the time I was beginning to experience hitchhiker despair, another bus stopped. It was destined for Wuhan, the capital of Hupei Province, 180 miles to the west. This time, a Huangmei fare of 30RMB was somehow worthwhile, and the conductor motioned for me to get on board. There was even an empty seat.

The bus resumed its pedal-to-the-metal momentum, but it didn't go more than five miles before it began slowing down. Our side of the expressway narrowed to one lane due to bridge construction. As we passed under a half-finished overpass, three more would-be passengers stepped out of the shadows and waved from the roadside. The driver stopped so suddenly, a truck behind us didn't have time to brake. Instead of rear-ending us, the driver veered into the construction area and smashed through several barricades before coming to a stop. While the three people climbed aboard, the truck driver jumped out and started running toward the bus with a tire iron in his hand. The bus driver closed the door and hit the gas, and that was the last we saw of that truck.

An hour later, as we approached the Huangmei exit, I reminded the conductor that was where I was getting off. He said there was a better place a bit further on. He knew the road. If I had gotten off at the Huangmei exit, it would have been a long walk to the tollbooth and an even longer walk to where I could catch some form of local transport into town. The better place turned out to be the Huangmei Travel Center a mile or so further on.

While the other passengers filed into the WC, the conductor told me to walk back to a road we just passed over and catch a local bus from there. When I got to the place he mentioned, there was another break in the fence at the bottom of the embankment. Someone, I thought, should compile a travelers' guide to expressway fences. But this time, as I climbed over the guardrail, my hold on it slipped, and I nearly ruptured myself. I would add a warning in the new guidebook. A pair of gloves would also be a good idea. Hell, why not wire-cutters as well? After standing there for a few minutes trying to catch my breath (what exactly, I wondered, was the connection between one's nuts and one's lungs?), I eased my way down the embankment and through the fence, tiptoed around some rice paddies and a fishpond, and finally out to the road. A minute later, a minivan picked me up. And it kept picking people up until there wasn't room to open the door. At least it was quick. Ten minutes later, I disembarked in Greater Huangmei.

Huangmei, or Yellow Plum, was one of those towns that no longer had a center, at least not one discernible to an outsider. It was developing in five directions at once. Even locals weren't sure which road led where. It took several three-wheeler rides before I tracked down the place where I could catch a minivan going west on the old highway. Once I found the right place, it was another quick ride, this time to the turnoff for Fourth Patriarch Temple, which was another six miles up a side road.

Four men were standing there next to their motorcycles. They made their living by taking people up the mountain, and I asked one of them how much he charged to the monastery. He looked at his colleagues, then said the rate was 15RMB. I offered 4RMB, and he eventually came down to 8RMB. But that was still double the rate I had paid the year before, and I wasn't in a hurry. Every once in a while, I refused to pay double just because I was a foreigner. After I stood there a few minutes wondering why I was making such a big deal over fifty cents, a truck turned off the highway and stopped to pick up some boxes at a small dry goods store. I went over and talked to the driver. He said he was carrying a load of produce and canned goods to the monastery and told me to hop in.

At least the road was paved. I'll never forget my first visit to Fourth Patriarch Temple in 1999 with my friend Mountain Dave. It made me rethink whether overland travel was a good idea at all. The road was all dried mud and deep ruts, ruts so deep we should have walked, and we would have walked, but our driver on that occasion was the temple manager of Fifth Patriarch Temple. He had just gotten his license and a new jeep. It took over an hour to go six miles.

This time the ride was smooth and quick. Fifteen minutes later, the driver dropped me off at the front gate of Fourth Patriarch Temple and the foot of Shuangfeng Mountain. After exchanging greetings with the Buddha of the Future and the Four Guardians of the Universe, whose statues form the welcome committee at most temples in China, I continued up the steps to the guest hall and met the guest manager. He was expecting me and led me to the lay quarters at the very back of the monastery and turned me over to the laywoman in charge of visitors. She handed me two thermoses of hot water and led me to a room with three beds. I chose the middle one for my afternoon nap and followed the nap with an afternoon coffee and my last pumpkin cookie in the sunlit bathroom that looked out on the bamboo-and pine-covered slopes of Shuangfengshan.

One pumpkin cookie wasn't enough. The thought of more cookies drove me outside and back down the long series of steps, out the front gate, and down to the shops by the monastery's ancient covered bridge where they sold incense and snacks to pilgrims. Unfortunately, my recent experience with pumpkin cookies had raised my expectations beyond what the vendors could supply. I moved on to other items, one of which was a copy of an out-of-print pamphlet about the temple. I hadn't seen it before and bought it in case it had something I could use in my own account. Since it wasn't quite dinnertime, I sat down on a bench under the bridge and read a few pages.

The covered bridge was a landmark in the area. It was built in 1350 and spanned a waterfall that once powered a waterwheel. In the past, the monks used the waterwheel to mill their rice, but no more. The monastery had lost its farmland, which was how it supported a community of several hundred monks in the past. That was what made Zen work: work.

No one has ever explained why Zen rose to such prominence, why the very word became synonymous with Buddhism in China. Most people have assumed it was the result of historical forces or ideology. But over the years, I've visited just about every site associated with the beginning of Zen in China, and I've concluded that the success of Zen was more a matter of location than anything else. And the location that made all the difference was just beyond the bench where I was sitting. Zen didn't amount to much until its practitioners started working the land. And the land they chose to work was the mountain basin: relatively flat, well-watered land surrounded by mountains. And the Yangtze watershed was one mountain basin after another.

In addition to possessing an ecological niche that didn't exist in the arid North and that only Zen masters had the good sense to exploit, the Yangtze watershed was

Fourth Patriarch Temple and former rice fields

far from the tiger's mouth and imperial whim, and also exempt from nomadic incursions. And it was where the emperor banished more wiseacre poets and political idealists than any other place in the empire. All of these factors helped. But they only helped because of what the Fourth Patriarch started. Tao-hsin was the one who introduced self-supporting communal practice as the Way of Zen.

When people think about Zen, they usually think of it in external terms: nonsensical talk, spontaneous behavior, or minimalist art forms. But that would be to look at it from the outside. If you look at it from the inside, from your mind, Zen is just a way of living. And that way of living is far easier to realize in a communal setting with the support of others than it is alone. Seclusion has its place, especially once a person has practiced in a community, but it was its communal approach to spiritual cultivation that was the strength of Zen. That was why it overwhelmed all other Buddhist sects in China, both in terms of numbers and in terms of influence. Its success was Darwinian. It produced a better-trained monk and more of them. Other sects were ideology-driven. Zen didn't have an ideology. Zen was life-driven. Its motto was "No work, no food." Zen monasteries in China were slowly getting back to this approach that had made them possible in the first place. But not all of them have been able to do so—even Fourth Patriarch Temple had not yet managed to recover the land that made the work and the food of Zen possible.

Thinking about the food part of the equation made me realize that maybe it was time to be getting back. Of course, I hadn't done anything to deserve it, but there were certain responsibilities that came with being a guest. I returned the way I came, through the front gate, past the welcoming committee, and back up the steps. As I walked around the outside of the main shrine hall, I met Ming-chi, the temple manager. He waved for me to follow him into the abbot's quarters. The abbot was Ching-hui, whom I had known since 1989, when I asked him if there were still hermits in China, and he told me there were and where to find them. Since then, we had become dharma friends.

When he was still a novice, Ching-hui was the personal attendant of Empty Cloud. Ever since then, he had been involved in Buddhist politics, and Buddhism had become a big deal in China. Unlike Taoism, which was viewed with a certain amount of trepidation, having spawned many of the uprisings in Chinese history, Buddhism was considered a source of social stability. The government liked the Buddhists. They were peaceful, they encouraged people to lead upright lives, and their monasteries and nunneries were just about the only communes left in the country.

In addition to serving as abbot of at least four monasteries that I knew of, Ching-hui was a vice director of the Buddhist Association of China, which was where the government and the Buddhists played out their political games. For many years the Association's director had been Chao P'u-ch'u. But when Chao died in 2000, Ching-hui's supporters vied with those of another vice director named Sheng-hui over the succession. The struggle was sufficiently intense that the post remained vacant for several years. Finally, in one of his last official acts before stepping down as president of China, Chu Jung-chi appointed Yi-ch'eng, aka the Eccentric Buddha. That, of course, did nothing to placate those who cared about such things. And such things were and are cared about. Every time I saw Ching-hui, I couldn't help wondering about the toll such power struggles took on him, or why he allowed himself to be drawn into them, or why he didn't retire to one of the handful of temples of which he was the abbot, like Fourth Patriarch Temple.

He usually stayed close to Beijing, and I was surprised to see him sitting there in the reception room talking to two laywomen. I was also surprised when he didn't get up, as he usually did when we met. He usually jumped up and grabbed my hand and didn't let go. This time I waited until he finished talking to his other guests, then I went over and sat down in the chair next to him. When I told him I hadn't expected to see him there, he said he was conducting a Shuilu ceremony at the monastery the following week and needed to oversee all the preparations, which were many.

The Shuilu was the mother of all Buddhist ceremonies and was first held by Emperor Wu of the Liang dynasty 1,500 years ago. Emperor Wu was always coming up with new ways to earn merit, and he asked Pao-chih, the same monk who established what later became Third Patriarch Temple, to put together a ceremony that would liberate beings in realms normally cut off from the Dharma—thus the name *shui*: "water" and *lu*: "land" to suggest the range of beings reached by the efficacy of such a ceremony. But it wasn't just one ceremony. It was a series of ceremonies that required the participation of at least one hundred monks and hundreds, if not thousands, of laypeople simultaneously chanting such sutras as the *Lotus*, the *Shurangama*, the *Sukhavativyuha*, and the *Avatamsaka* at seven different altars. It lasted from well before dawn to well after sunset for seven days and was so expensive to conduct that few temples attempted it. The part I liked, in fact the only part, was at the very end when the paper horsemen constructed for the occasion were set on fire and galloped off to rescue beings in less obvious realms.

Ching-hui said he was holding the ceremony to rouse the faithful in the Huangmei area. Fourth Patriarch Temple had only recently been rebuilt and restaffed. So this was tantamount to a coming-out party, a way to let people in the area know there was now a place they could come to wire money and merit ahead to the next life. That was the primary function of a Buddhist temple as far as most people were concerned, and some temples were viewed as having a better connection with the afterlife than others. And there was nothing like a Shuilu ceremony to get people's attention—assuming it didn't bankrupt the place.

When Ching-hui asked me what I was doing there, I told him I was collecting material about the early patriarchs of Zen. When I asked if he had time for an interview, he suggested I read *Record of the Masters of the Lankavatara* and his own essays. While we were sitting there, he had his attendant bring me a copy of a series of Dharma talks he had given at Fourth Patriarch Temple during the meditation retreats

Conclusion of Shuilu ceremony at Pailin Temple

he held there every winter. He said it had some information about Tao-hsin and his teaching of Zen that might be useful, and added that he had said all he wanted to say about the subject. He was looking very tired, and ill. His diabetic condition had been getting worse with the years and with the demands of his positions.

While we were talking, the dinner board sounded, and Ching-hui got up and asked me to join him. I couldn't help noticing how much slower he walked. He leaned on the arm of his attendant as much as on his cane. While Ming-chi and I followed behind, Ching-hui sighed, "How am I going to get through all those ceremonies? How am I going to do it?"

That was the part of being a monk I had trouble with. There have been times when I thought about saying "so long" to the world of red dust. I liked the spiritual community part. But the thought of all the ceremonies, daily and otherwise, always put an end to such daydreams. I know: rituals are part of every culture and efficacious in realms we can't see. And they also provide a way for participants to establish or reaffirm their sense of group identity. That's what people say. But it must be my karmic inheritance. I've always preferred to stand outside the shrine hall rather than inside: Tonio Kröger of the ritual world. Give me the wind in the pines any day, and a pumpkin cookie from time to time. I've always wondered what kind of ceremonies the Buddha performed in his day. I don't recall ever reading about any. Did he even say grace before meals?

As we followed Ching-hui and his attendant, I expected them to lead us into the mess hall or into the smaller dining hall for guests. But they led us instead to the rear entrance of the kitchen. Ching-hui had a table set up inside that was big enough for a dozen people, and that was where we all sat down: Ching-hui and his attendant, Ming-chi and a few other senior monks, several laymen who were living at the temple, and myself.

No one said grace. We all just started eating. But while we were eating, Ching-hui suddenly stopped to complain about Americans. I guess he didn't get many opportunities to be so direct. Normally he had to be polite with the foreigners he met. His position, and Chinese etiquette, required it. But we were friends, and I was his native informant and now his emissary conveying a message back to my people and its misguided rulers. Americans, he said, got things backwards. Americans paid attention to the outside instead of the inside. They were so aggressive. They were always ready to go to war.

I wasn't about to try to defend people whose policies were indefensible. I told Ching-hui we all voted, and the warmongers won. Maybe the next election, we'd throw the bastards out. And as far as getting things backwards, I said that not everyone got it backwards. But the karma of Americans, I added, was different from that of the Chinese. I decided I'd better stop right there. Fortunately, Ching-hui didn't ask me to explain what I meant and turned his attention instead to the infernal airplane and the even more infernal nuclear bomb. Finally, he pointed with his chopsticks at the plate of stir-fried pumpkin. The pumpkin, he said, was cold. And I was happy that it was. I was off the hook.

Afterwards, I returned to my room. Ming-chi had invited me to join him for evening meditation and said he would send someone to show me the way to the new meditation hall. But my guide never showed up, and it was too dark to try to find it on my own—the monastery used a minimum of lights at night. I wasn't sorry. It had been another big day, and I was glad to go to bed early.

. . . . .

I hadn't realized I was so tired. I slept for twelve hours and could have slept a few more. I had to force myself up the next morning. Even after a cup of coffee, I still felt groggy. I walked outside and started walking down the steps just to clear my head. I didn't have a plan for the day, but something always happened, and it did.

On my way past the main shrine hall, I met Master Hung-yung, the abbess to whose group of nuns I had given a talk on Prajnaparamita in Beijing. She said she had arrived the night before with her contingent for the Shuilu ceremony. It was all hands on deck. She said before things got too busy she and five other nuns were going on an excursion to Laotsu (Old Patriarch) Temple. She said there was room for one more in the temple's SUV and invited me to join them, which I did. I rode shotgun so I wouldn't have to sit next to the young nuns in back, for which they were no doubt grateful—not that I would have made them rethink their vows. But I would have made them feel uncomfortable.

It was a new vehicle—no doubt a present from some wealthy patron. I forget the brand; something domestic. And it was slick. It even had a map screen. But as soon as we returned to Huangmei and headed northwest into the countryside, the screen turned blank. I'm not sure what that meant: lack of concern for the rural sector, unwillingness to make information with strategic potential public, or simply the slow pace of digital mapping. Probably all three. And so we wound our way through the terra incognita of flooded rice fields and past the village of Kuchu, or Bitter Bamboo, and up the forested southern slopes of the Tapieh Range. At the 27 km marker and next to a sign that announced the future mountain resort of Napuyuan just ahead, we turned onto a dirt road and drove another two miles. The road ended at a construction site that overlooked a half-dry reservoir. It was another mountain basin, a high mountain basin.

That was our destination: the past, present, and future home of Laotsu Temple. The only structure, and perhaps it was all that had ever been there, was one small stone building where two monks were living until construction of a new monastery was finished. They were there to guard the building materials and the equipment, of which there was quite an assemblage, including a bulldozer and a backhoe.

The two monks and the foreman showed us around and kept pointing out the excellent fengshui of the site: the monastery would be set against a bamboo-covered hill and would face east toward the sun and moon rising out of the reservoir, which the foreman said would be full from spring rains by the end of May. The plan was to build a monastery with room for between fifty and a hundred monks. The living quarters, kitchen, mess hall, main shrine hall, dharma hall, and meditation hall were all expected to be ready by year's end. Everything, and that included the thirty member construction crew, was being paid for by one of Ching-hui's patrons.

The place was intended for monks who preferred a less distracting place to practice, not that there were a lot of distractions at Fourth Patriarch Temple. It was to be modeled on Zen monasteries of the past, where life revolved around meditation and manual work. In the past, the work would have consisted of growing rice and vegetables, chopping wood and carrying water. But the combination of electricity, natural gas, and plumbing would obviate the need for the chopping and carrying part. And at an elevation of more than 2,500 feet, there were only four frost-free months so rice was out, as were vegetables for most of the year.

The plan was to grow tea, organic tea, and to use the proceeds to buy everything they needed. I marveled at the idea. It was so simple, so perfect. The climate couldn't be better for a high-mountain oolong. However, I suspected they would produce green tea instead. Green tea was simpler: pick it, dry it, cook it, and sell it. I could see the label: "Old Patriarch's Tea, the taste of Zen in every cup." The Huangmei area was famous for its tea-picking songs, which inspired one of the most popular forms of Chinese opera. Maybe the monks, I thought, would contribute something new to the genre, inspire the development of Dharma opera. In addition to tea, they planned to grow medicinal herbs. Another great idea. According to the monks, the local government had agreed to give them forty acres. And they were negotiating for another ten. That much land, they said, could support anywhere from one hundred to two hundred monks.

After showing us around, our guides led us into the small stone building and pulled up some rough benches, and we all sat around the large wooden table that was the only other furniture in the kitchen/dining room half of the building—the other half was the two monks' sleeping quarters. While the monks served us tea and snacks, the foreman did most of the talking. He said an Indian monk named Pao-chang came there in the third or fourth century and lived there for several hundred years, which was why it was called Old Patriarch's Temple. No one batted an eye at the idea of someone living that long. The area around Huangmei had deep Taoist roots. Over the centuries, many Taoists had come there to practice—and many still did. The foreman said strange lights appeared in the sky at night over the mountain at different times of the year. It wasn't the Northern Lights, he said, but more like the lights that appeared over Wutaishan and other sacred mountains: more like balls of fire. He said they usually appeared in the south, and they lasted an hour or more. Once, he said, they lasted three nights.

It was obviously a great place to practice, just below the realm of the gods. But our time was up. We thanked our hosts and returned to Fourth Patriarch Temple just in time for lunch. Another group of visitors joined us in the kitchen: three professors and two graduate students from Wuhan University's Philosophy Department. They had come to invite Ching-hui to give a lecture on Zen. Ching-hui's Daily Life Zen was becoming popular.

But Ching-hui led them off in another direction. He said what was needed was a new edition of the Chinese Buddhist Canon. The old one edited in Japan between 1924 and 1934 was full of mistakes, and the new one being edited by Fokuangshan in Taiwan would take forever. China, he said, had the people who could do it, and do it quickly. I didn't know it at the time, but Ching-hui had sponsored their depart-ment's reediting of the Prajnaparamita volumes of the Canon that formed the scriptural side of Zen. The work was nearly done. So he was lobbying for them to continue their efforts with the remaining two hundred or so volumes.

Since they all had business to discuss, I excused myself from the meal as soon as I was done and returned to my room for what was becoming my regular afternoon nap, after which I decided it was time for a walk—nothing major, just a walk. Outside the monastery's front gate, I started up the stone steps that led to Tao-hsin's stupa on the small promontory that overlooked the temple. The steps were new and had replaced the old dirt trail that was so slippery after a rain.

The Fourth Patriarch's body was placed inside the stupa following his death in 651, just as the Third Patriarch's body had been placed inside his much larger pagoda. And like the Third Patriarch's body, it didn't stay there. It was taken out for use in ceremonies aimed at propitiating the local rain dragons. According to one account, the body self-immolated in 1519. According to another account, the body was taken to Tao-hsin's hometown and later cremated there. In either case, no one seemed to know what happened to his relics.

Fourth Patriarch's Stupa

Tao-hsin's hometown was the Yangtze port of Wuhsueh, twenty-five miles southwest of Huangmei. Not much is known about his early years other than that he became a novice when he was only seven. He must have been more than precocious. In 592, when he was twelve, he traveled to Tienchushan to pay his respects to Seng-ts'an and quickly became the Third Patriarch's chief disciple. Nine years later, when Tao-hsin was only twenty-one, Seng-ts'an transmitted the patriarchship to him, then left for Lofushan in South China.

A year later, Tao-hsin also left Tienchushan. He crossed the Yangtze and traveled up the Kan River all the way to Chi-an, where he was formally ordained. During his stay there, he reportedly saved the city from bandits by reciting the words *Maha Prajnaparamita* (Great Perfection of Wisdom) for a week from on top of the city wall. He must have been a charismatic person and seems to have impressed people wherever he went. In gratitude for his miraculous intervention, the people of Chi-an fixed up a temple on a mountain outside the city for him. Later on, a group of laypeople in Chiuchiang invited him to become abbot of Talin Temple on Lushan. And later still, another group of laypeople invited him to build a monastery near his hometown. After constructing a small temple in Meichuan (Plum River), just north of Wuhsueh, Tao-hsin happened to travel to Huangmei in 624. As soon as he saw the setting at the foot of Shuangfeng Mountain, he knew he had found the place he was looking for. That was the origin of Fourth Patriarch Temple and also the beginning of the communal practice that put the Z in Zen.

Up until then, Zen masters such as Bodhidharma, Hui-k'o, and Seng-ts'an wandered from place to place and occasionally gave lectures on the Dharma. But whenever they settled in one place for long, they either lived in hermitages with a handful of students or they stayed in monasteries at the pleasure of others. Tao-hsin changed this. He created the first self-supporting monastery where life revolved around meditation and manual work. It would still be another one hundred and fifty years before Pai-chang's detailed code for such a community would be compiled, but the communal practice established by Tao-hsin attracted adherents immediately. By the time he died, there were more than five hundred monks living at his monastery.

And his reputation spread far beyond the Yangtze. He was invited to lecture at court three times. But he was not interested in entertaining the ruling elite, and he turned down each imperial summons. The emperor, however, was not amused and sent an emissary to tell Tao-hsin that if he could not come in person, then to send his head. When the emissary delivered the emperor's message, Tao-hsin stretched forth his neck. The emissary returned to the capital without the patriarch's head but with the story of Tao-hsin's willingness to send it along. The emperor sighed in admiration and conferred on the Fourth Patriarch the title of National Master.

Although Tao-hsin didn't travel to the capitals of Loyang or Ch'ang-an, he did travel to Nanching on at least one occasion. According to an account in a number of early Zen annals, one day when Tao-hsin was in Emperor Wu's old capital, he happened to notice the sky above Oxhead Mountain south of the city. It looked so unusual, he decided to investigate and saw a monk meditating at the bottom of a cliff.

When Tao-hsin approached him and asked what he was doing, the monk said, "Contemplating the mind."

Tao-hsin asked, "Who is it who is contemplating, and what sort of thing is the mind?"

The monk stood up and bowed. After discovering the identity of his visitor, the monk asked Tao-hsin to instruct him. The Fourth Patriarch then gave this explanation of the path to buddhahood:

"The hundreds of thousands of doors to the truth all depend on this one square-inch. The rivers of mystery and virtue all have their origin here in the mind. Every power and expression of morality, meditation, and wisdom are already fully present and inseparable from this mind of yours. All afflictions and obstructions are essentially empty and still. Every cause and every effect are but dreams or illusions. There is no Triple Realm to escape from, nor any enlightenment to attain. Humans and non-humans have the same nature and attributes. The Great Way is perfectly empty, free of thought and reason. You have already attained the Dharma and lack nothing. How could you differ from the buddhas? There is no other Dharma. Just let your mind be. Don't contemplate or purify your mind. Don't become angry or greedy and don't harbor cares. Float along unobstructed. Let your mind go where it will. Don't do good. And don't do evil. Whether walking, standing, sitting, or lying down, whatever you see, whatever happens, it's all the sublime work of the buddhas. Someone who is happy and without regrets, that is what we call a buddha."

The monk said, "If the mind is already complete, what is the buddha, and what is the mind?"

Tao-hsin said, "What is not the mind doesn't ask about the buddha. What asks about the buddha is nothing other than the mind."

The monk said, "Since I shouldn't engage in contemplation, how should I deal with my mind when confronting the world?"

Tao-hsin said, "The world has no hold on you. Whatever has a hold on you comes from your mind. Don't let your mind force names on you. Where do you think delusions come from? When delusions no longer arise, the true mind will fill you with knowledge. Just let your mind be. Don't try to control it anymore. This is called the ever-present, never-changing dharma body. I received this direct teaching from Master Seng-ts'an, and I am now passing it on to you. Pay attention to what I have told you."

The monk's name was Fa-jung (594–657), and he became the founding patriarch of the Oxhead Zen School, named after the mountain where he lived. But when it came time for Tao-hsin to choose a successor, he chose another monk as the next patriarch. Not far from the stupa that once contained his body, there was another shrine that marked the place where Tao-hsin transmitted the patriarchship to Hung-jen. I paused to pay my respects and considered the memory of events that made a pilgrimage like mine possible, the connection of the past with the present, and the need I felt to end their separation. It was a fine day to be a pilgrim, and there was still plenty of it left. From the place where somebody remembered and commemorated the transmission of the Dharma from one mind to another, I looked up at the summit and couldn't resist. It looked so close.

. . . . .

I walked back down the steps to the road that led past the stupa and continued on toward an adjacent peak. It was the kind of road that saw a vehicle every hour or so, and it would have been a pleasant enough walk. But it didn't lead to the summit of Shuangfeng Mountain. As soon as it began leading in another direction, I took the first trail I saw and followed it around the edge of rice fields still waiting to be plowed, and past a couple of farmhouses. And that trail led to another trail, which led to another trail, and I seemed to be making progress, until I ran into a water buffalo that wouldn't budge. The trail was too narrow, and the grass was too high on either side to go around. I had to walk back and bushwack my way through an opening that turned out to be illusory. I was soon engulfed in grass taller than me and had no idea which way to go. I figured that going uphill was the best policy and struggled onward. Every time I paused to catch my breath, I thought about returning to see if that water buffalo had moved. But I had gone too far, and I doubted if I could find my way back. As I worked my way up the slope, I had to lean into the grass to make any progress. It was so thick. And I kept slipping on it as I tried to plant my feet on the stalks. I missed my staff and wished I had given my outing the forethought it deserved. But the grass finally ended, and an actual trail appeared, and it led toward the summit, which I could see again—though not for long.

The trail soon turned east and started skirting the mountain. A couple of zigs and zags later, it led past a hermit's hut, and the hermit was home. She was dressed in traditional dark blue Taoist garb, and her hair was done up in a topknot. She was carrying a few sticks of wood to stoke the fire inside. When she saw me, she waved for me to join her, which I gladly did. She was making lunch for a farmer, who was sitting on a short stool next to the stove. He pulled out another stool, and I sat down and heaved a long sigh. I was out of breath.

Despite their lack of means, hermits are never without social graces. I was so thirsty I could barely speak. But I didn't need to. As soon as I sat down, the woman handed me a bowl of hot sugar water: the special occasion drink of hermits throughout China. She said she lived there with a Taoist priest, but he had gone down the mountain for provisions. She said she was from the local area, and the two of them had lived there for fourteen years.

I was too exhausted to ask anything more than if the trail led to the summit. She said it did, but it continued around behind the mountain, where there was a side trail to the top. She said it would take me another hour, maybe two. She filled my bowl again, and I drained it, and I could have drained another. But I wanted to press on. I thanked her for her kindness and returned to the trail. I went on a bit further, until I reached a spot where I could see the summit again. I knew I didn't have time to go around behind the mountain, so I decided to bushwhack my way straight up the slope. It was another struggle through brush and over one rock ledge after another. It was one of those stupid decisions one somehow survives. I had to keep stopping to catch my breath and once again regretted that I had gone off without my staff, and also without my gloves. But stupid or not, I persisted.

Persistence, I think, is the one virtue I have cultivated above all others. In this case, half an hour of unflagging boneheadedness got me to the top. As soon as I reached the summit, I collapsed on a flat rock and didn't think I would ever be able to get up again.

The top of the mountain consisted of two piles of rocks less than a hundred feet apart. That was why it was called Shuangfeng, or Twin Peak. According to that thin little volume about Fourth Patriarch Temple I bought the day I arrived, a young girl was once chased up to the summit by a lecherous landlord and his henchmen. As she reached the top, two Taoist immortals, Lu Tung-pin (author of *Secret of the Golden Flower*) and Iron Crutch Li, happened to be passing by overhead. On seeing the girl's plight, Lu grabbed his partner's crutch and cracked the skulls of the landlord and his henchmen and also inadvertently shattered the peak. And it had been that way ever since. That was also the origin of the mountain's other name: *Po-o-shan*: "Cracked Skull Mountain."

One of the reasons I wanted to climb to the summit was to see if I could see Fengmao Mountain nine miles to the northeast. That was where the Fifth Patriarch built his temple, and I had read that it was visible from the summit. But the clouds had rolled in, so I just sat there gasping for air and listening to the wind. Suddenly, a peal of thunder rippled through the sky. A weather front was moving through. I lingered just long enough to take a reading with my GPS—the elevation was 1,800 feet, which was 1,500 feet higher than the temple. After considering my options, I decided it was too dangerous to go back down the way I had come up without my staff or gloves. I opted for the trail that went down the backside, the one I should have come up.

Not many people hiked to the summit, and the trail was faint. It led through a pine forest and kept disappearing beneath pine needles. Fortunately, it kept reappearing and eventually widened into a regular path. At some point it led past a Taoist hermitage, which was a bit more substantial than the earlier hut (walls of stone instead of mud bricks) where I had stopped to ask directions. A few minutes later there was another hermitage. The gate of the first one was locked, but there was smoke coming from the second one. It even had a name. It was called Chunyangkung (Pure Yang Temple). Ch'un-yang was also a name used by Lu Tung-pin, the leader of the Eight Immortals who shattered the peak. I thought I'd better make sure I was still on the right trail and yelled, "Is anyone home?" A few seconds later, a Taoist priest and a nun appeared at the doorway. When I asked them about the trail down, I couldn't understand a word they said. We made a few more attempts at communication, but without success. I smiled, and they smiled, and that was good enough. I pressed on as ignorant as before.

I was encouraged, though. From their hermitage, the trail of dirt and pine needles turned into a trail of stone steps, suggesting that pilgrims frequented that part of the mountain. And pilgrims had to come from somewhere. As I continued on, the stone steps disappeared, and whenever I came to a fork in the trail, I took it. Before long I was completely lost, and the clouds were too thick to know which way was east or west. But the rumbling of an approaching rainstorm spurred me on.

Finally the trail widened into a rutted path, and I met a farmer hauling firewood down the mountain in a cart that looked older than he, and he was about seventy.

Taoist hermits on Shuangfengshan

When I asked him how to get to Fourth Patriarch Temple, he pointed west. I had come down on the eastern flank of the mountain, and the temple was on the southwestern flank. I followed the farmer's finger across two ridges and an intervening valley, and after an hour I finally came down behind the temple. Its yellow-tiled roofs were a welcome sight. As I walked through the front gate and past the fat buddha and his bodyguards, the monks were coming out of the main shrine hall. The evening ceremony was over, and I was just in time for dinner.

Ching-hui was more affable this time, but I didn't tell him or anyone else about my little adventure. After dinner, I showered and washed my clothes and went to bed. But I didn't get to sleep for several hours. As soon as I lay down, the thunder that began when I was at the summit erupted in a torrential rainstorm that lasted most of the night. It finally stopped around daybreak. The birds sounded relieved. There was even a ray or two of sunshine. My clothes, though, were still soaked from washing them the night before—too soaked to try wearing. After more than three weeks, it was finally time for the reserves to take over as the outfit du jour.

There wasn't much going on in the monastery. Everyone was getting ready for the Shuilu ceremony. I could hear the nuns in the courtyard below practicing mantras. The monks were setting up a sound system in the main shrine hall. I went outside and walked around and ran into Ming-chi, the temple manager. He invited me to join him for tea.

Ming-chi was thirty-five and from the northeast part of China, the industrial part, the really industrial part. He said he was working in a power plant when he became interested in Buddhism. He heard Ching-hui give a talk in 1995, and he became a monk the following year, over the strong objections of his family. Ching-hui had told me about Ming-chi and said it was hard to get him out of the meditation hall. But when Ching-hui took over Fourth Patriarch Temple from Pen-huan in 2003, he pried Ming-chi off his cushion and brought him there to serve as temple manager.

Ming-chi said that originally Pen-huan had planned to rebuild Fifth Patriarch Temple, but the local official in charge of religious affairs had pleaded with him to rebuild Fourth Patriarch Temple instead. Fifth Patriarch Temple was still a functioning monastery at the time, but Fourth Patriarch Temple wasn't. So in 1994 Pen-huan led the fund-raising drive to rebuild one of the most important monasteries in the history of Zen.

Pen-huan lived in the Kuangchou–Hong Kong corridor, which was one of the wealthiest parts of China, and he raised forty million RMB, or five million dollars, for the project. Once construction was finished, he turned the temple over to Ching-hui. Ching-hui had dozens of young, well-educated monks he was training and to whom he was transferring temples such as this. Ching-hui was also no slouch when it came to raising money. He had done the same thing with Chaochou's Pailin Temple and then turned it over to Ming-hai once it was up and running. It was a Zen fraternity.

Although Fourth Patriarch Temple had been rebuilt, it was so new it was still half empty. There were only about fifty monks and a dozen or so lay residents when I visited, but that was enough to conduct retreats, of which they had three every year: a four-week retreat in winter and two three-week retreats in spring. And they were planning to hold another three-week retreat in summer as well. Ming-chi said Ching-hui was also building a nunnery a mile or two up the road—the road I didn't follow the previous day. He said the slopes outside Huangmei at the southern edge of the Tapieh Range had been home to many famous Buddhist and Taoist masters in the past. Nine Buddhist patriarchs had been enlightened there, and thirteen Taoist masters had ascended to heaven.

He suggested I walk up the road to the Taoist center at Kuanyinai, where eighty Taoist priests were living. He said the priests there were famous for curing illnesses, which they did with all sorts of spells and concoctions but most famously with the branches of medicinal plants that they used to flagellate those who came for treatment. Ming-chi said it was only an hour walk and he would ask someone to accompany me there. But since there were still rumblings going on in the heavens and I was down to my reserve set of clothes, I demurred. I spent the day, instead, catching up in my journal.

After dinner Ming-chi once again invited me to join the monks in the meditation hall, and this time he made sure someone came and showed me the way. I always enjoyed taking part in the evening meditation, the pain in my knees notwithstanding. Life in every Zen monastery revolved around its meditation hall, and it was always in the least accessible part. Most monasteries didn't allow laypeople access, but Ching-hui's teaching of Zen was very much lay-oriented, and his monasteries always had a place for laymen to meditate—if not with the monks, then in a separate hall. Some of his temples also had a meditation hall for laywomen, but not at Fourth Patriarch Temple, at least not when I was there.

I stepped through the doorway and joined a solar system of more than forty orbiting monks and laymen. Everyone walked at his own pace and followed his own route around the statue of Shakyamuni in the middle of the room. Old-timers seemed to prefer the orbits of Neptune and Uranus, while the younger monks zipped around in the paths of Mercury and Venus. I ended up somewhere between Jupiter and Saturn.

At exactly 7:15, the *wei-nuo*, or religious affairs manager, entered the doorway and struck the wooden board next to his seat. Everyone froze in place. He said something, but I didn't understand a word. I didn't feel bad, though. I had heard that his dialect was so difficult that most of the time no one else knew what he said either. Somehow it seemed appropriate for the meditation hall, where language was on a par with the wind. After he said whatever it was he said, everyone walked to their seat on the long bench that circled the room and arranged themselves on their cushions.

The bench was about three feet wide and was covered with a padded blanket. And every few feet there were a couple of cushions people used to prop up their rear ends before crossing their legs. Once their rears were propped and their legs were arranged, they covered their knees with a small blanket—arthritis was an occupational hazard of work in the meditation hall, and the blankets helped.

And thus the evening meditation began. It lasted an hour, which was fifteen minutes longer than my knees and I were accustomed to. The period ended when the monk in charge struck a small hand chime and talked for five minutes in his wind-in-the-pines voice, then struck the wooden board again. Everyone got up and rearranged their knee blanket and cushions and resumed orbiting the buddha sun. Once the circulation had returned to their legs, they peeled off one by one and exited the hall. Those who wanted to could stay for another meditation period, and a few did, but everyone else left, including me.

Shortly after returning to my room, I went to bed, but once more I didn't fall asleep. This time, though, it wasn't because of the thunder. This time it was a group of professors from Central China Normal University who were given two rooms just down the hall from mine. I'm not sure what they were doing there. They were really loud. Even after the evening patrol went around beating the goodnight board, they continued as if they were at a convention. Finally, at ten o'clock, after lying in bed for an hour, I got dressed and stepped into the hallway.

I was surprised to see Layman Heng-chang pacing outside their door. He was editor of the temple's bimonthly magazine, *Cheng-chueh*: "True Enlightenment." He had a room on the same level and probably felt responsible for what was going on in an area of the monastery where he was usually alone. But that night, he wasn't alone, and he didn't know how to deal with the situation. Should he say something or not?

As I walked past him, he grabbed my left arm and tried to restrain me. But with my free right arm, I reached toward the offending door. A couple of loud knocks silenced whatever was going on inside. A few seconds later, one of the professors opened the door. I stepped past him into the cigarette smoke and told the conventioneers that this was a monastery and even the birds knew enough to stop chattering when the sun went down. They were dumbfounded. I turned and went back to my room. The barbarian had struck again. After I left, Heng-cheng went into their room and probably apologized for my rude behavior but glad, no doubt, I had resolved his problem. Silence reigned in the monastery once more.

I knew it would be a while before I could fall asleep, so I took out the book Ching-hui had given me with his Dharma talks on the Fourth Patriarch. They began with Tao-hsin's *Essential Means for Entering the Path and Stilling the Mind*, in which the Fourth Patriarch said his teaching was based on the *Lankavatara Sutra* and *The Prajnaparamita Sutra Spoken by Manjushri*. The *Lanka*, he said, taught that nothing was more important than the mind. And Manjushri's sutra taught that all practices came down to one practice, the practice of mindfulness in whatever one did. Together they supplied the theory and practice of Zen: the vision and its realization.

In explaining his approach, Tao-hsin quoted *The Perfection of Wisdom in 25,000 Lines*:

"To think of nothing is to think of the buddha." So what does to think of nothing mean? What thinks of nothing is the mind that thinks of the buddha. Apart from the mind, there is no buddha somewhere else. And apart from the buddha, there is no mind somewhere else. To think of the buddha is to think of the mind. To search for the mind is to search for the buddha.

That was enough work for one night.

9 NO DUST OR MIRROR

It sounded like a monastery when I woke up. The visiting professors were sleeping late. And I wasn't, for a change. My clothes were dry, at least dry enough. I got dressed, packed up, and went to say goodbye to my hosts. My next destination was Fifth Patriarch Temple, nine miles to the northeast, as the magic staff flies. I knocked on Ming-chi's door. He was expecting me, but goodbye was premature. He said he had to go there on temple business and would give me a ride.

While Ming-chi was getting ready, I walked down to the abbot's quarters to say goodbye to Ching-hui. He was looking a bit better, a bit livelier. During the brief conversation I had with him when I first arrived, I mentioned that I was hoping to visit a Zen nunnery. There were plenty of nunneries in China, and I knew of several where meditation was part of their practice. But I wondered if any of them were devoted to the communal practice of Zen and not simply the occasional meditation period. The sound of the dinner board had put an end to that conversation. This time Ching-hui handed me a slip of paper with a name and a phone number. He said the nunnery was near Nanchang, which wasn't that far out of my way. Once again I was in his debt. I thanked him and wished him well in all the ceremonies he would be conducting over the next week. I guess somebody had to do it. I'm just glad I was taking a nap when they handed out the ceremonial gene.

When I got to the temple parking lot, three young monks and two elderly lay-women were also waiting there. They had arrived the night before and had come for the ceremony. Since it was still a few days off, they wanted to take the opportunity to visit Fifth Patriarch Temple, and Ming-chi had invited them to come along. A few minutes later Ming-chi showed up, and we all got into the temple's SUV. Ming-chi sat up front with the driver, the three young monks sat in the backseat, and I joined the two laywomen in the middle.

It was a quick trip down the mountain and back to Huangmei. This time, instead of heading northwest to Bitter Melon and the future mountain resort of Napuyuan, we headed north, into another blank map on the vehicle's GPS. While we were bumping along a more or less paved road, one of the laywomen said she had flown down from Beijing for the ceremony, and she asked me what I was doing there. I told her I was collecting material for a book about Zen. It was sort of a sequel, I told her, to an earlier book I had written about China's hermit tradition. When she asked me the name of the earlier book, and I told her the Chinese title, she grabbed my hand and didn't let go. She said it was one of her favorite books. I thought she was being polite. But she proceeded to recount two of my interviews, almost verbatim. I should have felt grateful for her appreciation, but it made me feel disembodied. Sometimes I wished I didn't publish what I wrote. I enjoyed the writing part. But once my work was published, it was like it entered a realm to which I no longer had access. It was like I had this friend, this friend who was alive, then wasn't. It's hard to explain. I enjoyed the writing part. It certainly wasn't for the money.

From Huangmei, it was five miles to Fifth Patriarch Village, and another three to the temple. Just past the village, the road turned steep, and the mountain disap-peared in the fog. Visibility was no more than thirty feet, if that—just enough for the driver to see the rocks and the pine trees that marked the edge of the road, which dropped off on either side. For some reason, the thought of stopping never occurred to him, or to anyone else, except me. Fortunately, there was no traffic coming down the mountain, and at least the driver slowed down. When the monastery wall finally appeared, the driver honked, and a monk inside opened the side gate. We parked next to the temple's rose garden, and Ming-chi told everyone to meet back at the SUV in an hour. While they all went off to see the sights and pay their respects,

Ming-chi took me with him to meet Wei-tao, the temple manager. I was hoping to see the abbot, but Ming-chi said he wasn't there.

The abbot was Chien-jen. He was the temple manager the first time I visited, which was in 1999, when I was traveling with Mountain Dave. Dave was making his first trip to China after being deported from Taiwan for overstaying his two-month tourist visa by thirteen years. That demolished the old record of seven years set by Bob Benson, another friend who couldn't deal with the bureaucratic requirements of visa extensions and residency permits. For people like Bob and Dave and myself, Taiwan was a welcome refuge and a hard place to leave. We never heard any good news from fellow Americans who went back home. Just the opposite.

Someone once asked a Tibetan yogi the easiest way to attain Enlightenment. He said, "Leave your country." Living as a foreigner, one had the opportunity to reconsider the attractions of one's own culture and to choose new, less debilitating ones with which to outfit one's life. I chose Chinese poetry and Buddhist sutras, oolong tea, and the afternoon nap—ostensibly harmless stuff.

Dave and I also chose Seven Star Mountain just north of Taipei. I lived on the sunny side just below the summit at a place called Bamboo Lake. The lake had been drained long before I got there. It was, instead, a sea of cabbages and calla lilies. The converted farm shed I rented looked out across all of Taipei Basin, and the view of the city at night was like a jewelry store window. Chiang Kai-shek's old summer home was a mortar lob below. At 2,500 feet, it was the only place in North Taiwan that stayed cool in summer and the only place where it snowed in winter. Whenever it did, enterprising taxi drivers would drive up the mountain, pile as much snow as they could on their hoods and roofs, then drive back down to the city and sell their crystal treasure in front of the Taipei train station. Most people in Taiwan had never seen snow in those days. Now they go skiing in the Alps.

The weather wasn't the only blessing the mountain provided. The mountain was volcanic, and the farmers jerry-rigged a long series of pipes from some fumaroles further up the mountain to a makeshift bathhouse a short walk from where I lived. During the winter I took a couple of baths a day to keep my fingers flexible enough to work my typewriter keys. A bath was good for a few hours, which usually allowed me to translate a Cold Mountain poem or a Stonehouse gatha. And the bathhouse was never closed. Lounging in the steaming water by candlelight, it was hard to imagine ever going back to the States. But the bathhouse was gone now—code violations—and the farmers had turned their houses and sheds into restaurants that catered to flatland visitors coming up to visit what was now called Yangmingshan National Park.

Dave lived on the shady side of the same mountain in a small farmhouse built by an orchid grower. The owner preferred to stay in Taipei to enjoy the conveniences of city life and to peddle his flowers. In exchange for watching the place, Dave got free rent. He didn't have any neighbors as far as he could see in any direction, and he liked it that way. Dave was a hermit. He picked wild plants for food, and whenever he went into town, he hit the dumpsters outside supermarkets. Occasionally he made some money by giving acupressure massages in the city or helping someone with their English. Otherwise, he lived on good fortune.

Every once in a while, the foreign affairs police would visit and threaten him with deportation for overstaying his visa. But Dave was such a convincing hermit, the police always ended up simply telling him to get a new visa, then leaving him alone. Finally, a new chief of police heard about Dave and needed to establish his credentials, so Dave had to go. After the police chief finally met Dave, he invited him to dinner and told him how sorry he was he had ordered him deported, but it was too late to revoke the order. He told Dave how to get back into the country: just change your name and get a new passport, he said. But once Dave left, he never went back. Sometimes you can't.

Since he was being deported the same week I was heading off to China, I invited him to join me on a Zen trip. While we were getting our visas in Hong Kong, I gave a talk about our upcoming adventure to my former colleagues at the Foreign Correspondents Club. I called it my "Fifty Days, Fifty Zen Masters" trip. And by the time we got to Fifth Patriarch Temple, we were somewhere in the twenties.

That was when we met Chien-jen. We had such a good time together, he gave us his cell phone number when we left. We were surprised. Cell phones were still fairly new in China in 1999—there were only forty million subscribers then, compared to five hundred million in 2007. We were even more surprised when he told us to call him anytime we needed money. I guess we looked like we could use some. He said he could wire money to us anywhere in China. That was the first and only time anyone in China has ever extended such an offer. I was hoping to see Chien-jen again, not that I was looking for money. I was just hoping to see him.

The reason he wasn't there was that he was a disciple of Ch'ang-ming, and

Ch'ang-ming lived in Wuhan, the capital of Hupei. Ch'ang-ming was easily the most famous monk in the province, but he was getting on in years and was relying more and more on Chien-jen to get things done. When Ch'ang-ming was asked to take over as abbot of Fifth Patriarch Temple in 1994, he made Chien-jen temple manager, even though he was only twenty-eight and had only been a monk for four years. Seven years later, he made Chien-jen abbot. It was a nationwide phenomenon at monasteries and nunneries—the old masters were appointing young, competent successors for the new age, people who could talk to the times.

Since Chien-jen was gone, Ming-chi had arranged to meet with the temple manager. He knew the way, and I followed him through the maze of corridors in which I'd gotten lost the last time I was there. Wei-tao was waiting for us in a room that served as his office as well as his bedroom. He looked even younger than Ming-chi, and Ming-chi was thirty-five. He was pudgy for a monk, but he was so cherubic, his pudginess suited him. When he laughed, which was often, his eyes disappeared.

Ming-chi was there to line up more monks for the Shuilu ceremony. As soon as we sat down, Wei-tao started working his cell phone, calling other Buddhist temples in the area. He was really good at it. Ming-chi had only been in charge of Fourth Patriarch Temple for three years, and he didn't have the connections Wei-tao had. He also lacked Wei-tao's directness. In his phone conversations, Wei-tao didn't waste words. He specified monks, rather than nuns, and, if at all possible, light-skinned ones. I could understand the preference for monks over nuns; China was still a patriarchal culture. And I suppose dark-skinned monks gave the impression of a lack of refinement, of having spent more time working outdoors than practicing indoors. We were, after all, sitting in the same temple where Hui-neng, the future Sixth Patriarch, showed up in 671 and was derided for looking like a "jungle rat." If he had been there that week, he wouldn't have made the cut for the Shuilu ceremony. But then, ceremonies were about image, not awareness.

While his fellow temple manager stayed on the phone, Ming-chi made us all tea. By the time we finished the fourth pot, Wei-tao had lined up a contingent of two dozen light-skinned monks and promises of more. Ming-chi looked at his watch and said he had to get back. I walked with him as far as the magnolia tree outside Wei-tao's residence. That seemed like a good place to say goodbye. Afterwards, I sat down on a bench next to the tree and waited for Wei-tao to finish another phone call. The petals had turned the ground white, and the fragrance was transporting.

It reminded me of the magnolia I lived above at Haiming Monastery in Taiwan before I moved to Bamboo Lake. Sometimes I had to close my window, it was so overpowering.

This time there was no window to close, and I had to be rescued by Wei-tao. He led me to the guest quarters and turned me over to Mrs. Shih, who handed me a pair of thermoses and showed me to a room with five beds. Before I had a chance to choose, I heard the sound of the lunch board and joined the monks and laypeople in the mess hall. It was the standard monastery meal: tofu, shitake mushrooms, bean sprouts, cabbage, even a few hot peppers, and a steamed bun to make sure everyone was full.

I returned to my room and chose the bed nearest the window for my nap. But just about the time I was falling asleep, a group of pilgrims arrived. My window overlooked the final steps of the old trail that began far below, near Fifth Patriarch Village. Most visitors came up in cars or buses, but these people were there to gain merit, so they walked up. And to make sure the gods noticed, they announced their arrival with several long strings of firecrackers, which also drove off any malevolent spirits that might have followed them. It also drove off any hope of a nap. I gave up and spent the rest of the afternoon hiking around the mountain visiting the sites associated with the Fifth Patriarch.

And there were lots of sites. Hung-jen spent his whole life in the area and fifty years of it on the two mountains where he and Tao-hsin lived. He was born just outside of Huangmei in 601. And when Tao-hsin established the country's first Zen center at the foot of Shuangfengshan in 624, Hung-jen became one of its first residents. He was still there when Tao-hsin died in 651. Up until then, Zen masters were always striking out on their own after receiving the Dharma from their teachers. Bodhidharma, Hui-k'o, Seng-ts'an, and Tao-hsin all parted ways after the transmission of the patriarchship. Hung-jen was the first Zen master to stay with his teacher until the latter's death. It was another indication of the change from personal to communal practice. Zen was becoming residential. It was also becoming popular. There were more than five hundred monks living at Fourth Patriarch Temple at the time of Tao-hsin's death, and there were more than a thousand at Fifth Patriarch Temple when Hung-jen died.

After building a stupa to hold his teacher's body, Hung-jen stayed at Shuang-fengshan for another three years. That was the customary period of mourning for a parent or a teacher. When it was over, he decided to establish a second Zen center. Since he was familiar with the terrain in the area, he chose a place a half-day's walk east of Tao-hsin's temple, and one that was capable of replicating what Tao-hsin had started.

Tao-hsin had chosen not only a site that was remote but one that also had enough land to support a community of monks. He called his monastery Yuchu (Secluded Residence)—although most people referred to it as Fourth Patriarch Temple. Hung-jen found a similar site just below the summit of Fengmaoshan. The mountain belonged to a man named Feng Mao, but when Mr. Feng heard about the Fifth Patriarch's plan, he gave him the mountain. Hung-jen called his Zen monastery Chanting (Meditation Samadhi).

As Zen developed over the next two hundred years, we see this phenomenon over and over: the conscious selection of a mountain basin, and whenever possible, a high mountain basin, remote, well watered, and with sufficient arable land to support hundreds of monks and sometimes more than a thousand. We see it at the monasteries established by almost every monk who was instrumental in the early development of Zen. Yang-ch'i, who was even more important than Lin-chi

Fifth Patriarch Temple and Fengmaoshan (East Mountain)

in establishing the Linchi (Rinzai) lineage, actually built his center inside an extinct volcano.

This process of selecting a specific ecological niche for the site of a monastery began as an experiment on Shuangfengshan, but it became a tradition on Fengmaoshan. Because Fengmaoshan was more or less east of Shuangfengshan, it became known as Tungshan, or East Mountain, and the variety of Zen practiced there became known as East Mountain Zen. Less than six years after Hung-jen established Chanting Monastery, even the emperor had heard about it, and he asked Hung-jen to come to court to lecture about Zen. But the kind of Zen Tao-hsin and Hung-jen practiced wasn't something you lecture about to the curious. It was something you lived, and Hung-jen declined the invitation.

When someone asked Hung-jen why he didn't establish his Zen center in a city instead of in the mountains, he said,

> The timbers you see in a great building originally come from remote valleys.
> You don't find them where people live. It's because they grow far from human-

Home of Linchi/Rinzai Zen on Yangchishan

kind that they don't get chopped down and gradually grow big enough to serve as beams. This is why we settle our spirit in remote valleys far from dust and noise, why we nourish our nature among the peaks cut off from the world of mundane affairs. When distractions no longer come before our eyes, our minds become still. Thus does a tree of the Way flower and a Zen grove produce its fruit.

It was the selection of such sites that made communal practice possible, and it was communal practice that enabled practitioners to extend their spiritual awareness beyond the meditation hall to their daily lives. This was what Tao-hsin and Hung-jen taught their disciples, teaching them to practice everywhere, regardless of what they were doing. Tao-hsin explained it as "guarding the one." Hung-jen called it "guarding the mind." They told their disciples to be mindful in all that they did or said or thought to the point where the distinctions between doing and saying and thinking disappeared.

Other than a few scattered statements, the only record we have of Hung-jen's teaching is his *Discourse on the Supreme Vehicle*, which begins,

> The key to cultivating the Way is knowing that your own mind is originally pure, that it is neither created nor destroyed, and that it is free of discrimination. The mind whose nature is perfectly pure is your true teacher and superior to any of the buddhas of the ten directions you might call upon.
>
> And how do you know your mind is originally pure? The shastras say "Within the body of every being is their adamantine buddha nature. Like the sun, it fills the world with its perfect light. But because it's covered by the dark clouds of the Five Skandhas [Form, Sensation, Perception, Memory, and Consciousness], it can't shine forth, like a lamp inside a jar." For example, when the clouds and mists of the world arise in every direction and turn the sky dark, does the sun stop shining? The reason there's no light isn't that the light has been destroyed but that it's been covered up by clouds and mist. The pure mind of every being is like this. It's just obstructed by the dark clouds of attachment, delusion, and affliction. If you can concentrate on guarding the mind, delusions will no longer arise, and the reality of nirvana will spontaneously appear. Thus you should know that your mind is originally pure.

When it came time to choose a successor, Hung-jen asked his disciples to write a poem to demonstrate the depth of their understanding. This occurred in 672. His chief disciple at that time was a monk named Shen-hsiu, who heard about Hung-jen in North China and moved to East Mountain in 655. He had been there for seventeen years, but he offered a poem that has since become famous for its misunderstanding of Zen:

> The body is our Bodhi Tree
> the mind is like a standing mirror
> always try to keep it clean
> don't let it gather dust.

Another person who heard about Hung-jen was Hui-neng. He had traveled all the way to East Mountain from South China, and he had been there less than nine months. When Hui-neng heard Shen-hsiu's poem, he offered this rejoinder:

> Bodhi doesn't have any trees
> this mirror doesn't have a stand
> our buddha nature is forever pure
> how can it gather dust?

The dark-skinned newcomer understood what Hung-jen meant by "purity," and Shen-hsiu didn't. And so Hung-jen passed on the patriarchship to the illiterate jungle rat from South China.

While I was wandering around after dinner, I looked inside the building where Hui-neng's stone wheel had been preserved, as if he had just taken a break. I also ran into Wei-tao again, and he invited me into his room for tea. He shared a quality typical of temple managers I noticed throughout China: he was ready for anything. He also made a good pot of tea.

Wei-tao was born in 1975 in Yincheng, a small town seventy miles northwest of Wuhan. He said he became interested in Buddhism as a youth, and his first Buddhist master was a hermit who lived on a mountain near his home. His master instructed him in meditation and Buddhist texts for a few years, then sent him to Fifth Patriarch Temple for ordination in 1998. Wei-tao had been there ever since.

He said his parents still weren't happy about his decision to become a monk. Times were changing, he said, but not that fast in the town where he was from.

Although Fifth Patriarch Temple hadn't been destroyed during the Cultural Revolution, all the monks had been forced to leave. It wasn't until 1979 that the central government "reaffirmed" the freedom of religious practice, and it wasn't until the following year that monks were allowed to return, although not many came back. There were only seven or eight monks living there when Ch'ang-ming became abbot and began rebuilding the place in 1994, the same year Pen-huan began rebuilding Fourth Patriarch Temple.

Although the number of monks in residence had increased to seventy, and that figure was expected to double, Fifth Patriarch Temple hadn't yet reestablished itself

Hui-neng's old rice pounding stone

as a Zen monastery. Still, it was headed in that direction. There were half a dozen monks who basically lived in the meditation hall, and the rest of the residents took part in two meditation periods a day, one in the morning and one in the evening. There was also a three-week retreat every winter. But not all the monks practiced Zen. Some practiced Pure Land and chanted the name of Amitabha in one of the shrine halls. Fifth Patriarch Temple hadn't yet developed its "style." But a much larger meditation hall was being built, Wei-tao said, and the focus of practice in the future would be on Zen.

He said the abbot also planned to build six or seven huts for those who wanted a more secluded place to practice. The huts were going to be built near the summit where the monastery was originally located. There wasn't that much room at the summit, and the monastery was moved halfway down the mountain one structure at a time in the ninth century to its present location.

The move made the temple more accessible to patrons and pilgrims and, more importantly, reduced the distance to its growing inventory of fields. It had become so famous that emperors began bestowing land on the monastery as early as 763, when Tai-tsung donated 375 acres near the foot of the mountain to go with the 100 or so acres the monastery already farmed in a basin on the backside of the mountain at a place known ever since as Tsaitien: "Vegetable Fields." Subsequent emperors added to that amount, as did wealthy benefactors. During the T'ang and Sung dynasties, the fields owned by the monastery, not including its forestland, exceeded five thousand acres. Most of that was spread over a thirty-mile radius, and it wasn't land the monks worked, but was land they rented to farmers. Of course, collecting rent was never easy, and could be dangerous, even fatal. That much land must have generated a huge income, and I wondered how it affected the communal practice of those who lived there. What did they do with all the money? Did they give it to the destitute? Or did they use it to build more shrine halls? Surely the thought must have occurred to some members of the sangha: "Why work if you don't have to?" And surely the same thought was occurring to members even now.

After a few cups of tea, Wei-tao led me outside and into the hall constructed around the Fifth Patriarch's stupa. The stupa that held Hung-jen's remains was first built in 674, the year before he died. Originally it was also further up the mountain, but was moved down to its present location when everything else was moved downhill. The hall that was built around the stupa had been destroyed and rebuilt several times, and what appeared to be the body of Hung-jen on the altar was a plaster replica made in 1938. The fate of Hung-jen's physical body was unknown. According to some records, it was destroyed by fire. But Wei-tao said the patriarch's body was still inside a subterranean vault below the stupa, or so his predecessors had told him.

It's hard to overestimate the impact Hung-jen had on Zen. His disciples founded both its Northern and its Southern schools and lectured before emperors and court officials. They were the first harvest of the Zen grove, and they were responsible for spreading Zen throughout China—not just north and south, but east and west. Thus, Hung-jen's admirers were many, and many came to pay their respects. Among them was the poet Pai Chu-yi (772–846), whose descendents I had met eight days earlier in Loyang. In 815, Pai was banished to Chiuchiang, across the Yangtze from Huangmei, for being too frank in urging reforms and criticizing abuses at court. Following his visit, he wrote this short poem entitled "East Mountain Temple":

I looked all around me and up to the bluest heaven
the moon shone alone through a veil of white clouds
in this boundless world and infinity of people
how many men are worthy of their stature?

Hung-jen's stature and the communal practice he fostered attracted people from all over the country. What attracted them wasn't an ideology or a set of ascetic practices or something magical or mysterious. What attracted people was simply a way of life. I suspect that while many pilgrims who showed up at the monastery had the *Diamond Sutra*'s teaching of nonattachment in mind, even more had Lao-tzu's *Taoteching* echoing between their ears. I could certainly hear the penultimate verse between mine:

Imagine a small state with a small population
let there be labor-saving tools
that aren't used
let people consider death
and not move far
let there be boats and carts

but no reason to ride them
let there be armor and weapons
but no reason to employ them
let people return to the use of knots
and be satisfied with their food
and pleased with their clothing
and content with their homes
and happy with their customs
let there be another state so near
people hear its dogs and chickens
and live out their lives
without making a visit.

Tao-hsin and Hung-jen didn't start this. But they did provide the old Tao with a community setting. I lit some incense and bowed to the Triple Gem—the Buddha, the Dharma, and the Sangha—and thanked Wei-tao for his hospitality. It was getting late. I went back to my room and filled in a few pages in my journal and had no trouble falling asleep to the sound of the rain. During the night, I heard a nightingale. A couple of hours later, the morning patrol sounded the wake-up board, which was promptly answered by roosters far below. I turned over and went back to sleep, content in the knowledge that Wei-tao had arranged for the monastery jeep to take me as far as the Yangtze after breakfast.

10 NO DAY OFF

This was going to be a day off. I envisioned getting a ride down the mountain in the monastery jeep—the morning vegetable run—and spending the day on the south side of the Yangtze immersed in the urban comforts of the big city of Chiuchiang, or "Nine Rivers." But the driver left before, instead of after, breakfast. I waited in bed for his knock, but it never came.

Finally, at eight o'clock I began working on a new plan. I got up and got dressed and packed my bag and returned my key to Mrs. Shih. Then I walked over to the dharma hall, where Wei-tao's room was located. I knocked on his door, but there was no response. I figured he hadn't gone far, and I decided to wait. I sat down on the bench in front of the building again. I was drawn once more to the magnolia tree that dominated the garden. The fragrance was so strong it was pungent.

While I was trying to decide whether dizziness was a good or a bad thing, an electrician showed up and went inside the building. He knocked on Wei-tao's door. Still nothing. Unlike me, he had work to do. Instead of joining me on the bench, he went around to the side of the building. Through a window just above where Wei-tao's bed would have been, he yelled, "Master Wei-tao!" When he didn't hear anything, he motioned for me to join him and asked me to yell too. I guess he thought a foreigner's yell might carry more weight. So we both yelled. Nothing happened. But we kept yelling.

Just when we were about to give up, we heard noises inside and walked back around and into the building. As we turned the corner, Wei-tao opened his door. He said he had been meditating. As soon as he saw me, he asked me why I was still there. I told him the jeep left early. Unfazed, he reached into the pocket of his robe and took out his cell phone. A minute later, a black sedan appeared outside. It was like magic. That was another ability that distinguished temple managers through-out China: a knowledge of the phone mantra that called forth such things as black sedans—in this case, one with faux burl paneling on the dash.

The driver was an architect who had also spent the night at the monastery. Wei-tao said his firm was building the monastery's new meditation hall and also its Buddhist academy. When I first started traveling in China in 1989, there were fewer than ten functioning Buddhist academies in the whole country. Now there must be fifty. It seemed like every monastery or nunnery of any size was opening one. It was another way to attract the new generation of monks and nuns: offer an education.

Since the architect was ready to go, I thanked Wei-tao and rode down the moun-tain in far greater style than I had expected. The luxury was short-lived. Fifteen minutes later, my benefactor dropped me off at a bus station in Huangmei. The sta-tion was so run-down I concluded I was in the original center of town. And the bus I boarded must have been the station's original bus. I could see the road below my feet. The sign in the bus window said CHIUCHIANG, so at least it was going where I wanted to go. But I should have looked closer, at the small characters underneath. The bus was going toward Chiuchiang, but only as far as the Yangtze bridge, which was where it dropped me off. Chiuchiang was on the other side of two and a half miles of water.

The north side of the bridge was not a good place to try to catch a bus. There were plenty of buses going across but none that stopped. I stood there waving in vain for thirty minutes before a local bus finally deigned to pick me up. And the only reason it picked me up was that it was letting off passengers and only going as far as the other side of the bridge. So it, too, left me short of my destination, in the middle of a low-income housing project. I decided to put an end to what seemed like a haywire morning. As soon as I saw an empty taxi, I flagged it down.

I had been to Chiuchiang the previous year and told the driver to take me to the same hotel I had stayed in then. It was in the center of the old part of town a couple of blocks from the river. Ten minutes later, I entered the lobby of the White Deer and walked up to the front desk. The assistant manager remembered me—it was the beard, and I didn't have to bargain. She gave me the discount rate of 260RMB, or thirty-five bucks, which was still a bit high for my budget, but low for Chiuchiang. For centuries Chiuchiang had existed as just another port on the Yangtze. But with the completion of a bridge across the river in 1995, it had become a major transportation hub for overland traffic in Central China. The city had exploded, and so had prices. But for all its slick new façades, the old part of town was still the old part of town.

After dropping my bag in my room, I ventured out. I started at an Internet cafe directly across the street and checked my e-mail. After making sure all was well back home, I recrossed the street and walked down the lane behind the hotel to find the tea shop where the year before I bought some unusually fine Iron Goddess—the kind of tea I seldom found in China, in Taiwan but not in China. When I got to what I thought was the location, it wasn't there. I walked another block just to make sure I

Old section of Chiuchiang on the Yangtze River

wasn't mistaken. Nothing looked familiar, so I walked back to where I remembered it. Apparently, it had been replaced by a shop that sold women's fashions. When I went inside and asked the salesgirl, she said the tea shop had indeed moved, but she didn't know where.

It was called Chayuan (The Tea Connection), and it specialized in Iron Goddess, or Tiehkuanyin, which was processed as an oolong in terms of exposure to heat and treatment of leaves. The Goddess of Mercy herself had bestowed the variety of tea bush from which the tea was made on a farm in Anhsi County of Fukien Province centuries ago. And it has been grown there ever since. Fukien was the next province to the east, and the owner had connections with a grower—hence, the name of the shop.

Whenever I travel in China, I always try to bring back the finest tea I can find, or afford. It's a small indulgence. I knew I would have to settle for something less this time. I was bummed. Mrs. Ts'ao, the lady who ran the tea shop, sold the best Iron Goddess I had ever tasted or inhaled—even better than the tea served by Shaolin's master-at-arms. I walked back outside and stood there for a moment. I sighed and moved on to the next item on the day-off agenda.

I walked into the convenience store next door. I was hoping for an afternoon snack, something like the pumpkin cookies I found in Chienshan. But everything was so packaged I lost all enthusiasm. I settled on a yogurt drink. When I went to pay for it, I asked the owner if he knew what had happened to the tea shop. I was still feeling bummed. He said it had moved to a new part of town. He didn't have the address. I sighed again. But he said he knew the woman who ran it, they were old friends, and he had her number. He took out his cell phone and called her. Five minutes later, her younger brother showed up in a taxi and took me to the new shop. I was transported.

When I entered her new tea shop, Mrs. Ts'ao smiled and told me how happy she was to see me again. I wasn't a big customer but I was an appreciative one. I sat down on the tree stump next to the huge burl that served as the table for her tea paraphernalia and prepared to renew my acquaintance with the Goddess.

It was March 23, and Mrs. Ts'ao said the spring crop wasn't due for another month. And she knew I wouldn't be interested in what was left over from the previous summer's crop, when the Goddess turned into Cinderella. The fall was when Iron Goddess attained the ethereal qualities for which she was named. Mrs. Ts'ao said the fall crop was sold out. The winter crop would have to do, and she made a pot. It was nice, but after the exhilaration of finding her store, I couldn't help feeling disappointed. We chatted for a while, and I was ready to buy some winter tea, just because it was there, and so was I. But she could see my heart wasn't in it. She got up and walked over to the huge tea canisters where she stored her tea, reached into one of them, and came back with another bag.

Mrs. Ts'ao leaned back and smiled. She said she wasn't completely out of fall tea. She had a small stash of Iron Goddess known as "red twig." I had heard of red twig. It was more like a wild tea and only grew on the steepest slopes. When it was picked, which was with difficulty, the twig from which the leaves grew was left in place to enhance the flavor. Normally the presence of twigs was a sign of a lesser-grade tea. But in the case of Iron Goddess, it was just the opposite. Something in the twig smoothed out the flavor. Unfortunately, it also reduced the tea's life expectancy to less than a year. After six months or so, the twig began to turn the tea bitter, and within a year its fragrance was a memory, or so it was said. Very little red twig was produced and even less reached the marketplace. I had never had any, not even in Anhsi, where Tiehkuanyin was produced. She got it, she said, because she knew the grower.

She made a pot, and neither of us said a word. It was incredible. The fragrance was both overwhelming and subtle, unlike the magnolia I had sat beneath earlier that morning. It was a fragrance I could have smelled for hours, one I could have fallen asleep beside. I've never been to a tea competition in China, but in Taiwan 50 percent of the points are awarded on the basis of fragrance. Only 25 percent are based on taste, and the remaining 25 percent on the appearance of the brew. There weren't enough points to measure what I was inhaling. And the taste was, indeed, incredibly smooth—not a hint of astringency.

I asked her how much of it she had and how much it cost. She said she only had one and a half kilos left (a market kilo = 600 grams), and a kilo cost 1,000RMB, or a hundred and twenty-five bucks. I didn't stop to consider if I could afford it. I told her I wanted all she had. She smiled and said since I was an old customer, and since the tea was already four months old, she would lower the price for the whole bag to 500RMB. Somehow, without any effort on my part, I had become a master of negotiation. She vacuum sealed it for me, all 1,500 grams, into fifteen tiny bags. I figured at one bag per week, I could look forward to a whole summer of afternoons among the tea immortals. I even had a book of poems waiting at home to accompany the tea: the poetry of the T'ang-dynasty poet Wei Ying-wu. I'd been planning to translate his poems. And now I had a reason to begin.

While she was packaging the tea and I was envisioning my summer of red twig poetry afternoons, her brother showed up again. In the course of conversation, I told him about my current trip, visiting Zen temples. As soon as I did, he said something to his sister and made two calls on his cell phone. He, too, knew the phone mantra. A few minutes later, a new SUV pulled up outside the store. The vehicle belonged to their uncle. The brother said he knew a monk on Lushan and wanted to take me to meet him. How could I refuse?

After saying goodbye to Mrs. Ts'ao, I left with her brother and their uncle's driver. We headed south on the highway that skirted the east flank of Lushan. Lushan was one of the most scenic mountains in China, known for its mists and waterfalls and ever-changing, ever-hidden face. The name meant "Hut Mountain," and it was once a favorite refuge of recluses. But that was in the past. It was now a mountain overwhelmed by tourism, and I was glad we weren't taking the main road that led to the top of its long, rambling summit.

The road we took led to Hsingtzu, or "Starlet" (named for a meteor that fell there), near the southern end of the mountain. Just past the 17 km marker, we turned off on a cement road just wide enough for one vehicle and drove toward the mountain through a countryside of safflower in bloom and villages of mud-brick houses. After a couple of miles, the cement road ended and was replaced by one of rocks and mud. A light rain began to fall, and the last part was so slippery we had to get out and walk behind the vehicle and provide an occasional push. At least we didn't have to walk far. A few hundred yards later, the road ended just past a small reservoir at a rustic temple. It was called Huijih, or "Sun of Wisdom." Somewhere in the mist above its roofs loomed Lushan's Elephant Peak. But there was no sign of the sun that day.

The temple walls were made of stone and were a welcome change from all the imperial-style monasteries I had been visiting. The surrounding bamboo and pine forests nodded in agreement. In addition to two small one-story buildings with corrugated roofs, the temple included a bell tower and a drum tower made of wood. As we walked across the open courtyard, a young monk appeared in the doorway of one of the buildings. His name was Wen-hsi.

Wen-hsi turned out to be another tea nut, which was why Mrs. Ts'ao's brother knew him. After exchanging introductions, he led us past the building that served as a shrine hall into the second building, which served as his reception hall, office, and bedroom. While we all sat down on stools around the room's lone table, Wen-hsi put on a CD of Chinese zither music and got out his tea paraphernalia. He made us a pot of Chinmao, "Golden Fur." It was a red tea, and he said it was from Tanhsiashan. Tanhsiashan was a mountain just north of Shaokuan in Kuangtung Province. Normally, I didn't like red teas, but this one was exceptional. It smelled like honey and approached Oriental Beauty in flavor. I had never heard of Chinmao and asked Wen-hsi how he knew about the tea. Mrs. Ts'ao didn't sell it.

He said he learned about it while he was attending the Buddhist academy at Yunmen Temple, which was just west of Shaokuan. I had also been to Yunmen. And when we compared notes, it turned out he was there the day I visited in November of 2001. I was with a group of American Buddhists, and while we were looking around, we met a short saffron-robed monk picking oranges in the temple's orange grove. The monk was Master Yi-hsing, or Thich Nhat Hanh, who was there to give a lecture

Huijih Temple at the foot of Lushan

that day to the students. Unfortunately, we had tickets on an afternoon train and couldn't stay for his talk. Wen-hsi said we didn't miss anything, that it was disappointing. He didn't think much of Thich Nhat Hanh's Buddhism. By the time we left, he made it clear he didn't think much of my understanding of the Dharma either. But I had met so many accommodating Zen masters, it was somehow refreshing to meet a jerk. And a jerk who served such fine tea was worth enduring.

When I asked him if he remembered what Thich Nhat Hanh talked about that he found so objectionable, he said the only thing he remembered was that the Vietnamese monk kept using metaphors rooted in dialectics and talked about Enlightenment as something accomplished in stages. He said the monks at Yunmen were too polite to raise questions. But it was nearly five years ago, and he didn't remember enough to provide details. I think his problem wasn't so much his memory as it was his disdain for foreigners. Or maybe in Thich Nhat Hanh's case, it had something to do with China's brief but disastrous war with Vietnam. The month-long conflict occurred at the beginning of 1979 and cost the lives of twenty thousand Chinese troops, most of whom were from units stationed near Kuangchou. Wen-hsi would have only been three at the time, but his home, he told us, was in Toumen County, just south of Kuangchou. Perhaps he lost a family member in the fighting.

When one of my companions asked what Wen-hsi did before becoming a monk, he said he was a student and specified "a student of Chinese culture." That was an unusual area of study in modern China, where everyone was concentrating on international trade or computer science. But it helped explain his cultural myopia, which became more evident the more he talked. After college, he became a monk. And after he graduated from the Buddhist academy, he was ordained. Since then, he had been living on Lushan. He was clearly well educated, but everything he said was so strident and condescending, I had no choice but to turn to the tea for solace. And fortunately, he never stopped pouring.

I thought back to when I studied philosophy for one semester in the winter of 1973 at Taiwan's College of Chinese Culture on Yangmingshan. I was between monasteries and hoping to improve my spoken Chinese, as we didn't do a lot of talking in the monastery. I lived in the dorm with the other philosophy graduate students, and every Sunday they all took a bus down the mountain to Taipei and another bus across town to study the Confucian classics with K'ung Te-ch'eng. Master K'ung was the senior lineal descendent of Confucius, the eldest male heir of the seventy-seventh generation. The Nationalists made sure they brought him with them when they fled to Taiwan in 1949. Even though he was only twenty-nine at the time, they needed people like him to support their claim to represent traditional Chinese culture—they also brought an older brother of the last emperor, just in case the republican form of government didn't work out.

As K'ung Te-ch'eng came of age, he became sufficiently well versed in his ancestor's teachings that attending his weekly class was considered mandatory among philosophy graduate students in Taiwan. I had great respect for the teachings of Confucius, and I asked my classmates if they could ask Master K'ung if I could join his Sunday soiree. But when they conveyed my request, he told them that a foreigner couldn't possibly grasp such profound teachings. And so I spent my Sundays instead with the girl who sat behind me in the class on Alfred North Whitehead taught by Hsieh Yu-wei, who had studied with Whitehead and Russell at Harvard. I don't remember much about Whitehead, but I did learn about Confucian virtues first-hand. It took seven years before the girl's parents finally agreed to let her marry a foreigner with no credentials and no ambition to acquire them.

Wen-hsi shared K'ung Te-ch'eng's perception of the cultural abyss. It didn't matter what I said that day, I was wrong. Almost all Chinese make a conscious effort to be polite. But Wen-hsi was an exception. I couldn't possibly understand something as ancient as Chinese culture. And I mixed up all the religions. I thought everyone cultivated the Tao. And how could someone who wasn't a monk understand Zen? I didn't dare suggest otherwise and stuck with the tea.

When my companions told him I had just come from Fifth Patriarch Temple and was going to . . . where was it? I volunteered, "To Tachinshan Temple, near Nanchang. It's a nunnery," I said, "the only Zen nunnery in China." Wen-hsi turned to my companions to avoid confronting me directly and said, "He doesn't really understand China, does he." It was a statement, not a question. "China has lots of Zen nunneries."

When I asked him if he had been to any, all he would say was that he was sure there were lots of them. I told him I had met nuns who practiced Zen, but they did so in their rooms or in hermitages in the mountains, not in a community devoted to the practice. But it wasn't a point worth pursuing.

His argumentativeness aside, he expressed himself well—although it seemed as if he was parroting his teachers at the Buddhist academy. When my companions asked about different schools of practice, Wen-hsi said, "It all depends on your mind. If you chant the name of Amitabha, you practice Pure Land. If you meditate on a koan, you practice Zen. When people study Buddhism, they study many kinds of Buddhism. But when they practice, they need to choose one kind. Lots of people nowadays want to practice Zen, but it's hard to find someone who can explain it. You have to experience it before you can talk about it.

"When the Buddha held up a flower, there were five hundred monks present, but only one of them understood his wordless teaching. That was the beginning of Zen. When the Buddha transmitted Zen to Kashyapa, he gave him his robe and bowl as a sign of transmission. And these were transmitted from one generation of disciples to the next until Bodhidharma brought them with him from India. Once they were in China, they were transmitted up to the time of the Sixth Patriarch. After the Sixth Patriarch, there was no need to pass on the robe and bowl anymore because Buddhism had spread everywhere in China. So from that time on, only Dharma certificates were transmitted, not the robe and bowl.

"Zen means meditation," he said. "But it also has another meaning, it also means to become aware, self-aware. And this requires a quiet place, such as a meditation hall, where our delusions gradually fall away as we become more and more aware and we finally give rise to our innate wisdom. This wisdom is our original face, our original nature." Again, it sounded as if he was repeating something from memory. But he was young and sincere, and he served such good tea.

When I told him that I was a translator and that I translated Buddhist texts, he shook his head. He said, "The Buddhist texts we have in China contain the same teaching as that taught by the Buddha. But Western languages are incapable of conveying their profound meaning. And translations into Western languages can't possibly be as rigorous as those put into Chinese over a thousand years ago. Even Chinese monks can't understand everything they read in a sutra. If a Chinese monk has such problems, how can a Westerner, and one who isn't even a monk, possibly understand enough to produce an accurate translation?"

What could I say? I told him that translation was my practice. It wasn't about the words. Finally, he stopped. He decided he had said enough and asked, at last out of politeness, if I had any other questions. I saw my opening and took it. I told him I had come to taste the tea, and having done so, it was time to leave. I thanked him for his hospitality, and we all got up and walked outside. As we were saying goodbye in the courtyard, I congratulated him on his choice of building materials and told him I wished more temples were built as simply. Apparently, he took what I said as a backhanded compliment. He said the buildings and towers were just temporary. He had plans for a much bigger temple, one that would be made of cement instead of wood and stone and whose roofs would be covered with glazed tiles instead of corrugated plastic. I held my tongue one last time, and we headed back to Chiuchiang.

My companions dropped me off at my hotel, and I thanked them for their kindness. The day was so unexpected. Instead of going up to my room, I went to take care of the woes of the road. In one of the lanes behind the hotel, I approached a man sitting in a stairwell next to a sewing machine. It was his after-hours job. I told him I needed a new zipper for my parka, and he installed one in ten minutes. He also sewed up two tears in the fabric and charged me 20RMB, or two-and-a-half bucks. I couldn't imagine traveling without my parka. It was purple and as light as a cloud. It was made in France of Gore-Tex and cost two hundred bucks. It was the most expensive piece of clothing I'd ever owned. It cost more than the suit I got married in. Every time I put it on, I felt ready for adventure. I bought it at a mountaineering store in Taiwan in the spring of 1991 with money I got from Winston Wong.

Two years earlier, I was interviewing Winston for my weekly radio program at ICRT, the English-language radio station in Taiwan. Every week I interviewed someone in the news who could speak English, and Winston was in the news. He was the eldest son of Y. C. Wong, and his father had given him control of Nanya Plastics, the biggest private employer in Taiwan and one of the world's biggest producers of plastics. At the end of the interview, I asked him if he had ever seen the movie *The Graduate*. He said, "Of course." So I asked him what advice he would offer a graduate today. Without pausing to think, he said, "I would tell them to follow the Tao." I was impressed with his remark and also with his candor during the interview. He had a really quick mind. Afterwards, I turned off the tape recorder and we chatted for a while, and I told him that was one of the last interviews I would be doing. I had applied to the Guggenheim Foundation for a grant to search for hermits in China, and I was expecting the award letter the following week. Again, without pausing, he said, "That's a great idea. If they don't give you the money, I will." And he did.

Two years later, shortly after I sent the manuscript about my encounters with hermits in China to the publisher, I phoned him again. I told him I had another idea, and it was even better. I wanted to explore the origins of Chinese culture by traveling from the mouth of the Yellow River to its source on the Tibetan Plateau. When he asked how much I needed, and I told him, his only question was whether I wanted that in cash or traveler's checks. His secretary, he said, would take it out of petty cash. Who needed the Guggenheim? Even in swirling snow at fourteen thousand feet, that parka kept me warm, and I was glad to have it back in good shape again ready for the next time the weather changed.

With my attire cared for, I moved on to the attiree. I had been to Chiuchiang before and knew where to go, approximately, which was back across the street from the hotel and down a lane. But which lane? It took a few tries, but once I spotted the appropriate sign, I followed it down an alley, then turned down an even smaller alley, and finally walked up a pitch-dark metal staircase—which was more of a fire escape. At the top of the landing, I pushed open a makeshift door and walked into a room almost as dark as the landing outside. As my eyes began to adjust to the light, I could see a woman sitting on a couch. She got up and led me into the next room, where I hung up my purple parka and lay down on a table covered with a sheet and waited. A minute later, a blind masseuse felt his way in and made all the bad roads and hard beds go away. It had been two weeks since my last massage.

Afterwards, I retraced my way back to the main street and stopped somewhere for dinner. It was sufficiently unnoteworthy that I erased all memory of it. Before returning to the hotel, I decided to check my e-mail once more. I had one message. It was from my friend Nic Gould in Taiwan. Nic and I were once the local news team at ICRT. Nic married an intern whose father was a member of Taiwan's Paiwan tribe and whose mother was Chinese. And Mike Ryan, the station's music producer, married her sister, so Nic and Mike were brothers-in-law.

Life was good in those days, those days being the eighties. We all made more money than we knew how to spend and enjoyed such benefits as business-class plane tickets anywhere in the world once a year for ourselves and our families. But times changed. The Taiwanese finally gained control of the government from the Mainland Chinese and eventually asserted their control over what was once a U.S. Armed Forces radio station by replacing all but a handful of foreigners.

I followed the station's American boss to Hong Kong and became a flash-in-the-pan radio raconteur for two years, which began with an account of my trip up the Yellow River. Nic stayed in Taiwan and flourished as a promoter of foreign phantasmagoria. But Mike got caught in a syndrome of bad business decisions, depression, alcohol, and fucked-up dreams. And he finally got tired of it. In his e-mail, Nic said Mike committed suicide the day before. He left a note saying, "no job, no money, no hope." He also left an estranged wife and a six-year-old daughter.

I walked back across the street to the hotel. I hadn't had a bath in eight days. A shower was okay for getting clean, but a shower wasn't a bath. A bath washed away more than dust and sweat. It washed away long rides on bad buses. It also washed away the troubles and sorrows I picked up along the way. Afterwards, in my journal that night, I wrote, "Why isn't love enough?"

II NO PEACH BLOSSOMS

I packed up, checked out of the White Deer, and took a taxi to the Chiuchiang bus
station. It was only about ten blocks from the hotel, and I could have walked but my
pack was getting heavy again, and I had a shopping bag full of books and tea. I was
on my way to Nanchang, the provincial capital of Kiangsi, and buses left every half
hour. Mine left ten minutes after I got there, just before eight.

From Chiuchiang, the expressway skirted the west side of Lushan. As usual, the
mountain was veiled. I had visited Lushan many times, but I had only seen it once.
That was on a fall day in 1992. I was passing by Hotspring Village at the foot of the
mountain's southeast corner and stopped briefly to visit the place where the poet T'ao
Yuan-ming (365–427) spent the last half of his life. I went back to the village again
in the spring of 2005, but the mountain was gone. I was there with my friend Tony
Fairbank and hoping to visit T'ao Yuan-ming's grave. It was only two miles from the
village, but it was on a naval firing range, and my previous attempts to gain access had
failed. I failed that time too. One of the villagers told me I was also out of luck if I was
hoping to talk to the poet's last lineal male descendent, as he died the previous week.
While I was wondering what to do next, the man asked me if I had visited the place
where the poet and his friends used to drink. I hadn't and asked him to take us there.

He led us out of the village, past an illegal hot spring hotel that had been closed down, and along a stream into the foothills. He said only farmers used the trail, farmers and water buffaloes and snakes. I can still see him nonchalantly reaching down and picking up a cobra by the tail, then grabbing its head before it could react. He said he could get 50RMB for the snake in Hsingtzu, the nearest town. We told him we would give him the money then and there if he would let it go. He looked at us as if we were touched in the head, then smiled and threw the snake a healthy distance away. It reared up and showed its displeasure before disappearing into the tall grass. We paid him and continued on until we came to some huge boulders next to a small waterfall. He said that was where T'ao Yuan-ming sat with his friends and drained a river of wine on moonlit nights. He wasn't just making that up. The Neo-Confucian poet Chu Hsi (1130–1200) also visited the spot in 1180 and left an inscription on the rock. More than eight hundred years of rain had obliterated most of it, but I could still make out Chu Hsi's name.

It would be hard to name a poet who had a greater influence on Zen than T'ao Yuan-ming. He didn't cultivate any of the practices advocated by organized religions. He simply followed the Tao of simple living and wrote poems that have inspired people ever since to do the same. He summed up the life he chose in his own eulogy, which he wrote just before he died:

The weather is getting colder and the nights longer. The wind moans and sighs. Geese are on the move, and the leaves are falling. Master T'ao is about to depart from this traveler's inn and return forever to his original home. Old friends have come to sympathize, and clan members have gathered tonight. I'm embarrassed by their offerings of fine food and wine. Their faces are growing dark, and their voices faint. Alas, it has come to this! The Earth is so vast, and Heaven is so distant. Of the ten thousand creatures, I was born a human. But my fate was to be a poor one. I have often been short of food and drink and have worn threadbare clothing in winter. And yet I have laughed while carrying water and sung while hauling firewood. Though I have lived in obscurity, I have stayed busy night and day. As the springs and autumns have passed, I have worked in my garden weeding and hoeing, fertilizing and tilling. For pleasure, I have read books. For tranquility, I have played my seven-string zither. I have sat in the sun in winter and bathed in the stream in summer. I have done what needed doing, and my mind has always been at ease. I have been content with the lot I received from Heaven and have lived out my years. Alas, people are in love with their lives. They worry they haven't accomplished enough and begrudge their time here. They value worldly treasures and never stop to think. I only sigh that I have met so few of whom this isn't true. As to this transformation of mine, I have no regrets.

You can't begin to practice Zen if you don't get your life in order. The simpler your life, the easier it is to begin. T'ao Yuan-ming didn't practice Zen, but anyone who did owed him a debt of gratitude for helping clear the trail. Rare was the Zen master who didn't know and admire and quote his poems. And try to find anyone in China who doesn't know his story about Peach Blossom Spring.

T'ao Yuan-ming's drinking rock

It's about a fisherman who tries to find the source of the peach blossoms he sees floating in a stream. He rows his boat upstream as far as he can go, then he walks along the shore and eventually works his way through a cleft in the rocks and comes out into a hidden valley whose inhabitants have been spared the ravages of the past few centuries. After the fisherman returns home and tells others of his discovery, they try to find the opening, but they can't. Since my previous visit, I've learned that some Chinese scholars think the inspiration for T'ao Yuan-ming's story was at the headwaters of the creek where we were standing. I've visited a dozen places in China that claimed to be Peach Blossom Spring, but it never occurred to me that T'ao Yuan-ming's bucolic land of peace and harmony was just upstream from his old drinking rock.

As I passed by the mountain a year later, a poem by Li Pai entitled "Conversation in the Mountains" came to mind:

> You ask why I stay in the mountains
> I smile without speaking, my heart content
> peach blossoms in the stream float into the distance
> there's another realm beyond the world of man.

Lushan's true face was still hidden. In its place, everyone was watching *Tomb Raider* on the TV monitor. I sought refuge in the expressway traffic. As we sped south, we must have passed a dozen tractor-trailers packed with pigs. It was like a migration. They were probably on their way to Nanchang, the same as me, where four million people would be welcoming their arrival. Pork has always been the meat of choice in China. According to archaeologists, the pig was first domesticated from wild boars in North China around seven thousand years ago, and the rise of Chinese civilization was based in large part on its fat and protein. Still, one would have thought their subsequent devotion to Taoism and Buddhism would have inspired more Chinese to follow a vegetarian diet. After all, they've had tofu for nearly 2,200 years. But the Chinese are second only to Americans in their consumption of meat, and every year they consume more than 120 billion pounds of pork, which comes to about 100 pounds per person.

I tried to imagine it: assuming an average weight of 300 pounds per pig (they grow them big in China), it would take 400 million pigs to total 120 billion pounds.

And assuming an average length of five feet, those 400 million pigs lined up snout to tail would have a length of two billion feet, or 380,000 miles, and would circle the Earth's circumference of 25,000 miles fifteen times. I tried to think of it another way. I imagined the Chinese pork consumer as a huge Pac-Man eating its way around the Earth fifteen times in the course of a year. Since fifteen times around the planet was 380,000 miles, dividing that by 365 days in the year, our Chinese Pork-Man would have to travel a bit over 1,000 miles a day and consume pigs at a rate of more than 40 miles or 42,000 pigs per hour, twenty-four hours a day. My imagination shuddered before the thought of it all. I was glad we didn't pass any trucks full of chickens.

It was ten o'clock when we finally pulled off the bad karma expressway and into the Nanchang bus station. Provincial capitals were always good places to get things done. From the bus station, I took a taxi to the post office near the train station, piled up my excess baggage on the appropriate counter, and the clerk boxed everything up. It took about ten minutes to inspect, pack, address, and ship twelve pounds of books and tea. Sending it all home cost 170RMB, or just over twenty bucks.

When I hoisted my pack, my back felt much better. And gone was the shopping bag I'd been lugging around. From the post office, I didn't have to walk more than a hundred yards. Off to one side of the train station was a parking lot full of buses headed for towns inside the province. A bus for Fuchou was waiting with its engine running—and it was the local, which my prospective hosts had instructed me to take. I don't think I spent more than thirty minutes in Nanchang. If someone was on my tail, I gave them the slip—it was a recurring image that had stayed with me since 1989, when it wasn't a fantasy, and when plainclothes police were everywhere.

The Fuchou bus left a few minutes after I boarded, and it left half-empty. But like most buses in China, it picked up more passengers on the way out of town. By the time we were finally beyond the city's blighted outskirts and rolling along on the old highway, there wasn't an empty seat. Still, the bus continued to stop every time someone on the roadside waved. As more people got on, they simply pulled out wooden stools from underneath the seats and sat in the aisle. My memory of empty buses was growing faint.

At some point, a young girl dressed from top to bottom in denim boarded and sat down on a stool next to me. She was also wearing a bracelet and necklace of opalescent pink plastic and a white beret that said, "Smile." She radiated such happiness

I had to look away. I thought she might have been a factory worker going home for a few days and planning to impress her friends with big city fashions. She never stopped singing along to the music videos playing on the TV at the front of the bus. I imagined her memorizing them at night in the factory dormitory. What else was there to do?

Ninety minutes after we left Nanchang, the conductor yelled that it was my stop. We had been rambling through the countryside, and there wasn't anything to suggest a stop except for a couple of small roadside stores. Amazingly, the girl in denim also got off. It was the stop for Tachinshan Temple. As we both watched the bus continue on toward Fuchou (aka Linchuan), I asked her where she was going. I thought maybe she was visiting someone at the temple. But I was wrong. And I was also wrong about my factory dormitory fantasy. She said she lived with her husband near Nanchang. But it was a Saturday, and during the weekends she stayed with her mother-in-law and helped take care of the family's dry goods store. The store was across the highway next to the road that led to the temple.

While I was looking around for local transport, of which there was none, she went into her mother-in-law's store and made a phone call. A minute later, a fifteen-year-old boy drove up on a motorcycle and said he would take me to the temple for 8RMB. The price was steeper than the road. It was less than two miles. But even with my lighter pack, I didn't feel like walking, and I really couldn't refuse the arrangement. I waved goodbye to Smile and headed off on the back of the motorcycle to meet the Zen nuns.

The road was paved, the ride was quick, and both ended in front of the huge new shrine halls of Tachinshan, or Greater Gold Mountain Temple. The walls of all the buildings were oxblood red, the pillars were scarlet, and the roofs were covered with green ceramic tiles. It was a stunning yet subdued look. Along the ridge of the mountain rising behind Tachinshan was the original Chinshan, or Gold Mountain Temple. I learned later that Chinshan had gone through a dozen incarnations since it was first built in the eighth century, and the temple was about as big as it had ever been. But due to its precarious location, it only had room for a hundred nuns, and the abbess had big plans. These new buildings at the foot of the mountain were already home to two hundred more. By the time the expansion is complete, the whole place is expected to house more than a thousand nuns, which would make it two or three times bigger than any monastery in the country. So far the project had cost several million U.S. dollars, with most of that coming from a single donor, the same maker of denim apparel who had financed a number of Ching-hui's projects, including Pailin Temple, one of the biggest monasteries in China. It was Ching-hui who introduced his Hong Kong connection to the abbess, Yin-k'ung.

It was a typical Chinese network. Yin-k'ung's teacher was Pen-huan, the monk who rebuilt Fourth Patriarch Temple, then turned it over to Ching-hui. Pen-huan and Ching-hui were old friends. They were both from Hupei Province, which was always an important consideration. And they had known each other for over fifty years, ever since Ching-hui was Empty Cloud's personal attendant at Yunmen Temple and Empty Cloud asked Pen-huan to take over the abbotship of Nanhua Temple, the Sixth Patriarch's old temple. The two temples were less than thirty miles apart, and monks were always going back and forth. That was how things happened in China. Relationships. Without a relationship, it was hard to do anything. This trip would have been just another fantasy.

While I was walking around one of the buildings, a nun saw me and motioned for me to follow her inside a four-story structure built around a central courtyard. It housed the nunnery's dormitory and classrooms on its upper floors and its kitchen, mess hall, offices, and meeting rooms on the ground floor. She led me into the guest hall and introduced me to the guest manager, Miao-wei. Miao-wei told me to wait while she went to find the temple manager. While she was gone, I struck up a conversation with another nun. Her name was Tun-hui, and she taught calligraphy in the nunnery's Buddhist academy. She was from Beijing, and her first Buddhist teacher, she said, was Ching-hui, which made us dharma kin.

While Tun-hui and I were exchanging family news, Miao-wei returned with the temple manager. Her name was Tun-ch'eng, and she led me into an adjacent room that was completely filled by one very long table with chairs around it for about forty people. The Chinese love meetings and get-togethers, and the nunnery, no doubt, used the room to welcome large groups of lay visitors in a more private setting. We both sat down at one end, and I told her I was gathering material for a book about Zen. When she asked me how she could help, I told her that the practice at the other nunneries I had visited in China was Pure Land Buddhism. I wondered what attracted her and the other nuns to Zen.

She said it was different for everyone, but it always involved karmic connections. She said in her case it was because she was from Kuangtung Province and happened to meet Yin-k'ung in Kuangchou, the provincial capital. She was so impressed with Yin-k'ung, she became a nun, and Yin-k'ung became her teacher. Since Yin-k'ung was a Zen nun, that became her path too. She had been with Yin-k'ung ever since and followed her north in 1985 to help rebuild Chinshan Temple. She had also become Yin-k'ung's dharma heir. I didn't ask how old she was, but I guessed about forty-five.

When I asked if their practice differed at all from that of Zen monasteries, she said it was the same. Everything revolved around meditation, she said. They were still using the meditation hall at Chinshan Temple up on the ridge. But it only had room for eighty nuns, so everyone had to take turns. However, they were building a much larger meditation hall behind the dormitory at Tachinshan, and it would have enough room for two hundred. She said the monks at Chenju Temple on Yunchushan had been acting as their advisors. They had already helped set up the meditation hall on the ridge, and would be doing the same when the new meditation hall was finished. The two communities had become brother and sister Zen temples.

When I asked Tun-ch'eng how much time they spent in the meditation hall, she said all the nuns had to attend at least one meditation period every day regardless of their duties. For those attending the Buddhist academy, that was about all they had time for. But everyone else, except those whose duties required them to be elsewhere, took turns taking part in the remaining periods, which totaled fourteen a day. That was a lot of meditation, but not for a place that billed itself as a Zen nunnery.

Tun-ch'eng said they also conducted a seven-week retreat every winter, from late November to mid-January, timed to end just before the Lunar New Year. All the nuns at the temple, except for the kitchen crew and a few others, were required to attend. Nuns from other temples in China also came to take part. But due to the limited space, everyone had to take turns.

During the retreat, the number of daily meditation periods increased from fourteen to twenty-four, with their length varying from sixty minutes at the beginning of a cycle to forty-five, thirty, and finally twenty minutes. Then the cycle began again. Between sitting periods there was a ten-minute walking meditation, which gave those who needed it a chance to use the restroom. There were also breaks for meals. That left less than four hours for sleep. It was a grueling seven weeks, which was, of course, the idea—wear down the resistance of the delusional self. During the retreat everyone also had a weekly meeting with one of the meditation instructors to assess their progress. And usually once a week, the abbess gave a Dharma talk.

Tun-ch'eng said, "Nuns don't have the strength that monks have in doing physical work. But in the meditation hall, there's no difference. Most nuns prefer the devotional path of Pure Land Buddhism. They chant the name of Amitabha. Not many nuns are willing to give up their reliance on Amitabha and rely on themselves instead. This is why there aren't so many nuns who practice Zen. But this is changing.

"We get a lot of nuns who come here out of curiosity. Most of them have never practiced meditation before, and they sit for a few periods in our meditation hall, then leave. It takes a special person to practice Zen. In addition to meditation, we study sutras, especially the *Diamond Sutra*, the *Vimalakirti Sutra*, and the *Shurangama Sutra*. And we study the teachings of Zen masters of the past.

"Some nuns come here because they know this is a Zen nunnery, and they're ready to practice Zen. Others come for instruction, then become interested in Zen. That's why we established a Buddhist academy. That way, nuns can find out more about Zen before they start spending their days meditating. Everything we do here has to do with Zen. And we put special emphasis on the precepts and the monastic code as well. The code we use is the one developed at Zen monasteries like Chenju Temple on Yunchushan. We follow the same rules."

When I asked her how she gauged the level of understanding among the students, she said, "There's no one way of determining how much someone understands. But we can usually tell when we give them a task they've never done before. Someone whose practice is good isn't easily upset when things go wrong. Someone who doesn't practice or who doesn't practice correctly is constantly upset. Just because you sit in the meditation hall doesn't mean you're making progress. This is why we watch and listen to the nuns who study and practice here to decide how best to help them. Some of them understand right away. Others seem to take forever. In any case, we tell them to be patient. Zen isn't for people in a hurry."

She said, "Nowadays, most of the people attracted to Zen are intellectuals, people with an education. We're seeing more and more nuns and laywomen who have been to college." When I asked if it wasn't a contradiction for educated people to be practicing Zen when the intellect posed such an obstruction to understanding, she said, "No, the level of education doesn't seem to matter in practicing Zen. But it does make a difference as to who wants to practice. Educated people are more likely to want to practice Zen instead of Pure Land.

"In any case, once people start practicing, everyone needs to study texts at some point, and the disciples of many Zen masters have recorded their teacher's words. We encourage the nuns to read those kinds of texts. But words are only used to direct people to their own minds. Our focus is on the mind, not on words. If people read books and think they're enlightened, we say they're walking blind. My favorite text is the Sixth Patriarch's *Platform Sutra*. It was the first Buddhist text that made sense to me. But reading texts is no substitute for meditation and practicing Zen. If you read a book about a place, and you want to go there, you don't keep reading the book. You have to travel. That's what practice is about. Traveling. Walking the path."

I asked her if she knew of any other Zen nunnery in China. Tachinshan was the only place I'd heard about, and that only recently. She said she had heard there was a group of nuns practicing Zen on Mopanshan near the North Korean border, but she wasn't too clear whether it was the whole nunnery or just a group of nuns within the nunnery. That was the only other place she had heard about.

When I asked her if I could meet Yin-k'ung, she said the abbess was in Fuchou for the day and she wasn't sure when she would be back. Instead of letting the matter drop, she took out her cell phone and called her. During the ensuing conversation, Yin-k'ung asked Tun-ch'eng to arrange accommodations so that we could meet later that evening after she got back. Just then a large group of laywomen arrived, and the commotion outside put an end to our conversation. But before sending me off to my room, Tun-ch'eng gave me a brochure about Yin-k'ung and also went and got her own copy of a book about Zen Buddhist nuns in China and gave it to me.

Buddhist nuns had been so overlooked by those who compiled religious histories, finding anything in print was rare. The book she gave me was titled *Ch'an-lin chu-chi pi-ch'iu-ni*: "Bikhuni Pearls of the Zen Forest," and it contained the biographies of twelve nuns, seven of whom lived during the Ch'ing dynasty (1644–1911). It was published in Taiwan in 1994, but I had never seen it there. The book was probably already out of print, and I only accepted it when she assured me that she had another copy.

Tun-ch'eng then led me back into the guest hall and turned me over again to Miao-wei, who led me to the temple's reception room for distinguished guests. It was a huge room full of desks and tables and sofas and armchairs. Off to one side there were two beds, and there was a bathroom with a shower. It wasn't exactly what I was expecting, but it was a place to spend the night. Obviously, they didn't get many male visitors. Perhaps a building for male guests—outside the nunnery wall—was somewhere in the expansion plans.

I tried out the bed, and it seemed to work, at least for a nap. Afterwards, I made a cup of coffee and began reading the book Tun-ch'eng had given me. It began with an account about a nun named Mo-shan, but I didn't get past the first page. Someone knocked on my door. It was Miao-wei and another nun. They said Tun-ch'eng had asked them to take me to Chinshan Temple on the ridge above Tachinshan. The

Trail to Chinshan Temple

coffee wasn't that good anyway. The water in the reception room thermoses was only lukewarm. I followed my guides along the courtyard corridor and through the door at the rear of the building, which was the only entrance into the compound. The building had clearly been designed to limit access.

Once outside, we walked past the construction site for the new meditation hall. As we did, I paused. I looked at the dirt. It was the color of burnt sienna and moist from a recent rain. The clay content was sufficiently high that it squished under my shoe. It was perfect. I reached into my shoulder bag and took out a Ziploc bag I had prepared for such an occasion and filled it with a couple of pounds of squishy mud. An artist friend had asked me to collect exactly that kind of soil from an appropriate site in China. She was putting dirt from different places of the world into her baths and photographing the residue. The higher the clay content, she said, the better. And what site could be more appropriate, I thought, than the foundation of a Zen nunnery's meditation hall. I didn't ask questions. I gave friends a lot of leeway, especially artist friends. The nuns looked at me as if I was crazy, but they didn't say anything.

Just past the future meditation hall, we started up the trail of stone steps that led to the ridge. It was a good hike up a mountain of bamboo and pine, and we had to pause a few times to catch our breaths. We also had to step aside several times to let nuns pass who were coming down the trail. They had their carrying sticks with them for hauling provisions back up. Living on the ridge may have looked idyllic, but there was a lot of work involved.

It took us about ten minutes to reach the top. Once we did, my guides led me past a series of buildings perched along the edge. The structures were strung out in layers, the result of disparate building projects over the past twenty years. Squeezed in between them were several shrines to local deities. Seeing them there reminded me that mountains have always been sacred in China. Chinshan was the only mountain around for miles, and people must have been coming to its summit to commune with spiritual forces long before the first Buddhists arrived. No doubt the gods they called upon had changed names a few times, but they were still there.

Eventually we wound our way to the guest hall and went inside. A few minutes later, we were joined by the guest manager and the chief meditation instructor, a nun named Tao-wu. The guest manager said the place was nothing but rubble when the local authorities asked Yin-k'ung to return to rebuild it in 1985. All traces of the temple's previous incarnations had been obliterated by the Red Guards. Once

Yin-k'ung returned, one new structure had followed another, until the buildings occupied most of the ridge. The idea of living in such a setting, on the edge of the wind, must have appealed to Yin-k'ung and her disciples at first. But it didn't work for a large community. So the plan, the nuns said, was for everyone to move down to Tachinshan and for those who preferred a more secluded place to live at Chinshan.

While we were talking, Tao-wu asked me if I wanted to see the meditation hall. Usually I had to ask at a monastery, and I wasn't always allowed, as access to that part of any monastery was restricted. But the nuns were clearly proud of theirs. Naturally, I agreed, and she led me outside and through a series of archways and courtyards and finally into an octagonal four-story building. The meditation hall was on the second floor.

I walked inside and circled the sitting area. It didn't look any different from the meditation halls I had seen in monasteries. The board used to summon nuns to meditation looked exactly like the ones used in meditation halls belonging to the Linchi School of Zen—rectangular with its top corners lopped off. When I asked

Chinshan Temple meditation hall

Tao-wu about that, she said the abbess was a forty-fifth-generation dharma heir of Lin-chi, which gave her the right to use the board. That was the only real difference, as far as I could tell, between the various schools of Zen in China: different boards.

From the meditation hall, Tao-wu led me up the steps to the next floor, which was a shrine hall for chanting and was designed around a reclining buddha. Reclining buddhas weren't that common in China, because a reclining buddha represented the Buddha as he entered Nirvana. Thus, it reminded some people of death, and some might have considered it *pu-chi-hsiang*: "inauspicious." But the nuns of Chinshan Temple had no such qualms. That was, after all, why they were there: to confront the suffering inherent in life and death. This was the hall where laypeople came for memorial services. For 60RMB per year, laypeople could also keep their names or those of their loved ones affixed to the wall on paper strips so that they could share the merit accruing from the daily services. Red was for lengthening a person's years, yellow for improving the rebirth of a loved one. There were several hundred of each color.

We continued to the top floor and yet another shrine hall. But this one was different from any I'd seen elsewhere. Its walls were lined with niches filled with foot-high wooden buddha statues. They were gilded, and there were a thousand of them. It was very impressive, but it wasn't unusual; the unusual part was in the middle of the hall. Hanging from the ceiling were huge gilded chandeliers of intricate design that held a galaxy of lights. It must have looked like a planetarium at night. Below the universe of light were four large, gilded, wooden buddhas. They were about twelve feet in height, and they were seated on wooden lotus thrones. What was unusual was that the thrones were designed to rotate. Unfortunately, the mechanism was broken. It was a wonderful idea that must have looked good on paper. But it didn't work, even for buddhas.

The day was getting late, and I thanked Tao-wu for showing me around and headed back down with my two guides. We arrived just in time for dinner. I was about to enter the mess hall, but my guides directed me instead into a dining room for guests. On the room's lone table someone had laid out seven or eight plates of some of my favorite vegetarian food, including stewed potatoes, fried wheat gluten, and dried tofu with black mushrooms. It was a feast. And I was the only guest. While I was eating, one of the cooks came in and asked me if the food was okay and urged me to eat more. She was about seventy, and despite her near-total lack of teeth she had the most infectious smile. I apologized for not being able to eat as much as she thought I should. I considered dumping the mud I had collected earlier and replacing it with leftovers. But when would I eat them? I was too well cared for to need leftovers. So I kept the mud.

Afterwards, I returned to my room and took a shower. As I was writing in my journal, there was another knock. One of the nuns yelled through the door that the abbess was back. I dressed and was ushered into the set of rooms on the first floor where Yin-k'ung lived. She was eighty-five and quite short, but she was a dynamo and the linchpin of the place. Everything revolved around her. And she clearly enjoyed watching her Zen solar system. She asked me to sit down in the chair next to hers. The room swirled around us as we talked. There were a dozen other nuns in the room chatting and laughing, watching a Buddhist ceremony on TV, eating snacks, coming and going. It was more like a clubhouse than an abbess's private reception room.

Although Yin-k'ung wasn't reluctant to talk, I had a hard time understanding her. She spoke in the Kiangsi dialect of the Kan River watershed, the watershed where *Ch'an* was still pronounced *Zen*. The brochure Tun-ch'eng had given me earlier supplied an outline of Yin-k'ung's life, so I didn't have to ask about that. She was born in 1921, just down the road from Tachinshan, and she decided to become a nun when she was nineteen. The monk who shaved her head was Pen-huan, who was living at Paoen Temple in Hsinchou, northeast of Wuhan, at the time.

The following year Yin-k'ung returned to the Fuchou area to raise funds to rebuild Chinshan, which was a remarkable undertaking considering that she did this in the middle of the Second World War. It took her six years, but by 1947 she had completed a set of buildings big enough to house sixty nuns. In the wake of "Liberation" and with the advent of Communism, she organized the temple's nuns into a textile production unit. Everyone chanted the name of Amitabha while they wove cloth. But as Buddhist groups began to confront their new government's aversion to religious practice, Yin-k'ung looked for advice on what to do next.

In 1955, she traveled to Yunchushan, sixty miles northwest of Nanchang, and asked Empty Cloud for advice. The old Zen master was 116 at the time and still recovering from the beating he received several years earlier at the hands of Communist cadres at Yunmen Temple. He had begun sending senior disciples to other countries and remote places in China to weather the coming storm. After Yin-k'ung returned to Chinshan, Empty Cloud wrote and told her to go stay with Pen-huan in Kuangtung Province. She did as he suggested, and she later became Pen-huan's dharma heir.

During that time, Chinshan was destroyed by the Red Guards, and her fellow nuns were forced to return to lay life and undergo reeducation. Yin-k'ung refused to give up her practice, and in 1985, with the members of the Gang of Four in prison or dead and the principle of religious freedom once more affirmed by the central government, the authorities in Fuchou asked her to come back and rebuild Chinshan. By that time there was only one small building at the summit with room for three or four nuns. It took her eight years, but she more than accomplished her goal of restoring the temple to its T'ang-dynasty glory—far outdoing her earlier efforts at rebuilding the temple during the Second World War. After that, she decided to build a Buddhist academy to train all the nuns who were arriving. It opened in 1994. Three years later, she also built a meditation hall for nuns. And in 1999, she began holding meditation retreats during the winter.

As the number of nuns increased, Yin-k'ung decided to move her community down the mountain and began construction of Tachinshan. She said she was also building a retreat center on Chiufengshan, or Nine Peak Mountain, where the Zen nun Mo-shan once lived. It was ninety miles southwest of Nanchang, in Shangkao County. Yin-k'ung said it would operate on the same model as Yunchushan's Chenju Temple. The plan, she said, was for nuns to go to Chiufengshan for several years of practical training after they studied three to nine years at Tachinshan's Buddhist academy. It wasn't just Marx who combined theory and practice. It was Bodhidharma's teaching too.

Yin-k'ung said the retreat center on Chiufengshan, like Yunchushan's Chenju Temple and Zen centers of the past, was being built where there was enough land to support the nuns who lived there. She said, "Living in a place like that, where you can support yourself with your own effort, is important. Zen involves training the body as well as the mind. Zen is about everyday living. That sort of training takes time. You can't accomplish much in a few days or a few weeks. It takes years. It takes a lifetime. It takes patience. People who aren't patient can't practice Zen. People who aren't patient give up and go back to Pure Land practice and chant the name of Amitabha. It takes great determination to practice Zen. It's not something everyone is ready for."

She said, "Pure Land practice is like Christianity. It's devotional. Zen is different. Zen is self-reliant. It depends on you." Then she told me my tea was getting cold and if I didn't drink it, I wouldn't know how it tasted. I took a sip and realized it was late. I thanked her and went back to my room, where I finally had a chance to read about the nun who had inspired Yin-k'ung and the hundreds of other nuns living at Chinshan and Tachinshan, and probably those up there on the Korean border too.

Her name was Mo-shan Liao-jan, and she lived in the latter half of the ninth century. She was from Kao-an, thirty-five miles southwest of Nanchang, and she studied with Ta-yu, the Big Fool, on Big Fool Mountain just outside her hometown. She became Ta-yu's dharma heir, and eventually built her own hermitage on Chiufengshan, fifty miles southwest of Kao-an. Chiufengshan was also called Moshan, and that was where she got the name most people still knew her by. She was a forceful teacher, like Yin-k'ung. Before long she gathered five hundred disciples around her, and her hermitage became a major nunnery.

Her reputation finally aroused the interest of a dharma heir of one of Lin-chi's students. His name was Kuan-hsi Chih-hsien (d. 895), and he decided to find out for himself what kind of teacher she was. After arriving at her temple, he stood outside and yelled,

"If your meditation hall suits me, I'll stay, if not, I'll knock it down." Then he walked inside.

Mo-shan's attendant asked him, "Did the venerable master come for the scenery or for the Dharma?"

Chih-hsien said, "I've come for the Dharma."

Mo-shan then walked over to the chair reserved for Dharma talks. After sitting down, she asked, "Where has the venerable master come from?"

Chih-hsien said, "From where the road began."

Mo-shan said, "Why don't you go back?"

Chih-hsien made no response and bowed. Then he asked, "What is it like on Moshan?"

Mo-shan said, "The peak isn't visible."

Chih-hsien said, "Who's in charge of Moshan?"

Mo-shan said, "Neither man nor woman."

Chih-hsien scoffed, "Why don't you change into something?" [Ed: This is a reference to a female deity in chapter seven of the *Vimalakirti Sutra* who changes her gender and form in order to teach Shariputra the illusory nature of such attributes.]

Mo-shan said, "I'm not some kind of spirit or ghost. What could I possibly change into?"

Chih-hsien finally admitted he had met his match, and he stayed there and worked in the garden for three years. Later on, he told his own disciples, "I received half a ration from Old Man Lin-chi and another half from Old Lady Mo-shan. I put the two together in my bowl and haven't been hungry since."

I, too, went to sleep with a full belly.

12 NO EAST OR WEST

I woke up in a nunnery to the sound of the breakfast board. I don't usually eat break-fast when I'm traveling—it slows me down. I opted, instead, for a cup of coffee in bed. The nuns had refilled one of the thermoses in the room. But there was a knock on my door again. The nun on the other side said, "Your breakfast is ready." If it had just been "breakfast," I could have declined, and would have. But it was "my" break-fast. I had no choice. I got dressed and returned to the scene of the previous night's meal in the dining room reserved for guests.

My breakfast was waiting: a large bowl of hot millet gruel, a plate of stir-fried mustard greens with red peppers, and a big steamed bun. It was far more than I was prepared to eat. But the ever-smiling kitchen bodhisattva kept checking to make sure I had enough, and I had no choice but to eat it all. Afterwards, I went back to my room and lay down and took a nap, which reminded me why I didn't eat break-fast on the road but also what a privileged life I was living—the morning nap being the prerogative of those who had successfully dodged the ranks of the more-or-less employed.

It was nine o'clock by the time I finally got up, packed my bag, and went to the guest hall to announce my departure. When I told Miao-wei I was leaving, she called

Yin-k'ung, and the old master appeared a few minutes later. She asked me to stay longer. And she meant it. But I told her I had to leave, that I was on a mission. I said I would be back, and I wanted to visit the retreat center she was building on Moshan. She told me not to wait too long. The way she said it sounded like, "While we're both still alive." Then she said, "Let's take a picture together in front of Kuan-yin"—the Bodhisattva of Compassion, the Goddess of Mercy, the female face of Buddhism in China. Usually I had to ask for a photo, and I was always reluctant to do so. But Yin-k'ung was the kind of person who preferred to initiate action rather than wait for it to happen. She grabbed my arm, and we walked together out the back door of the compound and down to the bottom of the steps that led to the main shrine hall.

While we were walking, I told her I was surprised that the land around the mountain and all the way out to the highway was uncultivated and wondered if there were wild animals. She said there were still tigers on the mountain when she returned in 1985. The South China Tiger was the species from which all other tigers evolved. It was smaller than other tigers but bigger and more dangerous than a wolf. She said the tigers were all gone now, but there were still boar, and they were more dangerous than tigers. They foraged in packs.

When I asked why there weren't any farms, she said it was because the local authorities had agreed to set aside all the land around the mountain to provide the nunnery with as much seclusion as possible. I could imagine her meeting with local officials. And I could not imagine any of them telling her "no." She was on a mission too. As we finally reached the bottom of the steps, one of her attendants took our photo with my camera. Then I took one of Yin-k'ung by herself. Right on cue, the nunnery truck pulled up, and I got in. I waved goodbye, and Yin-k'ung kept waving back until I was out of sight.

The truck dropped me off on the highway and continued on to Fuchou for provisions. I thought about going over to the dry goods store and thanking Smile for arranging my ride to the nunnery the previous day. But I decided it would only result in an invitation to stay for lunch. I was still full from breakfast and had a long way to go. There was no shortage of buses passing by, and I stuck out my arm. But it was Sunday, and everyone was going somewhere. The buses were packed.

Until modern times, there was no such thing as a "workweek" in China, at least not for most people. People worked every day, except during the Lunar New Year and one or two other holidays. Only officials got a day off, and those occurred every ten days. The seven-day week didn't appear in China until the beginning of the Republic in 1912. I'm not sure when people started taking one of those seven days off. It probably began when someone complained that the Christian convert down the alley wasn't working on Sunday, so why should they? As for taking Saturday off as well, that didn't begin until the government promulgated a law to that effect in 1995. Of course, many workers were still required to work on weekends to maintain production schedules or public services. Theoretically, though, everyone had a two-day weekend. And they filled the buses that ignored my outstretched arm. I waved anyway.

Finally a bus stopped that was as packed as any bus could be and still manage to open its door. What the hell, I thought. A ride is a ride. I prepared for ninety

Master Yin-k'ung in front of Tachinshan Temple

minutes as a sardine. But as soon as I got on, the conductor turned and told a young girl to get up and give me her seat. I was surprised, and I protested—but too feebly to do any good. Of course, I was glad to sit down, but I wondered if it was because I was a foreigner or if it was because of my beard and gray hair. The Chinese still respected the elderly, especially in the countryside. While I was wondering about this, the young girl told the driver to stop, and she got off. So it was simply that the conductor knew that she had almost reached her stop. I felt much better, and younger too.

It didn't even bother me when the bus broke down. I had a seat. No one else seemed bothered either. Half the people on the bus had cell phones, and they used the break to check in with friends. There were so many people talking at once, it sounded as if we were all in the same phone booth. Meanwhile, the driver opened up the engine cowling and decided there was something wrong with the fuel line. Then he sorted through a bunch of metal tubing he kept behind his seat. Apparently there was a design flaw, and he was ready for it. When he found a length he liked, he bent down and replaced the defective section. When he fired up the engine again, gas spurted everywhere. He calmly bent down and tightened the nut that connected the line to the engine, closed the cowling, and off we went.

Almost all roads of any significance in China were toll roads, and I had been on thousands. But as we approached one tollgate, the driver introduced me to a new twist. He stopped a hundred yards short of the gate and told all the people sitting on benches in the aisle to get off the bus and walk a hundred yards past the gate. We then proceeded through and waited for the bench-sitters to walk down the road and retake their seats. Apparently, the officials at that particular tollgate were actually enforcing a law about passenger limits on buses. Strange but true.

Even with the breakdown and the tollgate delay, it took less than two hours to reach the Nanchang train station, from which I had departed the previous morning. From there, I took a taxi to the long-distance bus station and bought a ticket on the next bus to Wuhan, the capital of Hupei Province. Wuhan was one of the biggest cities in China, and I was headed there fifteen minutes later.

Once more I left whoever might have been following me to explain to their superiors how I had given them the slip. The driver hit the gas, and we were gone. A lot of people in China still weren't used to the speeds that the new roads made possible—that and the constant switching of lanes. A woman sitting behind me got sick as soon as we were on the expressway. Many buses, I noticed, now had barf bags in the pocket behind each seat in anticipation.

We drove north for two hours and past the invisible mountain of Lushan, and I sat through another rerun of *Tomb Raider*. As soon as we crossed the Yangtze, we turned west. A few miles later, the driver made his only concession to passenger needs and stopped at the same travel center where I had nearly ruptured myself the week before trying to climb over the guardrail. While we were waiting to reboard, I noticed a column of geese overhead, flying back north. Summer was just ahead.

Four hours later, we began to arrive. Wuhan was a city where one never really arrived, because it wasn't one city but three: Wuchang was on the south shore of the Yangtze, and Hanyang and Hankou faced each other on opposite sides of the Han River on the north shore. We began dropping off passengers in Wuchang. Then we crossed the Yangtze again, this time on the city's new Number Two Bridge, and continued dropping off passengers in Hankou. I got off a block from the Hankou Holiday Inn and started looking for something within my budget.

I flagged down a taxi and asked the driver to take me to a three-star hotel, which was my usual price range. The first place he took me to had rooms for 230RMB, but not with bathtubs. The second one was 350RMB for a standard room, which was too much for too little. And the third one turned out to be a brothel. I went back to number two, the Hsunlimen, and tried to get them to lower the price. It was Sunday, and weekend rates were always higher. They finally came down to 270RMB, or thirty-five bucks, for a deluxe, which was a good deal. I felt like I needed a deluxe after the long ride. As a gesture of appreciation, I told them to keep the breakfast coupon.

After dropping off my bag in the room, I walked back outside. It had been a while since I had seen so many lights. The city was so dazzling I sought refuge in a nearby alley and found a place that served a decent plate of fried noodles. That was enough nightlife for me. I went back to my room and ended the day with a long soak and a washing of the clothes—both sets. Before I went to sleep, I made a few notes in my journal, including one whose origin remains a mystery to me: "Watersheds, phonemes, and dharmas, they all depend on disharmony, the flux of high and low, without which," I wrote, "nothing flows, not even the Tao." It was a long bus ride. I also wrote: "If I have to watch *Tomb Raider* again, I'll barf."

When I woke up the next morning, it wasn't to the sound of a nun at my door but the hotel maid vacuuming down the hall. I was once more in the world of red dust. I got up, made a cup of coffee, and looked at my itinerary. I suddenly realized I was five days ahead of the schedule I had drawn up six months earlier. I deserved a day off.

Instead of checking out and heading for my next destination, I went down to the front desk and told the receptionist I would be staying another night. Then I asked directions to the nearest ticket office. She said there was one a few blocks away on Liberation Road. I had seen similar offices in other major cities, like Shanghai and Beijing, and was grateful that Wuhan also had them. In the past a person had to go to the train station to buy a ticket for the train—or to a travel agency that then sent someone to the station. But these small private ticket offices were now selling plane and train tickets directly—all made possible by the computer and the opening up of the travel industry. There wasn't even a line. In less than two minutes, I was able to buy a hard-seat ticket to Tangyang for the next morning. And since I had to return to Wuhan and head south three days later, I also bought a soft-sleeper ticket to Shaokuan, where I hoped to meet the final Zen patriarch on my itinerary. I felt relieved. Trying to buy tickets at the train station was always traumatic, and getting soft-sleeper tickets was impossible.

Having taken care of travel arrangements for the next three days in the blink of an eye, I felt so light-headed, I stopped in a liquor store and bought a bottle of wild grape wine fermented with mountain honey. Unfortunately, wild grapes, I learned later at bathtime, don't have a high sugar content, and that particular bottle (I should have looked) only managed 5 percent alcohol—even with the honey. The label said it was made from wild grapes picked in the "deep forests" of the Changpai Mountains, which were up on the Korean border where that group of nuns was meditating.

According to recent archaeological discoveries in Central China, the ancestors of the Chinese were making wine from grapes as early as anyone, maybe earlier. Traces of fermented grape wine have been found in nine-thousand-year-old pottery jars at Chiahu in Honan's Wuyang County. Also unearthed at the same site were the world's earliest known musical instruments: some very fine bone flutes. Music, wine, and domesticated wild boar; civilization was just a building permit away.

Strangely, grape wine disappeared from the Chinese diet during Neolithic times and didn't reappear until it was reintroduced via the Silk Road around two thousand years ago. Even then, it didn't make much of an impact. The Chinese have always preferred much stronger stuff made from grain. Not all discoveries are fully appreciated in their time.

I went back to my hotel room, dropped off the wine, and considered how to squander the day. My itinerary didn't include days off, and I suppose I should keep that in mind in the future. But days off are hard to schedule. They can only be taken when the stars align, which was why my earlier attempt to take one in Chiuchiang had failed. This time I decided to do something simple, something that required no effort. I even decided to visit a place I had visited before, a place that had nothing to do with Zen. It was in Hanyang across the Han River from Hankou, only five minutes by taxi from my hotel. The place was inside a park near the Hanyang train station. At the far end of the park there was a small hill, and on top of the hill there was a marker that said *Ku Cheng T'ai*: "Ancient Zither Terrace." That was the place.

I paid the park entrance fee and walked up the steps to the terrace. It was a windy day, and the leaves that had managed to hang on all winter were finally letting go to make room for summer. They were swirling around me, and it was a fine sunny day. There was a memorial hall on the terrace, and the man in charge had set up a zither on a table outside where for 2RMB people could have their photo taken. I sat down

Author playing "High Mountain" at Hanyang's Ancient Zither Terrace

on the bench before the instrument, and he arranged my fingers on the strings. He told me I was playing "High Mountain." And that was what I did on my day off. I played "High Mountain."

It was an old tune first played on that very terrace 2,300 years earlier by a man named Yu Po-ya. If you were Chinese, you would know the name. Yu Po-ya was a famous zither player. On that hill overlooking the confluence of the Han River and the Yangtze, he played his zither whenever the weather permitted. He preferred to play alone because he had never met anyone whom he felt understood the tunes he played. Then one day a man gathering firewood on the hill paused to listen. When Yu Po-ya finished, the man sighed that he had never heard such music.

Yu Po-ya was surprised that a firewood gatherer could appreciate something so subtle, and he decided to test the man. He played a piece he had composed called "High Mountain," and he asked the man what he heard. The man said he heard the soaring peaks of Taishan. Yu Po-ya was stunned. He retuned his zither and tried another composition called "Flowing Water." Again he asked the man what he heard. The man said he heard the surging current of the Yangtze. That was too much for Yu Po-ya. He had finally met someone who felt what he felt, and the two became fast friends. In fact, to this day, the Chinese say the most intimate of friends, the truest of friends, is a *chih-yin-chih-yu*, a "friend who knows your tune," referring to the firewood gatherer, whose name was Chung Tzu-ch'i.

But that wasn't the end of the story. Due to his fame, Yu Po-ya was invited to serve as an official in North China, and he left Hanyang. But as the years passed, he became homesick, and he missed his friend. Finally, he quit his post and returned to Hanyang. When he got back, he learned that Chung Tzu-ch'i had died. He went to visit his friend's grave and was so overcome with grief he smashed his zither and never played again. He didn't think there was anyone else worth playing for.

I had been to Zither Terrace four or five times, but I had never visited Chung Tzu-ch'i's grave. It wasn't because I hadn't tried. I had never met anyone who knew where it was. I had seen an old map of Hanyang once with an arrow pointing toward his grave. It pointed to the west, but off the map. The last time I was there, the custodian at the park entrance told me the grave had been demolished during the construction of apartment buildings five years earlier. I was too late, she said.

After the man took my picture, he led me inside. The place was as much a store as it was a memorial hall. There was a counter on one side where he sold soft drinks and books. Off to the other side, another man was sitting at a table on which several zithers were displayed. The man in charge of the hall introduced me. The other man's surname was Wu, and he used to be in charge of the place, but he had retired. After all these years, I finally got the story straight.

First, he said their names were Po Ya and Chung Ch'i, not Yu Po-ya and Chung Tzu-ch'i. The names were changed by the author of the *Chingshihtungyen* (1624). He was the one who added the surname *Yu* and the honorific *tz'u*. And Chung Ch'i may have gathered a bit of firewood in his day, but members of his family had been court musicians for three generations, and he was a skilled musician himself. Mr. Wu likened him to Beethoven. But the two men did indeed meet on that terrace in the year 278 BC.

Mr. Wu said his information was from a detailed history of the Wuhan area based on local records, some of which had only recently been unearthed. He showed me the book. There was another copy for sale at his friend's side of the hall, but it was too big to lug around, so I simply read the relevant sections and made notes in my journal.

Mr. Wu said he made his living, or at least kept himself busy, selling replicas of famous zithers of the past. They all had names, like Bell Ringer, Ceiling Circler, Green Beauty, and Burnt Tail. He told me the stories associated with each of them. Burnt Tail, for example, was made by a Han-dynasty zither master from a plank of paulownia wood that he pulled out of a fire. Mr. Wu said he made his replicas from wood he got from ancient buildings that had been torn down, and all the zithers on display were made from wood at least two thousand years old. He sold them for 4,600RMB, or less than six hundred dollars. I would have bought one then and there if I had really known how to play "High Mountain" instead of just pretending.

In the course of conversation, I mentioned to Mr. Wu that I wished I had come earlier so that I could have visited Chung Ch'i's grave. He asked me what I meant, and I told him what the custodian at the entrance had told me on my previous visit. He said she was wrong. The grave was still there, and he even offered to take me there the next day. When I told him I had to leave the next day, he wrote down the location on a piece of paper and told me to show it to a taxi driver. I thanked him profusely and floated out of the hall on the swirling wind.

On my way out, I stopped to buy a map of the Wuhan area, just in case. It turned out the lady selling maps also knew about the grave. She had even been there once when Chung Ch'i's descendents came to Wuhan to pay their respects, which they did, she said, every year. It's funny how I didn't seem surprised that a man who lived 2,300 years ago was still being honored by his descendents. It was China. And who wouldn't want to honor an ancestor who was one of their country's heroes, a hero whose great accomplishment was to understand what was in someone else's heart.

A taxi was waiting at the curb, and I got in and showed the driver the slip of paper with the location Mr. Wu had written down. He had never heard of the place, and the map didn't help either. Finally, he called his dispatcher. A few minutes later, the dispatcher called back with directions, and off we went on the old highway leading west from Hanyang. About thirty minutes later, where the highway passed north of a lone mountain, we turned toward it and followed a tunnel straight through Ma-an-shan, or Saddle Mountain. It wasn't very big, and the tunnel soon brought us out on its south side. Just past the tunnel exit, we stopped and asked a farmer for directions, and he pointed to a dirt road that ran east, parallel to the mountain. We followed the dirt road, and less than two hundred yards later a small pavilion came into view.

The driver parked, and I walked along a dirt trail that led past a grove of peach trees in bloom and the edge of a pond and the stream that fed it to the pavilion. Below its small roof, some government agency had erected a commemorative stele in 1983 that recorded the story Mr. Wu had recounted at Zither Terrace. Just past the pavilion was the grave mound. It was obscured by a year's worth of weeds, but Chung Ch'i's name was clearly visible on the tombstone. Grave Sweeping Day was still ten days away—usually it fell on the fifth of April. That was the day Chinese visited their ancestral graves and cleared away the weeds that had grown up since their last visit. I presumed that would be when Chung Ch'i's descendents would make their annual pilgrimage.

Having finally found the grave, I bowed to Chung Ch'i and Po Ya and the trans-mission of understanding that takes place between one person and another. So my day off was about Zen after all. After paying my respects, I walked back and sat down on the bench below the pavilion and listened to the water flowing by and the wind coming off the mountain. While I was sitting there, I watched a man and a young boy walk toward the grave, but from the other side. There must have been another road closer to the mountain. As they stood in front of the weed-covered mound, the man showed the boy how to hold his hands and how to bow. He bowed three times, and the boy followed his lead. Afterwards, they walked back the way they had come, and I did the same.

As I walked through the grove of peach trees, I surprised a pheasant and turned to watch it fly toward the mountain. When I reached the dirt road again, a farmer was talking to my driver. He said from the top of the mountain, the area around the grave looked like the head of a phoenix, limned by the course of the stream. He also said there used to be a Buddhist temple at the foot of the mountain. It was called Chunghsing Temple, but it was destroyed by the Red Guards in 1968, and the monks had never come back. He used to play in the ruins and recalled ringing the bell and waiting until the sound became too faint to hear, then ringing it again.

As I got back into the taxi, the driver turned around and told me how excited he was to have finally found the grave. He said Yu Po-ya and Chung Tzu-ch'i were his city's two greatest heroes. He couldn't wait to tell his family he had been to Chung Tzu-ch'i's grave. He said he planned to bring them there on his next day off. Then he said he wanted to show me another part of the city. He was still excited

Grave of Chung Ch'i (Chung Tzu-ch'i)

about his discovery. Instead of returning to the old highway, he took another way back. He wanted to show me the new industrial zone and the East Hawaii Housing Development southwest of Hanyang. I tried to look interested.

Thirty minutes later, he dropped me off at my hotel and only reluctantly took my money: 140RMB, a good deal for us both. On my way into the lobby, I finally saw a foreigner, the first one I had seen since Loyang. He was wearing a suit and tie and standing outside smoking a Gauloise. The smell was unmistakable. I nodded hello, but as soon as he saw me, he turned away. I must have looked like a firewood gatherer fresh from the countryside.

At the front desk, I asked a receptionist if there were any blind masseuses in the area. After the long bus ride from the nunnery, the muscles in my lower back were going south again. She sent me back down Liberation Road. But she had misunderstood my real need. The only places offering massages were brothels. I spent an hour going up one street and down another and was about to give up when I came across a place on Taipei Road that advertised itself as an East-West clinic. It was late in the day, and the place looked closed, but I pushed the door, and it opened. I yelled to see if anyone was there, and a man wearing a white frock came out from behind a curtain. His name was Chang Chien-min, and the clinic was his.

When I told him I needed an acupressure massage, he said he had something better—something that would go beyond the surface to the root of the problem. He sat me down and took hold of my wrists and checked my pulses. I've always liked that part of Chinese medicine. It was so personal—much better than an icy stethoscope on the chest. The examination of a person's pulses to get a sense of the varying flows of *ch'i* in the body and thus the obstructions that caused illness was an old specialty of the Wuhan area. In fact, Wuhan was where the technique began back in the third century. On a previous trip, I spent a day taking local buses and hiking through the countryside thirty miles northeast of Wuhan to another grave, the grave of Wang Shu-ho. It was Wang who first developed pulse diagnosis, who discovered how to hear the tunes of which our bodies are made. He was the Chung Ch'i of Chinese medicine.

Once Doctor Chang finished with my pulses, his assistant came in and took my blood pressure (100/80). I guess that was the other half of the East-West diagnosis. Doctor Chang then said that my kidneys were deficient, and my blood was sluggish. To inspire confidence in his treatment, he showed me a pile of magazine and newspaper articles testifying to his accomplishments. Then he told me to lie facedown on a treatment table and began with a sliding cup treatment, which was quite painful when the cups caught on my skin and wouldn't slide. Then came acupuncture needles along the spine and some major jolts. Finally, his assistant gave me a couple of injections in the butt. I didn't see them coming and didn't even ask what they were. It was too late anyway. They were probably vitamin shots. The whole process took an hour and cost 86RMB, or eleven dollars. Afterwards, Doctor Chang insisted we go outside and have our picture taken together in front. The sign behind us said it all: EAST–WEST UNIVERSAL LOVE CLINIC—a noble sentiment too seldom realized.

13 NO NORTH OR SOUTH

I woke up in Hankou with a spasm-free back and a reserved-seat ticket on the morning train to Tangyang. Doctor Chang asked me to call him in the morning, which I did—to tell him whether his treatment worked, which it did. After thanking him, I made a thermos of coffee and took a taxi to the train station. There was one in each of Wuhan's three cities. My train left from Wuchang on the other side of the Yangtze. It was a brand-new double-decker, and all the seats were in four-seat configurations, facing each other across a small table. It was an arrangement I've never liked. There was always the negotiation to find a place for one's feet, and by the time we left, there wasn't an empty seat.

At least I had a seat next to a window and could lean against it should the need to nap arise. Sitting next to me was a twenty-year-old student majoring in international trade at Nanchang University. She had a week off and was on her way to visit a friend studying the same subject at Three Gorges University in Yichang. Yichang was the home of China's Big Dam and the train's final destination. It was two hundred miles to the west, and Tangyang was the stop just before it. As soon as the train pulled out, my seatmate took out some mini cupcakes and insisted I share a few. The Chinese still haven't learned how to make a decent cupcake.

I got mine down with coffee. She did the same with a yoghurt drink.

Sitting across from us was another girl about the same age who kept quiet the whole time, as if she was trying to keep her parents' admonition about not talking to strangers in mind. Several times she looked as if she was about to say something, then she would catch herself and look away. Sitting next to her was a guy not much older who spent the first hour reading a newspaper article several pages long about the recent trip to the U.S. by Taiwan's Ma Ying-chou (aka Ma Ying-jeow). Our seats were so close I had no trouble reading the pages as he finished them.

Ma was the chairman of Taiwan's Nationalist Party (KMT), the party of the Mainland Chinese who fled to (or invaded) Taiwan in 1949. Ma's fellow Mainlanders had lost their hegemony when Chiang Ching-kuo brought the Taiwanese into the government after his father's death. The Taiwanese-led Democratic Progressive Party (DPP) had since ousted the KMT from the presidency. The KMT still couldn't believe it had happened, and they were now trying to regain control by telling people in Taiwan that they would do a better job of dealing with the Mainland than the DPP. The Chinese liked Ma. He may not have been pushing hard for reunification, but at least he wasn't pushing for independence.

Ma was the last person I interviewed when I was working as a journalist in Taiwan. When I told him I was quitting my job to go look for hermits in China, he shook his head and said there weren't any real monks in China, much less hermits. That was in 1989 when he was in charge of Taiwan's Mainland Affairs Commission, which was why I was interviewing him. I was hoping he actually knew something about China. Presumably, he's learned more since then.

The newspaper article was about Ma's (or the KMT's) policy of Five Don't's, which were intended to prevent Taiwan independence, and its counterpart: the Five Do's, which were aimed at fostering reunification with the Mainland. The Chinese have had a hard time getting it through their heads that the Taiwanese—and Ma was the son of Mainlanders—didn't want to be part of China. Life was fine in Taiwan and had been ever since Chiang Kai-shek died and his son took over. Once a person looked past the surface of China's current economic prosperity, it was still a brutal and a brutalizing society. The Mainland government had exchanged one form of dictatorship for another, while Taiwan had developed into a very odd kind of democracy, but a democracy nevertheless.

After a few pages, I turned to the window for relief. For the first hour, we passed through a flat landscape of waterways and ponds for raising carp and lotuses and water chestnuts, and rice paddies being plowed under—the water buffaloes were finally getting back to work—and fields of safflower in bloom and orchards of peach trees in flower. Images go by so fast on a train. Suddenly in the middle of nowhere, there was a tramp walking across a field with his bindle over his shoulder. When I first started traveling in China, I used to see lots of men, and also women, riding freights, but not lately; whether because of the advent of the container car or because the yards weren't as open as they used to be, I don't know. But there were still ragamuffin men tramping across the countryside in the middle of nowhere, gone in a flash.

During the second hour, the Tahung Mountains appeared in the distance to the north. Along the tracks the countryside turned hilly, the endless floodplain of fields and waterways gave way to terraced patches surrounded by hillsides of bamboo and pine, and the villages were replaced by lone farmsteads.

The girl who never said a word got off in Chunghsiang, where we crossed the Han River and turned southwest, and the guy got off in Chinmen. When he did, the girl sitting next to me moved over and took his place. At first I thought she just wanted to look out the window. But she wanted to look at me, which was as disconcerting as it was curious. She put her elbows on the table and cradled her chin in her hands and looked at me for the rest of the trip—which lasted another forty minutes. I had no idea what was going through her head or why she was so unabashed. She was a lovely girl, but I felt compelled to look out the window when I talked to her.

While we were pulling out of Wuchang and still eating our cupcakes, she said she had an important English exam coming up the following month, but she didn't speak a word of English the whole trip. Now that our seatmates were gone, she confided that she was interested in visiting scenic places and that she felt the need for more beauty in her life. When she said this, she lowered her voice. Even though it wasn't necessary, it was an old habit in China. She and her friend, she said, were planning to visit the Three Gorges and the new dam, and she asked me if I had time to join them. I told her I had a date with some monks. She said she didn't know anything about Buddhism but that it must be interesting. She remarked how happy I seemed and asked me if it was because of Buddhism. I told her it was because I didn't have high standards and was adept at avoiding anything that looked like trouble. When I was in school, my favorite sport was dodge ball. Four hours after leaving Wuchang, I wished her luck and got off in Tangyang.

As soon as I arrived, I checked on trains going back to Wuhan. I needed to be there two days later to catch an evening train to Shaokuan. Unfortunately there was only one train a day to Wuhan, and it left too late to get me there in time. I would have to take a bus. I went outside, but there was nothing there; no buildings, no signs, nothing but vacant land. Fortunately, there were a couple of men sitting in their cars who looked like they were waiting for fares. I went over and asked one of the drivers if he would take me to the long-distance bus station, which he agreed to do for 8RMB. I asked him what happened to the town. He said nothing happened to the town. They built the new train station far enough away so no one would be bothered by the noise. I tipped my hat to the local authorities.

The town was two miles to the south, and I had no problem buying a ticket for two days hence at the long-distance bus station. Buses for Wuhan left every hour or so, and I bought a ticket for the 9:20—a civilized time, I thought. I went back outside and told the same driver I wanted to go to Yuchuan Temple. It was seven miles southwest of Tangyang, and he said he would take me there for 30RMB. Half that would have been more reasonable, but I didn't feel like negotiating or looking around for another form of transport, so I proceeded to the monastery. Tangyang wasn't a big town, and most of the seven miles was through a countryside of rice fields waiting to be planted and safflower waiting to be harvested.

The road ended at the temple entrance and the foot of the mountain after which it was named. Since the temple was being rebuilt, I had the driver drop me off a couple hundred yards short of the gate at the place where lay visitors usually stayed. When I walked inside, I was surprised to see a monk behind the counter. The place used to be a private hostel, and I asked him what had happened. He said the monastery owned it now. Yuchuan was the most famous monastery in Hupei Province, but it had been in serious need of restoration, and the previous abbot had turned it over to Ching-hui two years earlier. The monk said since Ching-hui became abbot, the monastery had taken over all the private businesses that previously catered to tourists. Ching-hui was turning the place into a Zen monastery again. The monk also said the local government had ceded the monastery control over the adjacent forest and farmland as well. I was liking the local authorities more and more.

The hostel included a pair of three-story buildings. The monk said the one we were in was now for short-term visitors, and the building next door had been turned into a long-term residence for laywomen; there were about thirty of them when I was there. After I filled out the registration form, the monk led me to a room on the third floor and I dove into a nap, which was necessarily short. The lobby of the long-term residence next door had been turned into a shrine hall for chanting, and the afternoon session woke me up—not the chanting, but the drums and chimes that went with it.

There was still some coffee in my thermos, so I got up and took it with me onto the sunlit patio in front of the building. One of the laywomen was hanging up sheets. She said all the laywomen pitched in and took turns with the chores. She said if she hadn't been washing bedding, she would have been chanting with her fellow lay-women. She had a clear view of whatever she did as practice. She said it didn't matter where she was, the shrine hall, the meditation hall, the kitchen. She was grateful, she said, to Ching-hui for providing her and the other women with a place to practice what Ching-hui called *Sheng Huo Ch'an*: "Daily Life Zen." After she went back inside, I sat down at a table someone had set up on the patio and sipped my coffee while I read about Yuchuan Temple in a booklet I picked up at the front desk.

The name *Yu-ch'uan* meant "Jade Spring." It was one of several names by which the mountain was known, and it referred to the quality of the mountain's water. Particularly famous among local tea cognoscenti was Pearl Creek, which flowed past the temple's front gate. The first monk who settled on the mountain built his hut on its bank, just upstream from where the temple was later constructed. His name was P'u-ching, but he wasn't a Zen monk. Buddhism had only been in China a century or two, and Zen was still three centuries away. But P'u-ching practiced meditation. One day while he was meditating, the spirit of Kuan Yu appeared before him. The year was AD 219, and Kuan Yu had been beheaded a few days earlier just southeast of Tangyang.

Kuan Yu (aka Kuan Kung or Kuan Ti) has since become China's greatest folk hero, and his feats have been immortalized in the historical novel *Romance of the Three Kingdoms*. Over the centuries he has become the patron deity of just about every fraternal organization in China, from police to criminals, from employers to workers, from gamblers to philanthropists, from students to soldiers, from Buddhists to Taoists—anywhere loyalty and righteousness are prized. His is the statue with the red face and the long black beard.

That was what P'u-ching suddenly saw while he was sitting outside his hut watching the water of his mind flow by. P'u-ching had saved Kuan Yu's life on a previous occasion, and Kuan Yu's spirit sought him out again. He begged the monk to help him recover his head. But P'u-ching was unmoved. He recited the names of Kuan Yu's fellow soldiers who had also been beheaded during the war that followed the collapse of the Han dynasty. Hearing their names, Kuan Yu suddenly understood the emptiness of self-existence, and his spirit vanished, or at least appeared to vanish.

The people of Tangyang insist Kuan Yu's spirit has remained in the area and has continued to protect them. Tangyang was, after all, where the worship of Kuan Yu began. It began with the construction of a shrine next to P'u-ching's old hut and another much larger one just outside of town, where Kuan Yu's headless body was buried—his head was later taken to Loyang and buried there. Since then, shrines to Kuan Yu have appeared in every village, town, and city in China. Not even Buddhism's Goddess of Mercy sees as many supplicants or inhales as much incense in the course of any given day.

As pilgrims began visiting the site where Kuan Yu's spirit first appeared, a few hermitages and small temples were also built on the mountain, but nothing major until Chih-yi (538–597) arrived in 592. Chih-yi would later be honored as the principal patriarch of the Tientai School of Buddhism, named for his residence on Tientaishan in Chekiang Province. Tangyang was his hometown, and several years before he died, he returned. With funds supplied by Emperor Wen, the founder of the Sui dynasty (581–618), he built Yuchuan Temple. Chih-yi hadn't been back since he was fifteen, and he only stayed three years, but it was long enough to deliver two of his most famous presentations of the Tientai doctrine, namely his philosophical exposition of the teaching behind the *Lotus Sutra* (*Fa-hua-hsuan-yi*) and his guide to meditation (*Mo-ho-chih-kuan*).

The temple he built and where he delivered these sermons became one of the four most famous monasteries in China, and it has been rebuilt many times. The only thing left from its initial manifestation was an iron rice cauldron cast in 615. It was big enough to feed five hundred monks and suggests the size of the community that lived there even after Chih-yi left. Ching-hui showed it to me when I visited the temple two years earlier, just after he became abbot. This time I was waiting for the temple manager, who showed up halfway through the second cup of coffee. He had spent the day supervising construction of Tumen Temple, a subsidiary temple belonging to Yuchuan. He pulled up in front of the hostel in the temple jeep and waved for me to get in. His name was K'uan-hsiang, and he said he wanted to show me the new buildings at Yuchuan.

K'uan-hsiang said the older buildings were so dilapidated that most of them were unlivable, and only twenty-five monks were staying there until construction was finished. When it was, he said, Yuchuan would be the biggest monastery in the province and would have enough room for two hundred monks. Ching-hui's Hong Kong connections were once more supplying a major part of the funding. After parking the jeep at the temple entrance, we bypassed the front gate and the six-hundred-year-old shrine halls and scrambled up the dirt slope behind them to several new halls being built on the hillside where Chih-yi once lectured.

Sui-dynasty rice cauldron at Yuchuan Temple

The stone platform was still there where he delivered his discourse on the *Lotus Sutra* over the course of ninety days in the summer of 593. It wasn't a line-by-line explication—he had already done that in Nanching in 587. This time his exposition unfolded the flower of the Dharma petal by petal from the time of the Buddha's Enlightenment to its culmination in the teaching of the *Lotus*. The following summer from the same platform, he explained the stages of cultivation that brought an end to discursive thought and fostered an insight into the nature of reality. His detailing of that process and the objects and states of meditation provided something that Bodhidharma and his followers had avoided like the plague. Zen masters pointed to the mind. They didn't like to talk about it. Chih-yi talked about it in detail. That difference in the two approaches was to persist and deepen as Chih-yi's teachings developed into Tientai Buddhism and Zen split into its Northern and Southern schools.

As K'uan-hsiang showed me around, I was surprised that all the new buildings were being built out of granite, even the pillars and the intricately carved windows and doors. He said the stone was from the coastal province of Fukien, as were the workers, of which there were several dozen. He said the decision was made to use stone instead of wood to avoid termite damage, which was a problem in the older buildings being restored down in the main courtyard. It rained a lot. The temple was, after all, in the Yangtze watershed, which carried more water than any watershed in the world.

By the time I had seen what there was to see, it was time for dinner back at the hostel. Before sending me off, K'uan-hsiang invited me to join him later that evening in the meditation hall, and I told him I would be there. Back at the hostel, the only thing noteworthy about dinner was that it included a variety of wild fern the lay residents picked earlier that day. Otherwise it was leftovers from lunch. Afterwards, I waited until the light began to fade from the sky and walked back to the monastery while I could still see the way.

As I stepped inside the meditation hall, there were already several dozen monks and laypeople circling the buddha statue in the middle of the room. I joined those in the slowest, outermost orbit. It was an old custom among sun-worshipping peoples, circumambulation in a clockwise, sundial direction, and the practice arrived in China along with Buddhism. Fifteen minutes later, a whack on the board stopped us all in our tracks. After a few words from another meditation master whose dialect I didn't understand, we took our seats.

It was the usual arrangement: a three-foot-wide bench on the room's perimeter with a motley assortment of cushions filled with cotton wadding. I arranged a couple under my butt and covered my crossed legs with a thick blanket that was also filled with cotton wadding. The first sit lasted forty-five minutes, which was fine. Then we got up and orbited the buddha for ten minutes and returned to our cushions. The second sit lasted seventy-five minutes, which was not so fine. The last fifteen minutes were agonizing, and I wondered how, since my legs were completely numb, they could be the source of so much pain.

Once the evening meditation ended and feeling returned to my legs, I walked out onto the road that led back to the hostel. The night was pitch black, but I decided not to use my flashlight. I simply followed the river of stars between the trees on either side of the road. There weren't that many, but the ones I could see were as big as fireflies.

When I finally reached the hostel, the front gate was locked, and no one responded to my knocks or yells. Earlier, from the window of my room, I had seen a gate that separated the rear courtyard of the hostel from the front yard of a small farmhouse. With the help of my flashlight, I found my way through a thicket of bamboo and knocked on the farmer's door. He didn't look surprised when I asked him if he had the key to the gate. He did, and he came out and unlocked it. Apparently, lockouts had occurred before. Once inside, I went upstairs to my room and tried to take a bath but the water heater didn't seem to work, so I gave up and went to bed.

When I woke up the next morning, the weather had changed again. The previous day, sitting out on the patio, I was down to a T-shirt. As soon as I got up, I put on my parka and tried to warm my hands around a cup of coffee. After a second cup, I decided to face the day. I walked over to the monastery and tracked down K'uan-hsiang. He was in the guest hall looking at brochures for monastery bells. He was ordering one for Tumen Temple and asked me if I wanted to see the construction site. I told him that was why I was there, and he led me outside and fired up the temple jeep.

Tumen Temple was where the Northern School of Zen began back when Zen was just becoming Zen. From Yuchuan Temple, we took the paved road back toward Tangyang. But after two miles, we stopped and parked where a dirt road led off to the south. The ruts were too deep, even for a jeep, so we got out and walked. It was about five hundred yards to the cloud of dust that was the building site. Workers were unloading bricks from dump trucks, and a construction crane was moving them to two buildings that were already half finished. K'uan-hsiang said the workers, about twenty of them, were hired by a local construction company and were paid 50–60RMB a day, or about seven bucks. But they weren't locals. They traveled from site to site and specialized in building traditional-style temples out of brick and stone.

They had to start from scratch at Tumen. The only thing that even marked the spot was the hillock that contained the body of Shen-hsiu. Shen-hsiu was the disciple of the Fifth Patriarch who wrote the poem that made the mind into an object of meditation ("always keep it clean") and who failed to win the patriarchship. Bandits had looted his stupa, the Red Guards had finished the job of knocking down what was left, and farmers had carried off whatever materials were worth carrying off, which was everything aboveground.

But according to K'uan-hsiang, neither the looters, the Red Guards, nor the farmers knew about the burial vault belowground. He said that while workers were planting camphor and cypress saplings on the hillock, they had uncovered steps that

Tumen Temple under construction

led to the underground chamber, which appeared to be intact. When I asked K'uan-hsiang why he hadn't opened it, he said it would have required notifying a number of government agencies, which the monks didn't want to do until they were in a better position to control the situation. He said there was no hurry. Shen-hsiu could wait. His body had been there for thirteen hundred years. A few more wouldn't matter.

K'uan-hsiang showed me the place on the hillock where the workers found the steps. When Shen-hsiu's body was brought back to Tumen in 706, it was a big deal, and the burial vault must have been constructed in a manner befitting his status as preceptor to the royal family. Emperor Chung-tsung (r. 705–710) wanted the monk's remains buried closer to the capital. The bodies of the early Zen patriarchs—and some claimed Shen-hsiu was the rightful Sixth Patriarch—were thought to be imbued with special powers that could be called upon in time of need. But before he died, Shen-hsiu made it clear he wanted to be buried on the hillock he named Mount Lanka, after the mythical backdrop of the *Lankavatara Sutra*. The emperor relented and even saw the body off as it left Loyang.

Shen-hsiu was born a hundred years earlier east of Loyang near the city of Kaifeng. Not much is known about the first half of his life, other than that he grew up poor and left home to become a monk at the age of thirteen. He must have attached himself to a peripatetic Buddhist master, as he traveled widely, and he was considered erudite at twenty when he was finally ordained. That is all we know about him until he arrived in Huangmei at the age of fifty to study with the Fifth Patriarch. Hung-jen was impressed by his diligence and learning and six years later proclaimed Shen-hsiu his dharma heir. Shen-hsiu also became the monastery's chief instructor.

He was still there when Hui-neng left with the robe and bowl and the title of Sixth Patriarch in 672, but it isn't clear how long he stayed there after that. He might have left immediately, or he might have left when Hung-jen died in 675. Or perhaps he stayed to mourn his teacher, for which a three-year period of residence at the gravesite was customary. In any case, Shen-hsiu's next appearance in the historical record was when he arrived at Tumen Temple sometime between 676 and 679 and decided that was where he would live out his years.

Tumen was just an hour walk from Chih-yi's old temple, and Shen-hsiu was a great admirer of the Tientai master's teaching. The temple itself had never been anything more than a small hermitage ever since it was built in 528. But not long after

Shen-hsiu arrived, he began to attract disciples from all over China. Tumen kept getting bigger and bigger until there were more than four thousand monks in residence. Eventually word of his fame reached Empress Wu, and she summoned him to court in 700. Although Shen-hsiu was in his nineties, he accepted the invitation and arrived in Loyang the following year. He spent the last five years of his life traveling between the two capitals lecturing to audiences numbering in the thousands.

While we were standing on the hillock that still held Shen-hsiu's body, K'uan-hsiang pointed beyond the grove of cypress and camphor saplings to the tea plantation on the other side. He said the monastery was negotiating to buy the plantation

Mount Lanka and gravesite of Shen-hsiu's remains

so the monks could grow their own tea. He also said there was a trail that led through the plantation all the way back to Yuchuan Temple, and he preferred the trail whenever he wasn't using the jeep. But a walk would have to wait for another day. It was almost lunchtime, the big meal of the day. We returned to the work site and entered a small building where the two caretakers lived. They were both lay disciples of Ching-hui, and they were busy in the kitchen.

The building was divided into two rooms: one served as the kitchen and storeroom, the other served as bedroom, living room, dining room, and reception room. K'uan-hsiang sat down on one of the room's two beds and folded his legs in the lotus posture. He motioned for me to sit down on a bench next to the bed. One of the laymen brought us tea and kept returning periodically to refill our cups. It was a cold day, and hot tea was welcome.

I asked K'uan-hsiang how long he had been a monk. He said since 1993, when he was twenty-nine. He said his parents didn't agree with his decision at first. In those days, he said, not many people where he grew up were interested in cultivating a spiritual practice. The Cultural Revolution may have ended in 1976, but it took a while before people showed any interest in religion again. Once his parents met his master, though, they also became disciples, as did his two brothers and his sister.

His master was Ming-yu, who was abbot of Yuchuan Temple at that time. After Ming-yu died in 1998, K'uan-hsiang said he left to further his practice elsewhere. One of the advantages of being a monk or a nun in China was the freedom to travel to other Buddhist centers and to stay for extended periods. K'uan-hsiang spent a year in Fukien Province at the Buddhist academy of Kuanghua Temple, then a year in the meditation hall of Chenju Temple on Yunchushan, and finally a year in seclusion at a small temple near his hometown of Chunghsiang. Chunghsiang was the town where the girl who didn't talk got off the train. In 2003, K'uan-hsiang finally returned to Yuchuan Temple just before Ching-hui took over as abbot. He said now that he was responsible for overseeing construction of both temples he expected to be there for many years. He had no plans to leave.

K'uan-hsiang said Ching-hui's plan was to finish the construction work on both temples before the end of 2008, then to turn them over to someone else, just as he had done with Pailin and would be doing before long with Fourth Patriarch Temple.

K'uan-hsiang said Tumen would be like other temples in that it would have a couple of shrine halls where pilgrims could offer incense and where the daily ceremonies common to every temple could be held. But it was being designed to serve primarily as a Buddhist academy, and it would have enough individual rooms to accommodate up to sixty monks. That was also a sign of the times. In the past, only senior monks had their own rooms. Now it was normal for any monk who was a permanent resident.

While we were sitting there, K'uan-hsiang gave me a copy of the building plans. Looking at the blueprints with courtyards surrounded by individual monk cells, I was reminded of the ruins of Buddhist temples I had seen in India and of Christian monasteries in Europe. It was an architecture for a community of individuals living together with one purpose: liberation of the soul from the body or the mind from the dust—assuming, of course, one can find any dust or body from which to be liberated.

He also gave me a copy of a fifty-page booklet he was preparing on the history of Tumen Temple and of Shen-hsiu's Northern School of Zen. Buddhist academies were appearing all over China like mushrooms after a rain. But K'uan-hsiang said the one at Tumen would be unique. The emphasis of instruction would be on the Tientai teachings of Chih-yi and the Northern Zen teachings of Shen-hsiu and his followers. Both had had their moments in the sun, but neither school had attracted much interest since the T'ang dynasty. In China it was either Zen or Pure Land, and Zen meant the Southern School of Zen.

When I asked K'uan-hsiang about this, he said the Southern School of Hui-neng was for a wider public, people who lived ordinary lives, and the Northern School of Shen-hsiu and the Tientai teachings of Chih-yi were for a more highly educated audience, people with more time to devote to their practice. He didn't say this in a way that slighted the one or elevated the other, but simply as a matter of fact—or at least opinion. He thought it was time for practitioners to reexamine these teachings that had become of more interest to historians than those following a spiritual path.

Although the focus of study and practice at Yuchuan and Tumen temples would be Tientai and Northern Zen, K'uan-hsiang said most Buddhists in China preferred Pure Land practice. When they chanted the name of Amitabha, they could hear themselves chant. It was reassuring. People who practiced Zen couldn't hear a thing. Their focus was completely on the mind. There was nothing else to depend on. All there was was the mind.

The cultivation of the mind was what attracted K'uan-hsiang to Zen. But when he talked about meditation, he talked about stilling the mind and focusing on the mind. He talked about different samadhis, or meditative states. It was clear he had already been influenced by the Tientai teachings of Chih-yi and the Northern Zen of Shen-hsiu. It was also clear that these teachings were alive and not dead.

After a while, we both stopped talking and just sat there drinking tea and listening to the howling wind outside. Finally, the two lay caretakers brought in lunch. Considering the surroundings, I was expecting something simple. But it was a feast far beyond everyday fare: large plates of fried tofu, the Chinese version of Anaheim peppers, spinach, coriander in vinegar, black tree ears, a hot pot of vegetarian meatballs, noodles, and deep-fried rolls that had been previously steamed. It was sumptuous.

Afterwards, we walked back to the jeep and returned to Yuchuan, and I spent the rest of the afternoon writing in my journal. After a simple dinner of noodles with vegetables, I decided to forego evening meditation and heard a cheer from my knees. I went back to my room and finally figured out what was wrong with my bath-water the previous night. The gas tank, which was located in the hallway, was empty. I simply switched tanks with a room in which no one was staying. But when I filled up the tub, the water was scalding. The cold-water tap didn't work, and I had to wait an hour for the water in the tub to cool off. Only later did it occur to me that I could have turned off the gas at the tank and run the unheated water for a while. Sometimes I just stop thinking.

While I waited, I read about Shen-hsiu in K'uan-hsiang's booklet. The founder of the Northern School of Zen didn't leave nearly as much behind as his hero Chih-yi. Among the texts attributed to him was one called *Kuan-hsin-lun*: "Discourse on Looking at the Mind." Chih-yi had authored a text with the same title, and perhaps Shen-hsiu was simply following suit. Certainly the idea of treating the mind as an object of contemplation was shared by the Tientai and Northern School masters. But not everyone thinks the text attributed to Shen-hsiu was his. Possibly it was the work of one of his many students. One of the reasons for this assessment is that among the documents found in the Tunhuang Caves at the beginning of the last century was the Northern School text titled *Record of the Masters of the Lankavatara*, which listed Shen-hsiu, and not Hui-neng, as the rightful successor to Hung-jen, but which claimed that he didn't leave any writings. Still, even the author of *Masters of the Lanka* quoted a few words of Shen-hsiu: "The body is empty, and to see the body as empty is to be one with its subtlest movement. The mind isn't real, and to see the mind as illusion is to be one with its truest reality."

That was a fairly standard view. But Shen-hsiu was not averse to employing Zen-speak. He once asked, "You hear a bell when it's rung. But what about before it's rung? And what is the sound of that sound? And when a bell is rung inside a monastery, is its sound heard throughout the rest of the world or not?" On another occasion he said, "It's the body that perishes, not its shadow. It's the bridge that flows, not the river. My teaching can be summarized by the words 'body and function.' Or it can be called 'the darkness beyond darkness' or 'the turning of the wheel' or 'the path and the goal.'"

When people like Empress Wu asked what text they should read, he recommended *The Prajnaparamita Sutra Spoken by Manjushri*, while he himself relied on the teaching of the *Lankavatara*. His final instructions were a quote from the *Mahaprajnaparamita Shastra* of Nagarjuna: "It's a snake's nature to move in a crooked fashion. But if you put it in a bamboo tube, it becomes straight. The control of the mind through samadhi is also like this." This focus on controlling the mind was very much in keeping with the poem attributed to him, in which he tells us to constantly dust the mirror of our illusory mind in order to give rise to wisdom. His Zen was Tientai Zen. First you still the mind, then you look at the mind. But how can you still or look at what isn't there?

Once it was cool enough to get in, I stayed in the tub for an hour. When I got out, I was as red as a sunburn. Since the residents of both buildings were all in the shrine hall next door chanting, I walked out into the corridor and stood naked before the open window, watching the last light of dusk fade and the first stars appear over Jade Spring Mountain. After I had cooled off, I got into bed and unwrapped my last fun-size Snickers. I fell asleep savoring the taste and listening to the names of buddhas from next door.

14 NO FLOATING BELLY-UP

Later that night, long after the hot bath and chanting put me to sleep, I had a dream about my friend Mike Ryan, who killed himself a week earlier and left this summary of civilization and its fraudulent attractions: "no job, no money, no hope." He was lying dead at the bottom of a pool of water. People were looking down and pointing at him. Everyone was milling around, like at a cocktail party, and no one was doing anything but pointing. I had to summon all my strength, which is what it takes with dreams, to say something. But when I started to speak, I suddenly woke up to the sound of the Buddha's name. The morning chant had begun next door.

It was time to go. I got up and finished the last of the instant coffee, packed my bag, and headed back to the monastery to say goodbye to K'uan-hsiang. On the way, I stopped to talk to the woman who took care of the camel tethered to a post near the monastery's front gate. She and her husband took turns taking care of it during the day and charged people 5RMB to have their picture taken astride its two furry humps. They charged another 5RMB to dress up in one of the costumes they had hanging from a rack. The choices were a T'ang-dynasty princess or Kuan Yu (you supply the head). Anticipating my next question, she said they paid 9,000RMB, or about $1,100, for the camel, and that included the cost of bringing it there by truck all the way from the Silk Road province of Kansu. That was a lot of money. They could have bought a decent used taxi for that. Again, she seemed to read my mind. She said the camel was eight years old and would probably live another ten, which was a lot longer than a taxi would last. So maybe it was a good deal after all.

When she asked me if I wanted a photo atop the family meal ticket, I passed. I wasn't much into riding animals unless I had to. The last time I had to was fifteen years earlier in May of 1991. I had left my driver and the broken-down jeep I had hired and trekked off with one of my two guides to find the source of the Yellow River on the Tibetan Plateau. It took all day and all the energy we could muster, but we finally found the marker left by a group of Chinese adventurers whose members had subsequently tried to float down the river and drowned. By the time we started back, we were both exhausted—the elevation was over 14,000 feet—and the cobalt morning sky had given way to a late afternoon snowstorm.

As we came down from the heights, we decided to approach the camp of some Tibetan herders we had seen in the distance on our way there. As we started in their direction, my guide told me to get behind him, and he reached into his shoulder bag and pulled out a pistol. *What the hell is going on?!* I thought. With his other hand, he pointed at half a dozen small black dots near the yurts. The dots were headed our way, and they kept getting bigger. The dots turned out to be very large dogs, very large snarling dogs. As soon as they got close enough, he fired his pistol into the air twice. The dogs stopped their headlong rush and started circling. With his free hand, he reached into his bag again and took out a long rope. On one end was a heavy pyramid-shaped metal weight. He started swinging it over both our heads, letting it out gradually until the weight was swirling about thirty feet from us. As the dogs watched it whiz past their heads, they backed off, and we proceeded like that across the tundra toward the camp. When we got to within hailing distance, the herders called off their dogs, and my guide put away his weapons.

The herders lifted the flap of their yurt and invited us inside. We followed them in, sat down on the carpeted floor, and warmed our hands and feet near the metal stove that dominated the middle of the yurt. There wasn't any wood at that elevation, but dung from their herds burned just fine. While my guide explained what we were doing, one of the Tibetans went over to the big pile of yak butter near the entrance, scooped up a handful, put it in a kettle of hot water on the stove, and added a chunk of tea.

Once we had caught our breath and quenched our thirst on what the Tibetans called *pocha*, we asked them if we could hire their ponies to take us back to our jeep, which we were hoping would be repaired by the time we got there. The herders shook their heads. They said their ponies were their most valuable possession. And it was May. They were still weak from the winter. We were feeling sufficiently weak ourselves and persisted—or at least my guide did, at my urging. It was only with great reluctance and thirty bucks for three ponies—two for us and one for an escort to bring back the other ponies—that they finally agreed.

On our way across the tundra, I taught my companions the words to the only riding song I knew, which I edited for the occasion:

> One morning when I was out walking for pleasure, I spied a young herdboy a-riding along. His hat was pushed back, and his prayer beads did jangle, and as he approached, he was singing this song: 'Whoppie ti yi yo, get along little doggies, it's your misfortune and none of my own. Whoppie ti yi yo, get along little doggies, you know that Tibet will be your new home.'

I was pretty much on my own for the first part, but they rose to join me for the "whoppie ti yi yo" part. The herder also sang a couple of Tibetan songs, and my guide joined in. I gave up after a few tries and just bobbed along, letting the pony do all the work.

Tibetan ponies have short legs, to avoid the potholes in the tundra, but they cruise right along. We made it back to our jeep in less than two hours, just as it was getting dark. The vehicle had indeed been repaired, at least enough to get us back to the nearest trading post—but not until after midnight. By the time we arrived, my arm had lost all feeling from having to hold on to a wire that was jerry-rigged to the generator, which in turn made the lights work. So I wasn't opposed to riding, if the occasion demanded it. But I wasn't on the Tibetan Plateau, and my legs worked fine.

I proceeded through the monastery gate and found K'uan-hsiang in the guest hall again. I told him I had a ticket on the 9:20 bus to Wuhan and had come to say goodbye. He told me to come back again and stay longer. Then he escorted me back outside the gate. A minivan had just dropped off some pilgrims, and the driver was looking for a fare back to town. K'uan-hsiang told me to get in and shoved some money into the driver's hand, and off I went, waving a feeble goodbye.

I arrived at the bus station with half an hour to spare so I walked down the street and found an Internet cafe and checked my e-mail. There was a message from the girl I talked to on the train, the one studying international trade. I still wasn't adept at typing Chinese on the computer, so I responded in English: "I'm going back to Wuhan today. I will miss your cupcakes and your smile." Actually, she didn't smile that much, but I figured I'd encourage her. Where else was she going to find beauty?

The bus left on time, and didn't stop until we reached Wuhan. It took four hours, the same as the train, but it was far more comfortable. There was not only room for my feet, there was a row of empty seats at the back to stretch out across. Somewhere between Tangyang and Wuhan the weather turned warm again, and I took off my parka for what I hoped would be the last time. March was nearly over.

As we came into Wuhan, the bus crossed the Yangtze on the old Number One Bridge. When the bridge was first built in 1958, it was the only way for cars or trains to cross the river between its mouth and source, or for 3,500 miles. And it was still the only such bridge for over six hundred miles in either direction when the people of Wuhan decided to close it down with a human barricade on May 17, 1989. It was one of those days a person tends to remember. Steve Johnson and I had just arrived by train from Loyang on the Hankou side of the bridge. We were between hermits, and after checking into a hotel we were wandering the streets looking for a cold beer. We turned a corner and found ourselves on the edge of a crowd of a couple thousand people gathered in the old Hankou square. They were collecting money to send representatives to join protesters at Tienanmen. When I inadvertently contributed 100RMB instead of the 10RMB I had intended, I was literally carried up to the makeshift stage and was asked to address the crowd. After offering a few words of encouragement, I rejoined Steve, and we continued on in search of our own more modest goal.

Three weeks later, in the aftermath of Tienanmen, I returned to Taiwan and was sharing a few drinks with the CIA station chief. When I told him about our trip, including our day in Wuhan, he said he had heard about our little escapade. Sometimes the CIA can be really amazing. He said he had seen a dispatch about the events in Wuhan. Teng Hsiao-p'ing / Deng Xiaoping was there the same day meeting with military leaders trying to gather support for a crackdown on the democracy movement. None of the military commanders in the Beijing area were willing, so he had flown down to Wuhan. When an aide told him a foreigner was leading a rally in the city, he became furious, or so the CIA's informant claimed. I could just see him crushing his smoke, hocking a loogey into the nearest spittoon, and pounding the big table everyone was gathered around, giving vent to his sus-picions that foreign powers were somehow behind what was going on—when all it was was a quest for cold beer.

This time traffic was moving smoothly: cars on top, trains below. As we reached the Wuchang side of the bridge, I pictured Mao jumping into the Yangtze from the riverbank below. When it was built, the bridge was intended as a symbol of what the Chinese and Russians could do when they joined forces. But the Russians pulled out of the project during a diplomatic rift in 1956, and they took their plans with them. So Mao came down to Wuhan. It was a matter of national pride. To spur the workers on, he jumped into the river and swam across, and he did it two more times: in 1958, upon completion of the bridge, and again in 1966, to prove that reports of his ill health were greatly exaggerated. What nobody seemed to notice, or at least mention, was that the Yangtze makes a big bend just downriver from the bridge. Mao simply floated across with the current and reached the other side nine miles downstream just before the bend. It was such a Taoist thing to do and typical of the Great Helmsman.

Yangtze Bridge and Mao's swimming hole

A hundred yards from where Mao jumped in, we passed a newly rebuilt version of Yellow Crane Tower, where a Taoist once flew off on the back of a crane to join his fellow immortals. I suppose Mao was simply doing the same, riding the current of the world's mightiest river into his own sagehood. Just past the tower was the monument to the workers of Wuhan who started the revolution that brought the Ch'ing dynasty to an end in 1911. Wuhan's Number One Bridge and its long shadow spanned a Sargasso Sea of legerdemain and wrecked dreams.

A few minutes later, we pulled into the Wuchang bus station. It was only two blocks from the train station, but my train didn't leave for another six hours. I thought about visiting the provincial museum or getting another back treatment from Doctor Chang. But in the end, I decided on another afternoon of doing nothing. I walked across the street and checked into one of the gaudiest hotels I had ever seen in China. It wouldn't have looked out of place in one of the seedier sections of Las Vegas. It was called the Chiaho, and it was a three-star fuck hotel and spa. The spa took up two of its five floors, and that's where I should have spent the day. After all, every spa had a public room with lounge chairs where customers could nap for as long as they wanted. But I wanted some privacy and rented a room instead: four hours for 100RMB. It was a pretty good room, and I tried to take a nap. But there was too much street noise, so I spent the afternoon reading and catching up in my journal.

I checked out an hour before my train was due to depart and decided to try the food in the hotel's Thai restaurant to forestall a dinner of snacks. Despite the mystique of a foreign cuisine, it didn't look expensive. I sat down in the faux garden section beneath a plastic palm tree, and a waitress brought me a pot of chrysanthemum tea. The tiny white chrysanthemums grown around Hangchou were famous for reducing body heat, and the tea was a sign that someone besides me thought the cold weather was over.

The menu had pictures, and I pointed to one of vegetables and tofu. After about ten minutes the waitress put a small stove of liquid paraffin on my table and lit it. Then she brought a small wok full of smoked bamboo shoots, black tree ears, red onions, green peppers, and braised tofu. It was excellent. But I felt odd eating such a fancy meal beneath a plastic palm listening to piano renditions of "Let It Be" and "Masquerade" and watching customers get up from their tables to choose their meals from aerated tanks of turtles, eels, frogs, and everything else that swims.

After eating what I could—I couldn't finish it all—I walked across the street to the train station and sat down in the soft-seat waiting room. Wuhan was the fourth largest city in China, after Shanghai, Beijing, and Tienchin, but the station was falling apart. The attendant said it was due to be torn down the following year. Everything in China was being torn down. I was only surprised they had taken so long to get around to the city's biggest building. But maybe that was why. It was colossal—a great example of Soviet inspired architecture. I was glad when my train arrived.

I had a soft-sleeper ticket, and a ticket for a lower berth, which had the advantage of sharing a table with the other lower berth, not that I had anything to put on it. But my cabin mates did. A husband and wife and their adult son boarded with a bucket of KFC fried chicken and started eating as soon as they sat down. They all talked with their mouths full. That and their dialect made it impossible to understand more than a few words of what they said. All I knew for sure was that they were going to Shaokuan, the same as me, and they were going there to see their daughter's new baby—only nine days old.

After they were done with the chicken, the father and son both tried to light up in the compartment. I told them that smoking was only allowed in the space between cars, and they actually got up and went out. Things had certainly changed. A few years earlier they would have laughed and smoked anyway. The train's sound system had also changed. In place of ear-piercing Chinese opera and comedy routines with laugh tracks, they played easy-listening music featuring lots of accordion and harmonica pieces, and it was turned off at 9:30.

From Wuchang, we headed southwest parallel to the Yangtze. After an hour or so, we rambled past Chihpi, or Red Cliff. Chihpi was the scene of the most famous battle in Chinese history, where Chu-ko Liang and Kuan Yu routed the army of Ts'ao Ts'ao. It was shortly afterwards, while giving chase, that Kuan Yu was surrounded by the enemy and beheaded. An hour later, we stopped briefly at Yuehyang, where memories always rose from the waters of Tungting Lake. It was September 29, 1991. I was with Finn Wilcox and Steve Johnson, and we were high on poetry after visiting Tu Fu's grave earlier in the day.

The Chinese call Tu Fu (712–770) the Sage of Poetry and Li Pai (701–762) the Poetry Immortal. I was traveling through Hunan doing a radio series on Chinese culture for Metro News in Hong Kong and wanted to pay my respects to the Sage. He was buried in the province, but none of the officials in charge of cultural affairs I talked to in the provincial capital of Changsha knew where the grave was located—or maybe they just wouldn't tell me. Fortunately, I had an old map and a general idea, and we followed both from Changsha to the village of Anting. It just happened to be market day, and all the farmers were there with their rigs. One of them knew where the grave was and offered to take us there with his tractor. The grave was so far out in the countryside a tractor was the only way to get there. It was a slow, bumpy ride over four miles of rutted farm roads, but we finally arrived. The old shrine had been turned into a dirt-floor elementary school for farm kids. The school was so far out of touch with the times, they hadn't heard about China's split with Russia in 1956. Over the school's archway next to a portrait of Mao there was another one of Stalin. The principal said it had been over a year since anyone else had visited. He led us around back and helped clear the weeds from in front of the grave. When he died, Tu Fu was living on a small boat he kept moored at Yuehyang. Shortly after arriving in this river port where the borders of the ancient states of Wu and Ch'u once met, he wrote a poem entitled "Climbing Yuehyang Tower":

> I heard long ago about Tungting Lake
> here I am climbing Yuehyang Tower
> where Wu and Ch'u divide south from east
> and the sun and moon and the whole world drift
> of family and friends I have no news
> old and sick all I have is a boat
> warhorses block the way back north
> my tears fall on the railing.

After three bows before his weed-covered grave, we thanked the principal and got back into the tractor's carryall. As we pulled away, we waved goodbye to the whole school. We had stirred up so much excitement, the principal had no choice but to dismiss classes, and dozens of children chased after us as we drove away. A couple of kids even managed to catch up and grab hold of the railing and ride along.

The farmer took us all the way to the next town, which was Pingchiang, where we boarded a bus. An hour or so later, we were in Yuehyang and feeling so euphoric we checked into the swankiest hotel in town. Our room overlooked Tungting Lake, which was formed by the confluence of the Hsiang and the Yangtze, and we pulled the chairs in the room up to the window and drank the few cold beers we were able to find while we looked out across the water to the island where the two wives of Emperor Shun (c. 2200 BC) were buried. They were twin sisters, and when they heard their husband had been killed in battle near the headwaters of the Hsiang, they jumped into the river and became its resident spirits.

While we were sitting there looking out across the lake, Finn called home. His wife told him Miles Davis had died. The first record album I ever owned, and that would have been in 1957, was *Miles Ahead*, something he did with Gil Evans. Miles was our Tu Fu, and hearing that he died took the wind out of our sails. Every time I passed through Yuehyang, the mirror of Tungting Lake brought back that day.

It wasn't just Miles and Tu Fu and the Hsiang sisters who were under those waters, the spirit of China's first great poet was there too. His name was Ch'u Yuan, and he wrote this elegy to the two wives of Emperor Shun:

O daughters of the Lord on High
pity me with your gaze
the wind of autumn stirs

The place where Ch'u Yuan drowned in the Milo River

waves on Tungting and falling leaves
and me looking past the flowering sedge
to an evening planned with my lover.

But Ch'u Yuan's lover was not in this world. A few minutes after we pulled out of Yuehyang, we turned south and crossed the Milo River, where Ch'u Yuan drowned himself in 278 BC rather than continue living in an unrighteous world. His death is celebrated as Poet's Day in China. On the fifth day of the fifth lunar month, Chinese everywhere still re-create the event by going out on rivers and lakes and racing dragon boats in an effort to get to his body before the water dragons do. Just before he died, he wrote: "I'd rather jump into the Hsiang (of which the Milo was a tributary) and be buried in a fish's gut than let something so pure be stained by common dirt." For my friend Mike Ryan, it was "no job, no money, no hope."

. . . . .

Somewhere after we crossed the Milo, I fell asleep, and we spent the night clickety-clacking our way up the Hsiang, and across the Nanling Range, and down into South China. When I woke up the next morning, we were in a different world. The hillsides were covered with all kinds of trees—not just bamboos and pines, but loquats and litchis and bananas and tree ferns and palms and my favorite, *Acacia confusa*, whose little furry yellow balls were still a month away. Everything was green, except the rock formations, which were stupendous. It was one of my favorite landscapes, but one I had only seen from a train and had never explored. Maybe next time. And the air was demanding to be noticed. It was heavy and moist. The Tropic of Cancer was only a few degrees to the south.

Ten hours after leaving Wuhan, I arrived in Shaokuan and the parish of Hui-neng, the last Zen patriarch on my pilgrimage itinerary. Just outside the train station, I stopped long enough to buy a fried egg flatbread for breakfast and more packets of instant coffee. Then I hopped on the back of a waiting motorcycle and asked the driver to take me to Tachien Temple. It wasn't far, maybe half a mile, in an alley just off the main street that ran east-west through the peninsular city.

The temple wasn't much to look at. It had lost nearly all its land to apartment buildings and small factories over the past fifty years. All that was left was a narrow corridor of four-story buildings that featured shrine halls on the first floor and everything else upstairs. I was there because Tachien was where the Sixth Patriarch delivered the sermon that formed the heart of the *Platform Sutra*, the most influential text in the history of Zen. When I went inside, one of the monks told me the abbot was in Kuangchou and wasn't expected back for a few days. Ten other monks were living there, but the abbot was the only one I wanted to talk to. I told him I would be back.

I walked out to the main road and flagged down another motorcycle and returned to the train station. All the buses going to towns in the area were lined up in front of the station, and I boarded one going to Juyuan, twenty-five miles to the west. As I

Tachien Temple in Shaokuan

paid the conductress, I couldn't help noticing her nose. I asked her if she was a Yao, and she nodded "yes." There were three million Yao in China, and Juyuan was one of eight counties they self-administered. There were three kinds of Yao: Red, Black, and Striped. The names referred to their clothing, but the differences went beyond that. A Red Yao once told me an anthropologist who was visiting their village said the language spoken by the Striped Yao was related to that of a Native American tribe, but he didn't know which one. Looking at the conductress's nose, I guessed Navajo.

The Yao used to live along the Hsiang River in Hunan, the one with all the dead poets. In one of the poems Tu Fu composed in his little boat before he died, he wrote: "The Yao shoot wild geese with bows made from mulberry wood." Before they lived along the Hsiang, they lived along the Yangtze and as far downstream as Nanching. But they had been pushed steadily southward until they ended up in a region whose mountains were too steep and too forested for the Han Chinese to farm. As we snaked our way through a countryside no one else wanted, I imagined her ancestors parting at some fork in the trail, one clan going north across the Bering Strait, another south across the Yangtze, then down the Hsiang, and finally over the Nanling Range to the headwaters of the North River, where they lived today.

The way the Yao tell it, a long time ago, the area around Nanching was ruled by King P'ing. King P'ing's kingdom was repeatedly attacked by a kingdom to the north ruled by King Kao. Chinese historians think this occurred during the Chou dynasty about 2,700 years ago. King P'ing was so upset by the attacks, he promised to marry his daughter to anyone who could kill King Kao. Well, among King P'ing's prize possessions was a dragon-dog named P'an-hu. When P'an-hu overheard his master's promise, he crossed the Yangtze and traveled north, arriving seven days later at the palace of King Kao. Since he was only a dog, no one paid any attention to him until it was too late. P'an-hu rushed into the king's bed chamber, ripped off his head, and brought it back to King P'ing.

Since a promise is a promise, the king gave P'an-hu his daughter in marriage. Strangely enough, the princess fell in love with P'an-hu. But she wasn't completely happy. She told her father that her husband turned into a handsome man in a fur robe at night, but in the morning, he turned back into a dog. P'an-hu was enjoying the best of both worlds, but his wife implored him to become a man for good, and he agreed. The royal shaman placed P'an-hu in a covered cage and hung the cage over a boiling cauldron. The shaman said that after seven days of steaming with medicinal plants, P'an-hu would no longer be a dog. But after six days, the princess couldn't wait any longer. She was worried that the steam had killed her husband. She ordered him taken down and removed from the cage.

Not only was he still alive, he was a man. But since he was taken down early, he still had patches of dog hair here and there. To keep her father from finding out that P'an-hu was still part dog, the princess covered her husband's hirsute parts with a turban and pants. Meanwhile, King P'ing was overjoyed, and he turned over his kingdom to his son-in-law. In the years that followed, P'an-hu and his wife had twelve children, and their descendents lived for many generations along the Yangtze until they were overrun by the Han Chinese and migrated south. Some of them ended up in Juyuan: dragon-dog descendents with dragon-dog noses.

I was enjoying my reverie so much, the conductress had to nudge my shoulder to tell me we were at my destination. Less than an hour after leaving Shaokuan, I got off in a wide valley between bamboo-covered hills and walked up the newly asphalted road that led to the largest monastery in South China: Yunmen Temple. It was named after its founder, Yun-men Wen-yen (864–949), one of China's greatest Zen masters. His followers formed one of the most important schools of Zen, and anyone who used koans (*kung-an*) in their practice was indebted to him. Someone once asked him, "How can I find the Way?" He replied, "Start walking."

Yun-men's method of instruction was presaged by his own Enlightenment, which occurred when his teacher, Hsueh-feng Yi-ts'un, slammed the door on his foot and broke it. After that, Yun-men limped around China for many years, until he finally came to Yunmen Mountain in 923 at the age of sixty. He decided to go no farther and the mountain's name became part of his own. That was where he started handing out cookies with his koans, or was it the other way around?

One day he addressed the assembly, "All you need to know is how to get hold of a Zen monk's nose. And what exactly is a Zen monk's nose?" When no one answered, Yun-men yelled, "Maha Prajnaparamita (Great Perfection of Wisdom)! All of you get to work in the fields!" The road to the front gate led past the fields the monks at Yunmen had been working ever since. It was another place where if you didn't work, you didn't eat. Everyone worked.

I walked past the front gate and across the bridge that spanned the pond where pilgrims released fishes and turtles and continued through the hall that honored the Four Guardians of the Universe and the Buddha of the Future. I left my bag outside the guest hall and went inside to inquire about accommodations. One of the guest managers remembered me from a previous visit and led me into the business office to check the registry for availability. He said they had a couple of spare beds in one of the rooms in the new guest facility back outside the gate. Lunch was just beginning, so before sending me off to my room, he led me into the mess hall, which was for lay visitors—all the monks now ate at the Buddhist academy mess hall.

The hall was packed with several hundred laypeople. They were taking part in a ten-day recitation ceremony leading up to Grave Sweeping Day, which was still a week away. I wasn't that hungry and ate as quickly as I could. Afterwards, I went back to the guest hall, collected my bag, and proceeded to the new guest facility. The woman in charge unlocked one of the rooms. Two of the four beds were already taken, and their occupants were off chanting, but the bed by the window was vacant and worked fine. Suddenly I realized I had a headache. I rarely got headaches and figured it was the change in the climate. I was in the tropics now. A couple of aspirins and a nap made everything better.

Yunmen Temple and rice fields

After I woke up, I figured out how to use the hot water heater and took a shower and washed my clothes. Then I walked to the monastery store at the front of the guest facility and bought a metal cup—unlike hotels, there were no large cups in the room—and some sesame crisps to go with the afternoon coffee. I was out of tea. It was all on its way home. I also checked out the monastery bookstore next door and bought a copy of a commentary by Yin-shun to the Pali *Dammapada*. I could envision yet another translation project. I was going to run out of years before I ran out of stuff to translate.

I considered a walk in the hills. There were several waterfalls nearby. But a peal of thunder and a smattering of rain were enough to keep me on the veranda outside my room reading and writing. Despite the nap and lack of activity, I felt lethargic and went to bed right after dinner. I felt as if I was recuperating from something. Maybe it was the heavier air, and maybe it was the road—I had been traveling more than a month. During the night, I woke up briefly when my two roommates returned from chanting, but they were quiet, and I had no trouble going back to sleep. The thunder also woke me up, and the night was filled with the sound of frogs chanting. They had a three-beat chant: *croak croak-croak* and took turns all night with the rain.

Oblivious to it all, or at least undeterred, my roommates got up again at four o'clock and headed off for a predawn session. I got up at seven, had some coffee, and called Ming-hsiang, the new abbot. Ming-chi, the temple manager of Fourth Patriarch Temple, had given me his number. They were dharma brothers, he said. When Ming-hsiang answered, I asked him if I could meet Fo-yuan, the old abbot. He told me to come over right away. Fo-yuan was meeting some monks from Shantung Province, and I could join them.

When I walked outside, the rain had stopped, but there was a heavy fog shrouding everything. Visibility wasn't more than twenty feet. It was as if we were deep in the mountains. I worked my way through several courtyards to the abbot's quarters at the very back. Sitting on a vinyl sofa inside Fo-yuan's reception room were three young monks from North China. Fo-yuan wasn't there yet, and the sofa was sufficiently long that there was room for me as well. The monks were traveling around China on pilgrimage and visiting the great masters of the day. And in the realm of Zen, Fo-yuan had few peers. After a few minutes, Fo-yuan came in with an attendant on either side. We all stood up and bowed.

Fo-yuan was born in 1923 in Hunan and left home to become a monk in 1941 at the age of eighteen. After studying with a number of masters, he came to Yunmen in 1951 to study with Empty Cloud, who made Fo-yuan one of his attendants. Ching-hui was also one of Empty Cloud's attendants at the time. Later that same year, Empty Cloud made both monks dharma heirs of the Yunmen lineage.

Two years later, Empty Cloud went even further. He turned Yunmen over to Fo-yuan, who became abbot at the age of thirty, while Empty Cloud moved to Chenju Temple on Yunchushan. That also marked the beginning of one of the worst periods in Chinese history, at least for those devoted to spiritual practice. With the beginning of Mao's Great Leap Forward in 1958, Fo-yuan was jailed as a Rightist. He narrowly escaped execution and nearly starved to death in prison. In 1961, he was released and sent to join the work crew at Nanhua Temple, the Sixth Patriarch's old temple south of Shaokuan, where he remained for eighteen years. In 1979, when the government finally reaffirmed the right of religious belief and practice, Fo-yuan went on a pilgrimage to other Buddhist centers he had only heard about but had never visited. It was also a pilgrimage to the places where Empty Cloud had lived and practiced.

When Fo-yuan finally returned to Yunmen in 1982, there were only three other monks living there. Within a few years, there were more than a hundred. In 1992, he also took over Nanhua Temple and served as its abbot for eight years, until it was restored to its former prominence. Since then, he had devoted his energies to establishing Yunmen as one of the preeminent centers for Buddhist learning in China. The monastery's Buddhist academy was one of the best in the country, and famous monks and professors of religion came from all over China, and even from other countries, to address the students, which was what Thich Nhat Hanh was doing there when I met him.

I was hoping to see Fo-yuan alone, as were my companions. But given his age and poor health, that was now impossible. Fo-yuan told us to sit back down and asked the young monks if they had any questions. Fo-yuan was a Zen master's Zen Master, and people never knew what to expect from the Old Monk. He surprised the visiting monks by asking about living conditions at their monastery. When they said things weren't good and weren't getting any better, Fo-yuan told them it all depended on relations with the local authorities. If you messed that up, he said, there was nothing you could do. He also said that establishing a Buddhist academy was an important step. It brought in students and donors. And you needed land to farm, he added. He was concerned about what kind of soil they had and what kind of crops they grew. When the monks said that most temples in Shantung Province didn't have any land, Fo-yuan shook his head and told them they needed to invite the local authorities to their temple for an inspection tour and explain to them the importance of being self-sufficient.

They wanted something to fill their heads, but Fo-yuan wanted them to focus on their bellies. One of the hallmarks of Zen temples in China was the emphasis on manual work, and Yunmen was no exception. Everyone took their turn in the monastery's fields and orange groves. While I was sitting there listening to Fo-yuan lecture the young monks about monastic politics, I could smell the scent of orange blossoms coming from the trees on the hillside behind his living quarters. According to botanists, South China was one of several places where the orange was thought to have originated. The Chinese were fond of any fruit with a reddish hue. Red was the color of happiness, the color of life, and the orange was close enough. When Chinese visit one another, they often take oranges as a gift. Since Fo-yuan didn't ask me if I had any questions, and, in truth, I didn't have any, I allowed myself to be transported to the realm where buddhas taught by scent instead of sound, smells instead of words. It seemed like wherever Zen went in China, so did orange trees. Or maybe it was the other way around.

Fo-yuan talked with a great deal of animation, and his attendants were concerned that he had tuckered himself out explaining how to win over the authorities. They suggested he had said enough. As we all stood up to say goodbye, he gave each of us a bag of *hu-ping* cookies. It was an inside joke. A thousand years ago, one of Master Yun-men's favorite responses to questions about Zen was "*hu-ping*"—a *hu-ping* being a kind of flat pastry filled with honey and sesame.

When I first met Fo-yuan the year before, he was bouncing around like a pitchman at a carnival. He asked me, "What are you afraid of?" And before I could answer, he danced off and started talking to a group of laywomen until they were all giggling. Then he came back and asked me again, "So, what are you afraid of?" And he was gone again. This year he didn't bounce or dance or ask me any questions. He moved with difficulty, and his attendants hovered near him, as if anticipating a fall. When I told Fo-yuan that last year he seemed in better health, he laughed and said, "What do you expect: birth, illness, old age, and death. Wait until you're my age."

We all bowed, and Ming-hsiang ushered us outside. When I got back to my room,

I had a new roommate. He was lying in the room's last vacant bed. He said he was from Shaokuan and was there to give acupressure treatments to the monks taking part in the chanting. It was his way of earning merit. He said he had been up all night, and five minutes later he was snoring.

I sat up in bed and read the history published by the monastery about Yun-men and Fo-yuan, and all the monks in between. After lunch, I finally managed to catch Ming-hsiang again and sat down with him long enough to share a cup of tea in the guest hall. When I told him I would be leaving the next day, he offered to provide transportation to Tachien and Nanhua, the two temples in the area associated with the Sixth Patriarch. I could sense earlier that he was not happy with me when I raised the subject of Fo-yuan's deteriorating health. He told me to be there in the guest hall at eight o'clock. And that was it. No bobbing or weaving.

Since I didn't have anything else to do, I walked out to the highway and flagged down a ride in a minivan and went into Juyuan, which was only four miles away. After catching up on my e-mail, I stopped in a phone shop to add more time to my account. The wireless system in China was a mystery to me. It seemed like every province was independent. Once you were outside the province where you activated your phone, it was hard, not impossible but hard, to add money to your account. In this case, I had to buy a new number. Of course, the new number was activated in Kuangtung Province, which meant I would have the same problem adding money in another province. But that would be another trip. What I found remarkable, though, was how dependent I had become on a cell phone in China. But so had the other five hundred million people who had cell phones.

When I returned to Yunmen, as I was walking up from the highway, I saw a woman dressed completely in black coming toward me. I thought maybe she was in mourning. But when we passed each other and exchanged greetings, she turned out to be a foreigner and sounded European. We both proceeded in opposite directions, but later at dinner we shared the same table. Her name was Daniela Campo, and she was from Sicily. She was working on a PhD at the University of Paris, and the subject of her thesis was Empty Cloud. She was visiting all the temples where he had lived for any period of time. As far as I knew, no one in the West had ever written anything about him, other than the odd paean of praise. She said she had been working on the project for eight years. I was truly impressed. Empty Cloud was one of my heroes.

After dinner, we carried our conversation outside. While we were talking, one of the monks came up and invited us to visit the Buddhist academy later that evening. Normally it was off-limits to outsiders, but at the appointed time one of the monks found us waiting under the pavilion by the fishpond and escorted us to the academy's reception room. Waiting for us inside were Yunmen's chief guest manager, Wan-t'ai, and two of the academy's instructors. One of them taught the students the *Shurangama Sutra*. The other taught Vasubandhu's *Weishihlun Shastra* on the Mahayana's Mind Only philosophy. And presiding over the soiree was Ming-hsuan, the chief meditation instructor.

It was a free-for-all, and Ming-hsuan was a hoot. He was out of the same mold as Fo-yuan and practiced Take No Prisoners Zen: direct, challenging, and fun to a fault. His laugh was unforgettable. He was forty-five and was already down to three or four visible teeth. He must have lived on gruel and sweet dew. We went through pot after pot of Iron Goddess and could have talked all night. I finally called it quits around ten o'clock, but Daniela stayed for another hour. During the night, the heavens opened up and rained as if it was the end of the world.

. . . . .

The next morning, the monastery was still there. I packed up and went to the guest hall to meet the driver Ming-hsiang had assigned to take me to Tachien and Nanhua temples. Daniela was also waiting there with her bag. She said she was also planning to go to Nanhua and asked if she could join me. Except for Empty Cloud's few remaining disciples, she knew more about him than anyone alive. How could I refuse? After traveling alone for more than a month, suddenly I had a companion.

The driver finally arrived, and we left with a huge send-off. I didn't realize it, but Daniela had been escorted from Kuangchou by a group of professors and graduate students from Sun Yat-sen University. They looked concerned that they were now turning her over to another foreigner. They must have thought: "the blind leading the blind." I knew it was a waste of breath to suggest otherwise, but I told them not to worry. The bodhisattvas protected those who worked for the Dharma. And off we went, into a downpour that didn't let up until we reached Shaokuan.

As we drove through town, I asked the driver to stop at a post office so I could mail more books home—it was my third box, and it didn't take more than ten minutes to unburden myself. Our next stop was Tachien Temple, where I had stopped briefly two days earlier. This time there must have been a dozen beggars in front of the entrance. It was a Saturday, and Grave Sweeping Day was approaching. Time to get straight with the ancestors. After divesting ourselves of the coins in our pockets, we went inside and walked through the place. The buildings that once formed the rear of the temple had been knocked down to make way for a pagoda, yet to be built, and there was actually the appearance of space in what was otherwise a very narrow piece of property. The two bodhi trees planted five hundred years earlier were the only things left from whatever was there in the distant past.

The abbot had managed to reacquire some of the surrounding buildings built on the temple's grounds during the Cultural Revolution, and there was an architectural illustration on one of the walls showing how half the neighborhood would eventually be replaced by new shrine halls and residential buildings for the monks. While we were walking around, we met the guest manager. He said the abbot was still in Kuangchou, but he was due back the following day. He asked us to stay for lunch, but our driver was anxious to get back to Yunmen. We arranged to return at noon on the following day.

Entrance of Nanhua Temple

Our final stop was Nanhua Temple nine miles south-southeast of Shaokuan. Nanhua was where Hui-neng lived for forty years after becoming the Sixth Patriarch. The temple was a big draw in South China. Some days it saw thousands of pilgrims. Hui-neng was as close to a buddha as the Chinese have been willing to admit into the pantheon of enlightened ones. And he was a southerner.

The first time I was there, the area in front of the temple was occupied by hundreds of incense sellers. During that visit, the guest manager told me that once when the abbot decided to hold a seven-week meditation retreat and wanted to reduce the noise from pilgrims, he closed the gate, which so infuriated the incense sellers, they smashed it down. Since then, there had been some sort of accommodation. The area in front was now a parking lot, and the incense sellers had moved into permanent stalls along both sides. The abbot, I learned later, had agreed to keep the gate and the first set of shrine halls open year-round. Meanwhile, he was building an adjacent set of halls that could be used for retreats and to which visitors would not have access.

Instead of dropping us off among the incense sellers in front, our driver drove around to the side gate and honked. A monk swung the gate open, and the driver followed a winding road through a thinned-out pine forest to within a hundred yards of the guest hall. We got out, thanked him, and went to see about accommodations. With the approach of Grave Sweeping Day, I wasn't sure there would be room. I didn't have any contacts at the temple and hadn't called ahead.

We were in luck. The guest manager turned us over to the laywoman in charge of guest quarters, who led us to the second floor of one of the buildings set aside for lay visitors and gave us adjacent rooms. I was surprised by the adjacent rooms. In most monasteries, male and female visitors were put up in separate sections, or at least on separate floors. I was also surprised by the quality of the furnishings. Each room had two beds, a tea table, and two large armchairs, and they were all made of wood. And the bathroom had a hot water heater, laundry detergent, towels, and toilet paper. The only things missing were a bedside table and a reading light. But then it wasn't supposed to be a resort hotel. And most visitors were there to take part in ceremonies, not to lie in bed reading.

We were just in time for lunch, a nap, and a page in the old journal. I was finally writing in the present. When I knocked on Daniela's door, she was working on her journal too. She was only twenty-eight and apparently too young for naps.

She had filled up four pages. And they were much bigger pages. I suggested we venture forth and tour the grounds, which we proceeded to do. Daniela had to inspect every inscription, every date. She was working on a PhD. But I wasn't, so I wandered ahead.

Nanhua was one of several temples built in the area by an Indian monk named Chih-yao. After arriving in Kuangchou by sea from India, he sailed up the North River in AD 502. When he reached the place where the river was joined by the Tsaohsi, he took a drink and said it tasted like the water where he lived in India. He said surely there was an auspicious place upstream for a temple. At the time he was on his way to Wutaishan to pay his respects to Manjushri, the Bodhisattva of Wisdom, and he didn't stay to investigate. But when he returned from his pilgrimage, he built a temple near the headwaters of the Tsaohsi and became its first abbot in 505. It remained a modest temple, but Chih-yao was right. It was auspicious.

This time I bypassed the shrine halls and went straight to the patriarch's hall. In place of the usual buddha statue, the body of Hui-neng (638–713), the Sixth Patriarch of Zen, was in the middle of the altar. Flanking him were the preserved bodies of Tan-t'ien (d. 1614), about whom I knew absolutely nothing, and Han-shan Te-ch'ing (d. 1623), with whom I've long felt a strong connection and whose old hut I had tried but failed to visit on Wutaishan. Both monks were abbots of the temple during the Ming dynasty.

Hui-neng came to Chih-yao's old temple in 677, a few months after being ordained in Kuangchou. The temple at that time was called Paolin: "Forest of Jewels," and Hui-neng also found it to be an auspicious place. During the forty years he taught there, thousands of monks and nuns and laypeople came from all over China to learn the direct teaching of Zen from him. If any one person could be singled out as contributing to the spread of Zen, it was Hui-neng. Zen, I suspect, would have still flourished without him. But it would have been different. My guess is the practice would have been more cloistered, more superficial, and more full of itself. Hui-neng expanded it, deepened it, and emptied it.

Hui-neng's final advice to his disciples just before he died was:

Sit together in meditation, but remain free of stillness and movement, birth and death, coming and going, right and wrong, past and present. Be at ease and at peace. That is the Great Way. After I'm gone, simply practice in accordance with

the Dharma, the same as when I was with you. And if I were here, and you dis-
obeyed my teaching, even my presence would be of no help.

And what was his teaching? "See your nature and become a buddha." It was the same
teaching Bodhidharma brought to China. The words weren't so important as the
directness with which they were spoken.

In anticipation of Grave Sweeping Day, there were lots of visitors at the temple
lighting incense, but most of them stopped at the patriarch's hall. I only stayed long
enough to add a few more sticks to the pyre. Then I walked out the rear gate and
found myself nearly alone in a forest of gargantuan trees. Off to one side was the
Empty Cloud Memorial. Empty Cloud also rebuilt Nanhua Temple. He came there
in 1934, and when he was done, he turned the place over to one of his disciples in
1943 and then invited Pen-huan to take over in 1948.

The lay Buddhist master Nan Huai-chin told me a story about Empty Cloud's
penchant for rebuilding temples and turning them over to others. Master Nan was
over ninety when he told me this story. He recalled that during the Second World War
when he was still a young layman and accompanying Empty Cloud in Chungching,
he asked his teacher, "Master, why are you always rebuilding temples, then turning
them over to others without ever finishing them yourself? You leave all the temples
you rebuild half-done." Empty Cloud slapped his young lay disciple on the back of
the head and said, "You little smart aleck, if I finished rebuilding them, what would
the next generation have to do?"

After Empty Cloud's death in 1959 at the age of 120 (Daniela says he was 116), his
body was cremated, and his relics were distributed among the temples where he had
served as abbot, including Yunmen and Nanhua. Empty Cloud, some say, was Han-
shan Te-ch'ing in a previous life. Maybe that was why I felt such a strong connection to both monks. After paying my respects to his latest incarnation, I went to find
his biographer. She had finally satisfied herself that there were no traces among the
temple's inscriptions of his writings or calligraphy, and we returned to our rooms. I
pulled my table and two armchairs outside onto the veranda, and we discussed our
mutual projects.

Before long the sun reached the top of the temple roofs, and we heard the sound
of the dinner board. This time the layperson in charge of such things led us into
the VIP mess hall. That really bothered Daniela. Her sympathies were decidedly

proletarian. She couldn't bear the thought of receiving something other people weren't. So we dined in the adjacent hall on the more modest fare bestowed on the hoi polloi. And no way was she going to let someone wash her bowl.

Afterwards, we went for a stroll and happened to meet the temple manager. His name was Chao-yuan, and he invited us to his room. While he made some tea, I asked him how many monks were living at Nanhua. He said there were two hundred, and forty of them lived in the meditation hall. They didn't just spend time in the meditation hall, he said, they lived there, which was the way it used to be at Zen temples. There were always a few who preferred to do their work on a cushion. When I asked him about the meditation schedule, he said there were fourteen periods a day: seven sitting and seven walking. Walking periods at most places were usually ten minutes, but at Nanhua, he said, they lasted anywhere from twenty minutes to an hour.

He also said they had a new Buddhist academy. It only had fifty students, but that number was due to double with the construction of a new set of buildings. Every temple, it seemed, was embarking on a building project, which reflected the incredible amount of money that was pouring into religious centers in China from people who had been cut off from religion for decades. The first thing Chinese do when they become affluent, or maybe it's the second thing, is send money ahead—to the next life.

Chao-yuan also talked to us about Buddhism. But it was as if he was repeating something he had said to others, or had heard from others. He spoke impeccable Mandarin, and everything he said and did was very careful, very deliberate. He was ordained at Kaomin Temple, the West Point of monastic training outside Yangchou. But something was missing. If Fo-yuan had been there, he would have asked him what he was afraid of; either that or given him a cookie to go with the tea.

When I asked about the things the Sixth Patriarch had left behind, Chao-yuan said he couldn't show us anything unless the abbot was there. When I asked when the abbot would be back, he said he didn't know and added that he didn't dare ask. It would have been impolite. He must have thought that a couple foreigners didn't require a more reasonable explanation. Finally, he said there was nothing to see anyway. Of course, I had seen photographs of the things Hui-neng had left behind at the temple: his staff, his socks, the robe given to him by Empress Wu. But Chao-yuan was not about to admit their existence, much less show them to us.

We didn't stay for a second pot of tea and thanked Chao-yuan for his hospitality. We returned to our rooms and called it a night. After a hot shower—alas, there were no bathtubs—I lay down and listened to the monks chanting a memorial service, calling back and forth to each other. I didn't know if it was the text or just the way they chanted, but it reminded me of the way the hill tribes in the area used to sing, and maybe still did. They finally stopped around nine o'clock. As soon as they did, the frogs and crickets began. Then the bell and drum took over. The next thing I knew, it was morning.

. . . . .

The water in my thermos was lukewarm, so I walked down to the kitchen and filled it up with hot water from the boiler. When I got back, Daniela was sitting outside rolling a smoke. She said she must have looked as pale as a ghost. I hadn't noticed. She was still riding the wave of youth, and I thought it was the morning light. She said her mother called on her cell phone after she went to bed to tell her that her grandfather died. She said she cried all night. She and her grandfather were close. She cried, she said, because the path she had chosen had taken her away from her family and had kept her away. She said whenever there was a family tragedy or a celebration, she wasn't there. It also didn't help when she got a roommate during the night—a late-arriving pilgrim from Kuangchou.

While we shared a couple cups of coffee, she told me more about her grandfather. I told her that however much he would have enjoyed seeing her, he wouldn't have wanted her to turn back. Since I didn't have anything else on my agenda, and since our lunch date at Tachien Temple was hours away, I asked her if there was someplace in the area she hadn't yet visited where Empty Cloud might have left something behind. She said she had read about another temple he had rebuilt when he was abbot of Nanhua. That sounded good to me. That was, after all, what she and I were doing so far from home: following threads that might help us weave together our respective stories.

And that was what we did. We followed Empty Cloud through the monastery's front gate out to the highway and asked at the small stores that sold incense and snacks. Daniela found someone who had heard of the temple he rebuilt. It was twelve miles to the south. In the monastery parking lot, we also found a taxi driver—Mr. Yang—who agreed to take us there and back for 120RMB, or fifteen dollars. And off we went.

Even though the storeowner gave Mr. Yang directions, he kept stopping to ask along the way, which I've always taken as a good sign in a driver. He was determined to get us there, and he did. Just north of the village of Wushih, or Black Rock, we turned off near a coal-fired power plant and drove across a small bridge that spanned the Tsaohsi River, the same river that flowed past Nanhua Temple. Just past the bridge, we drove through an archway announcing Yuehhua, or Moonglow Temple. Another two hundred yards past the temple flowed the wide waters of the North River that had brought Chih-yao there 1,500 years earlier.

There was a new wall around the site and a pyramid-shaped shrine hall going up. It was only half-finished and was still surrounded by bamboo scaffolding. Other than that, the only other buildings weren't much more than sheds. Just inside the gate, a young monk was talking to a bunch of laywomen. They were engaged in fundraising and had a table set up with ledgers for writing down the names of donors and amounts donated.

After we exchanged introductions, the monk said he had only been there a month. He was from Shaolin Temple and had brought funds for rebuilding the temple. There were also two older monks, and they clearly had problems with the newcomer. It was unclear whether the Shaolin monk was really from Shaolin or how he had insinuated himself into the place. Shaolin was a zillion miles away, and why would the abbot of Shaolin send funds to rebuild a small funky temple in the middle of nowhere in the shadow of a power plant? It wasn't until later that I realized what was going on.

While Daniela poked around for inscriptions or relics of the past, I talked to a laywoman who seemed to know more than anyone else. She said that a temple was first built on the site by Chih-yao, the Indian monk who also built Nanhua. The two temples had been connected ever since. Whenever Nanhua was rebuilt, so was Yuehhua. Hui-neng rebuilt both temples, so did Han-shan Te-ch'ing, and so did Empty Cloud. In the past, monks and pilgrims from Kuangchou usually traveled by boat up the North River to that point. And because the North River then turned northwest away from Nanhua, they disembarked and followed the Tsaohsi River to Nanhua Temple's front gate. That was why Shaolin had sent down funds to rebuild Yuehhua Temple. The abbot of Shaolin had decided it would be good to have a Shaolin foot in the Nanhua door. And Yuehhua was its front gate. It was the board game known as Chinese Politics.

Although there was nothing left of the temple's previous incarnations, there was a statue of Chih-yao inside the shed that passed for the patriarch's hall. However, everyone disagreed as to whether it contained the actual body of the Indian monk, or whether Chih-yao's preserved body had been destroyed by the Red Guards. Since there was no way to settle the matter short of drilling a hole in the statue, and since there was nothing else to see, we paid our respects, thanked our hosts for showing us around, and walked back to our taxi.

As we were getting ready to leave, the laywoman I had talked to came over and whispered through the car's open window. She asked us if we had heard that the place where Hui-neng hid when he was being chased had been recently rediscovered.

Hui-neng's Refuge Rock

After Hui-neng became the Sixth Patriarch, people had tried to steal the robe and bowl he had been given by the Fifth Patriarch as signs of transmission. Near the end of Chapter One of later versions of the *Platform Sutra*, the text recounts an occasion when the people pursuing Hui-neng set fire to the mountain where he was hiding to flush him out. The laywoman said the place was across from Nanhua Temple and she would be happy to take us there. I told her to get in.

Her name was Li Sheng-hua, and she sat up front with Mr. Yang. When we got back to Nanhua Temple, she directed him to cross the small bridge that spanned the Tsaohsi River opposite the temple's main gate. Once across, we followed a dirt road that was thoroughly rutted from the deluge of the past few days. It led past a few farmhouses and halfway up a small mountain. We took it as far as we could, then we got out and walked up a dirt trail.

Just below the summit, the trail ended at a jumble of huge boulders surrounded by a brick wall. There was a gate in front, and a gate near the rear, and both were locked. The laywoman said the nun who took care of the place must have gone to town. While we paused to catch our breath and consider our options, Mr. Yang found enough footing to scale one of the boulders. Once he was high enough, he was able to jump over the wall. Then he opened the rear gate from inside. This was where Hui-neng crouched while the whole mountain went up in flames, and the imprint of his robe was still visible on a niche in the rocks. An altar had been set up in front of the niche, and the caretaker had provided incense for pilgrims like ourselves to light.

The amazing thing about the place was that it had only recently been rediscovered. An artist named Chu Te-jui tracked it down in 1978 using local records. Apparently it was known in the past but not considered significant enough to warrant a regular shrine. But times had changed. Not only was there a resurgence in Buddhist belief and practice throughout China, there was also a keen interest among local authorities in developing any site that might have tourist potential. In 2002, Mr. Chu finally gained their approval for protecting the site with a wall and for setting up a small shrine. According to a pamphlet next to the incense, the caretaker was a nun named Chih-sheng. She came there in 2005 on pilgrimage and was so moved, she decided to stay and take care of the place.

We lit some incense and left a donation. Then I checked the time on my alarm clock. It was nearly noon, when we were supposed to be at Tachien Temple. We hurried back down to the taxi and dropped off Mrs. Li in the next town, which was

Mapa. We tried to give her some money for her trouble, but she wouldn't take it. She was such an angel and looked the part, dressed in a pink and silver brocade jacket. She was thoroughly excited by our adventure together and in her part in it. Helping us, she said, was sufficient reward.

We arrived at Tachien Temple thirty minutes late, but not too late for lunch. The abbot was waiting for us, as was lunch. It was a feast: tofu shrimp, crispy tofu fish, fried wheat gluten, and four or five other vegetarian dishes. After making sure we ate all we could, he led us upstairs to his reception room. The abbot's name was Fa-chih. He looked to be in his fifties, but he had the energy of someone much younger. He told us he had been in Kuangchou for the past week studying Chinese medicine. He said it was one of the arts expected of a monk in the past, and he wanted to learn more in order to help his parishioners.

He made a pretty good pot of tea and poured us all cups, then gathered his legs into the lotus position and asked me if I had any questions about the *Platform Sutra*. Tachien Temple was where the sermon that formed its heart was delivered, and I had told him on the phone that I had recently finished a translation of the text. I surprised myself, and Fa-chih as well, I think. I didn't have any questions about the sutra. It was what it was. But I was curious about the temple. I asked him if it was in the same place when Hui-neng was there. I'm glad I asked. He said the original temple was about five hundred yards to the south, closer to the river. It had been washed away in a flood centuries ago. He wasn't sure exactly when, only that it had been rebuilt on higher ground away from where the two rivers meet and that the bodhi trees near the rear of the temple were grown from cuttings of the original trees. That was the only question I could think of. Otherwise, my mind was a blank.

Fortunately, Daniela had questions about Empty Cloud, and Fa-chih knew quite a lot. He even gave her the name and phone number of one of Empty Cloud's disciples who lived in the next county. During the third pot of tea, I finally mustered a question about the existence of the Sixth Patriarch's staff and robe. Fa-chih said they were still at Nanhua Temple in the second floor of the sutra library. He knew, he said, because he used to be temple manager of Nanhua. Obviously, the current temple manager did not share his openness.

After the fourth pot of tea, even Daniela was out of questions. Fa-chih was excited that a couple of foreigners were interested in Hui-neng and Empty Cloud. But he appeared disappointed that we limited ourselves to inquiring about their lives and not about their teachings. He seemed to be waiting for us to ask questions we never asked. I felt like a bump on a log. Finally, he had one of his assistants bring us bags of "Zen Tea" and told us to call him if we had any more questions. We thanked him and returned to Nanhua. At one of the stalls near the main gate, Daniela filled up a bag with small yellow mangoes. When we got back to our rooms, I pulled the table and chairs from my room onto the veranda again, and we sat down. Daniela reached into her boot, and pulled out a Uighur knife, the kind they used on the Silk Road for melons. She peeled and handed me mango after mango, and I wondered if there was any fruit more luscious. Having feasted at lunch and later on fruit, we skipped dinner and talked about Empty Cloud until it was dark. The laywoman in charge of guest quarters came by and said she would turn on the outside lights for us. We told her to let them be. The darkness was fine.

Author and Daniela Campo eating mangoes at Nanhua Temple

The next morning we called Mr. Yang and arranged for another excursion. Daniela left no stone unturned in her effort to learn all she could about Old Empty, as he was called. This time the stone was Liu Ts'un-chi, the disciple Fa-chih told us about the previous day. He lived in Lechang, thirty miles northwest of Shaokuan. It wasn't that far away, but after the recent downpours, the road was in terrible shape, and it took us two hours to get there. When we finally arrived, we called Mr. Liu, and he came to meet us on his motor scooter, with his three-year-old granddaughter standing between his legs. He told us to follow him and led us to his house just up the road from the town's morning market. I was expecting someone older. He was only sixty-eight and would have been nineteen when Empty Cloud died. He said he met Empty Cloud when he was in his early teens, and after becoming his disciple, he visited him often at Nanhua and later at Yunmen and even once at Chenju Temple on Yunchushan, just before he died.

Mr. Liu's accent was nearly impenetrable, and neither of us understood more than half of what he said. But of what we did understand, I finally heard what happened to the Sixth Patriarch's body during the Cultural Revolution. He said the Red Guards took the body from Nanhua Temple to Shaokuan. But before they did, they opened the back and dug out some of the desiccated insides and filled it full of straw. Then in Shaokuan, they took out the body in public and pulled the straw out to prove to people that the body they had been worshipping was a fake. Mister Liu said the arms were also knocked off and later reattached, but with the hands flat, when earlier they had been cupped. But the face, he said, wasn't damaged, and the body was later returned to Nanhua.

He also said the things Hui-neng left behind were still there at Nanhua. Even during the Cultural Revolution, they were never taken out from the second floor of the sutra library—only a set of copies. Although he was forthcoming about such things, he was reluctant to criticize the abuses of the Red Guards, and he skirted whatever political issues we brought up. Some lessons are never forgotten.

Mr. Liu didn't seem to have expected us to stay for lunch, which was very un-Chinese. We kept waiting. Finally at 12:15, he extended a feeble invitation. But nothing was going on in the kitchen, or we would have smelled it. So we thanked him and told him we had to get back. As he saw us off, though, he told our driver about a different route back via Yunmen Temple, which only took an hour, instead of two.

Back at Nanhua, Daniela went on one last inspection tour of the grounds, and

I recorded Mr. Liu's remarks, few though they were, in my journal. After dinner, while we were walking around, we met two young monks who told us the abbot was back. We asked them if they could arrange a meeting, and they said they would try. We also went to say goodbye to the temple manager and thanked him for his hospitality. He was a nice enough fellow but a black hole of misinformation. No doubt he had been hurt in the past by offering more help than he should have and wasn't taking any chances.

Meanwhile, back on the veranda, Daniela manifested another bag of fruit, more mangoes, and tangerines, too. We had a long discussion about Zen and Taoism. She was an advocate of the view current among most Western scholars—and some Eastern ones too—that Zen didn't come from India but resulted from the intersection of Chinese Taoism with Indian Buddhism. The proposition would be difficult, if not impossible, to prove either way, and would ultimately depend upon how one defined terms as much as the marshalling of so-called facts.

I've never liked the idea. Over the years, I've combed through the biographies of hundreds of early Zen monks. Among those who had an affiliation prior to becoming monks, most were Confucians. Taoists were rare. But I would suggest that Zen didn't derive in whole or in part from Taoism or Confucianism, or even from Buddhism as it existed in China at the time. Zen was something new. Who else besides Zen masters delivered wordless lectures or offered sermons in a cup of tea—no Taoist or Confucian I've ever heard of, and no Buddhist prior to Bodhidharma.

The Chinese are incurable record-keepers and couldn't avoid turning Zen into just another written tradition. But it was and remains the quintessential invisible tradition. It isn't a tradition in the normal sense. It's just the mind in action. I think it was more a matter of an invisible tradition, unrecorded in a land known for not keeping records, namely India, arriving in a land known for its record keeping. And when Zen finally ended up in the hands of the Fourth, Fifth, and Sixth patriarchs and their students, it went from the limited confines of private transmission to communal practice and spread throughout China, affecting everything from art to gardening. That was my view, and I was sticking to it. And thus we talked about Zen on the veranda of the temple where Hui-neng tried to get people to stop talking about it. Finally the evening bell sent us back to our rooms, while the crescent moon smiled above the temple roof. Goodnight, Hui-neng.

The next morning we packed up and were sipping our coffees when the two young monks we had met the previous evening reappeared and told us the abbot was ready to see us. They were as new as monks could be. One of them had only been a monk for three months, and the other's ordination was scheduled for the next auspicious day. They led us through a maze of corridors to the new buildings east of the main shrine halls. That was the monastery's solution to the distraction of the temple's own fame: a monastery within a monastery. We followed our guides up a series of huge steps to a mammoth set of doors. They knocked, and a monk inside squeaked open one of the doors. We stepped inside a courtyard covered with hundreds of potted plants in bloom. We were in South China, and it was early April.

The courtyard was surrounded by the wings of a three-story building. It was the new residence of the monastery's senior monks. The abbot's reception room was on the second floor, and he was waiting for us. His name was Ch'uan-cheng, and he looked to be in his late fifties or early sixties. He had a bad cold, and we kept our meeting with him short. Still, he confirmed the existence of the items that Hui-neng left behind: the socks, the staff, and the thousand-buddha robe presented to him by Empress Wu. And he confirmed the authenticity of Refuge Rock, where Hui-neng hid out and which we had visited two days earlier. He also confirmed Mr. Liu's story about Hui-neng's body being stuffed with straw and hauled out of the temple by the Red Guards and taken to Shaokuan for public humiliation.

Ch'uan-cheng was clearly not feeling his best, and we did not want to impose. But before we left, he gave us the Hong Kong phone number of Yi-ch'ao, one of the last disciples of Empty Cloud still engaged in teaching Zen. He said Yi-ch'ao knew as much as anyone left alive about Empty Cloud. Ch'uan-cheng loaded us down with bags of gifts commemorating the fifteen-hundred-year anniversary of Nanhua Temple, which was celebrated the year before. He also gave us his name card and wrote down his cell phone number, should we have any further questions. Such a welcome contrast to the temple manager.

We thanked him and walked back to the main shrine hall to pay our final respects to Hui-neng. After collecting our bags, we headed out of the monastery. Three guinea hens someone had "released" at the temple began following us. The Chinese called them "pearl-birds" because of the white specks that marked their plumage. They followed us as far as the huge pond where people released aquatic creatures to earn merit. Thousands of fishes were floating belly-up. When the weather turned warm, the water had needed changing, but the monks had been too busy with all the memorial services leading up to Grave Sweeping Day, which was the following day. Workers were draining the pond and netting the few fish that had survived. We walked out the front gate and looked for Mr. Yang.

15 NO END IN SIGHT

My pilgrimage was almost over. There was only one more page on my itinerary, and it began in Kuangchou. Mr. Yang was waiting for us outside Nanhua Temple and took us back to Shaokuan, where we caught a bus. Three hours later, Daniela and I found ourselves in the chaos of the Kuangchou bus station. The traffic and the crowds were overwhelming, and it was with difficulty that we finally managed to corral a taxi, which we took to Shamian Island. Shamian, or Sand Flat, was seventy-five acres of Pearl River mud connected to the southern edge of the old city by pedestrian and vehicular bridges. It was created by digging a channel parallel to the river, then piling up the resulting mud on the river side of the channel and building a granite embankment around it. This man-made island was one of the concessions won by the British and French as a result of the Opium Wars in the middle of the nineteenth century. It provided their officials and merchants with their own little world from which to sally forth and to which to retreat. There were still dozens of colonial mansions on the island, and a few of the larger ones had become hotels. I got out on the south side of the island at the Shamian Hotel, and Daniela continued on to the proletarian accommodations of the Sun Yat-sen University Hostel. We agreed to meet the next day at the place where Bodhidharma stayed when he arrived.

When I went inside the Shamian to get a room, I smelled glue. The hotel was under renovation. It was just as well. I had never been to that part of Kuangchou before and didn't realize the White Swan would be right across the street. I had heard about the White Swan. It was the first really big, really fancy hotel built in Kuangchou. In fact, it was China's first joint-venture hotel built with Hong Kong money. It catered to foreign tour groups. And there were foreigners everywhere, big crowds of big people. I had forgotten how big Westerners were, especially Americans. Outside on the sidewalk, I felt like I was swimming among manatees. And the surrounding lanes overflowed with shops selling the chintziest of souvenirs. It was too much too fast. After five weeks in the provinces, I needed something less brazen. I took a taxi to the quieter north side of the island and checked into the Victory. A room in the old building was a reasonable 280RMB, or thirty-five bucks. And there was a liquor store next door. The single malt was beyond my reach, but the port was a modest 110RMB a bottle. That night I didn't need the temple bell to put me to sleep. The ruby red and my first hot bath in a week were more than up to the job.

The next morning, I took a taxi back across the Pearl and about twenty blocks to the west. Just off the corner of Changshou and Kangwang roads, amid a gauntlet of jade shops, I met Daniela at the entrance to Hualin Temple, where Bodhidharma lived after he arrived from India.

Bodhidharma was the third son of the ruler of Pallava, which was a kingdom that occupied the eastern flank of India's southern tip. Its seaport of Mahabalipuram was a major embarkation point for merchants carrying goods between India and China, and that was where Bodhidharma sailed from at the urging of his teacher, Prajnatara. The trip was slow going, as ships in those days had to hug the coast, and he made a few stops along the way. It took him three years to reach Kuangchou, or Nanhai (South Seas), as it was called. According to the earliest account of his life, Bodhidharma arrived around AD 475 and stayed in Kuangchou for three years before heading north. Later accounts delay his arrival until as late as 520, apparently to make his meeting with Emperor Wu of the Liang dynasty plausible, as Emperor Wu didn't ascend the throne until 502. Either way, this was where he stayed.

It was hard to imagine what Hualin Temple looked like back then. I'm guessing it was bigger. Kuangchou in those days was as much a foreign city as it was Chinese. According to the estimates of early Chinese and Arab historians, there were anywhere from 100,000 to 200,000 foreigners living in the city between the sixth and tenth centuries. That was a lot of foreigners. But it was also a transient population. Most of them were merchants and seamen, and they were always on the move, traveling back and forth between China and the various kingdoms of South and Southeast Asia.

Since the temple was located in the part of the city set aside for foreigners, it's likely it began simply as a temporary residence for Indian monks. Eventually, though, the residence became a monastery—one of the four largest in the city. It was called Hsilai, "From the West," which was a reference to the place of origin of its residents as well as to one of the most popular koans given to students of Zen: "Why did Bodhidharma come from the West?" In the seventeenth century, the name was changed to Hualin, or Flowering Grove, when the land around the temple was planted with hundreds of fruit trees. Those days are long gone, as are the temple's park-like grounds. Although the temple was now actively engaged in recovering what it had lost to apartment buildings and shops, the process was a slow, building-by-building process. Until recently, it hardly looked like the place had ever been anything more than a neighborhood shrine.

We just happened to arrive on Chingming, or Grave Sweeping Day. Chingming was one of those ancient folk festivals not considered worthy of note until about two thousand years ago. No one knows when or how it began. Unlike other annual celebrations, it was a solar holiday, occurring fifteen days after the spring equinox. Thus, it usually fell on April 5.

Hualin was a cloud of smoke from the reams of paper money and bundles of incense people were setting on fire. To get away from it all, we entered the only shrine hall left from the temple's nineteenth-century incarnation. It was built just after the end of the First Opium War (1841). Instead of a single altar with one or more buddhas, the shrine hall consisted of corridors in the form of the "field" 田. The corridors were lined with five hundred life-size bronze statues of *arhats*. The Sanskrit term, meaning "free of passion," used to refer to the paragons of early Buddhism who had transcended the world of red dust. At least that was the original idea. Obviously, membership requirements had been relaxed. One *arhat* in particular looked out of place. It was a statue of Marco Polo. But then again, maybe it belonged. After all, he came from the West.

From the Buddhist Hall of Fame, we returned to the smoke-filled courtyard but sought refuge this time in the temple's newest shrine hall. It was built to honor Bodhidharma, and featured a bronze statue of the Indian patriarch that was twenty feet high. The statue must have cost a ton, and it wasn't badly made, but after seeing the human-sized statues of the other patriarchs, this superhuman one seemed un-Zen-like, as did all the worship that was going on before it. I could hear Bodhidharma: "Your mind is the buddha. Don't use a buddha to worship a buddha." (*The Zen Teaching of Bodhidharma*, p. 25)

One of the attendants, who was making sure worshippers didn't burn the place down, said there was a third, much bigger hall planned. As soon as a few adjacent apartment buildings were razed, the abbot was going to build a shrine hall for the relics of the Buddha that had been found in a stone crypt at the temple in 1965. The relics had been secretly sent there by Emperor Shun-chih in 1655 shortly after he founded the Ch'ing dynasty. There was no inscription about where he had gotten them or why he had them placed at the temple, only that they were the relics of Shakyamuni: twenty-two little granules (down to twenty-one, as one had since disappeared). The Chinese have often placed potent objects in places to ward off unwelcome forces or people. But if it was the emperor's intent to keep foreigners out, he picked the wrong objects. The Buddha was also from the West. After adding our sticks of incense to the pyre, Daniela and I moved on to another temple.

Two hundred years after Bodhidharma took his Zen seed north, Hui-neng returned to Kuangchou with the fruit. He showed up one day in 676 a dozen blocks northeast of the Indian patriarch's old residence. The place was called Fahsing Temple. The day Hui-neng arrived, the abbot was lecturing on the *Nirvana Sutra*. The wind was blowing a flag on the temple's flagpole, and two monks were arguing about what was moving. Presumably this was during a break in the lecture. One monk said it was the wind that was moving. Another monk said it was the flag that was moving. Hui-neng overheard them and said, "It isn't the wind that's moving, and it isn't the flag. The only things moving around here are your minds."

The temple's name had changed. It was now called Kuanghsiao, or Light of Piety. But the flagpole was still there—though not the flag. We walked past its long shadow, and through the courtyard, and into the main shrine hall. The walls inside were covered with thousands of slips of yellow paper, each with the name of someone who had died, and on the floor below the walls were offerings of flowers and fruit. The former abbot, Pen-huan, was one of China's great Zen masters, and he encouraged people to meditate in the hall instead of doing prostrations, so in place of kneeling cushions, the floor was covered with hundreds of sitting cushions. There wasn't a vacant cushion that day, but no one was meditating. It was Grave Sweeping Day, and people were just sitting there, talking in subdued voices. It was a communal wake.

Daniela and I decided not to intrude and walked around to the stupa behind the hall. Back in 676, when the abbot discovered Hui-neng's true identity, he shaved his head and ordained him right then and there. Prior to that the Sixth Patriarch was a layman. Apparently, the abbot preserved Hui-neng's hair, and it was later placed inside the stupa. The adjacent incense burner was roaring as people threw in bags of paper money.

Just beyond the stupa, there were a number of ancient trees, some of them a thousand or more years old. One of them was a cotton tree, the city tree of Kuangchou. Until modern times, Kuangchou was China's main conduit for goods from South Asia and beyond, and the cotton tree arrived about the same time as Bodhidharma. The tree was in bloom, and someone had collected the fallen blossoms and spread

Kuanghsiao Temple and flagpole

them out to dry. The reddish orange, dinner-plate-sized flowers were used in Chinese medicine to reduce inflammation.

Just beyond the tree, the monks had set up a table and were collecting donations for another shrine hall, one for Kuan-yin, the Goddess of Mercy. Kuanghsiao Temple had also embarked on an expansion program, but it was years ahead of Hualin, thanks to Pen-huan. When he was still in his thirties, Pen-huan shared the abbotship of Pishan Temple on Wutaishan with my old teacher, Shou-yeh. Then in 1948, Empty Cloud asked Pen-huan to take over the Sixth Patriarch's temple near Shaokuan, and

Master Pen-huan practicing Zen

he had been in South China ever since. Those were not easy years. In 1958, Pen-huan was branded a Rightist and was sent to a labor camp for fifteen years. Following his release, he served as abbot of half a dozen temples and finally Kuanghsiao, which was where I met him, wielding his calligraphy brush. Without his financial and spiritual support, Zen monasteries in China would hardly be enjoying the renaissance they were today. Among Pen-huan's dharma heirs were Chien-jen, the abbot of Fifth Patriarch Temple, and Yin-k'ung, the abbess of Tachinshan. I was sorry he wasn't there to thank. But he had moved to the quiet of a mountain temple near the Hong Kong border, where he just celebrated his hundredth birthday. Daniela and I contributed 100RMB, wrote our names on a roof tile, and called it a day.

. . . . .

After another night at the Victory, I checked out early and left my bag with the receptionist at the front desk. I told her I would be back the next day. I had one more excursion to make. It was to the town of Hsinhsing, a hundred miles to the southwest. Buses left every hour from the main station, and mine left just after eight. From Kuangchou, we followed the expressway west, across the Pearl and past duck farms and carp ponds and factories of all sizes. After crossing and recrossing the West River (which the North River joined just outside Kuangchou to form the Pearl), we turned south and followed the Hsinhsing River all the way to the town of the same name. As we entered the city limits, a big banner hanging across the roadway welcomed us to the HOMETOWN OF HUI-NENG, THE SIXTH PATRIARCH OF ZEN.

Outside the bus station, a dozen motorcycles were lined up waiting for fares. There were also a few ramshackle buses, and one of them went to Lungshan, which was eight miles south of town and the location of Hui-neng's old home. I opted for the bus, which took a roundabout route but eventually dropped me off at the base of the mountain, a few hundred yards short of Kuoen Temple. In 707, Emperor Chung-tsung ordered Hui-neng's old home made into a shrine and gave the place the name Kuoen: "Benefactor of the Nation." Hui-neng returned in 712 and died there the following year.

I walked up the road to the temple and eventually tracked down the guest manager. He wanted to take me back down the road to a hot spring hotel that the monastery owned, but I told him I would rather stay in Hui-neng's old temple if there was room. He shrugged and told me one of the laywomen would find a place for me after lunch. Everyone had already eaten, but he said there was still food. He led me to the mess hall, and I sat down by myself. A minute later, one of the laywomen in the kitchen brought me a plate of leftovers and a bowl of soup. The soup was great and included peanuts and lotus root, and the leftovers were good, too.

After I was done, another laywoman led me to a room at the back of the guest quarters. Her name was Mrs. Chang. She was a retired naval officer, and it was clear that her word was law. She showed me to a room with six beds, all of them with boards for mattresses. The boards were covered with sheets. And at the end of each bed was a folded blanket filled with cotton wadding and a pillow filled with dried beans and chaff. Everything smelled of mildew. I was in South China now. Just in case I had forgotten, it began to pour as soon as I lay down. It was a heavy tropical rain, but it didn't last long—neither did my nap. As soon as the rain stopped, someone set off a string of firecrackers that went on for three or four minutes and ended with a loud boom. I gave up on the nap, moved a chair from my room out to the veranda, and made a cup of coffee and then another as I watched the steam rise from the temple roofs.

Since I was up, and the rain had stopped, I decided to tour the grounds. I visited the grave of Hui-neng's parents and the adjacent pagoda built in their honor. I also stopped to admire the huge litchi tree Hui-neng planted before he died. The place was more like a park than a temple. Afterwards, I walked back to my room and met Mrs. Chang again. I asked her what else there was to see. She recommended I walk back down to the base of the hill and negotiate with one of the motorcycle drivers for a tour of Hui-neng's birthplace and the place where he "entered nirvana," whatever that meant. She told me not to pay more than 10RMB but when I walked down the hill, there was only one motorcycle driver, and he wouldn't go below 25RMB. What the hell. The weather was so oppressive. It was still steaming from the earlier downpour, and the ride on the motorcycle was the first breeze I felt all day.

We headed west until we reached the road that led back to Hsinhsing, then turned south. A few hundred yards later, we turned off and entered Hsialu Village, where Hui-neng was born. In less than a minute, I had attracted all the children in the village, and they led me up the hillside to a grave where one of Hui-neng's descendents was buried. Since they said that was all there was to see, I got back on the motorcycle and we continued south another two miles, then turned off on a narrow paved road that led east into the hills. After a mile or so, we parked next to a rushing stream and followed the trail that ran beside it to a set of stone buildings. They looked like they were once part of a Buddhist temple.

The name of the place was Tsangfoken: "Hidden Buddha Gully." The only person there was the caretaker, who introduced himself as Layman P'an Yun-sung. After offering me a cup of tea, he asked me to light some incense in the small shrine hall. It was something he insisted on. Only then was he willing to lead me to the spot further upstream where Hui-neng "entered nirvana." As Layman P'an described it, when Hui-neng died on his meditation cushion at Kuoen Temple, his body flew through the air like a skyrocket and came down on a rock in the middle of this stream still seated in meditation. His disciples followed the trail of light he left in the sky, recovered his body, and later transported it back to Shaokuan, where it still sits on the altar of Nanhua Temple.

As we approached the spot, the mountain erupted with cicadas. Living in the northwest part of America, I never hear their sound anymore, and I miss it. The Chinese associate cicadas with rebirth. After spending a year or more underground as nymphs, they appear in early summer, slough off their shells, and find a tree against which to sing to their fellow cicadas. I always felt sad when the forest below my farmhouse in Taiwan was down to its last cicada, which was usually toward the end of September. And I was always happy when I heard the first one the next year, which was usually in early May. But in Hidden Buddha Gully, they were singing in early April, the day after Grave Sweeping Day. And it wasn't just a few. It was the whole mountain.

After paying my respects, I returned to Kuoen Temple and arrived just in time for dinner. There were about twenty monks in the mess hall but twice as many laypeople. Some temples were like that. Some temples were as much old age homes as they were monasteries or nunneries. As I was going back to my room, Mrs. Chang said the temple turned on a generator at seven o'clock that pumped hot-spring water to all the bathrooms. The supply lasted for an hour. Since that was still two hours away, I thought it would be a good time to visit the abbot.

When I asked where I could find him, the guest manager led me to his reception room. I sat down, and a few minutes later the abbot came in. His name was Ju-ch'an, and he was short and looked to be about fifty. Kuoen Temple, he said, was where he became a monk in 1980. After he graduated from the Buddhist academy in Beijing, he returned to take over as abbot. Hsinhsing was his hometown, and he knew as much as anyone I had ever met about the *Platform Sutra*. He also suggested a few new twists to the traditional understanding of the little we know about Hui-neng.

At the beginning of the sutra, Hui-neng says he and his mother moved to Nanhai when he was young, and he sold firewood to support them. It was while he was making a delivery there one day that he first heard the *Diamond Sutra* and resolved to travel to Huangmei. Nanhai, of course, was the name for Kuangchou at the time. But Ju-ch'an said Nanhai was also the local name for a suburb of Hsinhsing, next to the river, and that the place where Hui-neng heard the *Diamond Sutra* was at a temple near there, not in Kuangchou. He wasn't just making this up. He showed me pictures of the places and inscriptions on the stelae. He also gave me a five-volume set of books he had published that contained just about every article ever written in Chinese about Hui-neng's text. He apologized and said it didn't have everything. One of the things he tried to get was Mao's edition of the *Platform Sutra*, which the Chairman had gone through and penciled in comments in the margins: things like "this doesn't make sense" or "this is good." Mao was an odd bird, but the radical, communal nature of Zen appealed to a lot of his fellow cadres as well. In fact, in some ways it was more Communist than the Communism they advocated.

Ju-ch'an was eminently affable, and we talked for quite a while, until I realized it was getting close to when they turned on the hot spring pump. I told him I should be getting back to my room to take a shower. He told me to get my stuff. He said he was taking me to a different room. At first I thought he meant another room in the temple. But after I collected my gear, he led me down to the hot spring hotel at the base of the mountain. He said a layman bought it and gave it to the temple, and they used it sometimes for guests. It would have been useless to object.

Ju-ch'an turned me over to the receptionist, and she led me to a room on the second floor. It was quite a change from the board mattresses and mildewed bedding of the lay guest quarters. Everything was hospital white: the floor was white, the walls were white, and the sheets, of course. The bed was made so tightly I could have bounced a coin on it. And there was an air-conditioner. Oddly enough, the bathroom didn't have a bathtub, only a shower, but by blocking the drain, I was able to slosh around a bit, and I lay on the floor letting the hot, sulphur-rich water beat on me for half an hour. Then I stretched out on the crispy clean sheets, cranked up the aircon, and wrote a bit in my journal. After a while the heavens exploded in thunder and lightning and pouring rain. I turned off the aircon and opened the window to let the suddenly cool air flow inside. Fortunately, the windows had screens and no holes. Sometime during the night the rain stopped and the frogs in the pond outside began a nightlong celebration.

In Hui-neng's day, most of Kuangtung Province was inhabited by ethnic minorities and not Han Chinese. I've always thought he was related to one of them through his mother. His father may have been from Beijing, but he was born right here in frogland. Listening to the croaking going on outside his old home, I think he would have been at home among the Chuang. The Chuang are still the biggest ethnic minority in China, with somewhere between fifteen and twenty million members, more than the Tibetan and Uighur minorities combined. And they have a special connection with frogs. The Chuang consider frogs sacred creatures, because frogs are children of the thunder god. When the Chuang need rain, all they have to do is tell the frogs, and the frogs tell the thunder god.

Back in 1992, when I was doing a series of radio programs on China's hill tribes, a

Chuang village

Chuang woman told me how this came about. She said a long time ago an old woman couldn't sleep because of the frogs croaking outside her window, and she asked her son to make them stop. Her son's solution was to pour boiling water outside the window. It worked, and the frogs that weren't scalded to death hopped away. And they kept hopping. And all the other frogs joined them. Soon there were no more frogs left on the mountain. When summer came, there was no rain, only the scorching heat of the sun.

In desperation, the son went to the village shrine and prayed to Pu Lo-t'uo and asked him what to do. Pu Lo-t'uo was the ancestor of the Chuang people, and he told the boy that the frogs he had killed were the children of the thunder god, and unless he asked for forgiveness and henceforth treated frogs as members of his own family, there would be no more rain.

The boy did as he was told, and ever since then, the frog festival has been the biggest festival of the year among the Chuang. It begins on the first day of the Lunar New Year. As soon as the village elders see the sun that day, they beat the village's big bronze drum. Chinese archaeologists have collected over five hundred of these huge drums from ancient Chuang sites dating as far back as 2,500 years ago. Bronze drums were incredibly expensive to make, but they made a great sound, and nothing was too good for the thunder god.

In any case, once the drum sounds everyone gathers in the village square, which nowadays is usually the basketball court in front of the village school. They all bring their hoes and farm tools, and after praying for good luck they head into the surrounding countryside to find a frog. They turn over rocks and dig beside streams and ponds, and the first man and the first woman who find a frog become the frog king and the frog queen. They bring their frogs back to the village and give them to the village shaman, who recounts all the stories about frogs and how important they are as messengers of the thunder god. Then he kills the two frogs and puts them inside a bamboo coffin, which he places in the village shrine, and the party begins. And it begins again every night for two weeks until the first full moon, when the two frog spirits go to Heaven and tell the thunder god to send down rain, and everything is okay in the Chuang world for another year. Obviously, it was going to be okay again that year.

I fell asleep listening to the frogs in the pond outside and dreamed about Empty Cloud that night. He was sitting in the open surrounded by Zen temples, half-finished Zen temples. It was a strange dream. I've never dreamed about him before or since. In the morning, the frogs had been replaced by birds, all kinds of birds. Nothing like a good rain to get everyone excited about another day. I took another shower, just for the hell of it, then packed up and went downstairs. At the appointed time, Ju-ch'an's driver picked me up and drove me back to Hsinhsing. A few minutes later, I was on a bus headed back to Kuangchou. Less than three hours later, I was back at the Victory. And shortly thereafter, five more pounds of books were gone from my pack and heading home. What can I say about another afternoon off: an air-conditioned nap, a couple of iced mochas, and a piece of tiramisu.

When the afternoon turned to dusk, I ventured back across the Pearl into the Chingping Market area and looked for a place to eat. The Cantonese, as the people of Kuangchou are known throughout the world, love to gamble, which probably has something to do with the easy, and often illegal, money that flowed through the city over the centuries. Chingping Market was full of people playing cards and mahjong. It was also the endangered-species section of town, and there were groups of men in the doorways of darkened-windowed vans with fists full of bills selling tiger paws and tiger penises and anything else that might make your dick harder or your life longer. If it wasn't already extinct, it was for sale. The cool air was moving in again, and there was a light mist, but no thunder. I dodged into a nondescript restaurant for an unremarkable dinner and went back to the hotel, ending the day with a couple of more glasses of port. The pilgrimage was definitely winding down.

. . . . .

The next morning I called up Daniela, and we arranged to meet again at Hualin Temple. The temple may have been where Bodhidharma lived when he was in Kuangchou, but I wanted to make one last excursion to the place where he most likely landed, and I hailed a taxi to take us there. I had been there once before, which was one more time than our driver. He stopped to ask directions half a dozen times, but he finally found the place, in the easternmost suburbs of Kuangchou in Miaotou Village. It was the Temple to the God of the South Seas. Inscribed on the archway at the entrance was the plea: MAY THE SEA BE FREE OF WAVES. This was where people came to give thanks for a safe arrival or to pray for a safe journey.

The temple was located there, on the north shore of Huangmu Bay, because that was where foreign merchants anchored and offloaded their goods. The God of the South Seas was originally an Indian prince who was elevated to the status of guardian deity of all those whose lives depended on the sea and its moods. No one knows when or how this began. The first official notice of this cult didn't occur until about a hundred years after Bodhidharma arrived in Kuangchou, when the Sui dynasty sought to reestablish the central government's control over the region. In 581, they built China's first customs house a few blocks from the temple. They also bestowed the title of Nanhaishen: "God of the South Seas" on the long-departed prince, thus giving this local cult official recognition. In 594, they went one step further and replaced whatever locals had been using up until then with a much larger temple. And it had been there ever since. It seemed like a good place to say goodbye.

The buildings had been renovated and expanded since my first visit. The local government had obviously recognized the temple's tourist potential. It now featured a series of halls and galleries that were lined with hundreds of stone tablets commemorating various efforts at pirate suppression and trade protection. The earliest stele was dated 892 and bore an inscription by Han Yu, the mentor of the poet Chia Tao, whose grave I visited at the beginning of my pilgrimage.

Other than the stele with Han Yu's inscription, the halls didn't hold much of interest. We walked back out the front gate and over to the hill that looked out on what was once the port where Bodhidharma and his fellow travelers came ashore. The combination of river silt and landfill had moved the bay more than a mile to the south, and the land in between was now occupied by a coal-fired power plant. In ancient times, people stood on top of the hill and waved goodbye or watched for the arrival of someone who had been away too long. There was still a spirit way of stone statues commemorating the spot but its connection with the sea was a distant memory.

I said goodbye to the Prince of India and the God of the South Seas and thanked them for granting passage to Bodhidharma and the wordless, buddhaless, mountainless, homeless, beginningless, formless, mindless teaching of Zen. Afterwards, Daniela and I walked back out to the road, flagged down a taxi, and went back to the city, where we shared a dinner of nouveaux Shanghai cuisine just down the promenade from my hotel. We talked about Empty Cloud one last time. I had planned to end my pilgrimage right there in Kuangchou. There were no more pages on my itinerary. But since I was also interested in finding out more about Empty Cloud, I told her I would go see Yi-ch'ao, his former attendant, in Hong Kong. Hong Kong was only 120 miles away, but the next day I flew instead to Shanghai. I had arranged earlier to meet with the lay Zen master, Nan Huai-chin, and to take some friends on a tour of Buddhist sites in the region.

Two weeks later, I finally flew to Hong Kong to complete my mission. I arrived late and got a room at the Mariners' Club. It was also called The Sailors' Home & Mission to Seafarers. There was cheaper lodging in the old colony, but nothing as nice at that price, which was about forty bucks. The room rate included a good breakfast, and there was a swimming pool and a chapel. And the location was hard to beat. It was on the Kowloon side close to the Star Ferry and even closer to the subway.

The night I arrived, there was a crack in the heavens. The morning paper said it was the biggest thunderstorm and torrential downpour in twenty years. But for Hong Kong it was no big deal. The water was back in the harbor by morning. As soon as it was reasonable, I called Yi-ch'ao. I wasn't just calling on Daniela's behalf, but also on my own. If any one person was responsible for the resurgence of Zen in

Spirit way outside South Sea God Temple

China, it was Empty Cloud, or Hsu-yun. The least I could do was try to meet someone who had been at his side for five years.

Yi-ch'ao was not only one of Hsu-yun's attendants, Yi-ch'ao was still an active Zen master. Since most of his disciples lived in Hong Kong, that was where he spent most of his time. But his disciples also included the wife and family members of China's former president Chiang Ts'e-min / Jiang Zemin. So Yi-ch'ao sometimes spent time in Beijing. But he was in Hong Kong that day, and he told me to come by right away. It was a two-minute walk from the Mariners' Club to the subway, a half-hour ride to the last station in the New Territories, Tsuen Wan, and a five-minute taxi ride to Bamboo Grove Temple on Lotus Mountain.

Yi-ch'ao was waiting in the temple's guest hall. He looked like he was pushing eighty, and he was wearing a T-shirt and pajamas. That was standard summer attire in Hong Kong, and also Taiwan, until people became concerned with looking modern. Now only poor people, old people, and monks could afford to be so sensible. Yi-ch'ao motioned for me to sit down in a wicker chair, and he sat down in another one next to me. He crossed his legs in the meditation posture and asked me what I wanted to know.

I told him I was helping a friend gather material for a PhD thesis she was writing about Hsu-yun, and the abbot of Nanhua Temple suggested I talk to him. I asked if he could tell me anything that hadn't found its way into the standard biographical accounts.

He said the whole time he was with Hsu-yun there was hardly a day when something strange didn't happen. When I asked him if he could remember anything specific, he said once when there was an ordination ceremony at Nanhua, as soon as one of the monks received his robe he suddenly vanished into thin air. When people started searching, they couldn't find the monk, but they found his robe. It was in the branches of a tree. The tree spirit wanted to be ordained by Hsu-yun. The tree was still there, he said, just inside the main gate in front of the pond where people released fishes and turtles.

Yi-ch'ao said things like that happened all the time when he was with Hsu-yun. Yi-ch'ao got up and went over to the guest hall counter and poured us both cups of tea, then came back and handed me one. After he sat down again, he said once Chou En-lai invited Empty Cloud to Beijing. He said, "Nobody knows about this. I've never told anyone. Chou En-lai sent word that the Old Master was to come alone and not to bring anyone with him except his attendant. When Chou En-lai heard that Hsu-yun was coming, he was very happy and was looking forward to their meeting. But when the Old Master was ushered into his office, the premier became very upset. You don't know about this. Nobody knows about this. Premier Chou said, 'I told you not to bring anyone, to come alone. Why did you bring all these people with you?' Hundreds of people had suddenly appeared in the room. Hsu-yun said, 'I didn't bring anyone. All the people you see here with me are people who have died. They're all ghosts.' Then suddenly they disappeared. Premier Chou was terrified. After that, he issued orders to protect all the temples where the Old Master had lived. He thought Hsu-yun was a bodhisattva."

I asked Yi-ch'ao how long he had been a monk and how he met Hsu-yun. He said, "I became a novice in 1940 here in Hong Kong, right here where we're sitting. When the Japanese invaded Hong Kong at the end of 1941, I fled to the Mainland along with thousands of other people. A few months later, I ended up at Nanhua Temple, and I was ordained there in 1944. Later that year, I went to Yunmen Temple, and that's when I became Hsu-yun's attendant. Life was really hard then. We barely had enough to eat. But we all worked together, Hsu-yun too.

"After the Japanese were defeated, some of the monks wanted to go back to Hong Kong or Kuangchou or Shanghai. But Hsu-yun told us not to. He said it was not a good time for monks to be living in those places. So I stayed with him at Yunmen until 1949. Then one day he told me to leave. He told me to go back to Hong Kong. I told him he said not to go to places like Hong Kong, and I asked him why I should go. All he would say was that I had to leave. In those days, we didn't have access to a radio or newspapers. We didn't know what was going on anywhere else. When I asked him what made him change his mind and why I had to leave, he wouldn't say. He just told me to go. He even told me which day. And so I left. Later that same week, just after I returned to Hong Kong, the Communists took over the country and sealed the border.

"Hsu-yun was always having premonitions like that. He knew when things would happen beforehand. Later he wrote and told me why he stayed behind. He could have left too. But he said if he left, Buddhism would disappear in China. He had to stay behind. That's why Buddhism is flourishing again. It's because of Hsu-yun.

"Two years later, in 1951 the Communist militia occupied Yunmen Temple and started beating all the monks, including Hsu-yun. They were looking for gold or treasure of some kind. But there was barely enough food, much less any valuables.

They killed several monks and beat Hsu-yun until he was almost dead. When word finally got out about what was going on, Mao and Chu Te sent a train to bring him to Beijing to recover. Chu Te was Commander-in-Chief of the Army, and Hsu-yun had a karmic connection with him. When Chu Te was a young man, he was an opium addict. He was living in Yunnan Province at the time, and so was Hsu-yun. Chu Te came to Hsu-yun and told him he wanted to become a monk. Hsu-yun told him he couldn't become a monk. He said, "You're not cut out to be a monk. Besides, you've got important work to do, and it's not as a monk.' He gave Chu Te twenty dollars, which was enough money for train fare to Shanghai. It was while he was in Shanghai that Chu Te was finally able to break the opium habit and also where he started reading the works of Marx. Mao Tse-tung, Chou En-lai, and Chu Te all held the Old Master in the highest regard. But those were not good times. Even with such protectors, he was always being harassed. It was not a good time to be a monk or a nun.

"Last year I attended a conference about Hsu-yun at his old temple on Yunchushan. Everyone was discussing the Old Master's meditative power and how great it was. When they asked me to say something, I said his meditative power wasn't great at all. When it comes to things like that, there is no great or not great. There is no suffering or joy. If Hsu-yun attained something, then he could also lose it. All dharmas are empty. The nature of all dharmas is the same. Hsu-yun was the kind of person who neither attained something nor didn't attain something. He was beyond attaining.

"This building we're in has doors and windows. If we close the doors and windows, we can't get out. People lock themselves inside a house of delusions. But they're only delusions. They can leave anytime. Actually there is no house to leave. There's not even any leaving. What we see are flowers in the sky, the moon in the water. As for the meditative powers of Zen masters like Hsu-yun, sometimes it's useful to meditate and sometimes it isn't."

Yi-ch'ao got up and came back a minute later with a photograph of himself as a young novice standing next to Hsu-yun. He turned it over and wrote this poem on the backside:

Layman Red Pine,
When your mind dwells nowhere
no corrupting thoughts arise
when you don't cling to the world

suffering and joy have no place to grow
every thought you think
becomes the cause of life and death
understand impermanence
and find your ever-present body.

He signed it and dated it "the twenty-third day of the third lunar month in the year 2006," which was April 25 in the West. He said he was fourteen when the picture was taken. I tried to remember what I was doing when I was fourteen.

Yi-ch'ao with Master Hsu-yun (Empty Cloud)

My monastery was a boarding school in Hollywood, and my fellow monks were sons of the nouveau riche, which was why I was there. The education part was okay. But it was a military school, and the options were to bully or be bullied. My Zen master, though, wasn't there. He was back home in Idaho, where we moved when I was eleven. My father was often away on business, and he hired a man named George Williams to organize his hunting and fishing trips. George knew how to do everything, but he was wanted for murder in Montana and Wyoming—he never went drinking without a pistol in his boot, and we only hunted or fished on private land in those states. But when you're fourteen you're glad someone wants to teach you something, and learning to use a fly rod and a shotgun was my world of Zen. It was not a religious experience. But then again, maybe it was. It got me into the wilderness and into being alone a lot, both of which I liked.

Yi-ch'ao handed me the photograph and said, "There is no self in anything. Whatever we see, we discriminate according to our delusions. It's because of our delusions that we wander in the endless round of birth and death. But if we can become aware of the true nature of things, we become free of birth and death. There is no self. Neither you nor I have ever been born, nor can we ever die. But we worry about birth and death because we are attached to a material world made of our own delusions. The reason Shakyamuni was able to get free of birth and death was that he finally understood the true nature of things. But this is something any of us can do."

I bowed, and we said goodbye, then I walked out to the road, caught a bus to the subway, and took a subway back to Kowloon. I spent the next ten days seeing friends in Hong Kong and Taiwan and buying more books and tea. But I felt my trip ended when Yi-ch'ao handed me that photograph and I thought back to what I was doing when I was fourteen. There is so much baggage we burden ourselves with over the years that keeps us from seeing things the way they are. Some baggage we carry with us for a single thought, some for years, and some for lifetimes. But there isn't one piece that isn't our own creation.

16 NO GOING BACK

In addition to all the books and tea I'd sent home from China, I checked two bags at the airport in Taiwan with more of the same. I knew I'd need it all if I was going to write about the past two months. I was taking a China Airlines flight from Taipei back to Seattle. I'd flown back to the States a couple dozen times, and every time I did, at some point I thought about my first trip the other way.

It was on September 1, 1972. My father took me to the Burbank Airport to catch a plane to San Francisco, where my flight to Taipei left from. Somehow he had come up with a one-way ticket. He'd been broke for years and probably borrowed the money from my aunts, Pearline and Pauline. They'd been supporting him ever since he lost his millions fighting over a divorce settlement with my mother that didn't end until there was nothing left to fight over.

While I was standing in line getting ready to walk out to my plane, which was what people did in those days, at least in Burbank, my father shoved two hundred-dollar bills into my pocket to go with the thirteen bucks I already had. I don't know if I was fearless or crazy in those days—or just younger. The thought of arriving in Taiwan with thirteen dollars and no ticket home hadn't bothered me at all. I figured I was going to Taiwan to live in a Buddhist monastery. Why would

I need money? I wasn't planning to come back anytime soon.

The previous day, I had gone to the hospital to say goodbye to my grandmother. She was 102 and was being treated for emphysema. I spent a lot of time with her when I was growing up. Even when I was going to boarding school in Hollywood, I often spent the weekends with her and Pearline and Pauline. They all lived together in a two-bedroom apartment in Glendale, and I slept on the pullout couch in the living room whenever I was there. Pauline tried marriage once. But she came back to the apartment the next week. They all liked to watch wrestling on TV, and roller derby. My grandmother dipped snuff, and there was always a coffee-can spittoon on the floor. She did all the cooking, while my aunts lived out their lives in romance novels. The shelves in the closet overflowed with them.

Everyone on my father's side was tough on the outside and sweet on the inside. They all grew up on a cotton farm outside Little Rock. But my grandmother sold the farm and moved to Detroit in the 1920s when my father was imprisoned there for bank robbery. He and his cousins had formed a gang and worked their way up north until the cops got wind of their next job and killed them all, except my father, who suffered the minor embarrassment of a shattered kneecap. Pearline and Pauline got jobs as waitresses in the Cadillac Hotel in Detroit, which was also where the governor ate. They were good-looking, and they weren't shy, and they asked the governor to help their brother. He obliged and reduced my father's sentence to six years.

When he got out of prison, my father used his share of the cotton farm money to buy a hotel lease down in Texas. One hotel led to another, and before long he moved everyone to Los Angeles, which was where I was born. My father made so much money I thought he had a printing press somewhere. He had a chain of hotels. But it was a juggling act and kept him away a lot, and I spent a lot of time at my grandmother's. When I said goodbye to her at the hospital, we knew we'd never see each other again, and she said so.

Afterwards, I walked to a park just down the street from the apartment building where they all lived. I didn't have anything else to do and just wanted to kill time. I bought a pocket chess set at a store near the hospital and pulled it out on a picnic table. I set out the pieces, thinking I would play a game against myself. A hobo who was sitting on another park bench came over and asked if he could play.

He said he wasn't any good. He just wanted to play. But I wasn't any good either. I told him I was leaving for Taiwan the next day and was taking the chess set with me in case I got bored. I'd never lived in a monastery before and didn't know what to expect. The moment the man heard where I was going, his eyes welled up, and he turned away. I thought he was going to get up and leave, but he didn't. He just sat there. After a minute, he turned back toward me and told me this story.

He said during the Second World War he was a fighter pilot, and one day his plane was shot down over the Philippines. He managed to bail out, but he came down in a jungle and was knocked unconscious when his chute caught in a tree and his body crashed against the limbs. The next thing he knew, he felt himself being carried away, then he passed out. When he woke up, he was surrounded by a bunch of small, brown-skinned people, naked except for a primitive cloth covering over their genitals. He was stretched out inside a lean-to constructed of limbs and vines and covered with palm bark. When he tried to move, he almost fainted again from the pain. His leg was broken and so were several of his ribs, and his face was caked with blood from a gash on his forehead. He just lay there and stared up at the faces of the people. He thought he was dreaming.

When he lifted his head to look beyond the lean-to, he realized he wasn't on the ground, but somewhere up in the forest canopy. The people who had rescued him, he said, were the Monkey People. They cared for him, and his leg and his ribs healed. Once he was able to move around, they showed him how to get up and down the trees, and sometimes he went hunting with them. One of the women who had helped care for him became his mate. He was there about six months, he said, and he felt like he had been reborn in another world—a world he never wanted to leave.

Then one day while he and the other males were out hunting, they heard a distant rumble. The Monkey People were frightened and scrambled up the nearest trees. But he had heard that sound before, and he knew what it was. He headed toward it. He followed the noise until he came out into a clearing and met a column of GIs working their way along what must have been an old logging trail behind bulldozers. He ran over and told them he had been shot down and rescued by the Monkey People. He was glad to see his fellow GIs, but suddenly he realized he had left the jungle and couldn't go back. The officer in charge of the column told him to fall in, and they would make sure he got back to his unit. He tried to explain that he wanted to go back to the jungle, to say goodbye. But the officer just laughed, and told him to get some clothes on and join the column. If he hadn't, he said, they could have shot him for desertion.

He never learned where he was shot down or where he met that column of GIs. Not long after he returned to his unit, the war ended, and he was sent home. After he got back to the States, he tried to work, but nothing made sense anymore. He just drifted. When I met him, he said he'd been a hobo for over twenty years, and he expected to die a hobo. He said, "At least I won't die inside some cracker-box house working some meaningless job. I guess one jungle is as good as another. I don't mind dying a hobo. But I should have never come back." Then he was silent for a while. Finally, he got up and said, "If you ever find the Monkey People over there, don't leave like I did." Then he walked back to the bench he had been sitting on earlier. I didn't feel like playing chess anymore so I went back to my father's apartment, opened a beer, and joined him staring at the TV. The next day I got on the plane and never saw my father again. Four years later, the abbot brought me a letter he sent the day before he died. He asked if it wasn't about time I did something useful with my life. I moved out of the monastery not long after that and began translating poems and sutras. Thirty years later, I still haven't found anything better to do.

Breakfast was over, and the seatbelt sign was on. I had a window seat and looked outside as the plane approached the sea stacks along the Washington coast. A few minutes later, we passed over Port Angeles and then Discovery Bay. Port Townsend was so close, I could see the forest of doug fir next to my house.

CHINESE LEXICON

The following lexicon is intended to provide readers with the Chinese characters for the names, titles, and terms used in this book. The characters are those of traditional and not simplified Chinese. Also, with a few exceptions, such as internationally recognized spellings like "Beijing" or "Zhang Yimou," names, titles, and terms that appear in the text are romanized according to a modified version of the more traditional Wade-Giles system rather than the Pin-yin system devised in China during the 1950s to help Russians pronounce and transcribe Chinese. However, in the list below, I have added the Pin-yin spelling after that of the Wade-Giles wherever the two differ to help those who have learned that system. Also, for place names and certain book titles, I have usually eliminated apostrophes and dashes, except where to do so might lead to some confusion or where I felt it was important to demarcate the individual syllables.

A Question for Liu Nineteen	問劉十九	Anyueh / Anyue	安岳
Abbot	方丈	Arbor Day	植樹節
Acacia confusa	相思樹	*Arhat*	(阿)羅漢
Afghanistan	阿富汗	Avalokiteshvara	觀音
Age of the Imitation Dharma	像法世	*Avatamsaka Sutra*	華嚴經
Age of the True Dharma	正法世	Bactria	巴克特里亞
Agency for Imperial Dependents	宗正寺	Bamboo Lake	竹子湖
Agency for Imperial Sacrifices	太常寺	Bank of Hell	地獄銀行
Agency for Tributary Envoys	鴻臚寺	Bear Ear Mountain	熊耳山
Air China	中國國際航空	Beijing	北京
alaya consciousness	阿賴耶識	Beijing International	
Allied Forces	聯軍	School	北京順義國際學校
Amitabha Buddha	阿彌陀佛	Beijing University	北京大學
Anathapindada	阿那他賓低	Bell Ringer	號鐘
Anching / Anqing	安慶	Bhagavan	世尊
Ancient Bell Museum	古鐘博物館	Big Bell Temple	大鐘寺
Ancient Zither Terrace	古琴臺	Bitter Melon	苦竹
Andersson (Gunnar)	安特生	Black (Davidson)	步達生
Angelica	當歸	Bodhgaya	菩提迦耶
Anhsi / Anxi County	安溪縣	Bodhi Tree	菩提樹
Anhui / Anwei Province	安徽省	Bodhidharma	菩提達摩
Anting / Anding	安定	*Bodhisattva*	菩薩

Bodhisattva Summit	菩薩頂	Chao P'u-ch'u / Zhao Puchu	超朴初
Bruce Lee	李小龍	Chao-chou / Zhaozhou	趙洲
Buddha (Shakyamuni)	佛	Chao-yuan / Zhaoyuan	照遠
Buddha (abbot of Shaolin)	跋陀	Chaohsien / Zhaoxian	趙縣
Buddha of the Future	未來佛	Chayuan Teashop	茶緣茶莊
Buddhacarita	佛所行讚經	Ch'en / Chen dynasty	陳代
Buddhist Association		Chekiang / Zhejiang Province	浙江省
of China	中國佛教協會	Chenchiang / Zhenjiang River	滇江
Buddhist Association of Honan / Henan		Chengan County	成安縣
Province	河南省佛教協會	Chengchou / Zhengzhou	鄭州
Buddhist Association of Hopei / Hebei		Chengchueh / Zhengjue	正覺
Province	河北省佛教協會	Chenju / Zhenru Temple	真如寺
Buddhist Canon	三藏	*ch'i / qi*	氣
Bureau of Religious Affairs	宗教事務局	Chi-an / Jian (abbot of Tinglin)	積安
Burnt Tail	焦尾	Chi-an / Ji-an (city in Kiangsi)	吉安
Ceiling Circler	繞樑	Ch'i / Qi dynasty	齊代
Cenozoic Laboratory	新生代研究室	Ch'i-fo / Qifo	奇佛
Central China Normal		*ch'i-kung / qigong*	氣功
University	華中師範大學	Chia Lan-p'o / Jia Lanpo	賈蘭坡
Chan-jan / Janran	湛然	Chia Tao / Jia Dao	賈島
Ch'an / Chan	禪	Chiaho / Jiahe Hotel	嘉和大酒店
Ch'an-lin chu-chi pi-ch'iu-ni / Chan-lin ju-ji		Chiahu / Jiahu	賈湖
bi-chiu-ni	禪林珠璣比丘尼	Chiang Ching-kuo / Jiang Jingguo	蔣經國
Chang Chi / Zhang Ji	張籍	Chiang Kai-shek / Jiang Jieshi	蔣介石
Chang Chien-min / Zhang Jianmin	張健民	Chiang Ts'e-min / Jiang Zemin	江澤民
Chang Heng / Zhang Heng	張衡	Chicken Bone Hill	鷄骨山
Chang Shun-p'ing /		chief instructor	首座
Zhang Shunping	張順平	Chien-jen / Jianren	見忍
Chang Chi / Zhang Ji	張籍	*chien-yuan / jian-yuan*	監院
Chang Chien-min / Zhang Jianmin	張健民	Chienchai / Jianzhai Bodhisattva	監齋菩薩
Chang Heng / Zhang Heng	張衡	Chienshan / Qianshan	潛山
Ch'ang-an / Changan	長安	Chienshui / Qianshui River	潛水
Ch'ang-ming / Changming	昌明	Chienyang / Qianyang International	
Changchiakou / Zhangjiakou	張家口	Hotel	潛陽國際大酒店
Changpai / Changbai Mountains	長白山	Chih-chien / Zhijian	智堅
Changsha	長沙	*chih-k'o / zhike*	知客
Changshou / Changshou Road	長壽路	Chih-yao / Zhiyao	智藥
Chanting / Chanding Temple	禪定寺	Chih-yi / Zhiyi	智顗

chih-yin / zhi-yin	知音
chih-yin-chih-yu /	
zhi-yin-zhi-you	知音之友
ch'ih-ch'a-ch'u / chi-cha-qu	吃茶去
Chihpi / Zhibi	赤壁
Chihsia / Qixia Temple	栖霞寺
Chin / Jin dynasty	金代
Ch'in / Qin dynasty	秦代
Chinchieh Shanchuang /	
Jinjie Shanzhuang	金界山莊
Chinese gooseberry	獼猴桃
Ching-hui / Jinghui	淨慧
Ching-shih-t'ung-yen /	
Jing-shi-tong-yan	警世通言
Ching-wan / Jingwan	靜琬
Ch'ing / Qing dynasty	清代
Ch'ing Kuei / Qing Gui	清規
Ch'ing-yuan / Qingyuan	青原
Chinghai / Qinghai University	青海大學
Chingping / Qingping Market	清平市場
Chingtzuyao / Jingziyao Mine	青磁窯礦
Chinhuakung /	
Jinhuagong Mine	晉華宮煤礦
Chinhuangtao / Jinhuangdao	秦皇島
Chinmao /Jinmao	金毛
Chinmen / Jinmen	荊門
Chinshan / Jinshan Temple	金山寺
Chiuchiang / Jiujiang	九江
Chiufengshan / Jiufengshan	九峯山
Chiuhuashan / Jiuhuashan	九華山
Chou En-lai / Zhou Enlai	周恩來
Choukoutien / Zhoukoudian	周口店
Chu Hsi / Zhu Xi	朱熹
Chu Jung-chi / Zhu Rong-ji	朱鎔基
Chu Kuei / Zhu Gui	朱桂
Chu Te / Zhu De	朱德
Chu Te-jui / Zhu Derui	朱德瑞
Chu Ti / Zhu Di	朱棣
Chu-ko Liang / Zhuge Liang	諸葛亮

Ch'u Yuan / Qu Yuan	屈原
Ch'uan-cheng / Quanzheng	傳正
Chuang / Zhuang tribe	壯族
Chulin / Zhulin Temple	竹林寺
Ch'un-yang / Chunyang	純陽
Chung Ch'i / Zhong Qi	鐘期
Chung Tzu-ch'i / Zhong Ziqi	鐘子期
Ch'ung-tu / Chongdu	崇度
Chungching / Chongqing	重慶
Chungfu / Zhongfu Temple	崇福寺
Chunghsiang / Zhongxiang	鐘祥
Chunghsing / Chongxing Temple	崇興寺
Chungnan / Zhongnan Mountains	終南山
Chunyangkung / Chunyanggong	純陽宮
Cicada	蟬
Cold Mountain	寒山
College of Chinese Culture	中國文化學院
Communist Party	共產黨
Confucianism	儒教
Confucius	孔子
Conze (Edward)	孔茲
cotton tree	木棉
Cultural Revolution	文化革命
Daily Life Zen	生活禪
Dancer in a Dream	夢中舞人
Darwin (Charles)	達爾文
Democratic Progressive Party	民進黨
Devas	天
Dhammapada	法句經
Dharma	法
Dharma Ending Age	末法世
Dharmaraksha	法蘭
Dhyana	禪那
Diamond Sutra	金剛經
Discourse on Contemplating the Mind	觀心論
Discourse on the	
Supreme Vehicle	最上乘論
Dragon Bone Hill	龍骨山
Dubois (Eugene)	杜博斯

East Is Red Tractor Factory	東方紅托拉機廠	Fa-lin / Falin	法林
East Mountain	東山	Fa-tsang / Facang	法藏
East Mountain Temple	東山寺	Fahsing / Faxing Temple	法性寺
East Mountain Zen	東山禪	Falunkung / Falungong	法輪功
East-West Universal Love Clinic	普愛中西醫結合門診部	Fayin	法音
Eastern Wei dynasty	東魏代	Fayun Temple	法雲寺
Eight Immortals	八仙	Feng Mao	馮茂
Eighteen Dhatus	十八界	Fengle International Hotel	豐樂國際大酒店
Eightfold Noble Path	八正道	Fengmaoshan	馮茂山
Ekottara-agama Sutra	增一阿合經	Fifth Patriarch	五祖
Elephant Peak	大象峯	Fifth Patriarch Temple	五祖寺
Emperor Chung-tsung / Chongzong	中宗	Fifth Patriarch Village	五祖村
Emperor Hirohito	裕仁皇帝	First Opium War	第一次鴉片戰爭
Emperor Hsiao-wen / Xiaowen	孝文帝	Five Do's	五要
Emperor Hsuan-tsung / Xuanzong	玄宗	Five Don't's	五不
Emperor Ming	明帝	Five Elements	五行
Emperor Shun	舜帝	Five Skandhas	五陰
Emperor Shun-chih / Shunzhi	順治皇帝	*Flowing Water*	流水
Emperor T'ai-tsung / Taizong	宋太宗	*Fo-chiao / Fo-jiao*	佛教
Emperor T'ai-wu / Taiwu	太武帝	*fo-hsing-ch'ang-ch'ing-ching / fo-xing chang qing-jing*	佛性常清淨
Emperor Yung-cheng / Yongzheng	雍正帝	*Fo-yuan / Foyuan*	佛原
Emperor Wen-ch'eng / Wencheng	文成帝	Fokuangshan / Foguangshan	佛光山
Emperor Wen	文帝	food manager	典座
Emperor Wu	武帝	Forbidden City	紫禁城
Empress Wu Ts'e-t'ien / Wu Cetian	武則天	Foreign Correspondents Club	外國記者俱樂部
Empress Dowager Hu	胡太后	*Forty-two Passage Sutra*	四十二章經
Empty Cloud	虛雲	Four Directions	四方
Empty Cloud Memorial	虛雲紀念堂	Four Guardians	四大天王
Empty Cloud Relic Stupa	虛雲舍利塔	Four Practices	入道四行觀
Erchan / Erjan Village	二站村	Fourth Patriarch	四祖
Essential Means for Entering the Path and Stilling the Mind	入道安心要方便	Fourth Patriarch Temple	四祖寺
Eurasian Plate	歐亞版塊	Fu Hsi / Fu Xi	伏羲
Fa-chih / Fazhi	法治	Fuchou / Fuzhou (Fukien Province)	福州
Fa-hua-hsuan-yi / Fa-hua-xuan-yi	法華玄義	Fuchou / Fuzhou (Kiangsi Province)	撫州
		Fujungshan / Furongshan	芙蓉山
Fa-jung / Farong	法融	Fukien / Fujian Province	福建省

Gandhara	犍馱羅	Hidden Buddha Gully	藏佛坑
Gang of Four	四人幫	*High Mountain*	高山
Ganges	恆河	Hofei / Hefei	合肥
Garma Chang	張澄基	Honan / Henan Province	河南省
Gauloise	古洛伊斯香煙	Hong Kong	香港
Genghis Khan	成吉思汗	Hopei / Hebei Institute of	
Gil Evans	吉爾艾文斯	Cultural Affairs	河北省文物研究所
God of the South Seas	南海神	Hopei / Hebei Province	河北省
Grand Canal	運河	Hopei / Hebei Provincial	
Great Leap Forward	大躍進	Museum	河北省博物館
Grave Sweeping Day	清明節	Hotang Yuehssu / Hetang Yuesi	荷塘月色
Great Helmsman	偉大舵手	Hotspring Village	溫泉村
Great Vehicle	大乘	Hsialu / Xialu Village	夏盧村
Great Wall	長城	Hsiang / Xiang River	相江
Great Way	大道	*hsiang-ku / xianggu*	香菇
Green Beauty	綠綺	Hsiangshan / Xiangshan Temple	香山寺
Gridrakuta	耆闍崛山	Hsiaoshihtzu / Xiaoshizi	小石子
guarding the mind	守心	Hsieh Yu-wei / Xie Yuwei	謝幼偉
guarding the one	守一	Hsien-pi / Xianbi	鮮卑
guest manager	知客	Hsientung / XiantongTemple	顯通寺
Guggenheim Foundation	古根海姆基金會	Hsilai / Xilai Temple	西來庵
Gunabhadra	求那跋陀羅	*Hsin-hsin-ming / Xin-xin-ming*	信心銘
Haberer (Karl)	哈白勒	Hsinan / Xinan	新安
Hai-ch'an / Haichan	海禪	Hsinchiang / Xinjiang Province	新疆省
Hai-ju / Hairu	海如	Hsinchou / Xinzhou	新洲
Halloween	萬聖節	Hsingtzu / Xingzi	星子
Han Chinese	漢人	Hsinhsing / Xinxing	新興
Han dynasty	漢代	Hsinhsing / Xinxing River	新興江
Han River	漢水	Hsinjung / Xinrong	新榮
Han Yu	韓愈	Hsinya / Xinya Bus Station	新亞車站
Han-shan Te-ch'ing /		Hsiung-nu / Xiongnu	匈奴
Hanshan Deqing	憨山德清	Hsu-yun / Xuyun	虛雲
Hangchou / Hangzhou	杭州	Hsuan-ts'ang / Xuancang	玄奘
Hankou	漢口	Hsuanhua / Xuanhua	宣化
Hantan / Handan	邯鄲	Hsuankung / Xuankong Temple	懸空寺
Hanyang	漢陽	Hsueh-feng Yi-ts'un /	
Heart Sutra	心經	Xuefeng Yicun	雪峯義存
Heng-chang / Hengchang	恆章	*Hsukaosengchuan /*	
Hengshan	衡山	*Xugaosengzhuan*	續高僧傳

Hsunlimen / Xunlimen Hotel	循禮門	Juyuan / Ruyuan	乳源
hu-ping / hubing	餬餅	Kaifeng	開封
Huai River	淮河	Kaiyuan Edition	開元大藏經
Huai-jang / Huairang	懷讓	Kan / Gan River	贛江
Huainan	淮南	Kangwang Road	康王路
Hualin Temple	華林寺	Kanlu / Ganlu Temple	甘露寺
Huang T'ing-chien /		Kansu / Gansu Province	甘肅省
Huang Tingjian	黃庭堅	Kao Shih-t'ao / Gao Shitao	高士濤
Huang-po / Huangbo	黃檗	Kao-an / Gaoan	高安
Huang-t'u / Huangtu	黃土	Kaomin / Gaomin Temple	高旻寺
Huangmei	黃梅	Kashyapa	迦葉
Huangmu Bay	黃木灣	Kaushala	憍薩羅
Huayen / Huayan School	華嚴宗	Kaushambi	憍賞彌
Huayen / Huayan Sutra	華嚴經	Ke Hung / Ge Hong	葛洪
Hui-k'o / Huike	慧可	Khitans	契丹
Hui-k'ung / Huikong	會空	Kiangsi / Jiangxi Province	江西省
Hui-neng / Huineng	惠能	Kiangsu / Jiangsu Province	江蘇省
Hui-ssu / Huisi	慧思	King Kao / Gao	高王
Hui-yuan / Huiyuan	慧圓	King P'ing / Ping	平王
Huijih / Huiri Temple	慧日寺	King Prasenajit	波斯匿王
Hunan Province	湖南省	King Udayana	優填王
Hung-jen / Hongren	弘忍	KMT	國民黨
Hung-lu-ssu / Honglusi	鴻臚寺	Kowloon	九龍
Huoshan	霍山	Kuan-hsi Chih-hsien /	
Hupei / Hubei Province	湖北省	Guanxi Zhixian	灌溪志閑
ICRT	台北國際社區廣播電台	Kuan Kung / Guangong	關公
Immortal of Poetry	詩仙	Kuan Ti / Guandi	關帝
Indian Plate	印度版塊	Kuan Yu / Guany	關羽
Inner Mongolia	內蒙古	Kuan-hsin-lun / Guan-xin-lun	觀心論
instructor (meditation)	班首	Kuan-yin / Guanyin	觀音
International Hotel	國際大廈	K'uan-hsiang / Kuanxiang	寬祥
Iron Crutch Li	鐵拐李	K'uan-jung / Kuanrong	寬容
Iron Goddess	鐵觀音	Kuangchi / Guangji Hermitage	廣濟茅蓬
Jen-ming / Renming	仁明	Kuangchiao / Guangjiao Temple	匡教寺
Ju-ch'an / Ruchan	如禪	Kuangchou / Guangzhou	廣州
Ju-man / Ruman	如滿	Kuanghsiao / Guangxiao Temple	光孝寺
jungle rat	猲獠	Kuanghua / Guanghua Temple	廣化寺
Jungyang / Rongyang	榮陽	Kuanyinai / Guanyinai	觀音崖
Jurchens	女真	Kuanyintang / Guanyintang	觀音堂

Kuanyinwang / Guanyinwang	觀音王	Lofushan	羅浮山
Kublai Khan	忽必烈汗	Lokashema	支婁迦讖
Kuchengtai / Guzhengtai	古琴臺	*Lotus Sutra*	妙法蓮華經
Kuchu / Kuzhu	苦竹	Loyang / Luoyang	洛陽
K'ung Te-ch'eng / Kong Decheng	孔德成	Lower Huayen / Huayan	下華嚴
kung-an / gong-an	公案	Lu Tung-pin / Lu Dongbin	呂洞賓
Kunghsiang / Kongxiang Temple	空相寺	Lungmen / Longmen Caves	龍門石窟
Kungkuyulan / Kongguyulan	空谷幽蘭	Lungshan / Longshan	龍山
Kuo Mo-juo / Guo Moro	郭沫若	Lushan	廬山
Kuo-le / Guole	果樂	Luyehyuan / Luyeyuan	鹿野苑
Kuo-ming / Guoming	果明	Ma Ying-chou / Ma Yingzhou	馬英九
Kuoen / Guoen Temple	國恩寺	Ma-an-shan	馬鞍山
Kushan Empire	月氏帝國	Ma-tsu / Mazu	馬祖
Ladies Street	女人街	Mahabalipuram	馬哈巴利普拉姆
Lankavatara Sutra	楞伽經	Mahakala	大黑天
Lao-tzu / Laozi	老子	Mahamati Bodhisattva	大慧菩薩
Laotsu / Laocu Temple	老祖寺	*Mahaprajnaparamita Sutra*	大般若經
Large Sutra on Perfect		Mahasanghika	大眾部
Wisdom	摩訶般若波羅蜜經	Mahayana	大乘
Layman Hsiang / Xiang	向居士	Mainland Affairs Commission	大陸委員會
Layman Red Pine	赤松居士	Maitreya	彌勒
Lechang	樂昌	man-t'ou / man-tou	饅頭
Leng-ch'ieh-shih-tzu-chi /		Manchuria	滿州
Leng-qie-shi-zi-ji	楞枷師資記	Mandarin	國語
Li Pai / Li Bai	李白	Manjushri	文殊
Li Sheng-hua / Li Shenghua	李勝花	Mao	毛
Li Shih-min / Li Shimin	李世民	Mapa / Maba	馬壩
Li-sheng / Lisheng	利生	Marco Polo	馬可波羅
Liao dynasty	遼代	Mariners' Club	海員俱樂部
Liao River	遼河	Marx (Karl)	馬克思
Liberation Road	解放路	master-at-arms	僧值
Lin-chi / Linji	臨濟	Matanga	迦葉摩騰
Linchi / Linji School	臨濟宗	Mathura	秣菟羅
Linchuan / Linchuan	臨川	*May the Sea Be Free of Waves*	海不揚波
Liu Sung / Liu Song dynasty	劉宋代	Meichuan	梅川
Liu Ts'un-chi / Liu Cunji	劉存基	Meng Chiao / Meng Jiao	孟郊
Liufang Nanli	柳芳南里	Miao-chiang / Miaojiang	妙江
Liuli Bridge	六里橋	Miao-wei / Miaowei	妙為
Loess Plateau	黃土高原	Miaotou Village	廟頭村

Miles Davis	邁爾斯戴維斯	Nanching / Nanjing	南京
Milo / Miluo River	汨羅河	Nanching / Nanjing University	南京大學
Mind Only School	唯識宗	Nanhai	南海
Ming dynasty	明代	Nanhaishen	南海神
Ming-chi / Mingji (Pailin Temple		Nanhua Temple	南華寺
supply manager)	明吉	Nanling Range	南嶺
Ming-chi / Mingji (Fourth Patriarch		Nanya Plastics	南亞塑膠
temple manager)	明碁	Nanyang	南陽
Ming-chieh / Mingjie	明潔	Nanyueh / Nanyue	南岳
Ming-ch'ing / Mingqing	明清	Napuyuan / Nabuyuan	挪步圓
Ming-hsiang / Mingxiang	明向	National Master	國師
Ming-hsuan / Mingxuan	明玄	Nationalist Party	國民黨
Ming-yao / Mingyao	明堯	Neng-wen / Nengwen	能文
Ming-yen / Mingyan	明影	Neo-Confucian	理學
Ming-yi / Mingyi	明一	New Chuho / Juhe Hotel	新聚和大酒店
Ming-yu / Mingyu	明玉	Nihowan / Nihewan Basin	泥河灣盆地
Minister of Works	司空	Nine Dragon Wall	九龍壁
Ministry of Culture	文化部	Nine Rivers	九江
Ministry of Forestry	林業部	Ningpo / Ningbo	寧波
Ministry of Propaganda	宣傳部	Nirvana	涅盤
Mo-ho-chih-kuan /		*Nirvana Sutra*	大般涅槃經
Mo-ho-zhi-guan	摩訶止觀	*no work, no food*	一日不作，一日不食
mo-ku / mo-gu	蘑菇	North River	北江
Mo-shan Liao-jan /		Northern Ch'i / Qi dynasty	北齊代
Moshan Liaoran	末山了然	Northern Chou / Zhou dynasty	北周代
Mongol	蒙古人	Northern Lights	北極光
Mongolia	蒙古利亞	Northern India	北印度
Mopanshan / Mobanshan	磨盤山	Northern School (of Zen)	北宗
Moshan	末山	Northern Wei dynasty	北魏代
Mount Lanka	楞枷峯	Nu Wa	女媧
Mount Sumeru	須彌山	Number One Bridge	
Mountain Gorge Temple	山谷寺	(Wuhan)	武漢長江大橋
Nagarjuna	龍樹	Number Two Bridge	
Namo Omitofo	南無阿彌陀佛	(Wuhan)	武漢長江二橋
Nan Huai-chin / Nan Huaijin	南懷瑾	*Omitofo*	阿彌陀佛
Nan-ch'uan / Nanquan	南泉	*On Trusting the Mind*	信心銘
nan-kua-ping / nan-gua-bing	南瓜餅	Opium Wars	鴉片戰爭
Nanchang	南昌	Oriental Beauty	東方美人
Nanchang University	南昌大學	Oxhead Mountain	牛頭山

Oxhead School	牛頭宗	peony	牡丹
Pac-Man	吃豆	People's Republic	人民共和國
Pai Chu-yi / Bai Juyi	白居易	Perfection of Wisdom	般若波羅蜜
Pai Chu-yi / Bai Juyi Research Association		*Perfection of Wisdom in Eight*	
of Loyang	洛陽白居易研究會	*Thousand Lines*	道行般若經
Pai / Bai Gardens	白園	*Perfection of Wisdom in Twenty-five*	
Pai-chang / Baijang	百丈	*Thousand Lines*	摩訶般若波羅蜜
Pai-ho / Baihe	白鶴	Pi / Bi River	淠河
Pai-ma-ssu / Baimasi	白馬寺	Pi-er / Bier	比兒
Pailin / Bailin Temple	柏林寺	Pien-ho / Bianhe	辮和
Paiwan Tribe	排灣族	Pin-yin	品音
Pakistan	巴基斯坦	Pingchiang / Pingjiang	平江
Pali	巴利文	Pishan / Bishan Temple	碧山寺
Pallava	拔羅婆	*Platform Sutra*	六祖壇經
pan-shou / banshou	班首	Po Ya / Bo Ya	伯牙
P'an Ku / Pan Gu	盤古	*po-ch'a / bo-cha*	酥油茶
P'an Yun-sung / Pan Yunsung	潘雲松	P'o-o-shan / Po-e-shan	破額山
P'an-hu / Panhu	盤瓠	Poet's Day	詩人節
Pao-chih / Baozhi	寶志	Pohai / Bohai Sea	渤海
Pao-ching / Baojing	寶靜	Prajna	般若
Pao-en / Baoen Temple	報恩寺	Prajna-paramita	般若波羅蜜
Paohua / Baohua Temple	寶華寺	Prajnatara	般若多羅
Paohuashan / Baohuashan	寶華山	Pratimoksha	波羅提木叉
Paolin / Baolin Temple	寶林寺	*pratyeka-buddhas*	緣覺
Paoting / Baoding	保定	*Pratyutpanna Samadhi Sutra*	般舟三昧經
Pataling / Badaling	八達嶺	Princess Chin-hsien	金仙公主
Peach Blossom Spring	桃花源	*pu-chi-hsiang / bu-ji-xiang*	不吉祥
pearl bird	珍珠鷄	P'u-ching / Pujing	普淨
Pearl Creek	珍珠泉	Puhua Temple	普化寺
Pearl River	珠江	Pure Land	淨土
peepal tree	畢鉢羅樹	Pushou Nunnery	普壽寺
P'ei Wen-chung / Pei Wenzhong	裴文中	*pu-t'ai / bu-tai*	補胎
Peking / Beijing Man	北京人	Putuoshan	普陀山
Peking Union Medical		*Record of the Masters*	
College	北京協和醫院	*of the Lankavatara*	楞枷師資記
Pen-ching / Benjing	本淨	Red Guards	紅衛兵
Pen-huan / Benhuan	本煥	red twig	紅枝
pen-lai-wu-yi-wu /		Red Yao	紅瑤
ben-lai-wu-yi-wu	本來無一物	Refuge Rock	避難石

religious affairs manager	維那	Shaolin Temple	少林寺
Rhapsody on the Western Capital	西京賦	Shen-hsiu / Shenxiu	神秀
Rightist	右派份子	Sheng Huo Ch'an / Sheng	
Rinzai	臨濟宗	Huo Chan	生活禪
River Garden	裕京花園	Sheng-hui / Shenghui	聖輝
Rockefeller Foundation	洛克菲勒基金會	Shensi / Shaanxi Province	陝西省
Romance of the Three Kingdoms	三國志演義	Shihchiachuang / Shijiazhuang	石家庄
Saddle Mountain	馬鞍山	Shihlou / Shilou Township	石樓鎮
Sage of Poetry	詩聖	*shou-tso / shoucuo*	首座
Saigon	西貢	Shou-yeh / Shouyeh	壽冶
Samadhi	三昧	*shravakas*	聲聞
Samyutta Nikaya	相應部	Shrine of Lord Chia / Jia	賈公祠
Sangha	僧	Shuangfeng Mountain	雙峯山
Sanmenhsia / Sanmenxia	三門峽	Shuangfengshan	雙峯山
Sanskrit	梵文	Shucheng	舒城
sarira	舍利	Shuilu	水陸
School of Emptiness	空宗	*Shurangama Sutra*	楞嚴經
Second Patriarch	二祖	Sian / Xian	西安
Second Patriarch Village	二祖村	Sinopec	中石化
Second World War	第二次世界大戰	Six Paramitas	六波羅蜜
Secret of the Golden Flower	金花之迷	Sixth Patriarch	六祖
Seeing Off Spring on the Last		Small Vehicle	小乘
Day of April	三月晦日送春	Snickers	士力架
seng-chih / sengzhi	僧值	South China tiger	南華虎
Seng-ts'an / Sengcan	僧璨	Southern China University	南澳大學
Seven Star Mountain	七星山	Southern Peak	南岳
Shaho / Shahe	沙河	Southern School (of Zen)	南宗
Shakyamuni	釋迦牟尼	*ssu / si*	寺
Shamien / Shamian Hotel	沙面賓館	Ssukungshan / Sikongshan	司空山
Shamien / Shamian Island	沙面島	Stalin	斯大林
Shan-hui / Shanhui	善慧	Stone Sutra Mountain	石經山
Shan-ku-ssu / Shangusi	山谷寺	Striped Yao	班瑤
Shanghai	上海	Strosser	施洛塞爾
Shangkao / Shanggao County	上高縣	Subhuti	須菩提
Shanku / Shangu Temple	山谷寺	*suffering, impermanence, emptiness,*	
Shansi / Shanxi Province	山西省	*no self*	苦空無常無我
Shansi / Shanxi Restaurant	山西飯店	Sui dynasty	隋代
Shantung / Shandong Province	山東省	Sukhavativyuha	無量壽佛經
Shaokuan / Shaoguan	韶關	Sun Wu-k'ung / Sun Wukong	孫悟空

Sun Yat-sen / Sun Yatsen	孫中山	Tao-hsin / Daoxin	道信
Sun Yat-sen / Sun Yatsen University	中山大學	Tao-hsuan / Daoxuan	道宣
		Tao-wu / Daowu	道悟
Sung / Song dynasty	宋代	T'ao Yuan-ming / Tao Yuanming	陶淵明
Sungshan / Songshan	嵩山	Taoist / Daoist Association	道教協會
supply manager	庫頭	*Taoteching / Daodejing*	道德經
Sutra on the Mahaprajnaparamita		Tapieh / Dabie Range	大別山
Spoken by Manjushri		Tatung / Datong	大同
文殊師利所說摩訶般若波羅蜜經		Tayushan / Dayushan	大愚山
Sutra on the Purity and Wonder of the Bodhisattva		Te-sung / Desong	德松
Manjushri	佛說文殊師利淨律經	temple manager	監院
Szechuan / Sichuan Province	四川省	Temple of Heaven	天壇
Szechuan / Sichuan University	四川省大學	Temple of the God of the South Seas	南海神廟
Ta-yu / Dayu	大愚	Teng Hsiao-p'ing / Deng Xiaoping	鄧小平
Tachien / Dajian Temple	大鑒寺	Theravada	上座部
Tachinshan / Dajinshan Temple	大金山寺	Thich Nhat Hanh	釋一行
Taheitien / Daheitian Bodhisattva	大黑天菩薩	Third Patriarch	三祖
		Third Patriarch Temple	三祖寺
Tahung / Dahong Mountains	大洪山	Thousand Buddha Pagoda	千佛塔
Tai-tsung / Daizong	代宗	Three Gorges	三峽
Taichi / Taiji	太極	Three Gorges University	三峽大學
Taihang Mountains	太行山	*Three Hundred Poems of the T'ang*	唐詩三百首
Taihochun / Taihechun	泰和春		
Taihuai	台懷	Three Periods	三世
Taipei / Taibei Basin	台北盆地	Three Poisons	三毒
Taipei / Taibei Road	台北路	Three Realms	三界
Taishan	泰山	Thunder Cave	雷洞
Taisho	大藏經	Tibetan	西藏
Taiwan	台灣	Tibetan Plateau	青藏高原
Taiyuan	太原	Tiehkuanyin / Tieguanyin	鐵觀音
Talin / Dalin Temple	大林寺	*tien-tso / dian-cuo*	典座
Tan-t'ien / Dantian	丹田	Tienanmen / Tiananmen	天安門
T'an-yao / Tanyao	曇曜	Tienchien / Dianqian	店前
tang-chia / dangjia	當家	Tienchin / Tianjin	天津
T'ang / Tang dynasty	唐代	Tienchushan / Tianjushan	天柱山
Tangyang / Dangyang	當陽	Tienmen / Tianmen	天門
Tanhsiashan / Danxiashan	丹霞山	Tientai / Tiantai School	天台宗
Tantric	密宗	Tientaishan / Tiantaishan	天台山
Tao-ch'uan / Daochuan	道川		

Tinglin / Dinglin Temple	定林寺	Vajrayana	金剛乘
Toba	拓跋	Vasubandhu	世親
Tokyo	東京	Victory Hotel	勝利賓館
Toumen / Doumen County	斗門縣	Vietnam	越南
Tourism Administration	旅遊局	Vihara	僧房
Treasury of Mahayana Sutras	大寶積經	*Vimalakirti Sutra*	維摩經
tree ears	木耳	*Waiting at Night for a Flute Player*	
Triple Gem	三寶	*Who Doesn't Come*	夜期嘯客不至
Triple Realm	三界	Wang An-shih / Wang Anshi	王安世
Tropic of Cancer	北回歸線	Wang Shu-ho / Wang Shuhe	王叔和
trusting the mind means no duality	信心不二	Wang Yu-fu / Wang Yufu	王玉夫
Ts'ang-ming / Cangming	藏明	Wei Ying-wu / Wei Yingwu	韋應物
Ts'ang-t'ung / Cangtong	藏通	*wei-nuo*	維那
Tsangfoken / Cangfoken	藏佛坑	Wei-shan / Weishan	溈山
Ts'ao Ts'ao / Cao Cao	曹操	Wei-tao / Weidao	惟道
Ts'ao-shan / Caoshan	曹山	*Weishihlun / Weishilun Shastra*	唯識論
Tsaohsi / Caoxi River	曹溪	Wen-hsi / Wenxi	聞熙
Tu Fu / Du Fu	杜甫	West River	西江
Tu Mu / Du Mu	杜牧	Western Pacific	
t'ui-na / tui-na	推拿	University	西太平洋大學
Tumen / Dumen Temple	度門寺	Western Paradise	西方極樂世界
Tun-ch'eng / Duncheng	頓成	Western Regions	西域
Tun-hui / Dunhui	頓慧	Western Wei dynasty	西魏代
Tung-shan / Dongshan	東山	Wheel of Rebirth	輪迴
Tungpaishan / Tongbaishan	桐柏山	White Deer Hotel	白鹿賓館
Tungshan / Dongshan	東山	White Horse Temple	白馬寺
Tungting / Dongting Lake	洞庭湖	White Swan Hotel	白天鵝賓館
Tunhuang / Dunhuang	敦煌	Wiman (Carl)	維曼
Tunhuang / Dunhuang Caves	敦煌莫高窟	Winston Wong	王文洋
Tunhuang / Dunhuang		World Buddhism Forum	世界佛教論壇
Museum	敦煌博物館	*wu-hsiang / wu-xiang*	無相
Twelve Ayatanas	十二處	*Wu-men-kuan / Wu-men-guan*	無門關
tz'u / zi	子	Wu-ming / Wuming	悟明
Tzukungshan / Zikongshan	紫宮山	Wuchang / Wuchang	武昌
Uighur	維吾爾	Wuchiang / Wujiang River	武江
Upper Huayen / Huayan	上華嚴	Wuhan	武漢
Uttar Pradesh	北方邦	Wuhan University	武漢大學
Vaipulya Sutra on the		Wuhsi / Wuxi	無錫
Pure Precepts	清淨毘尼方廣經	Wuhsiang / Wuxiang Temple	無相寺

Wuhsueh / Wuxue	武穴
Wushih / Wushi	烏石
Wutaishan	五台山
Wutaishan Buddhist Association	五台山佛教協會
Wuyang County	舞陽縣
Yama	焰摩天
Yang Chien / Yang Jian	楊堅
Yang Chung-chien / Yang Zhongjian	楊鐘健
Yang Hsuan-chih / Yang Xuanzhi	楊衒之
Yang Tseng-wen / Yang Zengwen	楊曾文
Yang-ch'i / Yangqi	楊枝
Yang-shan / Yangshan	仰山
Yangchou / Yangzhou	揚州
Yangke / Yangge	秧歌
Yangkao / Yanggao County	陽高縣
Yangmingshan National Park	陽明山國家公園
Yangtze	長江
Yao tribe	瑤族
Y. C. Wang	王永慶
Yeh / Ye	鄴
Yellow Crane Tower	黃鶴樓
Yellow River	黃河
Yen-tzu / Yenzi	延慈
Yen-ying / Yenying	延穎
Yi River	伊河
Yi River Bridge	伊河橋
Yi-ch'ao / Yichao	意超
Yi-ch'eng / Yicheng	一誠

Yi-hsing / Yixing	一行
Yichang	宜昌
Yiching / Yijing	易經
Yin-k'ung / Yinkong	印空
Yin-le / Yinle	印樂
Yin-shun / Yinshun	印順
Ying River	穎河
Yingcheng	應城
Yu	于
Yu Po-ya / Yu Boya	于伯牙
Yuan dynasty	元代
Yuchu / Yuju Temple	幽居寺
Yuchuan / Yuquan Temple	玉泉寺
Yuehhsi / Yuexi	岳西
Yuehhua / Yuehua Temple	越/月華寺
Yuehyang / Yueyang	岳陽
Yuehyang / Yueyang	岳陽
Yun-men Wen-yen / Yunmen Wenyan	雲門文偃
Yunchu / Yunju Temple	雲居寺
Yunchushan / Yunjushan	雲居山
Yunkang / Yungang Caves	雲岡石窟
Yungle / Yongle Bell	永樂大鐘
Yungning / Yongning Temple	永寧寺
Yunmen Temple	雲門寺
Zdansky (Otto)	師丹斯基
Zen	禪
Zen Tea	禪茶
zen-na / chan-na	禪那
Zhang Yimou	張藝謀

INDEX

A

Abbots, 105–6, 205
Affliction and Enlightenment, 152
Agency for Tributary Envoys, 86, 122
Amitabha Buddha, 44–45. *See also Omitofo*
Amongst White Clouds (documentary), 2
Ancient Bell Museum, 17–22
Ancient Zither Terrace, 253–55
Anhsi County, 218, 235
Anhui Province, 147, 149
Anting, 284, 325

B

Bactria, 36
Baggage, 330
Bamboo Grove Temple, 326
Bamyan buddhas, 42
Bear Ear Mountain, 128
Begging, 86
Beijing, 17–22; Bill Porter's arrival in, 2; dragon walls, 52; Hotang Yuehszu (Lotus in the Moonlight) vegetarian restaurant, 4; sites/sights nearby, 22–33
Bells, 18–22; Wuhsiang Temple, 152–53
Belly-up floating fish, 309–10
Benson, Bob, 203
Bicycle-powered rickshaws, 162, 177–78
Big Bell Temple, 18, 19
Big Fool Mountain, 245
Birth and death, 330
Bitter Melon, 202
Bodhidharma (First Patriarch), 2, 53–54, 128, 268, 312–14, 323–25; death, 115; and Emperor Wu, 165; and Hui-k'o, 113–14; meditation in caves, 140; portrait, 129, 131; statue, 324; text for teachings, 31; two feet, 131–32; writings, 130–31; at Yungning Pagoda, 127; and Zen practice, 8
bodhisattva: Chienchai (Meal Watching), 91; statue (Venus of the East), 50; two-armed Daheitien (Mahakala), 97. *See also* Kuan-yin (Bodhisattva of Compassion); Manjushri (Bodhisattva of Wisdom)

Bodhisattva Emperor, 165
Bodhisattva Summit, 67
Brothels, 174, 175, 258
Buddha: as the mind, 166, 191–92; "we are all," 158
Buddhacharita, 148
Buddha of the Future, 180
Buddha (Shakyamuni), 88–89; birthday, 1; explanation of language, 31–32; images of, 35–36, 42, 44–45, 49, 87–88; Little Richard as, 37; and origin of Zen Buddhism, 224; reclining, 242; relics, 314–15; seeing, 33
Buddhism, 127; Chinese government view, 182; Indian Buddhism influence on Zen Buddhism, 308; Mind Only School, 12; School of Emptiness, 12; Tientai School, 28, 266, 268, 274, 275, 276. *See also* Chinese Buddhism; Mahayana Buddhism; Pure Land Buddhism; Theravada Buddhism; Vajrayana Buddhism; Zen Buddhism
Buddhist academies, 216; in Beijing, 319; Kuanghua Temple, 273; Nanhua Temple, 300; Pailin monestary, 93–94; Pushou nunnery, 116; Tachinshan Temple nunnery, 235, 237; Tumen Temple, 274; Wutaishan, 74; Yunmen Temple, 292, 295
Buddhist and Taoist clerics: campaigns against, 3–4, 29, 39, 115, 167, 243–44; Tapieh mountains, 197.
Buddhist Association of China, 4, 100, 105, 109, 183;
Buddhist Association of Honan Province, 125
Buddhist Association of Hopei Province, 112
Buddhist Canon, 6; earliest Chinese, 30; Kaiyuan Edition, 29–30. *See also* Chinese Buddhist Canon
Buddhist Hall of Fame, 313
Buddhist monasteries, 86; first ones, 128; sources of income, 244–45. *See also* Zen monasteries
Buddhist teachers' lineage, 95
Buddhist temples, 86; bells, 20–21; Chinese politics among, 302; legal standing, 104–5; as old age homes, 319; sources of income, 109; welcoming statues, 180; in the West, 112

Burger, Ted, 2, 15, 34
Burning paper money, 152
Bus travel: Beijing and Tatung, 34; Chienshan
and Huangmei, 178–79; Chiuchiang and
Nanchang, 229–33; between Fuchou and
Wuhan, 249–51; Hantan and Loyang, 120–21;
Hofei and Yuehhsi, 147, 148–49; Huangmei
and Chiuchiang, 216; Kuangchou and
Hsinhsing, 317; Loyang and Hofei, 145–46;
Nanchang and Fuchou, 233–34; Shaokuan and
Juyuan, 287–89; station at Kuangechou, 311;
Taihuai and Shihchiachuang, 76–78; Tatung
and Wutaishan, 55–60; Wuhan and Tangyang,
261–64. See also Train travel

C

Calligraphy, 100, 171–72, 235; Pai Chu-yi poems,
140; Pen-huan practicing, 316, 317
Camel photographers, 277–78
Campo, Daniela, 294–325
Cantonese people, 323
Cauldron for Yuchuan Temple, 266, 267
Caves: Bodhidharma's, 113–14; Pao-chih's, 172;
Taihang Mountains, 29; where Bodhidharma
faced rock wall nine years, 140; "Zen caves"
near Tatung, 53–54. See also Hermits in China;
Thunder Cave; Yungang Caves
Cell phones, 204–5, 216, 250, 294
Central China, 217, 252
Ceremonies, 185, 205; burial of abbot of
Shaolin Temple, 134–35, 139; Frog Festival,
322; lay memorial services, 242; recitation of
Mahaprajnaparamita Sutra, 8, 13–16; Shuilu,
183–84, 196–97, 205; by Zen temples, 107–8.
See also Holidays and celebrations
Chan (Buddhist magazine), 2–3, 4
Ch'ang, 127–28
Chang, Lili, 40–45
Ch'ang-an, 115, 122, 127
Changchiakou, 34
Chang Chien-min, 258–59, 261
Chang Heng, 122
Ch'ang-ming (abbot), 204–5, 211
Changpai Mountains, 252
Changsha, 284
Chang Shun-p'ing, 15–16

Chan-jan, 169
Ch'an-lin-chu-chi pi-ch'iu-ni ("Bikhuni Pearls of
the Zen Forest), 238
Chanting (Meditation Samadhi), 207; by frogs,
291
Chao-chou, 10, 16, 84
Chaochou Bridge (oldest stone-arch bridge), 10
Chaohsien, 9–10, 84, 87–88. See also Pailin
Temple
Chao P'u-ch'u, 113
Chao-yuan, 300
Chayuan (The Tea Connection), 218–20
Chekiang Province, 266
Chengan County promo DVD, 116
Chengchou, 125
Chengchueh ("The Englightenment") magazine,
199
Chen-jen (abbot), 317
Chenju Temple, 95, 100, 236, 273, 292
Chiaho hotel (in Wuchang), 282
Chi-an, 128, 190; portrait of Bodhidharma, 129,
131
Chian Ching-kuo, 262
Chiang Ts'e-min, 326
Chia Tao, 26–27, 324
Ch'i dynasty, 165
Chienchai Bodhisattva (Meal Watching), 91
Chien jen (abbot), 203, 204–5
Chienshan, 161–63, 172–74, 177–78
Chienshui (Shallow Water) River, 161
Chienyang International hotel, 162–63
chien-yuan (temple manager), 104
Ch'i-fo ("The Eccentric Buddha"), 100
chih-k'o (guest manager), 94
Chihpi (Red Cliff), 283
Chih-sheng, 304
Chihsia Temple, 74
Chih-yao, 32, 298, 303
Chih-yi, 266–69, 271, 274, 275
China's Big Dam, 261
Chinchieh Shanchuang (Golden Realm Resort)
hotel, 61, 62
Chinese Buddhism, 29, 48; Huayen School, 29,
48, 71; as religion of spiritual elite, 169; Tientai
School, 28, 266, 268, 274, 275, 276
Chinese Buddhist Canon, 188–89

Chinese creation story, 76
Chinese culinary preferences, 232–33
Chinese gooseberries, 162–63
Chinese medicine, 258–59
Chinese seasons, 1–2
Chinese White lightning, 59
Ch'ing dynasty, 282, 314
Ching-hui (abbot), 8, 11–12, 85, 94, 182–86,
    187, 188–89, 196, 197, 199, 201, 235, 264, 267,
    292; calligraphy, 4; disciples, 5, 6; photo, 7
Chingming. See Grave Sweeping Day
Chingping Market, 323
Chingshihtungyen, 255
Chingtzuyao Mine, 45–46
Ching-wan, 28, 29, 30–31, 32
Chinhuakung Coal Mine, 45
Chinhuangtao, 23–24
Ch'in Kuei ("Rules of Purity"), 87
Chinshan Mountain, 240
Chinshan Temple, 234, 236, 239–42, 244
Chintzuyao Coal Mine, 58
Chiuchiang, 216–20, 226–27, 228; areas nearby,
    220–22
Chiufengshan (mountain), 244
Chiufengshan nunnery, 245–46
Chou dynasty, 115, 288–89
Chou-En-lai, 326–27, 328
Choukoutian, 22–26
Chrysanthemums, 282
Ch'uan-cheng (abbot), 309
Chuang people, 321–22
Chu Hsi, 230
Chu-ko Liang, 283
Chu Kuei, 51, 52
Chulin Temple, 74–76
Chung Ch'i, 255–58
Chunghsiang, 263, 273
Chunghsing Temple, 257
Chungnan Mountains, 3
Ch'ung-tu, 84, 88, 94
Chung Tzu-ch'i, 254
Chunyangkung (Pure Yang Temple), 194
Chu Te, 328
Chu Ti, 18, 19
Ch'u Yuan, 285–86
CIA station chief in Taiwan, 280

Cicadas, 319
Cold Mountain, 119–20, 123–24
Confucianism, 127
Confucius, 18; lineal descendent, 222–23
Cotton trees, 315–16
Cultural Revolution in China, 3, 73–74, 86, 104,
    211, 307

D

Dagoba. See Stupas
Darwin, Charles, 25
Dead Tree Zen, 113
Death, 330
Delusions, 330
Dhammapada, 291
Dharma certificates, 224
Dharmaraksha, 64, 122–24
Dharma (truth), 28–29, 35, 166; practicing
    according to, 131
dhyana, 8
Diamond Sutra, 320
Discourse on the Supreme Vehicle, 209
Dragon Bone Hill, 23, 25
Dragons, 50–52
Drive to North Terrace of Wutaishan, 63
Drums from 2,500 years ago, 321
Dust: illness from, 111, 121; huang-t'u
    ("yellow dust"), 84, 87
Dying, 230–31. See also Suicide

E

East Mountain Zen, 208
East West clinic, 258–59
Eight Immortals, 194
Emperor Chung-tsung, 271, 317
Emperor Hsiao-wen, 138
Emperor Hsuan-tsung, 154
Emperor Ming, 64–65
Emperor Shun, 285–86
Emperor Shun-chih, 314
Emperor T'ai-tsung, 124
Emperor Wen, 115, 266
Emperor Wen-ch'eng, 39–40
Emperor Wu, 128, 129, 164, 165, 183
Emperor Yung-Chung, 18
Empress Hu, 127

Empress Wu, 272, 276

Environmental protection in America, 126

Erchan Village, 26–27

Essential Means for Entering the Path and Stilling the Mind, 199

Exercise groups in China, 83

F

Fa-chao, 74

Fa-chih (abbot), 305–6

Fahsing Temple, 314

Fairbank, Tony, 229

Fa-jung, 192

Fa-tsang, 29

Fayin (Buddhist magazine), 4

Fayun Temple, 155–59

Fengle International hotel (in Hofei), 147

Feng Mao, 207

Fengmao Mountain, 207, 208

Fengmao (mountain), 194

Fifth Patriarch. *See* Hung-jen (Fifth Patriarch)

Fifth Patriarch Temple, 201, 202–14, 215–16

Fifth Patriarch Village, 206

First Patriarch. *See* Bodhidharma (First Patriarch)

Five Elements (Taoist concept), 164

Five Skandhas, 209

Forbidden City, 52

Foreigners: in Beijing, 17; encounter in countryside with, 258; expatriates, 203; prevalence in Kuangchou, 312

Forty-two Passage Sutra, 124

Four Guardians of the Universe, 180

Four Practices, 130–31

Fourth Patriarch. *See* Tao-hsin

Patriarch Temple, 95, 179–86, 190, 207

Fo-yuan (abbot), 291–93

Friendship in China, 254

Frog festival, 322

Fuchou, 234; temples nearby, 234–48

Fu Hsi, 51

Fukien Province, 218, 268, 273

G

Gandhara, 36

Gas stations in China, 36, 79

Girl with cupcakes on train, 261–63, 280

God of the South Seas, 324

Golden Fur tea, 221

Gold Mountain Temples, 234

Gould, Nic, 226–27

Government information fair, 83

Government purchase of land around monasteries/nunneries, 248

GPS systems in vehicles, 186–87, 202

Graves: Bodhidharma, 128–30; Chung Ch'i, 255–58; Hui-k'o (Second Patriarch), 116–18; Matanga and Dharmaraksha, 122–24; Pai Chu-yi, 134, 142–43; Shen-hsiu, 272. *See also* Human fossils; Pagodas; Shrines; Stupas

Grave Sweeping Day, 256, 290, 310, 313, 315

Great Leap Forward, 292

Great Vehicle, 74

Great Wall, 33, 34

Gridakuta Temple, 65

Guggenheim Foundation grants, 147–48, 163

Guides: police escort, 62; in Tibetan Plateau, 279–80

H

Hai-ch'an (abbot), 70

Hai-ju, 111–12

Han dynasty, 122, 127, 164

Hangchou, 282

Hankou, 251

Han River, 251, 263

Han-shan Te-ch'ing, 63–64, 67, 68, 298, 299, 302

Hantan, 111, 119–20

Hanyang, 251, 253–55

Han Yu, 324

Hengshan (mountain), 165

Hermits in China, 3–4; author's book about, 3; documentary about, 2; Lushan ("Hut Mountain"), 220; Shuangfeng, 193, 194; Tienchushan, 165; Tungpaishan mountains, 125. *See also* Caves

"High Mountain" (song), 254

Hofei, 147–48

Holidays and celebrations: Arbor Day, 109; Buddha's birthday, 1; by descendents, 256; Kuan-yin's birthday, 159, 161; Pai Chu-yi birthday, 142–43; Poet's Day, 286. *See also* Ceremonies; Grave Sweeping Day

Honan Province, 83

Hong Kong, 309, 325, 327

Hopei Province, 83

Hopei Provincial Museum, 82–83

Hotels: haunted, 163; hot springs, 319, 320

Hotspring Village, 229

Hsiang River, 284, 286, 288

Hsiangshan Temple, 113, 143

Hsiaoshihtzu ("Little Rock"), 54

Hsieh Yu-wei, 223

Hsientung Temple, 61, 64, 66, 67, 75

Hsilai monastery, 313

Hsinan, 133–34

Hsinchou, 243

Hsingtzu ("Starlet"), 220

Hsinhing River, 317

Hsinhsing, 317, 323

Hsin-hsin-ming ("On Trusting the Mind"), 166, 169, 171, 177

Hsinjung, 54

Hsiualu Village, 318

Hsuankung Temple, 57–58

Hsuan-tsang, 6

Hsu-yun (Empty Cloud), 67–68, 69–72, 95, 100, 235, 243–44, 294, 301–2, 316, 322–23; body, 307; disciples, 309, 325–30; photo, 329; relics, 299; staff and robe, 305

Huai River, 146

Hualin Temple, 312–14, 313–14, 323–25

Huangmei, 179, 202, 216. *See also* Fourth Patriarch Temple

Huangmu Bay, 323

Huang T'ing-chien, 166

huang-t'u ("yellow dust"), 84, 87

Huaoshan (mountain), 164

Huayen Sutra, 71, 72

Huayen Temple, 48–50

Huijih ("Sun of Wisdom") Temple, 220–22

Hui-k'o (Second Patriarch), 2, 113–15, 140, 146–47, 150, 157–59; gravesite, 116–18; meeting with Seng-ts'an (Third Patriarch), 166; relics, 117, 118, 157; teaching, 152, 169; written materials by, 118–19; at Wuhsiang Temple, 154–55. *See also* Wuhsiang Temple

Hui-k'ung (abbess), 116

Hui-neng (Sixth Patriarch), 2, 154, 274, 286–87, 297, 302, 303–4, 314, 315, 317, 320, 321–22; body, 298–99, 309; chosen for Sixth Patriarch, 5–6; old temple, 235; place where he entered nirvana, 319; poems, 17; pounding stone, 211; relics, 207, 309

Hui-ssu, 28–29

Human fossils, 22–25, 37. *See also* Shrines

Hunan Province, 165, 283, 288

Hung-jen (Fifth Patriarch), 2, 11–12, 192, 194, 206–10, 271; disciple, 270–71; impact on Zen, 213–14; stupa, 212–13

Hung-lu-ssu, 86

Hung-yang (abbess), 6

Hung-yung (abbess), 186

Hupei Province, 149, 264

hu-ping (cookies), 293

I J

International Hotel (in Shihchiachuang), 80

Internet cafe: with brothel, 61

Iron Crutch Li, 194

Iron Goddess (tea), 217–20

Japanese Zen, 3

Jen-ming, 151, 155

Johnson, Steve, 280, 282

Ju-ch'an (abbot), 319–20

Ju-man, 141, 143

Juyuan, 294. *See also* Yunmen Temple

K

Kanlu Temple, 74

Kan River, 3

Kao-an, 245

Kaomin Temple, 300

Kao Shih-t'ao, 112

Kashyapa, 224

Ke Hung (alchemist), 168

Khitans (nomadic tribes), 48

Kiangsi Province, 3;

King Kao, 288

King P'ing, 288–89

koans, 313

Kuangchiao Temple, 112–15, 116

Kuangchi Hermitage, 70, 71

Kuangchou, 100, 311, 312, 323
Kuanghsiao Temple, 100, 314–15
Kuanghua Temple, 273
Kuangtung Province, 244, 321–22
K'uan-hsiang, 266–68, 269–75, 279
Kuan-hsi Chi-hsien, 245–46
Kuan-hsin-lun ("Discourse on Looking at the Mind"), 275
k'uan-jung (abbot), 161, 170–72, 177
Kuan Kung. *See* Kuan Yu
Kuan Ti. *See* Kuan Yu
Kuan-yin (Bodhisattva of Compassion), 67, 92, 100–101, 316; birthday, 159, 161;
Kuan Yu, 265–66, 283
Kuchentai ("Ancient Zither Terrace"), 253–55
Kuchu (Bitter Bamboo), 187
Kunghsiang Temple, 127–33
K'ung Te-ch'eng, 222–23
K'un-ku-yu-lan ("Hidden Orchids of Deserted Valleys"), 3
Kuoen Temple, 317–18, 319–20
Kuo-le, 117
Kuo-ming, 117
Kushan Empire, 7

L
Language: Buddha's explanation, 31–32; purpose of Buddha's teachings using, 16; as vibration, 21; why humans began using, 25; on Yungle Bell, 19–20
Lankavatara Sutra, 31, 32, 114, 148, 199, 271
Laotsu Temple, 186–88, 292
Lao-tzu, 213–14
Large Vehicle, 74
Layman Hsiang, 157–58, 166
Layman P'an Yun-sung, 319
Laymen Heng-cheng, 199
Laywoman Liu, 85
Leng-ch'ieh-shih-tzu-chi, 118
Liang dynasty, 165, 183
Liao dynasty, 48
Liao River in Manchuria, 48
Lin-Chi, 33, 246
Linchi (Rinzai) monastery, 208
Linchuan. *See* Fuchou
Li Pai, 154, 232, 283

Li Sheng-hua, 303–5
Li-shen (guest manager), 98–99
Li Shih-min, 138
Liu Ta'un-chi, 307
Living buddhas, 40
Loess Plateau, 18, 79
Lofushan, 168
Lotus Mountain, 326
Lotus Sutra (Fa-hua-hsuan-yi), 266
Loyang, 86, 113, 121–27, 134–43, 145; history of religions in, 127.
Lungman Caves, 141, 143
Lungshan, 317–18, 320–21, 322–23
Lung Tung pin, 194
Lushan (mountain), 190, 220, 251
Lu Tung-pin, 194
Luyehyuan (Deer Park) Caves, 53–54

M
Ma-an-shan (Saddle Mountain), 256
Maha Prajnaparamita (Great Perfection of Wisdom), 190
Mahaprajnaparamita Sutra, 6, 276; recitation, 8, 9–16
Mahasanghikas, 37
Mahayana Buddhism, 7, 36
Manjushri (Bodhisattva of Wisdom), 61, 65, 66, 68
Mao-hwa, 9
Mao Tse-tung, 281–82, 320, 328. *See also* Great Leap Forward
Marco Polo, 313
Martial arts, 138–39
Massage: Chienshan, 172–74; Chiuchiang, 226; Shihchiachuang, 80–81; Wuhan, 258–59
Master-at-arms, 94–96
Matanga, 64–66, 122–24
Mathura, 36
Ma-tsu, 84
Ma-Ying-chou, 262
Medical clinic, 258–59
Meditation, 275; at Fourth Patriarch Temple, 198; at Nanhua Temple, 300; at nunnery, 236–37; periods, 101–2; powers of Zen masters, 328; scriptures about, 8
Meditation halls, 100–101; altars, 103; Chinshan

Temple, 236, 241; Fifth Patriarch Temple, 212; Fourth Patriarch Temple, 197; Pailin Temple, 99, 101; rules, 102–3; Shaolin Temple, 139; on Wutaishan, 75; Yuchuan Temple, 268; in Zen monestaries, 107

Meichuan (Plum River), 190

Miao-chiang (abbot), 72–76, 77, 126

Miaotou Village, 323

Miao-wei (guest manager), 235, 238, 239, 247–48

Milo River, 285, 286

Mind, pure, 209

Mines in China, 45–47, 58

Ming-chieh, 3, 6, 9

Ming-ch'ing (food manager), 89–93

Ming-chi (supply manager), 96–97

Ming-chi (temple manager), 182, 185, 196–97, 201, 205, 291

Ming dynasty, 51

Ming-hai (abbot), 10–11, 84, 87, 104–9, 111, 197

Ming-hsiang (abbot), 291, 294, 295

Ming-hsuan, 295

Ming names, 95

Ming-shen, 152

Ming-yao, 2, 3–6, 9, 12–13

Ming-yen, 93–94

Ming-yi, 94–96

Ming-yu (abbot), 273

Monkey People story, 333–34

Monks: advantages in China, 273; from Korea, 172–73. *See also* Buddhist and Taoist clerics; Zen monks

Mopanshan, 238

Mo-shan, 244

Mo-shan Liao-jan, 245–46

Motorcycle trips: cost, 179–80; to Fayun Temple, 156–57, 159; from Kuoen Temple to Tsangfoken, 318–19; to Tachinshan Temple nunnery, 234; to/from Tachien Temple, 286–87

Mountain Dave, 203, 204

Mountains, 70, 76, 232; use for Zen monastary sites, 207–9

Mount Lanka, 271

Mount Sumeru, 51

Mrs. Ts'ao, 218–20

Murphy, Dave, 8–9

Musical instruments in Chinese music, 43. *See also* Zithers

"Muslim cap," 11

N O

Nagarjuna, 276

Nanchang, 223

Nanching, 74, 191, 288

Nanhai (South Seas), 312, 320

Nan Huai-chin, 132, 299, 325

Nanhua Temple, 235, 292, 296, 297–301, 307–10, 326, 327

nan-kua-ping (pumpkin cookies), 162–63, 172, 180

Nanyueh (Southern Peak), 165

Napuyuan (resort), 187, 202

Native Americans from China, 288

Neng-wen (abbot), 149, 155, 156–59

New Chuho hotel (in Loyang), 121

Nihewan Basin, 37

Ningpo, 68

Nirvana Sutra, 158, 314

Nomadic peoples, 37–38, 39, 48; Tibetan herders, 278–80

Northern Ch'i dynasty, 115

Northern Chou dynasty, 29

Northern School of Zen, 268, 269, 274, 275

Northern Wei dynasty, 38, 42, 74, 114, 115

North River, 302, 317

Not One Less (movie), 34

"No work, no food," 289, 290; Tao-hsin (Fourth Patriarch), 182

Number One Bridge (Wuhan), 280–81, 282

Nunneries, 201; Chiufengshan, 245–46; Kuangchiao Temple, 116; Shuangfeng Mountain, 197. *See also* Pushou Temple (nunnery); Zen nunneries

Nuns: early Buddhist, 245–46; from Fourth Patriarch Temple, 6, 9, 186–88; procedure for staying at monestary, 99; who lived on Wutaishan, 61–62

Nu Wa, 51

Omitofo, 60, 100

108 (number) significance, 21, 152

On Trusting the Mind, 166, 169, 171, 178

Oxhead Zen School, 192

P

Pagodas: Chao-chou, 85; Seng-ts'an (Third Patriarch), 172; Thousand Buddha Pagoda, 156; Yungning Temple, 127. *See also* Shrines; Stupas

Pai-chang, 95

Pai Chu-yi, 134, 140–43, 213

Pai Gardens, 140

Pai-ho (White Crane), 165

Pailin Temple, 6, 84–87, 88–110, 197; recitation of *Mahaprajnaparamita Sutra,* 9–16

Pai-ma-ssu, 86

P'an-hu, 288–89

P'an-ku, 76

Pao-chang, 188

Pao-chih, 165, 172, 183

Pao-ching, 113

Pao-en Temple, 243

Paohua Temple, 59

Paolin Temple, 298

paramita, 7–8

Pataling, 34

Patriarchal culture of China, 205

Patriarchs of Zen Buddhism: most famous, 6. *See also* Bodhidharma; Hui-k'o; Hui-neng; Hung-jen; Seng-ts'an; Tao-hsin

Peach Blossom Spring, 231–32

"Pearl birds" (Guinea hens), 309

Pearl River, 311, 317

Peking Man (museum), 22–25

Pen-ching, 154

Pen-huan, 100, 196–97, 243, 244, 314–15, 316, 317

Peonies, 125

People's Republic of China, 71

Perfection of Wisom in 25,00 Lines, 199

Phone shops, 294

Pien-ho, 116

Pi River, 147

Pishan Temple, 59, 69–76, 78, 315

Platform Sutra, 11–12, 238, 287, 304, 320; gathas, 17

Poems: by candidates for Sixth Patriarch, 11–12; Chang Heng, 122; Chia Tao, 26–27; Gary Snyder, 136; Huang T'ing, 166; Hui-k'o (Second Patriarch), 155, 158; Hung-jen (Fifth Patriarch), 210; Lao-tzu, 213–14; Li Pai, 232; Pai Chu-yi, 134, 140, 141–42, 143, 213; Seng-ts'an (Third Patriarch), 166–69; Tao-ch'uan, 50; T'ao Yuan-ming eulogy, 230–31; Tu Fu, 284; Wan An-shih, 165–66; Yi-chao, 328–29. *See also* Songs (gathas)

Poetry, 26

Poetry Immortal (Immortal of Poetry), 283

Poet's Day, 286

Police escort, 62

Porter, Bill: army life experiences, 55–57; climbing of the mountain, 192–96; Dharma talk for nuns, 6–7; family, 331–34; funding for his translation work, 147–48, 163, 225–26; photos, 253, 306; *Road to Heaven,* 3

Post offices, 233, 295

prajna, 6–8

Prajnaparamita Sutra Spoken by Manjushri, 68, 199, 276

Prajnaparamita (the Perfection of Wisdom), 6–8, 15–16, 66

pratimoksha (code of conduct), 89

Provincial capitals, 233

Public transportation in China, 84

P'u ching, 265 66

Puhua Temple, 74, 75

Pu Lo-t'uo, 322

Pumpkin cookies, 162–63, 172, 180

Pure Land Buddhism, 5, 21, 100–101, 224, 237, 244–45, 274;

Pushou Temple (nunnery), 61, 116

Putuoshan, 67

R

Record of the Masters of the Lankavatara, 154, 184, 275

Red twig (tea), 219

Restaurants in China, 81–82

Rickshaws, 162, 178–79

Rivers in China, 146–47

Roads in China, 36, 250; on Wutaishan, 63

Road to Heaven (Porter), 3, 15

Robe and bowl, 224

Romance of the Three Kingdoms, 265

Ryan, Mike, 226–27, 277, 286

S

Sage of Poetry, 283

sangha (Buddhist assembly), 88, 166

Second Patriarch. *See* Hui-k'o (Second Patriarch)

Second Patriarch Village, 117

Self, 330

Seng-ts'an (Third Patriarch), 2, 116, 154, 155, 190; Layman Hsiang, 157–58, 166; pagoda, 172; poetry, 166–69; relics, 169; stupa, 173

Seven Star Mountain, 203

Shamian hotel (in Kuangchou), 311, 312

Shamian (Sand Flat) Island, 311

Shanghai, 325

Shang-hui (religious affairs manager), 99–103

Shangkao County, 244

Shanku Temple, 165

Shansi Province, 83

Shansi Restaurant (in Taihuai), 61, 62

Shantung Province, 83

Shaokuan, 286–87, 295–97; temples nearby, 289–95, 297–311

Shaolin Temple, 108, 113, 132, 134–35, 135–40, 302

Sheng Huo Ch'an ("Daily Life Zen"), 5

Shen-hsiu, 210, 270–76

Shensi Province, 83

Shihchiachuang, 80–84

Shou-yeh, 68, 69–72, 316

Shrine halls, 100; cost, 152; Hualin Temple; Kuan-yin, 316; Tachinshan Temple nunnery, 234; Tsangfoken, 319; in Upper and Lower Huayen near Tatung, 48–50

Shrines: Chia Tao, 26–27; Hui-neng's Refuge Rock, 303–4, 309; Manjushri, 67–68; T'ao Yuan-ming's drinking rock, 229–32. *See also* Graves; Pagodas; Stupas

Shuangfeng Mountain, 180, 197, 206, 208; climbing, 192–96

Shucheng, 148

Shuilu (ceremony), 183–84, 196–97, 205

Shurangama Sutra, 295

Sian, 3, 127

Six Paramitas, 131

Sixth Patriarch. *See* Hui-neng (Sixth Patriarch)

Small Vehicle, 74

Snyder, Gary, 136

Songs (gathas), 17; Cold Mountain, 119–20; evening song of offering, 153; relation with language, 25

Sounding boards, 102, 107, 241–42

South China, 286; dampness, 318

Southern School of Zen, 268, 274

ssu, 86

Ssukungshan (mountain), 147, 149, 154

Stele at Temple of the God of the South Seas, 324

Stele for Chung Ch'i, 256

Stone Sutra Mountain, 30, 32

Stupas, 66; Bodhidharma (First Patriarch), 128, 129; Hui-k'o (Second Patriarch), 117; Hung-jen (Fifth Patriarch), 212–13; at Kuanghsiao Temple, 315; Seng-ts'an (Third Patriarch), 173; Shen-hsiu, 270–71; Shou-yeh, 72, 73; Tao-hsin (Fourth Patriarch), 189, 206. *See also* Graves; Pagodas; Shrines

Suffering. *See* Affliction and Enlightenment

Suicide, 227, 285–86

Sui dynasty, 115

Sung dynasty, 124, 129, 165–66

Sungshan Mountain, 113

Sungshan National Park, 135, 138

Sun Yat-sen, 109

Sun Yat-sen University, 295

Sun Yat-sen University Hostel, 311

Sutra on the Purity and Wonder of the Buddhaland of Manjushri, 66

Sutras: carvings, 29; on Yungle Bell, 20

T

Tachien Temple, 286–87, 295–96, 305–11

Tachinshan Temple (nunnery), 223, 234–48

Tai chi, 83

Taihang Mountains, 28, 29, 78, 79

Taihechun hotel, 38–39

Taihuai, 60–62; sites/sights nearby, 62–78

Taihuai (pilgrimage center), 65–66

Tailor, 225

Taipei, 203

Tai-tsung, 212

Taiwan, 203–4, 280–81; Nationalist Party (KMT), 262

Taiwan's College of Chinese Culture on

Yanmingshan, 222
T'ai-wu (emperor), 39
Talin Temple, 190
T'ang dynasty, 124, 138, 148, 220
Tangyang, 263
Tanhsiashan (mountain), 221
Tan-t'ien, 298
T'an-yao, 40
Tao-ch'uan, 50
Tao-hsin (Fourth Patriarch), 2, 86–87, 167–68,
    185, 190–92, 206; Dharma talks on, 199–200;
    originator of "no work, no food," 182; relics,
    189; stupa, 189
Taoism: Chinese government view, 182; Five
    Elements, 164; influence on Zen Buddhism,
    308. See also Fu Hsi
Taoist Association, 105
Taoist clerics. See Buddhist and Taoist clerics
Taoist hermitages, 194–95
Taoist Immortals, 194
Taoists, 127; around Huangmei, 188; center at
    Kuanyinsai, 197; during Cultural Revolution,
    3–4; Ke Hung, 168; on Tienchushan, 164–65;
    on Wuaishan, 65
Taoteching, 213–14
Tao-wu, 240–42
T'ao Yuan-ming, 229–32
Tapieh mountains, 149, 161, 187, 197
Tatung, 33, 34–36; hotels, 38–39, 52; lunch with
    family of Mr. Chang, 47–48; Nine Dragon Wall,
    50–52; sites/sights nearby, 40–47, 48–50,
    53–54
Taxis: trip from Loyang to Ch'ang, 127–28; trip to
    Ching Chi's grave, 255–58
Ta-yu (the Big Fool), 245
Tea: first use in Zen schools, 16; Golden Fur, 221;
    Iron Goddess, 217–20; preparation in China,
    94; red teas, 221; red twig, 219; at Shaolin
    Temple, 136; as source of monastery income,
    187, 272–73; Tibetan, 279; "Zen," 306
Tea competitions, 219
Temple to the God of the South Seas, 323–24,
    325
Ten directions, 152–53
Teng Hsiao-p'ing, 280–81
Textile production by nuns, 243

Theravada Buddhism, 74
"the Way," 6, 137, 169, 209
Thich Nhat Hanh, 221–22
Third Patriarch. See Seng-ts'an (Third Patriarch)
Third Patriarch Temple, 161, 163–65, 169–72
Three Gorges, 263
Three Gorges University in Yichang, 261
Thunder Cave, 28–31
Thunder God, 321–22
Tibetan people in China, 321
Tibetan Plateau, 278
Tienanmen Square, 132, 280–81
Tienchien, 149
Tienchin, 24
Tienchushan Mountain, 190
Tienchushan (mountain), 163–65, 167
Tientai School of Buddhism, 28, 266, 268, 274,
    275, 276
Tientaishan (mountain), 123, 266
tien-tso (food manager), 89–93
Tigers (South China tiger), 248
Tinglin ("Meditation Grove"), 128
Tobas (nomadic tribe), 38, 39, 40, 48, 53–54,
    127
Train travel, 34–35; Beijing and Taiyuan, 59;
    smoking on trains, 283; stations in Wuhan
    area, 261, 283; Wuhan and Shaokuan, 283–86;
    Wuhan and Tangyang, 261–64, 280. See also
    Bus travel
Traveling in China: importance of relationships,
    235; in March, 146; planning ahead, 38; with
    a staff (walking stick), 133, 178; ticket offices,
    252. See also Bus travel; Motorcycle trips; Taxis;
    Train travel; Vans
Tsaitien ("Vegetable Fields"), 212
Tsangoken ("Hidden Buddha Gully"), 319
Tsaohsi River, 302
Ts'ao Ts'ao, 283
Tu Fu, 283–84, 288
Tumen Temple, 266–69, 269–75. See also
    Yuchuan Temple
Tun-ch'eng (temple manager), 235–38, 239
Tungpaishan (mountain), 125–26
Tungshan (East Mountain), 208
Tungting Lake, 283, 284–86
Tunhuang Caves, 118, 275

Tunhuang Museum, 11
Tun-hui, 235
Tzukungshan (Purple Palace Mountain), 64

U V

Uighurs, 11, 321
Vaipulya Sutra on the Pure Precepts, 66
Vajrayana Buddhism, 5, 75
Vans: between Chienshan and Tienchushan, 163–65; from road into Huangmei, 179; between Yuehhsi and Tienchien, 149, 155
Vegetarianism, 232–33
Victory hotel (In Kuangehou), 312
vihara (resting place), 88–89
Voice of the Dharma. See Fayin (Buddhist magazine)

W

Wan An-shih, 165–66
Wang Shu-ho, 259
Wang Yu-fu, 116
Wan-t'ai (guest manager), 295
wei-nuo (religious affairs manager), 99–103
Weishihlun Shastra, 295
Wei-tao (temple manager), 203, 205–6, 210–12, 214, 215–16
Wei Ying, 148
Wei Ying-wu, 220
Wen-hsi, 220–24
Western Wei dynasty, 115
West River, 317
White Deer hotel (in Chiuchiang), 217, 229
White Horse Temple, 64, 86, 121–27
White Swan hotel (in Kuangchou), 312
Wilcox, Finn, 283, 284
Wild grape wine, 252
Winston Wong, 225
Workweek in China, 248–49
World Buddhist Forum, 111–12
Writing and publishing, 202
Wuchang, 251, 282
Wu Ch'u-ch'i, 255
Wuhan, 251–58, 280; Chinese medical techniques, 258–59. *See also* Number One Bridge (Wuhan)
Wuhan University Philosophy Department, 188–89

Wuhsiang Temple, 149–55
Wuhsueh, 190
Wu-ming (abbot), 116
Wushih (Black Rock village), 302
Wutaishan (mountain), 28, 55, 63–69, 70; balls of fire, 61–62; origin of name, 62–63

Y

Yang-ch'i, 207–9
Yang Chien, 29, 31
Yangchou, 300
Yang Tseng-wen, 11
Yangtze River, 215, 217, 251, 280, 281–82, 284
Yangtze watershed, 177, 181–82, 268
Yao tribe, 288
Yeh, 115, 116
Yellow Crane Tower, 282
Yellow River, 18, 79, 121, 128, 278
Yen-tzu (temple manager), 127, 130, 132, 134–35, .348
Yen-ying (master-at-arms), 134, 135–39
Yichang, 261
Yi-ch'ao, 309, 325–30
Yi-ch'eng, 100, 183
Yi-hsing (Thich Nhat Hanh), 221–22
Ying River, 146
Yin-k'ung (abbess), 235, 236, 238, 241, 243–45, 248, 317; photo, 249
Yin-le (abbot), 125–26
Yuchi (Secluded Residence), 207
Yuchuan ("Jade Spring") Mountain, 265
Yuchuan Temple, 264–69, 273, 277–79. *See also* Tumen Temple
Yuehhsi, 149
Yuehhua Temple, 301–3
Yuehyang, 283, 284–85
Yunchushan, 95, 100, 236, 243–44
Yunchu Temple, 27–28, 29
Yungang Caves, 39–45, 73
Yung-hsing (abbot), 130
Yungle Bell, 18, 19–20
Yungning Temple, 126, 127
Yunmen Mountain, 289
Yunmen Temple, 221–22, 243, 289–95, 327–28
Yun-men Wen-yen, 289
Yu Po-ya, 254, 255

Z

Zen: Chinese spellings, 2–3; first nonlinguistic teacher, 84

Zen Buddhism: appeal to Communists, 320; attitude towards books, 139, 158, 238; attitude towards words, 2, 5–6, 10, 107; communal practice, 190, 206, 209; difference from other kinds of Buddhism, 169; East Mountain Zen, 208; introduction of communal practice, 182; level of interest in China in, 5; Linchi School, 33, 241–42; nun's practice, 235–38; origin, 2, 6–8, 224, 308; split into Northern and Southern Schools, 268–69; split with Tientai Buddhism, 268; success in China, 181; view of body and mind, 275–76. *See also* Northern School of Zen; Patriarchs of Zen Buddhism

Zen centers: first, 206; retreat center on Chiufenghan, 244

Zen lineages in China, 102, 118

Zen monasteries: first, 87; first self-supporting, 190; of Fourth and Fifth Patriarchs, 207; guest halls, 99; how they work, 88–110; with meditation halls, 75, 100–101; monastery store, 291; plan for Third Patriarch Temple, 171; rules, 95–96, 100; sites for, 207–9; sources of income, 107–9, 132, 187–88, 212, 240, 242, 243, 264–65, 267, 272–73; in a volcano, 208

Zen monks: financial support, 86–87; meetings, 87; old abbot's advice, 292–93; procedure for staying at monasteries, 98–99; rooms, 96, 136, 137; training, 133

Zen nunneries, 223–24; rules, 237; Tachinshan Temple, 223, 234–48

Zen practice, 8; origin of self-supporting, communal, 182; patience needed, 244–45

"Zen tea," 306

Zen teachers, 5; customary mourning period after loss, 206–7; nuns, 235–38, 240–42

Zhang Yimou, 34

Zithers, 254